THE NEW CITIZEN- SHIP

ORIGINS OF
PROGRESSIVISM
IN WISCONSIN,
1885 - 1900

David P. Thelen

UNIVERSITY
OF MISSOURI
PRESS

FOR ESTHER

ACKNOWLEDGMENTS

It is a real pleasure to thank publicly the many people who have contributed to whatever merit this book may have. Not only are they innocent of any flaws in the book, but some of them also dissent from its interpretations.

E. David Cronon has been a friend and sympathetic adviser. Stanley P. Caine, Clay McShane, John Holtzhueter, and William F. Thompson directed me to valuable sources. The Wisconsin Electric Power Company kindly permitted me to use the records of its predecessor corporations at its Milwaukee office, and The University of Wisconsin Alumni Research Foundation and the University of Missouri Research Council generously supported research for the book.

I am especially grateful to the many people who read and criticized various drafts of the manuscript. Allan G. Bogue, James P. O'Brien, Stanley I. Kutler, Fred Rich, and H. Roger Grant offered valuable suggestions; David Wigdor, Stanley Mallach, Michael J. Cassity, and Richard Jensen provided encouragement at crucial times and helped me through many interpretive and organizational problems. Graduate students at the Universities of Missouri and Wisconsin forced me to refine many interpretations. The friendly encouragement and critical advice of Richard S. Kirkendall have been a real comfort over the last five years. I count the friendship of Robert W. Griffith as one of the major blessings of my scholarly career.

The debt to my wife, Esther Stillman Thelen, is very simple—without her there would have been no book.

D.P.T.
Columbia, Missouri
May, 1971

Contents

LIST OF ABBREVIATIONS

The full citation for the most frequently used primary sources is given the first time that source is used, and short titles are used for each subsequent reference. This list provides a quick reference for some of those short titles:

Blue Book · *The Blue Book of the State of Wisconsin*

Handbook · Wisconsin Farmers' Institutes, *A Handbook of Agriculture*

League Bulletin · *The* [Milwaukee] *Municipal League Bulletin*

National League · *Proceedings of the* [number] *Annual Meeting of the National Municipal League*

Secretary, *Biennial Report* · *Biennial Report of the* [Wisconsin] *Secretary of State*

State Journal · *Madison, Wisconsin State Journal*

WWSA Proceedings · Proceedings of the Wisconsin Woman Suffrage Association

Large-scale industrial capitalism produced two basic economic identifications in society. Men and women could identify primarily with their roles as producers or as consumers. Those who identified with their producer roles emphasized their relationship to the ownership of the means of production and forged self-conscious social classes and interest groups on that basis.

The producer orientation has beguiled historians of the Progressive Era. The three basic approaches to the historiography of the period are based on the assumption that the producer role was the primary determinant of progressivism. The first historiographical approach—associated with such scholars as George E. Mowry, Richard Hofstadter, J. Joseph Huthmacher, and John D. Hicks—suggested that progressivism was rooted in the class and status perceptions of a particular social group: the urban gentry, manual workers, businessmen, or farmers. Each author painted a compelling portrait of the insecurities and tensions felt by the group he chose to place in the foreground of his picture of progressivism. The second historiographical approach—associated with such scholars as Samuel P. Hays and Robert H. Wiebe—argued that the most important development of the period was the formation of producer-oriented, national interest groups and professional associations to impose their values and needs onto government. The third approach—associated with such "New Left" scholars as Gabriel Kolko and James Weinstein—maintained that a producer-oriented social and economic corporate elite used government, particularly at the national level, to suppress the aspirations of the producer-oriented competitors and masses who presumably wanted to create radical changes.

Despite the obvious differences between these three approaches, the common emphasis on producer roles has led historians to examine the same developments. The independent regulatory commission, particularly at the federal level, seems to be emerging from the writings of historians as the Progressive Era's most significant legacy to the political economy of American capitalism. Regulation served the conflicting needs of all producer-oriented Americans.

Wisconsin's early progressives would have been astonished

1

by the focus historians have placed on producer identifications. They identified mainly with their roles as consumers and tax-payers, and they gravely doubted whether the existing political economy could ever meet their needs. Like many Marxists, they wanted to create a society in which artificial economic barriers would not divide men, in which each individual could achieve his fullest human potential. Unlike many Marxists, they believed that the economic basis of the classless society would be united consumers instead of united workers, and, unlike many Marxists, they did not particularly care who owned the means of production and distribution. Many of them favored public ownership of certain corporations because the particular relationship of those corporations to the political process made it impossible for consumers to receive redress in any other way. For these early progressives oppression resulted from "special privilege," not from relationship to the means of production. A socialist state could be as dominated by special privilege as a capitalist one, and it, too, could deny real power to consumers. Special privileges invariably prevented the aroused consumers and taxpayers—"the people"—from ruling.

The early progressives wanted to reintegrate a society that industrial capitalism had divided into competing producer-oriented classes and interest groups. Often inspired by Henry George and directly anticipating Huey Long's Share-the-Wealth program, they believed that taxation was probably the best way to cut down the rich and elevate the poor. They would have been surprised that historians have neglected their contributions to taxation—particularly the income tax—because they had so much faith in its potential ability to redistribute wealth and power.

But the progressives' fundamental demand—the one that makes them important precursors of today's radicals—was their insistence on giving power to "the people," by which they meant majority rule. They saw politics as a never-ending struggle between the aroused consumers and taxpayers ("the people") and a producer-oriented establishment that constantly thwarted the will of the majority. They believed that their most important contributions were the political reforms that they hoped would break the power of this establishment and give real power to the majority: direct primary, home rule for cities, initiative, referendum, recall, popular vetoes of judicial decisions, direct election of senators, woman suffrage, reform of the rules of the House of Representatives, and corrupt practices acts. These were the first steps to direct democracy.

Direct democracy was profoundly radical because it was thoroughly democratic. If the masses of men and women ruled directly—with no governmental structures and hence no special privileges between them and real power—they could produce fundamental changes in the political economy. The masses could—and most progressives believed that they would—enact the spirit of the Declaration of Independence. Progressives profoundly believed that the great majority of citizens were inherently progressive. Recent historians and liberals have come in the meantime to believe that "the people" are conservative, silent, or irrational and for that reason have ignored the progressive thrust toward direct democracy. This is a book about people with different ideas about democracy from those that prevail today.

Three introductory notes are needed here. The first concerns leadership. Assuming that the leader defined the political program and then sought popular backing, I began this study of Wisconsin progressivism as a biography of Robert M. La Follette. It was only after a good deal of research into La Follette's personality and the sources of his programs that I concluded that this approach would obscure more than it would reveal about the origins of Wisconsin progressivism. La Follette did not espouse progressive causes until 1897, and he ignored the legislative battles of earlier progressives until he became governor in 1901. He was, in fact, converted to progressivism by the voters and the earlier reformers. Although the progressives developed a new concept of leadership that endowed leaders with the superhuman qualities needed to break the hold of the establishment, they insisted that those leaders respond to voters in new, more direct ways. Tom Johnson's tent meetings in Cleveland and Hazen Pingree's protest rallies in Detroit had their counterparts in Wisconsin and reflected the new communion between "the people" and their leaders. The voters generated the progressive programs and, familiar with the devices by which older politicians had betrayed them, they insisted that progressive leaders keep their tent flaps open so that the voters could observe their methods and, if need be, discipline them. The early Wisconsin Progressives put more faith in developing new voluntary associations and the techniques of mass, popular, grass-roots pressure than they put in their leaders.

The second word of caution concerns the heavy emphasis on reform at the expense of reaction. This book discusses shifts in the ideologies, issues, and political practices of those groups that promoted change in Wisconsin between 1885 and 1900. While it discusses some of the actions taken by those who opposed those changes, it confines that discussion to the consequences of conservatism for reformers. More attention to the conservatives might well explain why the vision of institutionalizing the Declaration of Independence remained a vision. Reformers had vigorous critics, but this book is confined primarily to a study of reform.

The third introductory note concerns the use of terms. I have used the term *Gilded Age* to describe the 1885–1893 period in order to emphasize its continuity with the "old order" and to highlight the break with the past produced by the Panic of 1893. Many of the attitudes that Mark Twain and Charles Dudley Warner portrayed in *The Gilded Age* (1873) continued to influence reform between 1885 and 1893. While historians have usually reserved the term *mugwump* for those Republicans who preferred principle to party, particularly in 1884, I have broadened its use to include a set of prejudices toward change and politics. I have used the terms *mugwump* and *progressive* to describe ideological and political programs, not to describe social types. Since the term *progressive* did not come into usage as an ideological label until about 1906, I have capitalized it only to describe the party. Likewise, I have followed the contemporary practice of not capitalizing *mugwump*.

I | GILDED AGE REFORM, 1885-1893

On the eve of the Panic of 1893 Wisconsin seemed an un-
likely state to earn a national reputation as a leading progressive
state within a dozen years. In the early nineties, in fact, Wisconsin seemed very ordinary. The state's economy, people, and
politics lacked the extremes to be found elsewhere.

Wisconsin's population of 1,686,880 ranked it fourteenth
among the states in 1890. The state's boom days had long since
departed; it had taken the twenty-five years since 1865 just to
double the population. Unlike that of many other parts of the
country, Wisconsin's economy was remarkably diversified. Lumbering continued to dominate the state's industrial development
as it had since the 1870s, but during the eighties, when investment in manufacturing increased more than three times, such
industries as brewing, agricultural implements, carriages, paper,
machine products, and iron and steel arose to challenge the
supremacy of the pineries. Even with the growth of manufacturing in the eighties, however, Wisconsin remained predominantly agricultural, with almost twice as many farmers as
workers, a fact that partially explains the state's relative immunity from the industrial strife of other areas.[1] Wisconsin's
diversified agricultural sector differed markedly in political
climate from that of regions that depended on the vicissitudes
of a single crop. The farm protest movements that accompanied
years of failure in the wheat and cotton areas were notably
absent from the Badger State; at the same time, the state placed
great emphasis on agricultural education. More than thirty years
had passed since the state's leading newspaper had proclaimed
that "wheat is king, and Wisconsin is the center of the Empire,"
and in the intervening generation a number of aggressive dairy
propagandists had persuaded Wisconsin farmers that dairying
and scientific agriculture, not Granger movements, offered the

1. *The Blue Book of the State of Wisconsin, 1899* (Milwaukee: Northwestern Litho Co.) , 686–87, hereinafter cited as *Blue Book*. U.S. Department
of Commerce, Bureau of the Census, *Compendium of the Ninth Census of
the United States, 1870,* 872; *Tenth Census of the United States, Report of
the Manufactures, 1880,* 189–91; *Eleventh Census of the United States, Report on Manufacturing Industries, 1890,* 1:628–35; *Eleventh Census of the
United States, Population,* 2:624–25.

true "agriculture of survival."[2] As a result, the Alliance and Populist movements had almost no impact on Wisconsin farmers. From the quiet vantage point of Wisconsin it indeed appeared, as the state's labor commissioner wrote, that "the tillers of the soil have always constituted the conservative elements" of society.[3] Nothing in the state's industrial or agricultural development marked Wisconsin as a likely seedbed for reform.

The people who settled Wisconsin came from remarkably varied ethnic and religious backgrounds; some eastern editors were appalled that foreign-born voters outnumbered the native-born in the state. The New York *Post* suggested that Wisconsin should take the lead in restricting immigration because it had a higher proportion of immigrants than any other state, but, since the majority of Wisconsin's immigrants came from Germany and Scandinavia, the proportion of immigrants to the state's population had begun to decline by 1893 as fewer northern and western Europeans came to America. Wisconsin's native-born residents tended to emphasize the positive stereotypes of her immigrants: the hard-working, free-thinking Germans and the cooperative and assimilation-minded Scandinavians. The state experienced the usual conflicts between German Catholics and Lutherans, between English-speaking and German-speaking Catholics, and between Catholics and Protestants over such issues as parochial schools and politics, notably in 1890, but Wisconsin was still freer from these tensions than neighboring Michigan and Minnesota, where the nativist American Protective Association, for example, made a greater impact.[4] There was nothing striking in the relationships among the state's ethnic and religious groups, which would later presage an aggressive reform movement.

2. Eric E. Lampard, *The Rise of the Dairy Industry in Wisconsin: A Study in Agricultural Change, 1820–1920* (Madison: State Historical Society of Wisconsin, 1963), 2–242, Wilbur H. Glover, *Farm and College: The College of Agriculture of the University of Wisconsin, A History* (Madison: University of Wisconsin Press, 1952), 69–70, 89, 149–50. Frederick M. Rosentreter, *The Boundaries of the Campus: A History of the University of Wisconsin Extension Division, 1885–1945* (Madison: University of Wisconsin Press, 1957), 15–23. *Proceedings of the 21st Annual Session of the Wisconsin State Grange Patrons of Husbandry, 1892,* 9–10, hereinafter cited as State Grange, *Session.*

3. *Seventh Biennial Report of the Wisconsin Bureau of Labor, Census, and Industrial Statistics, 1895–1896,* 1850, 3, previously called the Bureau of Labor Statistics, both hereinafter cited as Labor Bureau.

4. U.S. Department of Commerce, Bureau of the Census, *Tabular Statements of the Census Enumeration . . . of the State of Wisconsin, 1895,* xii.

On the eve of the Panic of 1893 Wisconsin's politics were equally unspectacular. Most voters were partisans who rallied and shouted and voted for the traditions, symbols, and candidates of their party. Fancying themselves politicians, Wisconsinites gloried in the intrigues that attended the candidacies for nomination at the local caucuses. The caucus offered relief from the boredom of everyday life, and the best "lieutenants" of the victorious candidates could depend on patronage jobs as rewards for their loyalty and hard work. The better political managers rose in the party hierarchy; at the apex of the political pyramid were the men of great political and commercial acumen whom their rivals generally and sourly denounced as "bosses." For the past decade the Republican party had been commanded by Henry C. Payne, the unparalleled specialist in "the mathematics of organization"; Philetus Sawyer, the United States Senator who devoted much of his considerable fortune to the party; and John Coit Spooner, the parliamentarian and legal adviser. At the head of the Democratic party were Edward C. Wall, Payne's close friend and the party's leading professional, and Sen. William Freeman Vilas, the wealthy lawyer whose close ties to President Grover Cleveland assisted the state party.[5] In Wisconsin, as elsewhere, the bosses successfully silenced rumblings of discontent from men whose ambitions and principles conflicted with their own by identifying party unity as a necessity in order to defeat the opposition. In this era of intense partisanship such appeals were usually sufficient to defeat most doubters.

There was little in the state's economic, demographic, or political development to mark Wisconsin as a future Progressive state, yet within a few years the fury and desperation of the Wisconsin reformers would be unmatched anywhere. The full dimensions of the revolution these reformers were to produce

New York *Post*, in *Madison, Wisconsin State Journal*, March 16, 1887; hereinafter cited as *State Journal*. John Higham, *Strangers in the Land: Patterns of American Nativism, 1860–1925* (New York: Atheneum Publishers, 1966), 77–87; Richard T. Ely, *Ground Under Our Feet* (New York: Macmillan Co., 1938), 208–9; Robert M. La Follette, *La Follette's Autobiography: A Personal Narrative of Political Experiences* (Madison: Robert M. La Follette Co., 1913) 177, 222–23. The most useful case study is Robert J. Ulrich, "The Bennett Law of 1889: Education and Politics in Wisconsin" (Ph.D. diss., University of Wisconsin, 1965).

5. William W. Wight, *Henry Clay Payne: A Life* (Milwaukee: privately published, 1907), 179; Richard N. Current, *Pine Logs and Politics: A Life of Philetus Sawyer* (Madison: State Historical Society of Wisconsin, 1950), 236–42; Horace Samuel Merrill, *William Freeman Vilas: Doctrinaire Democrat* (Madison: State Historical Society of Wisconsin, 1954), 160, 170–97.

becomes clear only when contrasted with the motivations and grievances, the successes and failures, of the state's advocates of change in the years before the Panic of 1893.

The rapid urbanization and industrialization of Wisconsin in the Gilded Age gave impetus and set limits to the activities of reformers. Dozens of individuals and groups had programs to attack new problems. Advocates came forward in support of the eight-hour day, woman suffrage, civil service reform, factory inspection, enforcement of vice laws, wildlife conservation, nonpartisan local elections, tax reform, regulation of loan companies, abolition of child labor, businesslike local government, and railway regulation.

Behind such apparently diverse reforms were two sets of motives that affected nearly all Gilded Age reformers and largely shaped their activities. One group of reformers simply wanted to participate more fully in the benefits of industrialism. Inclined toward collective action and driven by self-interest, these reformers included some of the state's workers, farmers, and businessmen. The second group were the heirs of earlier moral reform movements—the mugwumps. More influential than the first reform group because many of their values and prejudices were more widespread, the mugwumps resented the politicians, who were tied through local saloonkeepers to the worst groups in society, and relied instead on the individualistic appeals of education and moral suasion. Mugwumps included many teachers, clergymen, editors, and businessmen.

The rapid economic transformation of the state, while thus motivating reformers to promote changes, also limited the Gilded Age reformers. It intensified the growing divisions between farm and city, worker and boss, native-born and immigrant, father and son, and these conflicts prevented like-minded reformers from working together and isolated them from mass support. Many mugwumps, in addition, reacted suspiciously toward the whole process of industrialization and attacked the new interest groups. The mugwumps' suspicions prevented them from working with people who shared many of their values, but not their backgrounds.

The antebellum reform tradition did not die at Appomattox. Many heirs of the reform movement that had leavened life in the decades before the war persevered in Wisconsin. During the Gilded Age they kept alive the antebellum faith in the infinite perfectibility of the individual, in treating social injustices as sins, in direct appeals to the consciences of men, in doubting the ability of political solutions to make lasting changes, and they continued to use the antebellum techniques of education and moral suasion. The rapid urbanization and industrialization of Wisconsin after 1865 forced reformers to develop new implications from the old heritage, and those new implications would make that heritage profoundly more conservative. By the time they had grafted their response to the social tensions of the Gilded Age onto the older heritage, they would have transformed it beyond recognition.

Victorian morality and the passion for social harmony, products in turn of accelerating economic and social dislocations, powered basic changes in the antebellum reform tradition. A few reformers developed their prejudices into an elaborate ideology. They viewed the ideal society as a pastoral community composed of independent individuals who owed loyalties only to their families and their communities. Men and women maintained what reformers called the vital "purity and integrity" of their homes and communities by accepting the moral truths of an earlier America. "Home and Heaven are two words very nearly akin to each other," observed a Platteville woman.[1] The community expected "social harmony" and "social purity" from its members, and individuals demonstrated their devotion to the community by resisting partisanship and sin with equal fervor. Members were expected to express in their lives only the "good" and "noble" instincts that would improve the moral position of the whole community. Society had failed, these reformers felt, to the extent that individuals strayed from their loyalty to the family and the community.

The antebellum reformers had assumed that these loyalties existed and had built their programs on them, but their in-

1. Wisconsin Farmers' Institutes, *A Handbook of Agriculture*, bull. no. 7 (1893), 145, hereinafter cited as *Handbook*.

heritors could make no such assumption. The Gilded Age reformers recognized the tension between their vision of the dominance of family and community and the realities of the emerging economic order. They sensed the inevitable conflicts that were rapidly destroying the reformers' ideal society by eroding men's loyalties to the family and community. Since the harmony and very existence of the community were at stake, reformers felt that they must banish the new occupational, political, ethnic, and religious groupings, on which they blamed the hated conflicts and divided loyalties. "The Christian community has rights which it is bound to protect to secure order, decorum, decency and tranquility," declared a Catholic editor in Milwaukee.[2] Indeed, these reformers tended to see the whole process of organization as evil because it subordinated the individual, the home, and the community to the interests of the group. The assumptions of the antebellum reformers thus became ends for their successors.

Perhaps because they sensed that they could no more destroy the new groups than repeal industrialization, the Gilded Age reformers focused very sharply on the problem of policymaking in the community. While the term "mugwump" has been generally applied to those reformers who exalted their ideals over the demands of their political party, particularly in 1884, it accurately captures the tone of these Gilded Age reformers. These reformers believed that the community should be governed by "the best men" and the "better element," by which they meant those people whose vision was broad enough to transcend the partisan prejudices and group allegiances of the secular society. Yet, in fact, wherever the mugwump turned, he found the politician in command, and the partisan politician, as a result, became the symbol of everything the mugwump hated. Politicians not only pandered to all the occupational and ethnic prejudices that repelled and frightened the mugwumps, but they also made close alliances with the community's worst elements—its saloonkeepers, gamblers, and prostitutes. The political machine itself epitomized the process of organization that subordinated the individual and the community to the group. Whether the reformer advocated civil service reform, enforcement of vice laws, woman suffrage, or the economical administration of local affairs, he found the root evil in the partisan politician.

The mugwumps' strategies for reform proceeded from their

2. *Milwaukee Catholic Citizen*, November 16, 1889.

yearning for the harmonious community and their emphasis on the individual. The way to reform society was to reform the individual—appeal to his best instincts while suppressing those forces that tempted him to forget his duties to home and community. The tactical weapons of the mugwumps were education and moral suasion, the same techniques used by the antebellum reformers to reach individuals directly. While many Gilded Age reformers would enlist constables to suppress divisive groups and enforce social harmony, they all believed that "character"—this generation's conservative twisting of the antebellum reformers' concept of the regenerated individual—could be built only upon immediate appeals to individuals.

Since few Wisconsin mugwumps justified their crusades with fully developed ideologies, the full contours of mugwumpery are best revealed in their varied reform movements—the vice crusades, the woman suffrage movement, the campaigns to purify local governments, and the civil service reform movement. These movements show not only the sources of mugwumpery in different settings but also the ways in which social conflicts and secular prejudices limited its effectiveness.

I

The noisiest of the Gilded Age mugwumps were the vice crusaders. Throughout the late nineteenth century, as in most eras, Americans felt a deep ambivalence about liquor, prostitution, and observance of the Sabbath. Although the saloon, the prostitute, and the Sunday baseball game rarely ceased to be the objects of highly charged local crusades, they continued as more or less common aspects of life in Wisconsin. As firmly as these features were accepted by a majority of citizens, they were just as firmly denounced by a fervent minority. The conflicting feelings of excitement and guilt elicited by a glass of whiskey, for example, could lead a great many citizens to simultaneous support of the saloonkeeper and temperance reformer. For this reason the local crusades embroiled everyone and settled nothing; as soon as the reformers had spent their energies, the community returned to it usual amusements.

In all such crusades, rooted as they were in moral suasion, the churches took the lead. As slavery had been the great sin of antebellum America, so intemperance was the great sin of Gilded Age America. "Since the abolition of chattel slavery," declared

11

the 1880 convention of Wisconsin Congregationalists, "the providence of God seems to be pressing the temperance reform to the front, as the next great question to be passed upon by the American people."[3] Few conventions of Protestant sects in Gilded Age Wisconsin felt "morally perpendicular" until they had denounced intemperance as "the gigantic evil of the day," "the Devil's most successful nineteenth century agency for the destruction of the bodies and souls of men," "the arch enemy of our civilization," or "a moral pestilence more to be dreaded than Asiatic cholera."[4]

The churches had little trouble persuading aldermen and legislators to pass laws and ordinances aimed against the saloon, desecration of the Sabbath, gambling, and other vices. In 1849, one year after Wisconsin's statehood, the legislature enacted the first Sunday law, which banned sports and amusements on God's day. Beginning in 1861 the churches secured laws prohibiting the sale of liquor near churches, schools, and public institutions. The most important of the vice laws were an 1874 act that allowed cities and towns to determine the amount of a saloon's license fee and an 1878 act that forbade the sale of liquor on Sundays. Few legislators dared resist the churches in the last half of the nineteenth century, and the statutes were often as Victorian as the ministers' resolutions.[5]

The real problem for the vice crusaders was not to secure legislation, but to persuade communities that the laws should be enforced. This was a problem of moral suasion and individual conversion. Law enforcement officials realized that to perform their duties in this area was to anger and alienate constituents who enjoyed their beers and Sunday ball games. Knowing that most officials would enforce sumptuary laws only when they could not evade angry citizens, the vice crusaders tried to arouse the conscience of the community. Whenever a minister felt that his flock was straying, he would launch a crusade for enforce-

3. *Minutes of the 50th Annual Meeting of the Congregational Convention of Wisconsin*, 1890, 32, hereinafter cited as *Congregational Minutes*.

4. *Ibid.*, 33. *Minutes of the 45th Annual Wisconsin Baptist State Convention*, 1889, 69, hereinafter cited as *Baptist Minutes*. *Minutes of the [Presbyterian] Synod of Wisconsin*, 1891, 35, hereinafter cited as *Presbyterian Minutes*. *Minutes of the Wisconsin Annual Conference of the Methodist Episcopal Church*, 1893, 64, hereinafter cited as *Methodist Minutes*.

5. Wisconsin, *Laws* (1849), chap. 139; (1861), chap. 279; (1874), chap. 179. *State Journal*, March 18, May 15, 1884.

ment of vice laws. In the spring of 1884, for example, six villages in Dane County alone were embroiled in such fights: Oregon held a referendum on saloon licenses; Deerfield closed its bars; Bristol withdrew the licenses of two saloonkeepers who had served liquor to minors; Mount Horeb rocked with near-revivalist fervor in temperance meetings; Stoughton arrested several saloonkeepers for selling without licenses; and Madison waged a fight over the Sunday closing law.[6] The Madison campaign typified hundreds of similar skirmishes. Headed by the Congregationalist, Presbyterian, and Methodist clergymen, the Law and Order League demanded "submission to the laws we now have, which are now boldly, openly and defiantly violated under the open gaze, and to the full knowledge of our city authorities and police officers." In response, the saloonkeepers organized a Personal Liberty Society and recruited German citizens whose cultural lives revolved around beer, bars, and Sunday sports. As in most such crusades, the reformers successfully closed Madison's saloons for several Sundays, but as their zeal waned the saloons resumed their Sunday business.[7] The perceptive Mr. Dooley, Finley Peter Dunne's fictional saloonkeeper in Chicago, commented after his saloon had been closed more than once by the vice crusaders that, although "as a people, . . . we're th' greatest crusaders that iver was—f'r a short distance . . . the throuble is th' crusade don't last afther th' first sprint. . . . Afther awhile people gets tired iv the pastime. They want somewhere to go nights. . . . an' wan day th' boss crusader finds that he's alone in Sodom."[8]

But the vice crusaders of Gilded Age Wisconsin never relented in the war against sin. The bitterest and most enduring struggles occurred at Racine, where a decade-long campaign against Sunday saloons, Sunday ball games, and "immoral" dance houses began in the late 1880s and included an attempt in 1891 to impeach Mayor J. I. Case.[9] At LaCrosse, Presbyteri-

6. *Madison Democrat,* May 8, 1884. *Stoughton Courier,* May 9, July 11, 18, 1884. *Mount Horeb Blue Mounds Weekly News,* May 16, 23, September 26, 1884.

7. For the Madison controversy, see David P. Thelen, *The Early Life of Robert M. La Follette, 1855–1884* (Chicago: Loyola University Press, 1966), 91–100.

8. Finley Peter Dunne, "The Crusade Against Vice," *Mr. Dooley's Opinions* (New York: R. H. Russell, 1901), 154, 156–57.

9. *Congregational Minutes,* 51st Meeting, 1891, 28; 52nd Meeting, 1892, 15. *Milwaukee Sentinel,* April 6, 1890, July 20, August 23, 1891, January 31, 1892, March 9, 1896, December 3, 1899.

ans led the 1887 fight that closed three saloons as "nuisances."[10] Between 1885 and 1890 the Fond du Lac Ministers' Association sponsored several temperance meetings, organized law-and-order movements, and brought pressure on the city council to curtail the number of saloons in their city.[11]

The vice crusaders were more successful in their fights over saloon licenses. Saloonkeepers generally had to reapply to city councils for licenses each year, and, after 1874, councils had the right to determine whether to charge high ($500) or low ($200) fees or to refuse to issue any licenses, which would theoretically abolish all saloons. The crusaders frequently persuaded the aldermen to hold advisory referenda on the license question and then inaugurated major campaigns to persuade voters to approve either high fees or no licensing at all. In 1888, for example, Marinette, Dodgeville, Fort Atkinson, Whitewater, and DePere were the scenes of successful fights for high license fees.[12] In 1892, five cities voted for high license fees, nine for no license, and only one for low license fees.[13] By the time the panic hit Wisconsin, the crusaders had accomplished little of permanent value in the decade since 1884, when the state president of the Woman's Christian Temperance Union had "confessed with sorrow that our Badger state is behind the sister states in the onward march of reform."[14]

Several factors accounted for this disappointing record. Some of the limits on the vice crusaders were political. The Republican party, born in the ferment of antebellum reform and appealing to the temperance sentiments of many Yankees, Englishmen, and Scandinavians, housed most of the crusaders. Republican leaders and candidates knew that temperance was one rallying cry expected by their constituents. The trouble came in the 1880s when radical vice crusaders, despairing of reforming their communities by piecemeal tactics, formed the Prohibitionist party and ran their first gubernatorial candidate in 1881. As state conventions of Protestants increasingly endorsed the Pro-

10. *Presbyterian Minutes,* 1887, 21.
11. Fond du Lac Ministers' Association, Minute Book, John N. Davidson Papers, Box 7, Manuscripts Division, State Historical Society of Wisconsin, 20, 51, 75, 97.
12. *Milwaukee Sentinel,* September 19, 1888.
13. *Ibid.,* September 21, 1892. *Congregational Minutes,* 52nd Meeting, 1892, 15.
14. *Minutes of the 11th Annual Meeting of the Woman's Christian Temperance Union of Wisconsin,* 1884, 4–5.

hibitionists in the 1880s,[15] Republican leaders began to fear that the temperance movement would recruit enemies instead of supporters. While they never expected that the Prohibitionists would win elections—and indeed the party rarely polled over 4 per cent of the state's vote[16]—Republicans knew that the new party siphoned off critically needed votes in the period's close elections. This fear became a nightmare in 1884 when New York's Prohibitionist voters deprived James G. Blaine of the Presidency. Republican publicists, responding to self-interest and to the party's moral origins, repeatedly lamented that the Prohibitionists had "absorbed the most of that labor which was devoted, with a considerable measure of success, to the promotion of temperance by moral suasion."[17] One temperance-minded Republican politician stopped attending temperance meetings in 1884 because they "nowdays run to the benefit of the Prohibition Party."[18] A Methodist layman protested privately in 1890 against the "Republican Sputterers here, that would dethrone and ostracise any man that persistently proclaimed prohibition principles from his pulpit."[19] Several Methodist clergymen converted to Congregationalism in the late eighties because they thought their new sect would allow them to attack saloons more vigorously.[20]

Crude efforts by Republican laymen to silence the more radical vice crusaders constituted only one problem. As the crusaders pondered their failures, they realized that the basic limits on their mugwumpery came from the collectivizing and secularizing results of the rapid growth of cities, pineries, and factories. Emphasis on the individualistic appeal of moral suasion came to sound increasingly alien to the crusaders' audiences; it appeared as though the basic goal of the crusaders was

15. *Methodist Minutes,* 1891, 62. *Presbyterian Minutes,* 1887, 22. *Congregational Minutes,* 50th Meeting, 1890, 32.

16. In gubernatorial elections Prohibitionist candidates polled 7.6 per cent in 1881, 2.7 per cent in 1884, 6.0 per cent in 1886, 4.0 per cent in 1888, and 3.6 per cent in 1890 and 1892. James R. Donoghue, *How Wisconsin Voted* (Madison: University of Wisconsin Extension Division, 1956), 77-82.

17. *Milwaukee Sentinel,* August 7, 1887.

18. Diary of Willet S. Main, October 15, also September 17, November 6, 1884, Main Papers, Manuscripts Division, State Historical Society of Wisconsin.

19. George L. Richards to Eugene G. Updike, January 11, 1890, Updike Papers, Manuscripts Division, State Historical Society of Wisconsin.

20. M. O. Milton to E. G. Updike, June 29, 1890, Updike Papers, 1890 Folder.

to repeal the whole process of secularization. "Divine enactments," proclaimed the state's Presbyterians in 1884, "are not
susceptible of improvement by advanced thought and modern
civilization."[21] Alienated by the greed and materialism of the
Gilded Age, a New Richmond Baptist preacher yearned for
"men who care most for souls and least for the almighty dollar,"
and a temperance-minded Catholic editor in Milwaukee trum-
peted for "higher ends than money-getting."[22] Identifying with
the biblical prophets, the crusaders lamented the "sort of go-as-
you-please morality, with little conscience and without the fear
of God" that accompanied secularization.[23] Knowing that it was
not easy for prophets to harken most Wisconsinites back to a
presecular morality, a Catholic editor admitted that "a certain
amount of radicalism is needed to work the Catholic masses up
to even a moderate attitude on this question."[24] The basic
problem, the crusaders realized, was the "persistent encroach-
ment of urgent and organized secularism."[25] Secularism had
produced the triumph of "the Moloch of our day, King Alco-
hol," according to the fifty local chapters of the Catholic Total
Abstinence Union, and this new Moloch demanded the sacrifice
of families and was guilty of "blighting the home and burning
out of the heart every moral virtue."[26] The crusaders' reliance
on moral inducement in a world increasingly dominated by
"urgent and organized secularism" makes them correspond
better than any other group of Wisconsin reformers to the
model of the status revolution. Unfamiliar with the concept,
they preferred to see themselves as prophets.

Since most of the pre-1893 vice crusaders were recruited from
Yankee Protestant and English-speaking Catholic sources—and
it is significant that there was no cooperation between the two
groups—they recognized that one of their goals was to control, if
not suppress, the strange ways of Wisconsin's new immigrants.
Their beloved, stable community of moral, law-abiding gentle-
men simply had no place for people whose cultural lives included a saloon and Sabbath breaking. Believing such people

21. *Presbyterian Minutes,* 1884, 6.
22. *Baptist Minutes,* 45th Meeting, 1889, 45. *Milwaukee Catholic Citizen,*
August 18, 1888.
23. *Congregational Minutes,* 53rd Meeting, 1893, 13–14.
24. *Milwaukee Catholic Citizen,* March 21, 1888.
25. *Congregational Minutes,* 51st Meeting, 1891, 46.
26. *Milwaukee Catholic Citizen,* April 8, 1893. *Methodist Minutes,* 1893,
64.

16

immoral and uncivilized, the crusaders frequently attacked the "barbarian elements in all our large cities" and wailed that "Europe pours into our lap her very dregs."[27] In these years before the panic, the vice crusaders made few efforts to reach the groups they hated and feared. They tried only to influence their own parishioners and to impose social controls from above and afar. Because of the crusaders' attitudes and methods, religious and ethnic tensions circumscribed at the same time that they helped to define the vice crusades.

Since they were movements predicated on mugwumpish appeals to an individual's loyalty to moral verities, his family, and a preindustrial definition of community, the vice crusades originated not in events of the temporal world but in the strength of the clergy's feelings that their congregations had strayed. The actual moral, economic, or political state of the community was irrelevant; that of the individual clergyman was paramount. Having rejected the secularization of society, the vice crusaders could easily ignore social and political facts as well. T. V. Caulkins, a Chippewa Falls Baptist preacher, underlined this point when he proclaimed that a clergyman should "forego the pleasures of startling—possibly pleasing—your hearers with the details, dangers and lessons of the latest political event; and instead, furnish an abundant supply of 'the spiritual milk, which is without guile,' that your people may thereby grow unto salvation."[28] Men would be damned or saved no matter how they felt about or acted in social and political events.

The vice crusaders fastened their frustrations with an increasingly alien world on the politicians as scapegoats. Their persistent and shrill attacks on policymaking by Gilded Age politicians were their major contribution to mugwumpery. The world of politics was "like a bar-room in the possession of hard characters," and saloonkeepers were "protected rather than exterminated by the 'strong arm of the civil law.' "[29] Spineless politicians built their organizations on the money and votes delivered by the merchants of vice. To right this wrong, the crusaders entered local elections to replace mere politicians with courageous, moral men who would enforce blue laws. Repeatedly

27. *Milwaukee Catholic Citizen*, July 21, 1888. *Presbyterian Minutes,* 1890, 8–9.

28. *Minutes of the 25th Annual Wisconsin Baptist Ministerial Union,* 1889, 12, hereinafter cited as *Baptist Union Minutes.*

29. *Milwaukee Catholic Citizen*, September 22, 1888. *Presbyterian Minutes,* 1891, 35.

they complained that politicians rejected the upstanding moral citizens and pandered instead to the community's worst elements. While many secular mugwumps doubted that the crusaders had located the basic evils of the age and therefore refused to cooperate with their campaigns, they shared and exploited the crusaders' efforts to discredit politicians.

II

As the Victorianism and ragged social conflicts of the Gilded Age had converted the temperance movement into vice crusades for the purposes of controlling new immigrants and rescuing policymaking from alliances between politicians and the community's least desirable elements, so the movement for woman suffrage underwent a similarly conservative transformation. Like the vice crusaders, the suffragettes would eventually become equally eager to control their inferiors and equally uncomfortable in the world of politics. By 1893 the woman suffrage movement was a product of two forces, one old and the other relatively new. The first was the movement's long heritage of moral suasion. In Wisconsin the suffrage movement grew out of the antebellum moral ferment that had bonded the suffragettes to the abolitionists and temperance reformers. When Reconstruction politicians seemed to ignore two of the antebellum reforms—temperance and woman suffrage—and to give their attention to the Negro, the suffragettes grew increasingly skeptical of politicians.[30] As a result, they intensified their faith in moral suasion and education as the levers that would move public support toward their cause. Relying upon what it saw as "the inherent sense of righteousness" in each voter, the Wisconsin Woman Suffrage Association devoted most of its energy in the late 1880s and early 1890s to exhibits at state and county fairs designed to educate voters to the ways in which women had improved social conditions. In 1888 the state organization held eighteen conventions throughout the state to appeal to the male voter's sense of rightousness.[31] The suffragettes' emphasis on conventions and exhibits, with their underlying faith in

30. Theodora W. Youmans, "How Wisconsin Women Won the Ballot," *Wisconsin Magazine of History,* 5 (September 1921), 3–8.
31. Proceedings of the Wisconsin Woman Suffrage Association, 1887, 31–32, 37–38; 1888, 53; 1891, 86–87, Ada James Papers, Box 36, Manuscripts Division, State Historical Society of Wisconsin, hereinafter cited as WWSA Proceedings.

education and moral suasion, had worked for the abolitionists before them, and from the success of the abolitionists the suffragettes drew their inspiration for actions in the Gilded Age.

A new force in the 1880s made the suffragettes more conservative. This new force was generated by the upper-middle-class women of leisure, more secular than devout, less concerned with saving souls than with relieving boredom and protecting their homes from foreign influences. Their husbands provided them with the comfortable homes and abundant free time. While some turned toward philanthropy, others found that the established charities were already dominated by the richest or oldest families in town. For such women, suffrage organizations offered an attractive alternative for their leisure time. In the 1880s, when the old suffrage movement was declining in Wisconsin, they formed vigorous new local associations and in 1885 captured the state organization for other women of their type. Mrs. Laura James, wife of a wealthy Richland Center merchant, typified these secular women as she headed the largest local organization and served as secretary of the state group. Her letters reveal a woman more interested in the romantic intrigues and travels of her friends and relatives than in saving souls. Like Henry Adams' Madeline Lee in *Democracy,* she was given to fits of melancholy. Such women naturally brought their other secular concerns to the suffrage movement. The 1892 state convention appealed to the interest of leisure-class women in dress reform when it proclaimed that "women will never be truly free til released from the bondage of superfluous drapery."[32]

As heirs of the antebellum movements and as good mugwumps, the suffragettes felt acutely that new forces were fragmenting the community and the family. Intemperance, of course, was the great wrecker of the family, and the state association rarely adjourned without pledging support to "all organizations which are working for the suppression of the saloon and drink traffic." At times the suffrage organizations were indistinguishable from the Woman's Christian Temperance Union; indeed, in 1888, all eighty members of the Marathon County WCTU were suffragettes. The first male group to endorse the suffragettes was the Good Templars, composed of temperance-minded business and professional men.[33] As liquor destroyed

32. WWSA Proceedings, 1892, 106.
33. *Ibid.,* 1886, 26; 1887, 40; 1888, 45; 1891, 82. Joann Judd Brownsword, "Good Templars in Wisconsin, 1854–1880" (M.A. thesis, University of Wisconsin, 1960), 5–6, 13, 108–10.

the family and community, so did the new immigrants who brought to Wisconsin their strange ideas about liquor and the Sabbath. Since the most vocal opponents of woman suffrage were immigrants, particularly Germans, the suffragettes frequently blasted them in nativist terms. They proclaimed, for example, that only native-born or naturalized citizens deserved the right to vote.[34] It was, after all, "social purity"—the restoration of the pure community—that had led these women to seek the ballot. They expected to find "an improvement of social conditions in direct proportion to the increase of woman's influence."[35]

The suffragettes saw the public school as a basic tool for restoring purity to the community and family, and its reform became their principal target. Vulnerable to taxpayers' movements and to pressures from mothers, the public school had been championed a generation earlier by educators like Horace Mann as a means for bringing together the community's increasingly diverse elements. Now, the need to control these elements became especially urgent as growing numbers of strange people moved into suffragette communities that had previously been homogeneous. The public school, as a consequence, became the chief agency for teaching children, and, hopefully, their parents, the evils of vice as defined by the reformers. As the opening wedge in their fight for social control over the schools, the suffragettes in 1885 persuaded the legislature to hold a state-wide referendum on whether women should be allowed to vote in school board elections. When voters approved the referendum in 1886, they opened the door for womens' participation in school management.[36] One immediate result of their new right to vote in school elections deeply gratified the women of leisure. Since women now attended its meetings, the Brodhead school board moved its meetings from a dingy downtown office to "one of the most elegant parlors in the city."[37] In this more congenial atmosphere the suffragettes

34. WWSA Proceedings, 1890, 65; 1891, 88.
35. *Ibid.*, 1886, 26; 1891, 79.
36. The suffragettes tested whether this gave them the vote at city and county elections, but the state supreme court ruled in 1888 that it did not. Olympia Brown to Laura James, January 3, 1893, unidentified note dated September 14, 1896, James Papers, Box 2. *Milwaukee Sentinel*, February 1, 1888. Donald J. Berthrong, "Social Legislation in Wisconsin, 1836–1900" (Ph.D. diss., University of Wisconsin, 1951), 291–300.
37. WWSA Proceedings, 1891, 79.

tried to infuse mugwumpery into the schools while continuing their battles to persuade politicians that the state could be purified if women could vote in all elections.

There were many similarities in motivation, tone, and popular attitudes toward vice crusaders and suffragettes in Wisconsin in the 1880s. Both groups wanted to suppress the new groups that were producing changes that increasingly undermined the old community; both built on the antebellum heritage of moral suasion and education; and both made it a more conservative heritage by turning its assumptions of a stable community into final ends and by transforming the earlier reformers' moral yardstick of "sin" into a class yardstick of "character"; both were basically divorced from the specific and immediate events of the secular and political world; and both shared the mugwumps' passion for the harmonious community and family and blamed politicians for the failures of their reform programs.

Popular attitudes toward both groups were also similar; indeed, woman suffrage was generally equated with temperance and prohibition. The same basic ambivalence toward liquor and observance of the Sabbath appeared in popular attitudes toward the role of women in policymaking. The president of the state suffrage association recognized that "popular prejudice" was overwhelmingly against full woman suffrage.[38] Voters were willing, however, to allow women to dominate the agency of education—the school—as they tolerated the vice crusaders in the agency of moral suasion—the church. This toleration seemed to result from the feeling that moral suasion and education were relatively harmless in the increasingly collective and secular 1880s. There were, however, limits to this toleration. As voters rejected political prohibition, so they rejected general woman suffrage. Denied political realization of their ideals, both groups drew upon their twisted Victorian views of the heritages of moral suasion and education and sourly denounced the politicians.

Mugwumps expressed passions for the harmonious, moral community and family, and their deep fear and hatred of politicians made the suffragettes and vice crusaders the purest of the Gilded Age mugwumps. For these reformers the partisan politician was fundamentally evil because his career depended on appeals to the prejudices of poor and immoral voters and because the formation of political machines subverted the

38. Olympia Brown to Mrs. Laura James, January 3, 1893, James Papers, Box 2.

character of men. They shied away from politics because their backgrounds and traditions led them toward church and school, toward moral suasion and education. Their pulpits and avenue homes removed them from direct contacts with the poor and immoral groups whose lives they wanted to control.

III

The mugwumps were limited by more than their individualistic and moralistic visions in an increasingly secular and collective world. The vice crusaders and suffragettes, in fact, were tolerated because a great many other Gilded Age Wisconsinites shared their quest for order and respectability and their judgment that politicians had corrupted policymaking machinery. As voters tried to restore respectability in their communities and set out to defeat partisan politicians, they revealed another, broader set of limits to mugwumpery. The spread of cities and factories widened the economic divisions between men, and it soon became clear that economic prejudices ran deeper than mugwumpish visions of the common good. In particular, the growing hatred between workers and capitalists, intensified by the rise of the Knights of Labor and several bloody strikes in the 1880s, prevented these two groups from cooperating politically even when they agreed that it was the politicians who had corrupted their communities.

The varied origins of and limitations upon Wisconsin mugwumpery before 1893 were displayed on the dirty battlegrounds of local elections. From the settled metropolis of Milwaukee to the raucous young mining city of Ashland, soldiers of reform marched to battle under the colors of mugwumpery and retreated under the banner of economic prejudice. In the end, the social conflicts that widened with the state's rapid economic transformation in the 1880s would prevail over mugwumpery.

The spectacular rise of Ashland typified the growth of industry along Lake Superior at the same time that it intensified the demands for reform. Most of Ashland's 10,000 residents had arrived with the mining boom of the 1880s. By 1890 Ashland was in the middle of what one observer called the typical "moral evolution" of the western city from its lawless "young and booming" stage to its ultimate position as "a quiet, respectable and law-abiding community."[39]

39. "Vox Populi," *Ashland Daily News,* April 17, 1890.

Ashland's 1890 reform movement was, on one level, an attempt to hasten that moral evolution. Settled residents of all classes feared the itinerants who frequented the emporiums of vice and menaced the safety of their wives and daughters. "The city," these residents felt, "has got to that age and position that it cannot prosper without the family and the home. Every effort must be made to protect these in purity and integrity." The challenge came from "The Hollow," that "sink-hole of inequity" where gamblers, prostitutes, and saloonkeepers controlled the ruling Democratic machine and blocked enforcement of blue laws.[40] Sharing many of the vice crusaders' prejudices, the leaders of the moral reform movement were the Catholic and Protestant clergymen, a group of young temperance-minded businessmen, and the city's righteous Democratic editor. Not surprisingly, the movement attracted to politics for the first time the city's settled, upper-middle-class women, who sought to protect their homes from immoral influences.[41] The movement also attracted a number of merchants and manufacturers whose opposition to the ruling Democrats was more secular and economic. These businessmen charged that the Democrats' corrupt, partisan, and extravagant looting of public funds meant higher taxes for the wealthiest taxpayers and repelled prospective businesses. Exalting "businesslike government" over partisan politics, these businessmen joined the mugwumps' campaign.[42]

In 1890, all these groups entered Ashland's political arena. The mugwumps formed the Citizens' movement and united behind the nonpartisan mayoral candidacy of L. C. Wilmarth, an established, wealthy Ashlander. Both the temperance-minded and the economy-minded agreed, according to the *Ashland Daily News,* that the 1890 election was "a test of the relative strength of the upper and lower elements of the community. The Democratic ticket will receive the support of at least three-fourths of the saloonkeepers and the lower classes generally, while the Citizens' ticket will be upheld by as great a proportion of the business men [and the] most thoughtful and public-spirited citizens." The Citizens' editor contrasted "the atmosphere of culture and refinement" at the reformers' meetings

40. *Ibid.,* March 21, April 2, 17, 1890.
41. *Ibid.,* February 23, March 13, 16, April 1, 1890.
42. *Ibid.,* February 23, 28, March 2, 13, 25, 1890.

with "the foul whiskey and tobacco laden air" that overhung the noisy Democratic gatherings.[43]

Still, their own class prejudices prevented the reformers from seeing that the 1890 campaign was not simply or even primarily a test between two economic classes. The mugwump appeal was broader. Organized labor, with its demands for the eight-hour day, realized that the businessmen in the Citizens' movement were not their allies. But many skilled workers felt the same yearning for respectability that had inspired the Citizens to organize. They did not identify with the itinerant miners and lumberjacks, whom they felt brought an immoral atmosphere to the town, and they, too, wanted safe streets for their wives and daughters. They also suffered from the Democrats' extravagance in the form of higher rents and taxes. Although the workers favored "the same thing exactly as the Citizens," they could not cooperate with reformers who condemned the lower classes in elitist terms as though they were even worse enemies than the politicians. On their side, the Citizens made no efforts to get support from the workers. As a result, the workers launched the Labor ticket, believing they could thereby punish the immoral Democrats without supporting the Citizens directly. The Democrats believed the same thing. Four days before the election, Labor's mayoral candidate Steven H. Smith announced that the Democrats had offered him $500 to withdraw from the race.[44] While the Citizens' 52 per cent of the vote assured their victory, Labor's 13 per cent showed that a large proportion of the city's settled workers was more interested in respectability and economical government than in maintaining a solid front against employers and mugwumps.[45] For many workers the merchants of vice and partisan politicians were real enemies.

Ashland's 1890 campaign demonstrated mugwumpery's broad appeal. Two-thirds of the voters in this boom town rejected the partisan machine and its alliances with vice lords, but the campaign also revealed that class and status tensions were too strong to bring political cooperation, even when men of different backgrounds could agree on the common enemy.

43. *Ibid.*, March 2, 13, April 1, 1890.
44. *Ibid.*, March 7, 9, 28, 29, 1890.
45. *Ibid.*, April 2, 1890, March 22, 1891. When Mayor Wilmarth strictly enforced the blue laws and refused to spend money for public improvements, many of the Citizens' leaders of 1890 turned against him a year later.

Class prejudices in the settled city of Milwaukee also retarded the spread of mugwumpery. With the aid of a growing number of German immigrants, a series of strikes and boycotts, and a group of able and aggressive leaders, Milwaukee's labor movement commanded respect—or fear—as soon as it entered politics in the 1880s. When the Knights of Labor nominated a city ticket in 1882, the Democrats endorsed it—and won the election. Seeking more direct political fulfillment of their goals after the brutal use of civil power to suppress a strike, Milwaukee's labor leaders launched their own labor party in 1886 and elected a congressman, seven legislators, and a majority of the county board. In 1887 labor leaders and socialists launched the Union Labor party, which seemed destined for a brilliant future.[46]

The spectacular rise of the Union Labor party reflected more than class appeals to other workers. Much of the party's attraction to workers came from its slashing attacks on partisan politicians, who used national symbols to distract attention from their failure to confront local problems. Believing that the patronage system was the lure for politicians and that policemen retained their jobs by campaigning for the bosses at the polls, organized labor led the successful drive that culminated in the 1885 law that introduced civil service reform to Milwaukee's fire and police departments.[47] Mugwump prejudices, it was clear, influenced even the state's most militant labor movement.

Although the city's business elite shared labor's hatred for politicians and the spoils system, businessmen hated organized labor even more. "In defense of the sacred rights of property . . . against the building up of a class party," Milwaukee's businessmen advocated the mugwump tactic of holding non-partisan elections to kill labor's political aspirations. Only by persuading Republican and Democratic bosses that the political menace of the lower class was greater than their partisan differences did the city's business leaders prevent organized labor from dominating Milwaukee politics. In the local elections of 1887 and 1888 Republicans and Democrats fused to form a

46. Thomas W. Gavett, "The Development of the Labor Movement in Milwaukee" (Ph.D. diss., University of Wisconsin, 1957), 105–48. Bayrd Still, *Milwaukee: The History of a City* (Madison: State Historical Society of Wisconsin, 1948), 282–84, 288–95.

47. Still, *Milwaukee*, 282–83. William Robert Johnson, "Municipal Reform in Milwaukee, 1900–1912" (B.A. thesis, University of Wisconsin, 1965), 2. Wisconsin, *Laws* (1885), chap. 378.

Citizens' ticket, which narrowly carried the judgeship in 1887 and the mayoralty in 1888 and rescued the city from dominance by organized labor.[48]

The success of the Citizens' tickets suggested to some conservatives that the "best men," as Horace Rublee termed them, could control politics whenever they wanted. Rublee regretted that the business leaders did not lead more nonpartisan tickets because partisan elections "divide the better citizens into two hostile camps, and the victory is likely to perch on the banner of the organization which can most successfully bid for the worst elements in the voting population." Nonpartisan tickets "ought not to require the menace of an organization effected with socialistic principles and seeking to gain control of the city affairs."[49] In truth, that was precisely what they required. For the next several years the conservative mugwump Rublee continued to press for nonpartisan local elections,[50] but when the socialistic menace disappeared as the labor movement fractured into opposing factions, the city's best men lost their interest in nonpartisan elections.

Milwaukee's best men did not, however, lose their skepticism toward partisan politicians. Distrusting the aldermen's projects and jobs created to reward the party faithful at the expense of higher costs and thus higher taxes for businessmen, they began devising ways of supplanting the ward heelers. A few months after the Citizens' ticket thwarted labor's political drive, a well-known businessman urged his colleagues to create "an association looking after the interests of taxpayers" in the deliberations of the city council. These businessmen soon formed a taxpayers' league, and by 1891 the Merchants and Manufacturers Association began sending a representative to the city council to protect its members' interests as leading taxpayers by preventing aldermen from creating unnecessary projects to compensate the political workers.[51] When this effort at lobbying failed, the merchants and manufacturers took more direct action. To replace partisan hacks with businesslike, tightfisted officials, they launched a drive that succeeded early in 1893 when Milwaukee elected a wealthy merchant and political

---

48. *Milwaukee Sentinel,* April 7, 1887. Still, *Milwaukee,* 284–86.
49. For examples, see *Milwaukee Sentinel,* April 7, May 7, 1887.
50. For example, see *ibid.,* February 1, 1892.
51. *Ibid.,* August 2, 1889, August 7, 1891. *Superior Leader,* July 9, 1893.

neophyte as mayor.[52]

In the years before the Panic of 1893, both organized labor and the city's leading businessmen had concluded that the partisan political system was an inadequate means for local policymaking, and together they had sponsored such mugwumpish programs as civil service reform, nonpartisan elections, and businessman mayors. If self-interest and moral outrage combined temporarily to suggest a lasting alliance between workers and businessmen to defeat the bosses, that alliance never developed. Many Wisconsinites were attracted to aspects of mugwumpery, but that attraction was not strong enough to overcome class prejudices. In cities like Ashland and Milwaukee meaningful political cooperation between workers and businessmen had to await development of the new attitudes that accompanied the depression in the years after 1893.

IV

While the state's rapid urbanization and industrialization in the 1880s promoted the growing secularization and class conflicts that severely circumscribed Gilded Age mugwumpery, they also produced attitudes that strengthened the adoption of mugwump programs. There were a few areas where politicians believed that reform programs would serve their purposes better than existing practices. Those mugwump proposals that aimed at streamlining and modernizing political machinery, at adjusting rural practices to increasingly urban circumstances, were rarely contested by politicians. Mugwump programs succeeded, in short, when they were adjustments rather than reforms.

One political area in which rapid urbanization demanded modification of existing practices was that of voting. Bosses joined mugwump reformers in promoting the secret ballot as a needed adjustment. Milwaukee's politicians of both parties were acutely aware by the mid-1880s of the mounting costs of printing tickets and rewarding voters, and of the necessity for curbing the violence and confusion that seemed to grow in proportion to the crowding of the city. Although mugwumps like Horace Rublee first championed the secret ballot because they hoped it would weaken the alliances among politicians, merchants of vice, and the "lower classes," partisan political leaders

52. *Milwaukee Sentinel,* January 22, 24, 25, February 7, 9, March 15, June 21, 1893.

provided the support that inaugurated a series of secret ballot laws in 1887. The first law applied only to Milwaukee, where increasing urban congestion had demonstrated the greatest need for modernizing the election machinery. The secret ballot, a voting method mugwumps championed to control their social inferiors and restrict the power of politicians, succeeded because politicians needed it to secure more effective control over the increasingly chaotic and expensive elections in the booming cities.[53]

The same process of adjustment was revealed in the capstone of political mugwumpery in Gilded Age Wisconsin—the 1885 state law that brought Milwaukee's fire and police departments under the control of a nonpartisan civil service commission. The mugwumps could not have succeeded, however, without the growing political power of organized labor, the transformation of the state's Republican machine that accompanied the rise of large corporations, and the manifest needs of the growing city for increased numbers and competence in its firemen and policemen. Civil service reform was the mugwumps' favorite crusade because they thought it would weaken the power of partisan politicians and restore policymaking to the most able men, instead of the most loyal. Reflecting mugwumpery's deeper sources in abstract desires for social control, the civil service reform movement had begun on the national level. By the mid-1880s its advocates could point to a major legislative triumph in the Pendleton Act of 1883 and a major political triumph in the election of Grover Cleveland in 1884. But this national focus paradoxically hurt the movement in the cities and states. All candidates for local and state office could safely use civil service reform as an abstract standard, like honesty or economy, for attacking the opposition. No one could readily prove whether the additional policemen appointed by the party in power were actually needed, or whether the men selected to the force were the best possible choices. As politicians appropriated the issue for partisan purposes, reformers lost the influence they might have wielded with its appeal. National reformers were further discredited after 1884 when they were forced to apologize for Cleveland's patent violations of their principles.

53. *Ibid.*, April 3, 1887, September 24, 1889. Emanuel L. Philipp and Edgar T. Wheelock, *Political Reform in Wisconsin: A Historical Review of the Subjects of Primary Election, Taxation, and Railway Regulation* (Milwaukee: privately published, 1910), 10.

The national reformers, too, seemed mere partisans.[54] Local politicians, whose machines depended more on local than on national patronage, were delighted to keep the issue alive at the national level because it would protect their local organizations. The approach worked well for every Wisconsin community except Milwaukee. All other Wisconsin cities escaped the reform hatchet until 1897, and Milwaukee, too, would have escaped had it not been for a series of developments that illustrated the interplay of mugwumpery with the larger economic and demographic changes in Gilded Age Wisconsin.

The state's rapid economic transformation stimulated the increasingly militant and political activities of Milwaukee's labor movement, and the first contribution to civil service reform came from the desire of the city's partisan leaders to thwart that labor movement. The bosses had ignored the birth of the Milwaukee Civil Service Reform Association in 1882 because its focus was national and its members seemed cranky elitists who lacked mass support. But when the newly formed Milwaukee Trade Union Assembly proclaimed that "honesty and capability should determine tenure of office, regardless of politics," in local city services, the bosses listened. Patronage would be useless if they lost the election. Democrats therefore endorsed labor's civil service demand in 1882, and they won the election. The Republican legislature, however, refused to pass a law for which Democrats would receive credit. Instead, the Republicans supported the civil service plank in 1884 and won that election. Only the pressures of organized labor had overcome what Rublee had called "the hopelessness of getting a party to commit itself to such a reform locally."[55]

The second change that contributed to passage of the 1885 law was the increasingly commercial outlook of the city and state Republican machines, an outlook that was also a product of rapid urbanization and industrialization. Politicians had broken promises before, and many people wondered whether Republican leaders would use their influence with the Republican 1885 legislature to implement their pledge to support civil service reform. They did; in fact, no one worked harder than Milwaukee's Republican boss, Henry C. Payne, to secure

54. See *Milwaukee Sentinel,* April 12, May 7, 25, 26, August 19, 1887, May 5, 1888, June 30, 1889, for examples.
55. Johnson, "Municipal Reform," 2. Still, *Milwaukee,* 282–83.

passage of the bill.[56] Although Payne well knew the uses of patronage in recruiting party workers, his order of priorities differed from that of earlier Wisconsin bosses who had placed their entire emphasis on patronage. Payne's sympathies were closer to those of the state's increasingly powerful quasi-public corporations, which had begun in the 1870s to finance political campaigns in order to buy protection against Granger-type movements that might develop in the future. His major goal was to win elections so that he could make policies sympathetic to his corporations, and he did not hesitate to sacrifice patronage employees to that end. Even if the party organization would suffer in the short run—and that was not clear, since Payne could always ask the corporations to hire the party faithful—it would profit in the long run, he hoped, by the votes of workers and mugwumps and the continued financial support of the corporations. When Payne rose to leadership in the city and state Republican party as the first of the new type of bosses who worked principally for the corporations, he supplanted the older bosses, men like Madison's postmaster Elisha W. Keyes, who were more interested in patronage alone.[57] Without this metamorphosis within the Republican machine, the 1885 law would never have passed.

The 1885 law also fitted Milwaukee's pressing need to expand municipal services to meet the demands of the city's rapid influx of newcomers. As Milwaukee's population nearly doubled during the 1880s, the new residents expanded the city's periphery at the same time that they crowded closer together in settled areas. Such close proximity vastly increased the threats and consequences of crime and fire, and incompetent firemen and policemen became an expensive luxury. After 1885 the nonpartisan Board of Fire and Police Commissioners, basing its appointments and promotions on competitive and practical examinations, filled an important institutional need as it transformed the police and fire departments into competent and modern bodies that could provide effective protection for the

56. John A. Butler, "The Place of the Council and of the Mayor in the Organization of Municipal Government," *Proceedings of the Indianapolis Conference for Good City Government* (Philadelphia: National Municipal League, 1898), 171, hereinafter cited as *Good City Conference*, Indianapolis. William W. Wight, *Henry Clay Payne: A Life* (Milwaukee: privately published, 1907), 34.

57. See chap. 8, sec. I, and chap. 12 for a further development of this point.

burgeoning metropolis. In the board's first three years, the city's police force nearly doubled from 94 men in 1885 to 181 by 1888, and the fire department grew from 119 men and a budget of $150,000 in 1885 to 174 men and a budget of nearly $250,000 three years later.[58] Civil service reform offered a "very quiet and inexpensive" way of bringing the needed increase in numbers and competence of policemen and firemen to meet the pressures of rapid urbanization.[59]

Mugwumpery was most successful when it mitigated the painful effects of growth processes of the modern city. The 1885 civil service law, like the secret ballot laws that began in 1887, resulted neither from effective mugwump tactics nor from a lessening of social tensions, but from the necessity of adjusting political machinery to an urban society. By flanking the labor movement, by helping bosses to control elections through the secret ballot, by providing large numbers of competent firemen and policemen, by easing such cities as Ashland in their transition from a frontier boom town to a respectable city, by allowing the new utility companies to maintain political immunity at the expense of party workers, mugwumpery demonstrated that it could triumph in an essentially noncontroversial climate where it served both urban dwellers and political leaders.

V

Mugwumpery provided a major thrust for Gilded Age reform. Even such diverse products of industrialization as the new groups of workers and businessmen shared contempt for the partisan politician and a yearning for an earlier time when men were loyal mainly to their families and communities. As a conservative and Victorian alteration of the antebellum attack on social injustices, mugwumpery tried to use what its supporters called "character" as a measure for social control and evaluation of men's purposes. The application of this measure provided the central tension in mugwumpery. However eagerly mugwumps might have wanted to reunite the community and family, to instill character into social inferiors, or to banish politicians, they recognized that industrialization

58. Laurence M. Larson, *A Financial and Administrative History of Milwaukee,* bull. no. 242 (Madison: University of Wisconsin, 1908), 120–21.

59. *Milwaukee Sentinel,* October 7, 1888.

had intensified the generational, religious, ethnic, and class conflicts that thwarted their desired social harmony and rendered obsolete the yardstick of character. In the end, class and ethnic loyalties transcended mugwumpish prejudices. Men increasingly measured their fellows by their occupational affiliations instead of how much character they had. Moreover, the radical mugwumps, like the vice crusaders, sounded increasingly irrelevant to an increasingly divided and secular society in their calls for social purity. The tools of moral suasion and education became daily more obsolete as industrialism transformed the face and loyalties of the community.

But mugwumpery had a real impact on the development of reform in Wisconsin. Civil service and secret ballot laws and the temporary defeat of some political machines testified to the desire to build modern and functional cities. Mugwumps were successful when their programs facilitated the process of urbanization. Even when they failed, mugwumps located the root problem in a community's policymaking and defined the yardsticks of economy and morality against which politicians could be measured. When the depression struck, Wisconsinites would turn first to mugwumpery as the familiar attack. The specific programs—law enforcement, nonpartisanship, economy, civil service reform—received their greatest trials in the years after 1893.

The second major thrust for reform came from the new interest groups that followed the common American tradition in which economic groups solidified their positions and sought aid from government. As industrialization drove deeper wedges between different kinds of producers, men organized to provide economic power and comradeship. Repelled by the nativism and elitism of the mugwumps and convinced that mugwumpery was irrelevant to their jobs, they formed groups to federate with like-minded producer groups. Social survival in the growing cities was perhaps as important a motive for these groups as economic self-interest. A Milwaukee craftsman maintained in 1883 that the city's trades assembly had served him best by breaking down his earlier sense of isolation. He had known only the people who worked in his shop in the years before the assembly was organized. Five years later, thanks to the assembly, he knew four-fifths of his fellow craftsmen throughout the city.[1] The Superior Trades and Labor Assembly also made use of its socializing function and held dances as well as grievance meetings.[2] Economic and social survival in an increasingly urban and industrial society dictated the formation of the new interest groups.

The first thrust of the new groups, especially in the building trades, was to secure economic control over their fields. When private contractors imported hundreds of new workers to Superior, twelve craft unions federated to form the Superior Trades and Labor Assembly. The assembly wanted to reach the new Superiorites before the contractors and to maintain job security for themselves by a program of introducing the city's new and old workers to each other and unionizing such unorganized workers as streetcar employees and newspaper workers.[3] At the same time, self-interest drove established groups of workers, merchants, and farmers to organize producers in related areas.

Once organized, interest groups followed the traditional practice of seeking support from the state and applied the pressures

1. Labor Bureau, *First Biennial Report, 1883–1884,* 123.
2. Superior Trades and Labor Assembly, Minute Book, Superior Trades and Labor Assembly Papers, Manuscripts Division, State Historical Society of Wisconsin, 9.
3. *Ibid.,* 3, 8, 28, 30-31.

that created most of the state's regulatory agencies. The Milwaukee labor movement secured state-wide factory regulation. Both the trades assembly, which by 1882 had drawn more than twenty unions into its orbit, and the rapidly growing Knights of Labor demanded a state labor bureau to collect statistics and enforce laws regulating child labor and factory conditions. So suddenly had organized labor gained significant economic and political power that the politicians could not ignore their demands. As a result, the 1883 legislature created a bureau of labor statistics.[4] When a single commissioner proved incapable of enforcing all the safety laws, organized labor led the campaigns to expand the commissioner's staff. In 1885 the legislature gave the commissioner an assistant and a factory inspector, and in 1887 a second inspector. In the meantime, the labor bureau worked diligently to enforce the laws. During 1891 and 1892, for example, the bureau issued 1,146 orders to employers to comply with state labor laws.[5] Even after they had secured a powerful labor commissioner and skeleton staff, the pressure groups continued to play a major role in state labor regulation. For instance, the Superior Trades and Labor Assembly contributed by appointing a committee in May of 1892 to investigate whether employers were working carpenters longer than the nine hours per day allowed by state law.[6]

Railroad regulation followed the same pattern. After the Granger movement collapsed in the mid-1870s, the Milwaukee Chamber of Commerce led the campaign for rate regulation. Dominated by the city's commission grain merchants, the chamber blamed the railroads for Milwaukee's steadily declining status as a midwestern entrepôt for the expanding wheat empire. The railroads had discriminated in favor of Minneapolis and Chicago, and Milwaukee's wheat receipts fell from 28,458,000 bushels in 1873 to 8,129,000 bushels in 1888. "Milwaukee's most formidable enemy," the merchants cried, was the Chicago and Northwestern Railroad.[7] After lobbying for

4. Labor Bureau, *First Biennial Report*, 2–3, 122. Donald J. Berthrong, "Social Legislation in Wisconsin, 1836–1900" (Ph.D. diss., University of Wisconsin, 1951), 178–80.

5. Labor Bureau, *First Biennial Report*, 169; *4th Report, 1889–1890*, vii; *5th Report, 1891–1892*, 145a; *9th Report, 1899–1900*, 123. Melvin W. Brethouwer, "Safety Legislation in Wisconsin" (M.A. thesis, University of Wisconsin, 1928), 1–5. *Milwaukee Sentinel*, June 13, 1887.

6. Superior Trades and Labor Assembly, Minute Book, 12.

7. Milwaukee Chamber of Commerce, *30th Annual Report of the Trade*

the creation of the Interstate Commerce Commission, the chamber was deeply disappointed when the new agency took years to process its complaints.[8] In 1888 the state railroad commissioner ruled that midwestern railroads had not discriminated against Milwaukee.[9] Denied redress from either federal or state regulators, the chamber drafted and lobbied vigorously in 1889 for a bill that would have set nondiscriminatory rates for Milwaukee.[10] But even the power of the Milwaukee Chamber of Commerce was not sufficient to influence legislators and to overcome Wisconsin's reputation as the most conservative railroad state in the West. While the chamber continued unsuccessfully to push the rate bill at subsequent legislative sessions, it also continued to return to the regulators with more complaints.[11]

The fight for conservation of the state's dwindling fish and wildlife populations was also championed by special interest groups. By 1887 organizations of sportsmen and resort owners had concluded that they were no longer capable of enforcing the state's fish and game regulations through their own private clubs. In that year they won a landmark victory when they persuaded the legislature to create a system of state wardens at the same time that the legislature enacted a great many more restrictions on hunting and fishing.[12]

---

and Commerce of Milwaukee, 1888, 20–22, 26, 27, 30–31; 31st Report, 1889, 55; 32nd Report, 1890, 26; 33rd Report, 1891, 22; 34th Report, 1892, 28; 42nd Report, 1900, 32. Milwaukee Sentinel, December 3, 1887. See also William Edward Derby, "A History of the Port of Milwaukee, 1835–1910" (Ph.D. diss., University of Wisconsin, 1965), 352–54, 364, 379–82, 399, 414.

8. For examples, see Milwaukee chamber, 31st Report, 1889, 22–23; 33rd Report, 1891, 28–29. See also various correspondence throughout Papers of the Milwaukee Chamber of Commerce, Milwaukee County Historical Society.

9. Milwaukee Sentinel, April 19, June 16, 19, 1888. Third Biennial Report of the Railroad Commissioner . . . Ending June 30, 1888, xxx–xxxv, hereinafter cited as Railroad Commissioner, Report.

10. Robert Eliot to Robert M. La Follette, December 22, 1904, La Follette Papers, Manuscripts Division, State Historical Society of Wisconsin. Milwaukee Sentinel, January 27, March 21, 23, 1889. Milwaukee chamber, 31st Report, 1889, 29–30. State Journal, March 21, 27, 1889.

11. The New York Financial and Commercial Chronicle explained the state's conservatism by citing the unfortunate Granger experience, the responsive state commissioners, and the high proportion of freight carried at interstate rates, as reported in Milwaukee Sentinel, March 21, 1889.

12. Milwaukee Sentinel, February 3, 15, 1887. Jackson T. Main, "History of the Conservation of Wild Life in Wisconsin" (M.A. thesis, University of Wisconsin, 1940), chaps. 1 and 2.

I

Although like-minded groups could occasionally work together to attain their political goals, as when labor unions
cooperated to secure organization of the state labor bureau, the
painfully obvious fact about the emerging pressure groups was
their isolation. Warfare between groups that represented similar
constituents and frictions within groups were more common
than unity. Groups with identical interests rarely came together
in united campaigns. As class tensions had prevented workers
and businessmen in Ashland and Milwaukee from mounting a
united campaign against the politicians, so geographical, personal, and class prejudices thwarted concerted action for the
development of reform movements in other areas.

Personalities, politics, occupations, and strategies were points
of division within the labor movement. When the Knights of
Labor gained hegemony over the Milwaukee labor movement
in the mid-1880s by trampling over the Trades Assembly, it
also established domination over organized labor's state-wide
political campaign of 1886 by suppressing D. Frank Powell, the
laborite mayor of La Crosse who had a wide popular following
and aspired to become governor. If Milwaukee's Socialist workers had cared more for organized labor's control over city
government than they did for doctrinal purity and personalities,
the city's long series of labor governments would have begun in
the late eighties instead of 1910. The recriminations growing
out of the Socialists' unwillingness to support the Union Labor
party's mayoralty candidate in 1888, which drained off enough
votes to defeat labor's man, became increasingly sharp, and the
Milwaukee labor movement splintered into one faction after
another. Disillusioned by the political failures of the Knights
of Labor, the craft unions soon departed, too. By 1891 the
hatred between the unions and the Knights flared into such
confrontations as a brawling fistfight on the Milwaukee water-
front between members of the Knights and members of the sea-
men's union. Since 11,000 of the state's 28,000 organized
workers in 1892 lived in Milwaukee and seemed to be constantly feuding, it is small wonder that out-state labor leaders
got no clear signals from the metropolis on what strategies to
develop for a state-wide movement. Although nearly one-third
of the state's workers belonged to unions in 1892, the geographical prejudices between Milwaukeeans and the rest of the

state's residents, the personal rivalry between the Knight's Robert Schilling and the Socialists' Paul Grottkau, the vacillation between economic and political goals, the war between skilled and unskilled workers—all reflections of the relative novelty of organized labor—prevented the development of a united labor movement.[13]

The fight for state railroad regulation illustrates the isolation that divided the new interest groups and their consequent failure to unite similar constituents. If the Milwaukee Chamber of Commerce could have rallied other merchant groups in the state—many of which shared its grievances with the railroads—its regulation bill would probably have passed. Both the Eau Claire Board of Trade and the La Crosse Manufacturers and Jobbers Union complained to the regulators that the railroads discriminated against Wisconsin cities.[14] Merchants from Appleton and the towns in the Fox River Valley lobbied strenuously for a bill to limit charges for switching cars,[15] but geographical rivalries prevented cooperation between these groups with shared grievances against railroads.

The Milwaukee chamber's problem with other merchants showed that the new groups sometimes valued workable relations with their adversaries over solidarity within their interest group. Many merchants wanted to remain in the good graces of the railroads, and when they realized that the chamber's 1889 bill would probably be defeated, they opposed the bill. Over 300 Milwaukee merchants joined the Green Bay Business Men's Association in publicly denouncing the rate bill.[16] Even though no one disputed the chamber's claim that Wisconsin shippers paid significantly higher rates than shippers in Illinois, the merchants could not unite to support the bill that would bring equitable rates to the state.

The chamber was even less successful when it tried to rally support for rate regulation from other groups. Edward P. Bacon, president of the Milwaukee chamber in 1891, claimed

13. Thomas W. Gavett, "The Development of the Labor Movement in Milwaukee" (Ph.D. diss., University of Wisconsin, 1957), 100–197. Milton M. Small, "Biography of Robert Schilling" (M.A. thesis, University of Wisconsin, 1953), 170, 188–227, 244–45. Labor Bureau, *5th Report*, 1891–1892, 116.

14. *Milwaukee Sentinel*, March 4, 1888, June 21, July 21, September 4, 1892.

15. *Ibid.*, April 10, 16, 1893. *Appleton Weekly Post*, April 20, 1893.

16. *Milwaukee Sentinel*, February 14, 24, March 23, 1889.

that the interests of his organization were "closely allied" to those of the state's farmers.[17] The farmers apparently disagreed. They refused to enlist in a campaign for rate regulation, and the Patrons of Husbandry, once the leading champions of regulation, failed even to discuss the subject during the 1880s and early 1890s. The dairy farmers, who preferred to negotiate directly with the railroads for such concessions as lower rates or more refrigerator cars, asked the legislature for help in their fights against the production of oleomargarine, but not against the railroads.[18] "Whatever the cause of grievance the farmers of other states may have against the railroads, the number in Wisconsin who cherish any feeling other than good will is extremely small," declared Charles R. Beach to the scientific agriculturists in 1891.[19] Therefore, the state's farm groups ignored the Milwaukee merchants' rate campaign.

Two prominent groups of passengers advocated rate regulation, but the Milwaukee chamber failed to coordinate its campaign with those groups. Just before the rate bill was introduced, the state's traveling salesmen formed the Travelers' Protective Association to take revenge upon the railroads that were "robbing us every day."[20] They wanted lower rates, but they did not join forces with the chamber. When the railroads refused to grant the customary rate reduction to members of the Grand Army of the Republic to attend the 1889 national encampment at Milwaukee, the old soldiers, at "a pitch of high indignation," demanded passage of the chamber's rate bill, but the chamber, which had accepted defeat two weeks previously, could not rally its forces.[21] Timing is essential to the legislative process, and the two most powerful groups did not coordinate their efforts. Both sought precisely the same goal, but each fought alone.

Many groups had begun to demand changes that would shortly produce unified reform campaigns, but in the years before the depression they were unable to see that their favorite reforms would also benefit others. This apparent blindness was especially true in the area of taxation, where many groups demanded

17. Milwaukee chamber, *33rd Report,* 1891, 27–28.
18. Eric E. Lampard, *The Rise of the Dairy Industry in Wisconsin: A Study in Agricultural Change, 1820–1920* (Madison: State Historical Society of Wisconsin, 1963), 126–27, 258–61, 384.
19. Beach, "What Can the Government Legitimately Do for the Farmer?" *Handbook,* bull. no. 5 (1891), 81.
20. *Milwaukee Sentinel,* December 28, 1888.
21. *Ibid.,* March 15, 27, 1889.

reform but none was able to develop a program around which others could rally. The state's farm groups compensated for their lack of interest in railroad regulation by the vehemence of their demands for tax reform. "The unequal and unjust burdens of taxation is a prolific source of discontent among farmers," declared Grange leader Washington Churchill to the 1892 convention. His proposal for a tax on mortgages was approved by the dairymen and scientific agriculturists, who also believed that farmers were unfairly taxed.[22] Despite their shared grievance, these farm groups never mounted a successful campaign for mortgage taxation. However strenuously the Milwaukee Trades Assembly and the Knights of Labor feuded over other issues in the 1880s, they agreed on the urgent necessity for a graduated income tax.[23] In their repeated attacks on the extravagance of partisan politicians, said papers in Ashland and Appleton, mugwumps of all types drew attention to the problems of taxation as they sought "protection to the tax-payer as against the tax-eater who now dictates the disbursements."[24] Temperance-minded reformers and suffragettes complained against tax dodgers,[25] and some state officials pointed to specific dodges certain groups used to evade their taxes. Throughout the late eighties and early nineties the state railroad commissioners repeatedly denounced the way railroads and sleeping-car and express companies juggled their returns to escape paying the taxes required by state law,[26] but none of these exposures resulted in tax reform.

Taxation was clearly one area that troubled many groups in Wisconsin. As events were subsequently to prove, however, tax reform was capable of drawing groups into close cooperation. The significant fact about tax reform in the years before the depression was the failure of these diverse groups to mount a united campaign; no major tax reform bills became law between 1885 and 1893. While many groups clearly felt that they were unfairly taxed, they could not agree on whether the best

22. State Grange, *21st Session, 1892*, 8. Beach, "What Can the Government Do?" 77–78.

23. Small, "Schilling," 220. Gavett, "Milwaukee Labor Movement," 94.

24. For examples, see *Ashland Daily News*, February 23, 1890. *Appleton Weekly Post*, January 1, 1891.

25. *Appleton Weekly Post*, October 22, 1891. Beach, "What Can the Government Do?" 78. WWSA Proceedings, 1892, Box 36, 102.

26. Railroad Commissioner, *2nd Report, 1886*, xiii–xv; *3rd Report, 1888*, xiv–xix; *4th Report, 1890*, 7–11.

reform would be to tax mortgages, incomes, breweries, or corporations. If there was one focus toward which most groups could channel their dissatisfaction with taxation it was probably the old demand for economical administration of government; but the groups failed to rally for attack on even this ever-popular target. The isolation of the various groups of tax reformers was demonstrated by the fate of a bill that was first introduced in 1889. Sponsored by K. K. Kennan, chief tax official of the Wisconsin Central Railroad, the bill proposed establishment of a state tax commission to survey the state's tax situation and propose needed reforms.[27] The different groups were unable to agree even on this minimal bill, and a concerted tax reform movement was to wait until citizens felt the depression's financial pressures.

II

This inability of the new groups to work together was one result of their leaders' strenuous efforts to nurture a sense of group consciousness and solidarity among their members. Because the major function and appeal of these groups was to offer a new sense of identity to people who felt isolated from the larger society, they understandably turned their faces inward and emphasized the homogeneity of their own groups. Charles R. Beach, speaking for many of the state's agricultural organizations, put the problem well in 1891: "Before we claim the privilege of reforming the government, ought we not to prove our ability to do so by reforming our practice as farmers?"[28] After complaining that "no man . . . needs to range up alongside of his neighbor more than the farmer," the state's most prominent farm leader, former Governor William D. Hoard, urged farmers to shun the larger society and develop a farmer consciousness: "We don't want to dabble in politics, we don't want to mix up in religion, we don't want to mix up with anything on earth, but stick to this. Give to me a larger judgment of my duty as a farmer."[29] The Patrons of Husbandry shared this group identity and its related isolation. In 1890 the state's farm groups began a crusade to wrest the college of agriculture from

27. Emanuel L. Philipp and Edgar T. Wheelock, *Political Reform in Wisconsin: A Historical Review of the Subjects of Primary Election, Taxation, and Railway Regulation* (Milwaukee: privately published, 1910), 109–11.

28. Beach, "What Can the Government Do?" 82.

29. *Handbook,* bull. no. 5 (1891), 19–20. *Milwaukee Sentinel,* May 31,

the state university and establish it as a separate agency to be controlled only by farmers. This move was only one campaign in the long battle by the state's agricultural groups to educate farmers' children, not in the liberal arts, but in how to become better farmers. The farmers had won significant victories in 1885 when the state began to subsidize farmers' institutes and short courses and in 1889 when a separate college of agriculture was established at the University of Wisconsin.[30] Such changes, they hoped, would encourage a group consciousness among farmers. Labor unions, of course, used social functions like dances to supplement their members' economic motives in building a sense of group identity. Even the Wisconsin Woman Suffrage Association felt this pervasive spirit when it resolved in 1890 to "keep the one object in view and whack away at that alone instead of dividing our forces by taking up other issues."[31] Leaders of all these groups seemed committed to the belief that exposure to the larger society, whether by studying liberal arts or entering politics, potentially undermined the frail sense of loyalty to the group.

Failure to win political goals intensified the sense of isolation and the yearning for group solidarity. When the Knights of Labor lost its political campaigns in Milwaukee in the mid-1880s, thousands of workers deserted that organization and joined the Federated Trades Council, which rejected politics and emphasized job consciousness instead.[32] After the defeat of the 1889 rate bill and the 1893 switching bill, merchants retreated from the larger world of politics and compromise into their local organizations, from which they filed complaints with

---

1890. See also T. J. Van Matre, "A Whack with the Shillalah," *Handbook,* bull. no. 7 (1893), 83.

30. State Grange, *19th Session, 1890,* 4–5. For the preference for education over politics, see State Grange, *21st Session, 1892,* 9–10. *Milwaukee Sentinel,* March 17, 1892. Frederick M. Rosentreter, *The Boundaries of the Campus: A History of the University of Wisconsin Extension Division* (Madison: University of Wisconsin Press, 1957), 17–18. Wilbur H. Glover, *Farm and College: The College of Agriculture of the University of Wisconsin, A History* (Madison: University of Wisconsin Press, 1952), 149–50. C. E. Estabrook, "Farmers Institutes: Their Origins in Wisconsin," *Handbook,* bull. no. 10 (1896), 193–98.

31. WWSA Proceedings, 1890, 70.

32. Gavett, "Milwaukee Labor Movement," 159. The close ties between the Federated Trades Council and the Socialists did not develop until after the depression hit Milwaukee. Frederick I. Olson, "The Socialist Party and the Union in Milwaukee, 1900–1912," *Wisconsin Magazine of History,* 44 (Winter 1960–1961), 110–12.

regulatory agencies. Political defeats strengthened those leaders who urged an exclusive group consciousness on producers.

A few leaders urged their members to seek broader political goals and to cooperate with other groups, but they were a distinct minority and failed to attract their members to wider areas. The most effective of these leaders was Milwaukee labor leader Robert O. Schilling, who had resigned from the coopers' union in the 1870s to help organize the broader Knights of Labor, an organization he hoped would remake industrial society. When the Milwaukee Knights turned increasingly from politics to unionism in 1888–1889 Schilling deserted that group to work for the Republican mayoral candidate and later still for the Populists. Rejecting job conscious unionism, Schilling found himself increasingly isolated from Milwaukee's workers by the late 1880s.[33] Milwaukee grain merchant Edward P. Bacon was no more successful than Schilling in his attempts to persuade the city's businessmen to "join hands in the common endeavor to advance the interests of all and promote the general welfare of the city at large." While Bacon went on to become a civic leader, his pleas in the 1891 presidential message to the local chamber of commerce "to be indifferent, in a measure, to what appears to be, at the moment, to one's individual interest, in order that some ultimate benefit may be secured for the many" were disregarded.[34] Voices like those of Schilling and Bacon became more muffled as the new interest groups rejected cooperation in favor of group consciousness.

Nowhere was this rejection more obvious than in the groups' negative attitudes toward politics. To coordinate a program with other groups and to mount a successful lobbying campaign a number of groups would have had to be willing and able to plan and look beyond their immediate contexts. But the reason they had formed their groups in the first place was that they felt isolated from the larger society. Their isolation as a group deprived them of the will and experience necessary to build successful political coalitions. As a major result, many of the state's most prominent group leaders were uneasy in the world of politics and politicians. The most notable example is that of Henry Smith, whom Milwaukee workers elected to the

33. Small, "Schilling," 11–12, 72–75, 107–8, 154–56, 165–66, 170, 197–98, 224–25. Gavett, "Milwaukee Labor Movement," 104, 155–68. Unidentified notes in Robert Schilling Papers, Manuscripts Division, State Historical Society of Wisconsin.

34. Milwaukee chamber, *33rd Report*, 1891, 29.

state legislature in the 1870s and to Congress in the late 1880s. At heart, Smith was unhappy in politics and preferred his circle of labor leaders in Milwaukee. "I curse the day that I was fool enough to allow myself to be led into politics," he confided to a friend from his seat in Congress. "It is nothing but mind torture. No fun in this."[35] Focused inward, the new groups were profoundly uneasy in politics.

The failure of the interest groups to develop common programs had other causes besides their self-imposed isolation. First, there were few objective evils around which they could rally. A series of spectacular events would be necessary before the groups would agree on the best way to remove the injustices in taxation, for example. New menaces and discoveries that accompanied the depression were to present new threats that would affect everyone and thus challenge the groups' inward directions. Second, groups could pursue their separate goals because the economy seemed to be progressing well. Commenting on the fact that wages in Milwaukee had increased 40 per cent since 1880 at the same time that living costs were declining, the *Sentinel* could plausibly state as late as 1892 that "the rich are growing richer, some of them, and the poor are growing richer, all of them."[36] The booming economy generated a feeling that problems resulting from industrialism might gradually disappear. The faith in a bright future blunted much of the desire to transcend special interests. Not until economic collapse shattered this illusion would the interest groups try to reintegrate themselves into and try to reform the society they had rejected. Those same social tensions that had retarded the development of mugwumpery inhibited the groups from cooperating in economic and political reforms. Finally, popular attitudes toward politics and reform sharply inhibited the political effectiveness of these groups.

35. Henry Smith to Gust A. Rahr, August 25, 1888, Schilling Papers. *Blue Book, 1899,* 191.
36. *Milwaukee Sentinel,* October 22, 1892.

REFORMERS AND THE PUBLIC IN THE GILDED AGE

Both the mugwumps and the new interest groups were repeatedly thwarted in the Gilded Age by old political habits and new popular prejudices. The first set of problems stemmed from widespread beliefs about the meaning and evolution of the American experience in the nineteenth century and the implications of those beliefs in a society that was rapidly becoming more urban and industrial. By the mid-1880s many Wisconsinites had developed ideas about reform and politics that severely limited opportunities for reformers. The second set of problems rose from the persistence of voting patterns and political allegiances that had originated before the Civil War. These allegiances undercut most reform of the 1880s, and since many reformers shared some of these traditions and values, they served as both internal and external handicaps.

I

Many fundamental Gilded Age values had a kind of independent life, rooted not so much in class conflict as in what seemed to be the evolution of the American experience. The first and strongest of these beliefs was that the whole thrust of American history was to liberate the individual from inhibitions imposed by a hereditary aristocracy and an arbitrary government. While this belief was common in Gilded Age Wisconsin, few people developed its implications as thoroughly and consistently as Horace A. Rublee. A former chairman of the Republican state central committee and still an important party spokesman, Rublee wielded further influence because his *Milwaukee Sentinel* was the most widely read newspaper in the state and Republican legislators frequently consulted the *Sentinel* to decide what laws to support.

As Rublee wrote one variation after another on the same theme, he showed the full contours of his prejudice, which hampered reformers. Finding "nothing but upward growth" in American history, he saw the basic cause for progress in America's greater "freedom of the individual—every man left free to pursue his own career, to get rich if he can, to get wisdom if he can and will, to waste his earnings or to save them as he will, to come and go at his ability and pleasure."[1] This meant that governments should encourage the liberation of the individual by protecting life and property while resisting all proposals that undermined individualism. "There is never a law that does not restrict liberty, from the law of gravitation down to the latest enactment of the Wisconsin legislature," he wrote in 1887.[2] Even when Rublee sympathized with a proposal, as he did with the idea of a national postal telegraph system, he opposed enacting it because "when we take one step it leads to another that was not contemplated and the multiplication of precedents tends to confer duties on the state that are inconsistent with the best development of individual character."[3]

As Wisconsin's leading disciple of Herbert Spencer ("the greatest living Englishman"), Rublee further maintained that experience had shown that legislation could not change men's behavior. Rublee stated through the *Milwaukee Sentinel* that science and experience both demonstrated that "the power of legislation to regulate conduct is painfully limited."[4] In his repeated attacks on Prohibitionists Rublee warned that "the return to violent methods of making men good, to the enactment of laws for the prohibition of that which a large proportion of mankind does not condemn, is the flinging away of all the results of long experience."[5] Child labor laws could never work because they could not alter "the rapacity of parents," which was "chiefly responsible" for that evil.[6]

How, then, was change to be accomplished? Rublee believed that the twin forces of education and moral suasion, with their direct appeals to the individual, would ultimately change public opinion and thereby render legislation superfluous. "Whenever we go outside the field of moral suasion, of education, and endeavor to make mankind good by legislative enactments," he warned, "we check the operation of the best methods of reforming men and induce evils vastly greater than those we attempt to destroy."[7] Since behavior was a product of the individual's will and character, not his environment, direct appeals could accomplish what laws could not. Believing that individual short-

1. *Milwaukee Sentinel,* May 9, 1889, March 16, 1887.
2. *Ibid.,* February 18, 28, 1887.
3. *Ibid.,* January 22, 1887, April 19, 1889.
4. *Ibid.,* September 16, 1887.
5. *Ibid.,* August 7, 1887.
6. *Ibid.,* April 9, 1887.
7. *Ibid.,* August 24, 1887.

comings caused poverty, Rublee contended that "nothing is more calculated to shake confidence in human nature" than work among poor people.[8] Change would come only when reformers persuaded enough parents not to let their children work or enough drinkers to quit.

While few Wisconsinites expressed these ideas as systematically as Rublee, this same philosophy operated frequently among the state's editors and reformers. Whether expressed as a coherent philosophy or a number of prejudices, the ideas Rublee expressed had three important effects on the pattern of reform in Gilded Age Wisconsin. First, the emphasis on moral suasion and education inhibited groups from seeking governmental assistance. Believing that only the education of individuals could alleviate poverty, the Milwaukee Associated Charities shunned legislation.[9] Charles Beach, speaking for the state's farm groups, put it bluntly: "Progress, wealth and civilization are not the result of governmental acts, but of individual effort. The individual is the unit of society."[10] Most of Wisconsin's predominantly immigrant-oriented religious groups opposed what a Milwaukee Catholic editor called "statolatry—the omnipotence of officialdom—the paternalism of the State—the expediency of intermeddling, fussing, interfering with and bossing a private concern."[11] Even the regulators had doubts. After many unsuccessful efforts to enforce laws to prevent food adulteration, Dairy and Food Commissioner H. C. Thom complained that "virtue and honesty cannot be legislated into the people."[12] Since the individual was the unit of society, reformers would have to appeal to him instead of the state.

Laissez-faire ideals restrained reformers in a second way: they prevented cooperation between like-minded groups. Even if a group could rationalize its own requests for government aid it believed that other groups should conform to the laissez-faire ideal. Fox River Valley merchants reasoned, in effect, that it was acceptable for them to seek state aid in their troubles with the railroads, but they petitioned against state aid for Milwaukee merchants. Denying the validity of other groups' appeals to the state, they naturally were incapable of working with those groups to generate a common program. At the very time that

8. *Ibid.,* January 22, December 8, 1889.
9. *Ibid.,* January 9, 1889.
10. *Handbook,* bull. no. 5 (1891), 81; bull. no. 7 (1893), 83, 84.
11. *Milwaukee Catholic Citizen,* April 5, 1890.
12. *Handbook,* bull. no. 5 (1891), 212.

an Appleton editor strongly condemned "the doctrine that every evil can be abolished by legislature," he was demanding a law to lower railway charges to his city's merchants.[13]

Rublee's editorials had a direct effect. Republican legislators used them as good reasons for defeating bills. State Sen. Edward Scofield merely echoed Rublee's editorials when he reported negatively on the railroad rate bill of 1889.[14]

If such laissez-faire ideals restrained the new interest groups, they would seem to support mugwumps in their direct appeals to individuals. While some mugwumps frequently invoked laissez-faire assumptions to buttress their moral and educational campaigns, they soon learned that the reasons Wisconsinites supported individualistic values often challenged cherished mugwump beliefs.

Ideas about the negative role of the state and the positive role of education were popular enough to limit the programs of groups, to prevent cooperation with other groups, and to restrain legislators. The main reason for this popularity was the acceptance of the legend of the self-made man and the resulting trust in individual mobility as the primary road to economic democracy and social progress. The American environment offered the opportunity. Hard work and virtue fattened the pocketbook while they steeled the soul. "Remember its a rule made by labor as well as capital that one must 'Paddle their own Canoe' to succeed," reminded a Wood County editor.[15] The farmers' institutes, more popular in Wisconsin than in any other state, perfectly combined faith in the self-made man with belief in the powers of education. They were predicated on the conviction that the farmer whose success was self-made would inspire other farmers to follow his example. A successful La Fayette County farmer told his audience of aspiring farmers that "the difficulty rests very largely with ourselves and may be traced almost directly to our own stepstones. . . . On a farm or elsewhere a man seldom rises higher than his aim."[16] Even many of the new groups, whose very existence implied the failure of the individual to achieve happiness through his own efforts, were strongly imbued with the faith in individual effort. This belief that men could get rich quick if they worked hard enough

13. *Appleton Weekly Post,* January 12, 1893.
14. *Milwaukee Sentinel,* March 15, 1889.
15. *Grand Rapids Wood County Reporter,* August 31, 1893.
16. *Handbook,* bull. no. 5 (1891), 202-3; bull. no. 10 (1896), 193–98.

—a belief that an environment of apparent opportunity reinforced—largely explained popular acceptance of Rublee's laissez-faire ideals.

This same belief, however, was one of the primary targets of mugwumps, who opposed its materialistic consequences. Horace Rublee himself found that the popular admiration for the self-made man that supported his arguments for laissez faire at the same time undercut his mugwumpish appeals to regenerate individual morality. He frequently protested "against the universal desire to 'get there'—against the delusive notion that riches are worth the getting at the expense of higher ideals."[17] Those other mugwumps who campaigned for moral reforms shared Rublee's conviction that the popular desire for "money-getting" turned Wisconsinites away from their crusades.[18] Mugwumps themselves were alarmed at the widespread support for the legend of the self-made man, which wrecked their goals in many ways.

Both the mugwumps and the new interest groups were thwarted by the popular belief that the nineteenth-century American thrust was toward liberation of the individual. Not only did conflicting ideas about the proper respective roles of education and legislation divide many interest groups from the mugwumps, but the reasons that most Wisconsinites accepted the legend of individual liberation also severely undercut both types of reformers.

II

The rapid growth of cities and industries in Gilded Age Wisconsin reinforced a second group of prejudices that retarded the growth of both mugwumps and interest groups. A large number of Wisconsinites came to believe that the worlds of reformers and politicians were alien to their own and that, as a result, they could wisely and safely ignore the efforts and programs of all types of reformers and politicians.

Reformers constantly had to battle the Gilded Age prejudice that they were somehow different men—cranky, nasty, ignorant, foreign, sinister—who deviated in fundamental moral or psycho-

17. *Milwaukee Sentinel,* May 19, 1887, December 13, 1891, December 4, 1892.
18. *Milwaukee Catholic Citizen,* August 18, 1888. *Presbyterian Minutes,* 1884, 6. *Baptist Minutes,* 45th Meeting, 1889, 45. *Congregational Minutes,* 51st Meeting, 1891, 46. *Baptist Union Minutes,* 25th Meeting, 1889, 12.

logical characteristics from the average citizen. When a Milwaukee Methodist preacher sought the reasons for his troubles with his congregation, a lay leader replied: "You are by nature a non-conformist, a round head—and an Independent, a social Reformer."[19] That was reason enough to reject anyone and his principles. A frequently made charge was that a reformer had an underdeveloped sense of humor and lacked a "cheerful and helpful confidence in the upward progress of humanity." "Is this world such a dreadfully serious thing," asked Horace Rublee, "is the task of regulating the universe such a solemn responsibility, that a Mugwump must abolish amiability, affability, geniality, benignity and all other qualities of good nature?" The state's established farm groups dismissed the Populists also as "chronic grumblers."[20] Many Wisconsinites were terror-stricken by union leaders and socialists whom they regarded as maniacs who plotted the overthrow of the established order.[21] Because reformers proposed programs to change other people they were often accused of being, in the words of a Catholic editor, "moral busybodies." Some Yankees charged that the suggestions of foreign-born reformers should be dismissed because their advocates did not understand the American heritage. Perhaps the most frequent charge of all was that reformers were too ignorant of the real world to suggest practical changes, and a great many Wisconsinites could join Horace Rublee in urging reformers to adopt "less of the profitless overstraining of the mind in dealing with abstractions and a vast increase in the amount of common sense."[22] Those people who advocated change, whether elitist mugwumps or union leaders, constantly had to confront the widespread impression that their peculiar personalities prevented them from being part of the mainstream of the times.

The increasing fragmentation of society that accompanied the state's economic transformation made the world of politics equally alien to a large number of Wisconsinites. The professional American politicians, explained a Catholic editor, were "a lot of drinking good fellows with easy-going notions on

19. George L. Richards to Eugene Updike, January 11, 1890, Updike Papers, Manuscripts Division, State Historical Society of Wisconsin.

20. *Milwaukee Sentinel,* May 18, July 11, 1887, December 7, 1888, May 9, 1889. *Handbook,* bull. no. 5 (1891), 82, 202.

21. *Milwaukee Sentinel,* January 5, February 16, May 19, 1887, February 5, 1889, July 7, 8, 1892.

22. *Milwaukee Catholic Citizen,* April 12, 1890. *Milwaukee Sentinel,* January 27, 1887.

morals and honesty, and wholly devoid of such qualities as courage, conviction and earnestness."[23] Local politics was dominated "by the voting rabble that flocks into [the cities] from all points of the compass" and that was composed, in the words of a county supervisor, of "the lower strata of society."[24] As a result, "moral men held aloof from politics, because looser morals were there more rampant than in business."[25] This distrust of politicians extended from business and religious circles to include many labor and farm leaders.[26] The aura of liquor, immigrants, and smoke and the emphasis on the negative role of the state repelled many reformers from the world of politics. Although the Ashland election of 1890 was an exception, the general reaction to the strange ways of the politicians was not to try to change those ways but to remain aloof. Not until new conditions virtually forced men to try to capture local politics would a great many Wisconsinites overcome their fear and hatred of the politicians and decide to attack, rather than withdraw. The dominant Gilded Age response to unresponsive politicians was retreat.

III

The most serious problem for Gilded Age reformers was the persistence of voting patterns that had been established in the pre-Civil War years. Wisconsinites in 1890 continued to support political parties on the basis of the responses those parties had made to the flood of immigrants and the moral issues of the 1840s and 1850s. Although the proportion of foreign-born residents to the state's total population declined from 36.2 per cent in 1850 to 30.8 per cent in 1890, the ethnic pattern of Wisconsin politics remained substantially unchanged. The Republican party's anti-Catholic and antislavery orientation attracted Protestants, whether born in Norway, Germany, or the United States, who burned with moral and religious indignation at the power of the Catholic Church and the slaveholders. In reaction, Catholic immigrants from Ireland and Germany turned to the

23. *Milwaukee Catholic Citizen,* January 11, 1890, also September 22, 1888, November 15, 1890.
24. *Appleton Weekly Post,* January 1, 1891. *Ashland Daily News,* March 2, 1890.
25. *Milwaukee Sentinel,* September 17, 1888.
26. *Ibid.,* January 25, February 8, 1893. State Grange, *20th Session, 1891,* 6.

Democrats for relief from the pressures placed on them by the moralistic and nativistic Republicans. For the next forty years politicians from both parties manipulated these ethnic and religious prejudices through such issues as temperance and schools and such techniques as patronage and nominations. While they succeeded in retaining the support of those groups that had supported them in the 1850s, they failed to dislodge any significant groups from the opposition. The ethnic and religious prejudices of the old and new worlds largely formed the political loyalties of most Wisconsinites in 1890.[27]

Ethnic and religious conflicts hampered reformers in several ways: they prevented reformers of different backgrounds from cooperating; they consumed energies that subsequent events would channel into reform movements; the noisy fights between ethnic groups drowned out many reformers; and ethnic prejudices conditioned reactions to economic events. When labor violence flared in Milwaukee in 1886, for example, commentators reminded their readers that the rioters were immigrants. The riot proved to a Madison editor that "the city of Milwaukee could well afford to ship every member of that murderous mob of Poles back to Poland and forever close its gates against them."[28]

The tasks of reformers became even more difficult in 1889 and 1890 as a result of two events that brought religious and ethnic tensions to a raging boil. The practice of reading the Bible in public schools had for decades been a serious point of division between Catholic and Protestant parents; the Catholics regarded it as a symbol of Protestant domination over public policy. The state supreme court ripped open the issue in 1890 when, in its most controversial ruling of the Gilded Age, it upheld the claim of Catholic parents that Bible reading in public schools was unconstitutional. Protestant leaders immediately blasted the decision as "unhistorical, illogical, unprecedented, un-American, unpatriotic and of immoral tendency," and found behind the decision "the antagonism and aggression of the Romish Hierarchy." Catholics replied that Protestant spokesmen were "bigots, nullifiers, rebels against the law and reverend enemies of our free institutions."[29]

27. Roger E. Wyman, "Voting Behavior in the Progressive Era: Wisconsin as a Case Study" (Ph.D. diss., University of Wisconsin, 1970), 26-69. *Milwaukee Catholic Citizen*, April 12, 1890.

28. *State Journal*, May 4, 1886.

29. *Presbyterian Minutes*, 1891, 15. Minutes of the Madison Convention

At the same time that Protestants battled Catholics over this ruling an event occurred that showed that ethnic and religious conflicts not only diverted popular interest from reform but also destroyed reforms. In 1889 Governor Hoard was deeply troubled that many children were not receiving educations because they had to work in factories, mills, and mines. He proposed that children be required to attend school for at least twelve weeks each year and that all instruction be in English. The legislature enacted the proposal without a dissenting vote. The law, Hoard hoped, would advance good citizenship at the same time that it helped to eliminate child labor. He could not have anticipated the result. German Lutheran churches and the Democratic party led a major crusade against Hoard and the Republicans for being nativists whose next program would be prohibition. Professing a reluctance "to get religious and racial blood up," politicians of both parties used the Bennett Law to exploit the ethnic antagonisms that undergirded Wisconsin politics. So successfully did they arouse voters over the possible nativist connotations of the law that very few people remembered that its primary purpose was to destroy child labor. The Democrats trounced Hoard in the 1890 elections and the 1891 legislature hastily repealed the Bennett Law.[30] When ethnic prejudices overwhelmed this humanitarian change, reformers concluded that such conflicts formed one of their most difficult problems.

Finally, ethnic and religious conflicts reinforced the grip of partisan allegiances over most Wisconsin voters in the Gilded Age. The symbols and traditions of parties were more important

of Congregational Churches and Ministers, 154–55, Wisconsin Congregational Church Papers, Manuscripts Division, State Historical Society of Wisconsin. *Baptist Minutes,* 47th Meeting, 1891, 31. *Milwaukee Catholic Citizen,* December 1, 1888, May 17, 1890. William Walter Updegrove, "Bibles and Brickbats: Religious Conflict in Wisconsin's Public School System During the Nineteenth Century" (M.A. thesis, University of Wisconsin, 1969).

30. *State Journal,* September 25, 1890. Horace Samuel Merrill, *William Freeman Vilas: Doctrinaire Democrat* (Madison: State Historical Society of Wisconsin, 1954), 159–69. Richard N. Current, *Pine Logs and Politics: A Life of Philetus Sawyer* (Madison: State Historical Society of Wisconsin, 1950), 254–55. Louise Phelps Kellogg, "The Bennett Law in Wisconsin," *Wisconsin Magazine,* 2 (September 1918), 3–25. William F. Whyte, "The Bennett Law Campaign in Wisconsin," *Wisconsin Magazine,* 10 (June 1927), 363–90. Robert J. Ulrich, "The Bennett Law of 1889: Education and Politics in Wisconsin" (Ph.D. diss., University of Wisconsin, 1965). Wyman, "Voting Behavior," 70–114.

than economic issues. Election statistics confirmed the observation of a Grand Rapids editor that "the natural tendency is to sustain by your vote that party to which your father belonged—into which you originally drifted without consideration, and in which you have remained by force of association and habit."[31] There were no major shifts in voting in the four presidential elections between 1880 and 1892; the state's Republican percentages were 56, 52, 53, and 49, respectively. None of the state's 68 counties deviated by more than 15 per cent in its party returns between 1888 and 1892, and only 8 counties fluctuated by more than 15 per cent between any two of the four elections. By comparison, between 1892 and 1896, when new problems and issues transcended traditional loyalties, no fewer than 26 counties changed their party votes by more than 15 per cent.[32] That men continued to vote the way of their fathers suggested that no reform issues were strong enough to overcome voting habits.

IV

Since the voters remained responsive to religious, ethnic, occupational, and partisan allegiances and issues, Wisconsin's reformers in the Gilded Age could not generate proposals or methods to bridge social and political barriers. Only a series of shattering events and discoveries would shake their widely held faith in individualism and the pervasive existence of opportunity and cast doubt upon the effectiveness of moral suasion and education to meet social and political realities. In the meantime, during the Gilded Age, mugwumpish individualism and the inward focus of voluntary associations led voters to avoid issues that would soon become matters of debate. The electorate agreed with the state official who declared in 1889 that "the public would not be justified in interfering" in labor disputes that were private quarrels between employers and their workers.[33] The general public lacked either the ideology or the sense of crisis to give them a stake in such problems as labor disputes. Those few reforms which were adopted were primarily noncontroversial adjustments to which all parties could agree, and the

31. *Wood County Reporter,* July 28, 1892.
32. James R. Donoghue, *How Wisconsin Voted* (Madison: University of Wisconsin Extension Division, 1956), 40–44.
33. M. Griffin to William D. Hoard, July 25, 1889, "Strikes and Riots," Box 1, Wisconsin State Archival Series 1/1/8–9.

voters lacked the desperation and conflict that were soon to accompany progressivism. Deflected by their faith in the self-made man, suspicious of reformers, beguiled by mugwumpery, distracted by bitter ethnic and religious conflicts, confirmed in partisanship, dominated by conservative machines and editors in both parties, led by education-conscious or group-conscious men in their business, farm, and labor organizations, Wisconsin's voters shunned popular revolts in the Gilded Age. The state was proud of its reputation as the conservative jewel of the Midwest.

II | THE ROOTS OF A NEW CITIZENSHIP AND SOCIAL PROGRESSIVISM, 1893–1900

The depression of 1893–1897 produced fundamental changes in the social and political ideas and institutions of Wisconsin. Before the depression men and women who desired changes acted mostly with people within their own class and status groups; men with similar programs but different backgrounds rarely acted together. Furthermore, they naturally entered the political party of their fathers and just as naturally accepted that party's economic and social programs. The rapid growth of cities and the widespread prosperity of the period reinforced an optimistic faith in the future that led them to fear and ridicule reformers of the Gilded Age.

The depression radically changed all that. As "the pinch of poverty begins to touch the richest as well as the poorest,"[1] men began to examine the causes of this catastrophe. "On every corner," declared the *Superior Evening Telegram*, "stands a man whose fortune in these dull times has made him an ugly critic of everything and everybody."[2] The results of the depression were so brutal and far-reaching that few Wisconsinites could escape them and avoid becoming ugly critics.

A profound sense of social unrest quickly overtook most areas of social and political debate. Men and women came to believe that established ideas and institutions failed to respond to the new discoveries they were making in the depression, and they felt that it was their urgent responsibility somehow to find and implement new diagnoses and cures. In this atmosphere a man's ideas became more important than his social background; it was unwise and unsafe to ignore any possible solutions. New local institutions—discussion clubs, reform leagues, university extension centers, church groups, farmers' institutes—arose to fill the widespread demand for places where men and women could share their puzzled quests for alternatives to the existing order. In the process of forging those alternatives they created a new civic consciousness that transcended the social barriers that

1. *Chippewa Herald,* quoted in *Grand Rapids Wood County Reporter,* August 24, 1893.
2. *Superior Evening Telegram,* March 21, 1896. See also *Appleton Weekly Post,* September 14, 1893.

had divided them in the years before 1893. Men and women began participating in solving new social and political problems with different people and in different ways than ever before. It all added up to a whole new pattern of citizenship.

The new citizens demanded that old ideas and institutions adjust to the new problems they discovered, and each social institution was expected to justify its existence. So rapid was the pace of change, so novel the directions, that most observers were content simply to insert the adjective "new" before their descriptions of each institution. The new citizenship thus brought forward the "New Woman," the "New Religion," and the "New Education," and they, in turn, led the emerging social progressivism.

The depression began as a severe bankers' panic. To fill the need for capital in the state's rapidly expanding economy, state banks had increased their assets five times between 1870 and 1890, and the number of state banks had risen from 29 in 1880 to 119 on the eve of the panic. Most people had assumed that the state's conservative banking tradition had made its banks strong and safe. This assumption was rudely disproved during a few months in 1893. The state's most powerful banks fell at the beginning. The Plankinton Bank of Milwaukee, with assets of over $2 million in 1890, failed on June 1, 1893. Less than two months later, on July 26, the Wisconsin Marine and Fire Insurance Company, long considered one of the Midwest's strongest financial institutions, collapsed under the weight of overextended loans. The demise of these two financial gibraltars toppled such other Milwaukee banks as the South Side Savings, the Milwaukee National, and the Second Ward Savings. During July alone the wave of failures engulfed banks at Manitowoc, Chippewa Falls, Port Washington, Sparta, Portage, Tomah, Washburn, Shell Lake, and Prescott. By the end of 1893 the year's casualty list totaled 27, over one-fifth of the state's banks.[1] Before the depression had run its full course it dragged under banks in such major cities as Superior and La Crosse.[2]

The bank failures revealed the fundamental unsoundness of the financial structure on which the state's economy depended and had tremendous ramifications for the rest of the state's economy. Local governments had deposited public funds in the banks, and each failure deprived the community of the money needed for the fire department, public schools, or the unemployed. The Superior school system was barely able to operate after two bank failures cost the board of education $34,000.[3] Such cities as Milwaukee and Oshkosh had to beg and borrow

1. Theodore A. Andersen, *A Century of Banking in Wisconsin* (Madison: State Historical Society of Wisconsin, 1954), 61, 67, 68–80. *Milwaukee Sentinel*, July 28, 1892, June 2, July 16, 19, 23, 26, 28, 29, 1893.

2. Andersen, *Banking in Wisconsin*, 83–84. *Superior Evening Telegram*, November 5, 1895. *Milwaukee Sentinel*, May 7, 1894, July 28, 1897.

3. *Superior Evening Telegram*, February 22, 1897.

enough funds to provide even rudimentary services.[4] Individual depositors suddenly found themselves penniless, and merchants and manufacturers discovered that the state's remaining banks were calling in loans and were reluctant to advance any more credit.[5]

As the bankers' panic broadened into a full-scale depression, the effects could be seen everywhere. By the summer of 1893 manufacturers were forced to fire workers and cut salaries. The huge E. P. Allis Company of Milwaukee, long regarded by workers as a sympathetic employer, fired 300 men and slashed the wages of the remaining workers by 10 per cent.[6] Workers struck a large Sheboygan shoe factory that cut wages by 20 per cent and the workday from ten to eight hours.[7] The paper mills, largest employers in the populous Fox and Wisconsin river valleys, began to close down,[8] resulting in unemployment in the northern pineries, where only half as many workers could find jobs in the winter of 1893–1894 as had been employed the previous winter.[9] The construction industry, which had boomed during the 1880s and early 1890s, languished during the depression.[10] The depression dragged on for four more grueling years. The *Appleton Weekly Post* reported that manufacturers came to "face the future with nervous forebodings"; workers stood "dazed in the enormity of their privations"; and everyone could only shudder as "this panorama of horrors is passing while the most hideous forms of unanticipated misfortunes are materializing.[11]

Authorities had difficulties getting an accurate statistical picture of the depression because people were reluctant to admit that they were unemployed and to apply for relief. At Milwaukee, with 38,850 wage earners in 1890, estimates of unemployment ranged between a police census of 11,200 unemployed males in December of 1893 and the typographical union's guess of 35,000 in the winter of 1893–1894. Most ob-

4. *Milwaukee Sentinel,* August 17, 27, October 1, December 13, 1893.
5. *Ibid.,* November 22, 1893, October 27, 1894.
6. *Wood County Reporter,* September 7, 1893.
7. *Sheboygan Herald,* August 12, 1893.
8. *Appleton Weekly Post,* August 16, 1894. *Milwaukee Sentinel,* June 18, August 13, 1893.
9. *Appleton Weekly Post,* December 14, 1893, October 25, 1894.
10. *Wood County Reporter,* September 7, 1893. Superior Trades and Labor Assembly, Minute Book, 64–65. Superior Trades and Labor Assembly Papers, Manuscripts Division, State Historical Society of Wisconsin.
11. *Appleton Weekly Post,* August 16, 1894.

servers estimated that 35 to 40 per cent of the city's workers were unemployed during 1893–1894. Charities officials made no guesses; they knew exactly how many people had applied for relief. In the prosperous times between 1887 and 1892 the Milwaukee County poor list ranged between 477 and 886 families; in January of 1894 that list numbered 3,430 families and as late as 1897 included 2,706 families.[12] Two hundred miles away, at La Crosse, a "conservative" estimated that more than half of that city's 3,844 workers were unemployed in the winter of 1893–1894; the story was the same at Beloit and Superior. The depression hit the mining towns along the Michigan border particularly hard. When Gov. George Peck stepped off a train bringing clothes and food to more than 20,000 unemployed miners, he was greeted by 1,500 jobless workers at Hurley.[13] The state labor commissioner reported that for a total of 62 industries wages had increased 35 per cent between 1888 and 1892, only to fall 18 per cent between 1892 and 1894.[14] A good guess would probably be that the state's unemployment rate fluctuated between 20 and 30 percent during the five-year depression.

Hard times affected rural areas as well. Farmers received lower prices for their products and had to accept payment in trade instead of cash. In the dead of winter they could be seen trying to clear land in summer rubbers because they could not afford overshoes. A small-town editor in the Wisconsin River Valley reported in 1895 that "we have been a resident of the Twin Cities for thirty-five years and never before have we noticed the results of hard times and poverty as we have noticed in this year."[15] Although urban editors urged the unemployed

---

12. U.S. Department of Commerce, Bureau of the Census, *Twelfth Census of the United States: Manufactures, 1900,* 7: cclii. *Milwaukee Sentinel,* November 2, 1887, May 18, 1888, February 21, 1890, January 23, 1891, February 14, 1892, April 22, 1894, January 1, 1895, November 1, 1896, January 20, 1897. Carlos C. Closson, Jr., "The Unemployed in American Cities," *Quarterly Journal of Economics,* 8 (January 1894), 196–97, 258 and (July 1894), 499. Leah Hannah Feder, *Unemployment Relief in Periods of Depression* (New York: Russell Sage Foundation, 1936), 82–83.

13. Closson, "Unemployed," 197, 258, 502. Albert Shaw, "Relief of the Unemployed in American Cities," *Review of Reviews,* 9 (January 1894), 187–88. *Milwaukee Sentinel,* November 27, 1893. U.S. Department of Commerce, Bureau of the Census, *Twelfth Census of the United States: Manufactures, 1900,* 7: ccli.

14. Labor Bureau, *7th Biennial Report, 1895–1896,* 339–40.

15. *Wood County Reporter,* February 7, 1895.

to return to the farms,[16] they failed to halt the movement toward cities during the depression. Conditions were so bad in the rural areas that the state's 112 cities and villages with over 1,000 residents grew more than twice as fast as the rest of the state between 1890 and 1895.[17] The depression was at least as severe outside the cities.

I

The mounting despair was sustained and intensified by the gradual realization that traditional political solutions could not end the depression. On the eve of the panic most Wisconsinites were confirmed partisans who never questioned the time-honored belief that the tariff and currency were the basic determinants of the business cycle. The tariff had again become the major point of division between Republican and Democratic economic policies. When the depression struck, the first response, especially among partisan editors, was to look to the familiar tariff and currency for an explanation. "Almost instant relief" would follow repeal of the Sherman Silver Purchase Act, declared Horace Rublee in August of 1893.[18] That same summer editors at Sheboygan and Grand Rapids confidently asserted that "all that is needed now to assure us prosperous times is to let the tariff alone."[19] But repeal on November 1, 1893, of the Sherman Act, which President Grover Cleveland had made his panacea for recovery, and the downward tariff revision in August, 1894, had no effect on the depression. Discussion of these old solutions, particularly the tariff, continued throughout the depression, but increasingly after 1894 or 1895 it was confined to the weeks before elections, and even the editors seemed more to be paying lip service to hallowed party symbols than to be proposing a solution for the depression. Partisans who still believed that the tariff was a burning issue could only lament that "there is a vast popular departure from old party moorings —a widespread political unrest" and that "the people in their

16. For example, see *State Journal*, quoted in *Appleton Weekly Post*, July 4, 1895.
17. The cities and villages grew 21.8 per cent and the rest of the state grew only 10.5 per cent. *Blue Book, 1901*, 455–91.
18. *Milwaukee Sentinel*, August 25, 1893.
19. *Wood County Reporter*, September 7, 1893. *Sheboygan Herald*, August 5, 1893.

manner of handling ballots, are as changeable as the inconstant moon."[20]

If Wisconsinites distrusted politicians because the old partisan answers could not stem the depression, they were even more disturbed because the leading state and national politicians seemed blind to the structural problems that the depression had exposed. Politicians continued to use the old symbols, but Wisconsinites were discovering layer after layer of problems that struck considerably deeper into the core of industrial society than the principles that divided the politicians.

The most obvious of these problems was poverty. In the prosperous times before the panic it was possible to believe that men were poor because of some individual failing. After the panic hit, when factories were idle and one-third of the community's workers were unemployed, when hundreds marched on local governments and thousands marched with Jacob Coxey to Washington, when 20 per cent wage cuts drove men out on strikes, it was impossible to ignore the plight of the poor. Because everybody was "more or less affected by" the depression, declared the Grand Rapids Epworth League, everybody could more readily sympathize with those who were starving or were without shelter.[21] Many Wisconsinites responded with simple compassion. For others the large numbers of unemployed and angry men raised the old fear, highlighted by such events as Chicago's Haymarket Riot of 1886, that the poor would resort to arms or at least rocks. "There is no reasoning with a hungry stomach," observed an Appleton editor. "Where men hang unemployed on street corners, or lounge near the door of the ever open saloon, it requires but a spark to ignite into passionate flame."[22] Obviously, some measures had to be taken to alleviate the lot of the conspicuous poor.

The first solution was to expand existing forms of direct public charity. Local governments had inherited the English tradition of supporting the poor out of public funds, and the result in the late nineteenth century was generally a war between the politicians, who saw in poor relief a source of funds to reward the faithful, and the city and county poor superintendents, who, in general, believed the public should support

20. *Milwaukee Catholic Citizen,* November 10, 1894. *Fond du Lac Commonwealth,* quoted in *Appleton Weekly Post,* August 22, 1895.
21. *Wood County Reporter,* November 23, 1893.
22. *Appleton Weekly Post,* August 31, 1893.

only those people whose health prevented them from supporting themselves.[23] As the panic became a depression thousands of people had to "swallow their pride and go onto the poor list."[24] Under the press of numbers, reported the *Appleton Weekly Post,* "the methods of the poor department have been considerably relaxed."[25] The costs of poor relief multiplied with the growing numbers. Milwaukee County, which had spent $30,277 for poor relief in 1891, disbursed $108,332 in 1895; Kenosha County increased its payments from $1,810 in 1891 to $7,033 in 1893; and Sheboygan County raised its poor relief budget from $5,776 in 1891 to $19,637 in 1895.[26] All traditional forms of charity were severely strained.

Most unemployed men and women did not consider themselves paupers; they wanted jobs, and they asked governments to provide those jobs. Hundreds of unemployed workers marched on city halls, and many unions petitioned city governments to create jobs.[27] Perhaps the stories of individual hardships were even more telling. "Scarcely a day passes that unemployed men do not flock to [the street commissioner] pleading for work and telling the most heart-rending stories of sickness, hunger and want," came the report from Appleton as late as the winter of 1896–1897.[28] These pressures from the unemployed corresponded with a deep-seated belief that public charity was a humiliating and expensive system that rewarded the least fit in the Darwinian struggle and bred a class of paupers.[29] The approved solution was for local governments to undertake extensive public works programs. Milwaukee hired its unemployed men to build a city hall and a library, to construct water mains, to improve parks, to sweep streets, and to begin street construction in the newer parts of the city. To accommodate the demand for jobs, the Board of Park Commissioners cut wages in September of 1893 from $1.50 to $1.25

23. *Milwaukee Sentinel,* May 18, November 29, 1888, July 24, November 19, 27, 1890, January 11, 1891.
24. *Appleton Weekly Post,* April 22, 1897.
25. *Ibid.,* July 22, 1897.
26. *Third Biennial Report of the State Board of Control,* 1896, 336–37.
27. Shaw, "Relief of Unemployed," 36. Closson, "Unemployed," 196–97. Superior Trades and Labor Assembly, Minute Book, 42.
28. *Appleton Weekly Post,* October 15, 1896.
29. *Ibid.,* February 8, 1894, April 9, 1896, April 22, July 22, 1897. *Milwaukee Sentinel,* November 29, 1888, November 19, 1890, December 4, 1893, February 6, August 19, November 12, 1894.

per day so that it could hire more men.[30] Oshkosh used its unemployed to improve the city's parks and appropriated $12,000 for that purpose in the summer of 1895 alone.[31] Superior hired men to clear stumpage in the parks and to remove snow in winter.[32] The *Wood County Reporter* stated that the city of Grand Rapids, with a population of less than 2,000, spent nearly $3,000 on a floodwall in order to give "quite a number of men an income from which they can live this winter."[33] Such projects seemed an ideal temporary answer to the immediate problem of starving men. When Appleton Democrats hoped for a taxpayers' revolt in the 1896 election by attacking the extravagance of the Republicans in spending money for public works, they discovered that the city's voters approved the Republicans' spending policy and voted the Democrats down.[34]

A great many Wisconsinites still believed that such public works projects were only token and temporary solutions to the larger problem of poverty in an industrial society that the depression had revealed. They began to ask questions that commissioners of public works could not answer. The specter of unemployment and starvation, of poverty, was one that haunted Wisconsinites as the poor drew attention to themselves.

The rich also drew attention to themselves. To a nation that had thought of rich men as the fittest citizens and as men who were endowed with superior intelligence, courage, industry, and thrift, the bankers' panic was a rude shock. In city after city—at Milwaukee, Superior, Madison, La Crosse, Manitowoc, Juneau, and elsewhere—the "robbed public" watched with horror and fascination as criminal proceedings disclosed that respected bankers had actually been thieves and embezzlers.[35] A troubled Horace Rublee could only ask: "What becomes of the popular confidence in the wise judgment of apparently successful busi-

30. *Milwaukee Sentinel*, August 20, September 2, 12, 1893, February 6, 25, April 22, September 6, 1894, March 29, 1896. Shaw, "Relief of Unemployed," 36. *Charities Review*, 8 (June 1898), 198–99. Feder, *Unemployment Relief*, 187.

31. *Milwaukee Sentinel*, July 1, 1894, June 23, 1895.

32. *Superior Leader*, March 13, 1895. Shaw, "Relief of Unemployed," 187–88.

33. *Wood County Reporter*, November 16, 1893.

34. *Appleton Weekly Post*, April 19, 1894, April 9, 1896, July 29, 1897.

35. *Milwaukee Sentinel*, July 13, 16, 19, September 10, 1893, January 25, May 7, September 12, 1894, May 22, 1895, February 17, October 14, 1896, June 4, July 28, 1897, February 4, 7, September 20, 1898. *Ashland Weekly Press*, November 2, 1895. *Ashland Daily News*, July 25, 1896. *Superior Evening Telegram*, March 12, 1896, February 22, 1897.

ness men?"[36] Fearing the intensity of popular indignation, the bankers persuaded the 1895 and 1897 legislatures to create the position of a state bank examiner and to "regulate" banking. The voters, still unappeased, rejected an 1898 referendum on the bankers' regulation plan.[37] Evidences of criminality were not the only magnet by which the rich attracted attention. While the elaborate expenditures and lavish parties of the wealthy were not new phenomena in the depression, they acquired a special significance during these years of general deprivation. "The ostentation of the rich is a leading source of such discontent as we have among us," declared a Catholic editor. It was, after all, not until after the depression that Thorstein Veblen labeled this kind of consumption as "conspicuous."[38] In the depression context it was equally difficult to ignore changes in corporate organization. The bankruptcies, business failures, and receiverships that accompanied the depression and the beginnings of a major new thrust toward monopoly in 1897 also brought financial practices of the rich into the spotlight. By 1897, when William Mylrea became the state's first attorney general to try to bust trusts, he was supported by most editors who declared that "the people are just in the mood to applaud action of this kind."[39] Corporation managers made themselves even more conspicuous when they lobbied to secure special privileges at a time when most people believed that they had received more than enough consideration from politicians. During the depression the rich could no longer escape criticism and censure of their dishonesty, ostentation, greed, and political power.

The most shocking discovery for the public was the appalling contrast between the ways of life of the rich and the poor, which not only accentuated the characteristics of each but also raised disturbing questions about the whole meaning of in-

36. *Milwaukee Sentinel*, August 13, 1893, January 20, 1894.

37. *Ibid.*, July 21, August 14, 1893, October 6, November 1, 1898. *Superior Evening Telegram*, April 1, 1897. Andersen, *Century of Banking*, 85–90. *Blue Book, 1899*, 257. Leonard Bayliss Krueger, *History of Commerical Banking in Wisconsin* (Madison: University of Wisconsin Press, 1933), 141–43.

38. Editors reported the affairs of "society" in detail. For a typical account of a party in a city of less than 15,000, see *Appleton Weekly Post*, February 6, 1896. *Milwaukee Catholic Citizen*, May 20, 1899.

39. *Manitowoc Pilot*, in *Appleton Weekly Post*, January 28, 1897. *Chippewa Independent*, in *Superior Evening Telegram*, March 29, 1898. *Milwaukee Catholic Citizen*, January 23, 1897, July 16, 1898.

dustrialism. While some observers had noticed this contrast before 1893, it was not until the depression that most editors and social groups discovered the urgency of the chasm between the rich and the poor. "Men are rightly feeling that a social order like the present, with its enormous wealth side by side with appalling poverty, its luxury for a few and its pre-mortem hell for many, with its war between labor and capital, cannot be the final form of human society," observed a Milwaukee Methodist preacher.[40] The State Grange bitterly contrasted the "misfortunes of the multitudes" with the "wealth of the favored few."[41] Even A Milwaukee woman's club, which had formerly discussed such topics as literature and the tariff, devoted an entire session in the winter of 1895–1896 to "The Idle Rich and the Idle Poor."[42]

The discovery of the social chasm meant different things about the social order to different people. To some it was a question of exploitation. "While thousands are starving no man has a right to be a sybarite, even though he have all the wealth of Croesus," declared a Catholic editor.[43] The contrast was "unrighteous and ungodly" to a minister in Superior.[44] To others it raised the fear of two classes "so antagonistic that a revolution would follow."[45] For nearly everyone the discovery of the gap between the rich and the poor challenged the whole meaning of American democracy. Did the steady erosion of the "old and much-vaunted equality of opportunity" mean that economic and political democracy could no longer survive? Patriotic citizens believed that the United States was the world's last, best hope, yet it seemed to be developing Europe's unbridgeable gulfs between rich and poor, between privileged groups and the masses, and between owners and toilers.[46]

These haunting social questions, accented by men's personal economic problems and the unresponsiveness of politicians, generated during the depression an atmosphere of profound social unrest. No one could escape what Charles K. Adams,

40. *Milwaukee Sentinel,* August 17, 1896.
41. State Grange, *22nd Session, 1893,* 7.
42. Milwaukee Social Economics Club, 1895–1896 program, Milwaukee County Historical Society.
43. *Milwaukee Catholic Citizen,* July 16, 1898.
44. *Superior Evening Telegram,* January 28, 1898. *Milwaukee Sentinel,* June 8, 1896.
45. *Wausau Daily Record,* April 1, 11, 1899.
46. *Appleton Weekly Post,* May 11, 1893. *Superior Evening Telegram,* February 22, 1898. *Wausau Daily Record,* April 11, 1899.

University of Wisconsin president, called "a general, all-pervasive, restless discontent with the results of current political and economic thought." President Adams told the 1894 graduating class:

As you go out from the halls of the university you will be confronted with some of the gravest questions that have yet perplexed the American people. You will see everywhere in the country symptoms of social and political discontent. You will observe that these disquietudes do not result from the questions that arise in the ordinary course of political discussion . . . but that they spring out of questions that are connected with the very foundations of society and have to do with the most elemental principles of human liberty and modern civilization.[47]

The winter of 1893–1894, as George D. Herron told an Appleton audience, had truly placed a severe strain on American institutions.[48] Editors of all shades of opinion repeatedly commented on the "manifest spirit of unrest and dissatisfaction among all classes of people."[49] To the more conservative Horace Rublee "the present is likely to be remembered in the history of the country as the era of crankism. It is as if multitudes of people had 'eaten of the insane root that takes the reason prisoner.' "[50]

The social unrest was so profound because the depression had uncovered structural problems—poverty side by side with splendor, monopoly in a society that treasured mobility, tax inequities in a nation born of a rebellion against unjust taxation, the rise of cities in a country whose political and economic values were agrarian, collectivism in a society of individualists—whose solutions were more urgent than merely ending the depression. "The time is at hand," warned a Superior editor, "when some of the great problems which the Nineteenth century civilization has encountered are crying for a solution."[51] Unlike a subsequent depression generation, which had decades of experiences to draw upon, this generation was confronting the problems of industrialism for the first time. Since national politicians were simply not talking about these things and seemed to lack the

47. *Milwaukee Sentinel,* June 19, 1893, June 18, 1894.
48. *Appleton Weekly Post,* February 22, 1894.
49. *Ibid.,* June 9, 1898. *Milwaukee Catholic Citizen,* April 7, 1894.
50. *Milwaukee Sentinel,* May 9, 1894.
51. *Superior Evening Telegram,* July 12, 1893. See also *Appleton Weekly Post,* September 14, 1893.

same sense of urgency and doubt that gripped ordinary men, Wisconsinites had to develop their own institutions and authorities in their search for new answers.

One group to which they now turned was the social scientists, particularly the younger economists who had for years been investigating precisely the conditions that most Wisconsinites were now discovering for the first time. Urging the State Grange in 1895 to study the writings of economists, a delegate from Milton said: "When the body politic is diseased we must look to men who have made a life study of the science of government. Our modern political economist can learn [sic] us much which we must learn."[52] A young economics professor at Lawrence University was astounded when Appleton newspapers wanted to report the discussions of his economics seminar to their readers.[53] Throughout the depression Wisconsin editors fed the interests of their readers by printing speeches and sketches of the dean of the new economists, Prof. Richard T. Ely of the University of Wisconsin. Ely's trial for economic heresy in the summer of 1894 on charges brought by a hack Democratic politician only intensified popular interest in his ideas. Most of the state's editors defended Ely, on the grounds that the problems he was investigating were so urgent that no ideas—however radical—should be muzzled.[54] The great interest shown in Ely's trial was intensified because of the new role to which Wisconsinites had assigned economists as explicators of their problems.[55]

In the yeasty ferment of the depression many citizens desired more direct contact with the new social scientists than books or newspapers permitted. Most Wisconsinites wanted to bring the new experts to them. "Nothing can be more useful than a scientific presentation of such [sociological] problems to popular audiences," declared one editor.[56] The highly successful farmers' institutes of the preceding decade provided the format for

52. State Grange, *24th Session, 1895*, 18–19.

53. Jerome H. Raymond to Richard T. Ely, September 22, 1893, Ely Papers, Manuscripts Division, State Historical Society of Wisconsin.

54. Theron F. Schlabach, "An Aristocrat on Trial: The Case of Richard T. Ely," *Wisconsin Magazine of History*, 47 (Winter 1963–1964), 146–59. Benjamin G. Rader, *The Academic Mind and Reform: The Influence of Richard T. Ely in American Life* (Lexington: University of Kentucky Press, 1966), 130–52. *Appleton Weekly Post*, August 23, 1894.

55. For example, see Mary Howe Shelton to Richard T. Ely, September 13, 1894, Ely Papers.

56. *Milwaukee Catholic Citizen*, November 24, 1894.

such presentations. Wisconsinites hastily formed university extension centers in cities and towns where they could hear the new social scientists. Beginning in the winter of 1890–1891 with one course offered by the state university, the movement filled such a popular need that by its peak in the winter of 1895–1896, when Wisconsin was "the best field in the country" for such courses, four colleges and universities gave over 100 courses throughout the state.[57] As the depression deepened, citizens increasingly demanded courses in economics, sociology, and political science, instead of literature and science. A Grange leader spoke for many when he wrote University of Wisconsin economist William A. Scott: "The science which you teach is the noblest of all professions and the hope of the future."[58] The demand was so great that the university had to hire additional lecturers in the social sciences to teach extension classes.[59] This enthusiasm for courses by the new social scientists, which probably reached forty or fifty thousand different citizens during the depression, suggests that a great many Wisconsinites had finally found people who, unlike the politicians, spoke directly to the depression's problems.

The profound social unrest of the depression gave a popular audience to the new social scientists who had been seeking acceptance for almost a decade before 1893. What must have struck them as most significant was their appeal to all classes; the social unrest cut across class lines. Sometimes, as at Kenosha, Ashland, Milwaukee, and River Falls, it was women's clubs that headed the movement for extension courses in economics. Business and professional men took the lead at Tomahawk, Philipps,

57. *Milwaukee Sentinel*, May 8, October 10, 1892, October 25, 1896. *Appleton Weekly Post*, November 15, 1894. Samuel Fallows to C. K. Adams, November 4, 1895, W. H. Hickok to Jerome H. Raymond, October 19, 1895, Lyman Powell to Raymond, December 13, 1895, B. E. Sheldon to University Extension, December 14, 1896, Raymond File, University of Wisconsin Extension Division Papers. Samuel Fallows to Richard T. Ely, November 8, 1897, Ely Papers. Frederick M. Rosentreter, *Boundaries of the Campus: A History of the University of Wisconsin Extension Division, 1885–1945* (Madison: University of Wisconsin Press, 1957), 39.

58. W. A. McEwan to William A. Scott, May 27, 1895; Samuel Fallows to C. K. Adams, November 4, 1895; Memo on "Prof. Freeman," and Memo on Scott dated August 28, 1895; Raymond File. Samuel Fallows to Richard T. Ely, November 8, 1897, Ely Papers. *Milwaukee Sentinel*, February 18, 1900. *Appleton Weekly Post*, December 14, 1899.

59. John A. Gaynor to Ely, April 27, 1899, Ely to C. K. Adams, November 2, 1894, Ely Papers. Gaynor to Jerome H. Raymond, July 16, ca. 1894, August 21, 1895, Raymond File.

Wausau, Sturgeon Bay, Fond du Lac, Omro, Hudson, and Milwaukee; farmers predominated at Milton, Cedarburg, and Waupaca; and workers took the initiative at Madison and Oshkosh. John O'Connell of the Madison Federated Trades Council underscored community-wide interest in economics when he wrote Ely that "our people here, not alone wage-earners but of all classes, would be pleased to hear you.[60]

University extension centers were only the most obvious expression of the popular groping for answers to problems the depression had made urgent. All over the state, citizens began forming discussion clubs where they could share the results of their search with others, exchange ideas, and discuss the writings of experts. Many established organizations created clubs where their members could discuss the relationship of the depression's new problems to their own activities. Labor unions formed many such clubs.[61] The Milwaukee Populist party in 1897 turned its ward clubs into "schools of political and social economy."[62] Women's organizations, from the Milwaukee Woman's School Alliance to suffragette organizations at Madison, La Crosse, and Racine, formed study clubs during the depression.[63] In the fall of 1894 the state's public schools began to give considerable attention to the new social scientists,[64] although church groups were perhaps the most sensitive of all to

60. W. A. Hilton to Richard T. Ely, September 6, 1893, John O'Connell to Ely, August 6, 1894, Ely Papers. H. F. Washburne to C. K. Adams, December 9, 1895, A. Bragden to B. H. Meyer, November 18, 1897, Mrs. E. N. Kimball to Meyer, December 2, 1897, letters to Jerome H. Raymond from: G. H. Jensen, September 24, 1895, E. E. Beckwith, October 19, 1895, John A. Carr, October 23, 1895, David L. Holbrook, November 1, 1895, W. A. McEwan, November 13, 1895, S. B. Tovey, November 17, 1895, Cimbra Daniels, December 10, 1895, F. G. Stark, December 20, 1895, D. E. McGinley, January 21, 1896, Theodore Johnson, September 7, 1896, N. B. Rosenberry, October 14, 1896, B. E. Sheldon, December 14, 1896, all in Raymond File. *Milwaukee Sentinel*, May 3, 1897, August 24, 1899, April 8, 1900. *Ashland Daily Press*, February 23, 1899. *Report of the President of the University of Wisconsin, 1895–1896*, 28, hereinafter cited as *President's Report*.
61. Superior Trades and Labor Assembly, Minute Book, 55, 57, unnumbered page for April 9, 1894. *Official Wisconsin State Federation of Labor Directory, 1896–1897*, 17.
62. William L. Pieplow, form letter, October 15, 1897, Pieplow Papers, Milwaukee County Historical Society.
63. Memo, November 25, 1898, Lizzie Black Kander Papers, Manuscripts Division, State Historical Society of Wisconsin. WWSA Proceedings, 1896, Box 36, James Papers, 2: 87–88.
64. Richard T. Ely, "Schools and Churches in their Relation to Charities and Correction," *Charities Review*, 4 (December 1894), 57–64.

the social unrest. They invited economists like Ely and activists like settlement leader Graham Taylor to address their ministerial councils. Pastoral organizations, like Sparta's Epworth League, representing three denominations, acquired "a broader outlook on the relation of man to man" by studying and discussing Ely's writings.[65] So many of the state's Catholics attended reading circles, summer school, and other organizations for adult education that by 1897 the editor of a Milwaukee church publication printed 50,000 copies of an issue of the *Catholic Citizen* that was devoted to the Catholic Chautauqua movement.[66]

The thrust of the general unrest was toward bridging social divisions. Citizens knew how people from their own backgrounds thought, and they hoped that someone else had somehow found answers to their questions. The clubs that typified this spirit of inquiry were not adjuncts to existing organizations but new clubs that grew up during the depression, and they provided forums where men of different backgrounds could trade solutions. They sprouted in nearly every community in the state. Believing that economics "is rapidly becoming the topic of the day," a group of men at Grand Rapids, a city with fewer than 2,000 residents, formed a discussion club.[67] Residents of Madison gathered at the Contemporary Club, the Historical and Political Science Association, the Literary Club, and the 6 O'Clock Club. In such gatherings manufacturers, workers, liberal and conservative professors, and clergymen exchanged ideas on such topics as the modern factory and monopoly.[68]

Milwaukeeans groped for answers at the Liberal Club, the Social Science Club, the Ethical Society, the Academy of Social

65. Milwaukee District Congregational Convention, Minute Book, 213, Madison Convention of Congregational Churches and Ministers, Minute Book, 186, Wisconsin Congregational Church Papers, Manuscripts Division, State Historical Society of Wisconsin. *Appleton Weekly Post*, March 11, 1897. H. W. Masters to Richard T. Ely, December 4, 1896, Ely Papers.

66. *Milwaukee Catholic Citizen*, November 17, 1894, July 20, 1895, July 25, August 15, 1896. Richard Jean Orsi, "Humphrey Joseph Desmond: A Case Study in American Catholic Liberalism" (M.S. thesis, University of Wisconsin, 1965), 21–22, 118–34.

67. *Wood County Reporter*, October 18, 1894.

68. Madison Literary Club Record Book, II; 6 O'Clock Club, Minute Book, 15, 46–53; both in Manuscripts Division, State Historical Society of Wisconsin. *State Journal*, January 18, February 27, 1900. Charles N. Gregory, *The Corrupt Use of Money in Politics and Laws for Its Prevention* (Madison: Historical and Political Science Association, 1893). Rader, *Influence of Ely*, 115–16.

Science, the Church and Labor Social Union, the Economic League, the Social Economics Club, the College Endowment Association, the People's Institute, the Christian Labor Union, and the Forum Club, all but one of which formed after the panic. At a meeting of the Liberal Club Victor Berger argued for socialism to an audience including leading bankers, merchants, and lawyers. Wealthy banker John Johnston used a meeting of the Church and Labor Social Union to call for "men to help create the new society [where] class privileges will be abolished because all will belong to the human family," and he was joined in his appeal by Populists, Socialists, clergymen, and a conservative editor. A Methodist preacher formed a Christian Labor Union in 1895 to "furnish a bond of reciprocal sympathy and information between the church and working men," and the Federated Trades Council attended as a body. The call for the Social Science Club reflected the new mood when it declared that "we are . . . serious students of the society in which we live and we gladly welcome all who will join us with the same spirit and purpose."[69]

The extension centers and discussion clubs reflected a new social pattern of political discussion in Wisconsin. In the crisis atmosphere of social unrest a man's ideas and solutions became more important than his social background. Many Wisconsinites felt a deep need to emerge from the social seclusion that had isolated them and their class from the larger society. Since politicians ignored the new spectacle of the yawning chasm between rich and poor and since Wisconsinites recognized their own individual incapacities to solve the new dilemmas, they had to develop new ways of solving social problems.

II

The most significant result of the social ferment was the development of a new spirit of change. Once they learned that others shared their own doubts and hopes, many Wisconsinites cooperated with others to establish reforms. They had been thrust together at centers and clubs because the problems they

69. *Milwaukee Sentinel,* February 3, March 2, April 30, May 5, December 18, 1894, March 4, May 20, December 8, 13, 1895, May 15, October 26, 1896, January 11, February 7, May 3, November 29, Decamber 27, 1897, August 24, 1899, February 18, 1900. *Appleton Weekly Post,* December 19, 1895. *State Journal,* April 27, 1897. Minutes of Social Economics Club, 1893–1900. *Milwaukee Daily News,* March 1, 1894.

discovered in the depression troubled them deeply, and they had intended discussions to be first steps toward change. Because local observations and problems had originally sparked their dissatisfaction with established principles and because they found national politics irrelevant, Wisconsinites directed their reform energies toward local and immediate problems. Rather than heeding principles, they earnestly sought to solve problems in any way that would work. "Everywhere is met a spirit of investigation, inquiry and experiment," declared a speaker before the 1895 farmers' institute.[70] Lacking any real experience and knowing only that some measures had to be taken, they set out to remake their communities without considering the social origins of their coworkers or the established principles and practices they defied. Their repeated emphasis after about 1895 on the importance and value of things new—the New Religion, the New Woman, the New Education—reflected the activities of men and women who sensed only that old ways threatened conscience and public safety. "The present time is fecund of 'movements,' which is indicative that society is undergoing a process of fermentation," wrote one editor in appraising the trend.[71] The widespread unrest presented ample opportunity for experimentation: "Never before in the history of the world were people so willing to accept true teaching on any of these subjects and give to them a just and practical trial," declared a Superior editor.[72] This new sense of the urgency for change, this creation of new institutions outside political parties where backgrounds were less important than the solution of local and immediate problems created a kind of civic consciousness that had never before been experienced in Wisconsin.

The depression and its social unrest had only shortly begun before this civic consciousness began to appear. A Milwaukee editor well expressed the resulting mandates for reform: "Every man owes it to himself and the community in which he lives to oppose wrong in all its forms and do his utmost to bring about the universal reign of right and justice and there is no obligation that he can assume that will relieve him from this responsibility."[73] An Appleton editor warned conservatives that "the

70. *Handbook,* bull. no. 9 (1895), 136.
71. *Appleton Weekly Post,* August 8, 1895.
72. *Superior Evening Telegram,* July 12, 1893.
73. *Milwaukee News,* in *Appleton Weekly Post,* March 19, 1896.

Juggernaut of reform is in motion and they will do well to keep out of its way."[74]

The restless eagerness for change bred a kind of pragmatism that cavalierly cast aside traditional principles. No one exemplified the new spirit better than Horace Rublee, long-time defender of the *status quo* from his position as editor of the state's leading Republican paper. For years the state's leading exponent of social Darwinism, Rublee began to question the validity of those Darwinian ideas as he observed the effects of the depression in Milwaukee. In the fall of 1893 Rublee suddenly announced that "Herbert Spencer's belief that more is to be expected from the selfish interest of men than from enlightened benevolence is put to a severe strain in practical life."[75] Expounding a new-found pragmatism by the summer of 1894, Rublee declared: "The extension of government management into other fields, is a question to be decided, not in accordance with theory, or any immutable principle, but with regard to circumstances."[76] By 1896 few readers could discern even vestiges of his once-rampant social Darwinism.

In one area after another, in fact, men and women were declaring that tradition and formalism were themselves the major causes of present problems. No less a professional than the superintendent of Madison's public schools identified the "hampering formalism of the traditional school" as the main stumbling block to operation of good schools and loaded his annual reports with phrases like "tiresome, listless word drills," "machine-like methods," "rote-learning," "dry memorization of useless stuff," "technicalities and arbitrary rules," "parrot-like reproduction," and "dull, mechanical exercises" and warned that "only those [teachers] who are thoroughly imbued with the progressive spirit of the times should be allowed to remain."[77] The defiance of tradition at Superior's First Ward School shocked the woman appointed to inspect it in 1898: "Our graded school presents to my mind a similarity to a charity hospital in the hands of a corps of medical students. It is all experimental, and if the child, or the patient, comes out with

74. *Appleton Weekly Post,* April 11, 1895.
75. *Milwaukee Sentinel,* September 24, 1893.
76. *Ibid.,* August 25, 1894.
77. Richard B. Dudgeon's *Annual Report of the Public Schools of the City of Madison, Wisconsin, 1892–1893,* 20, 24–25; *Annual Report, 1893–1894,* 36; *Annual Report, 1894–1895,* 25, 28; *Annual Report, 1896–1897,* 34; *Annual Report, 1898–1899,* 26, hereinafter cited as *Madison Schools.*

a well trained mind, or a sound body, it is more owing to his own mental or physical endurance than to the treatment he has received."[78]

While the rejection of traditional practices was not as complete everywhere as in the schools of Madison and Superior, a new-found sense of the urgency for change sprang up throughout Wisconsin. The very centers where citizens had gone simply to understand the new problems often developed into spearheads for local reform movements. Men and women who had turned to the new social scientists for answers to questions the politicians did not ask soon learned that the speakers had solutions. Extension lecturers rarely closed their courses without advocating municipal ownership of utilities, more equitable taxation, or changes in the environment of the poor. Some auditors criticized them for being outspokenly radical.[79] The Economic Leagues of the University Association of Chicago, with thirty centers in Wisconsin, frankly propagandized for specific reforms and proclaimed that their "sole aim" was "to arouse public sentiment in each community to the need of unity of action" on those reforms.[80] The courses produced positive results. At Grand Rapids, for example, Henry H. Swain's course on the evils of private ownership of utilities greatly stimulated a movement for local and popular ownership of telephones and electric lights.[81] Observing the spark that these courses gave to local reform movements, a Madison editor correctly claimed that "university extension acts chiefly as leaven."[82]

The impact of social unrest on civic consciousness could be seen even more directly in the programs of the less formal discussion clubs. The clubs turned from general study and discussion to investigations of local abuses and from investigations to

78. *Superior Evening Telegram,* August 1, 1898.
79. Summaries of these courses are in the following syllabi published by the University of Wisconsin Extension Department: Richard T. Ely, *Socialism* (Syllabus 4, 1892) ; William A. Scott, *Economic Problems of the Present Day* (Syllabi 1, 1892, and 26, 1894) ; B. H. Meyer, *An Introduction to Economic Problems* (Syllabus 31, 1895), University of Wisconsin Archives. See also Rosentreter, *Boundaries,* 35–36. *Wood County Reporter,* January 9, 1896. *Appleton Weekly Post,* January 2, 1896.
80. Samuel Fallows to C. K. Adams, November 4, 1895, Raymond File. *Appleton Weekly Post,* December 14, 1899. *Milwaukee Sentinel,* February 18, April 8, 1900.
81. *Wood County Reporter,* January 9, 1896.
82. *State Journal,* February 7, 1900. See also *President's Report,* 1895–1896, 28.

action. The Ethical Society, West Side Literary Club, Sociological Club, and College Endowment Association explored conditions of child and woman labor in Milwaukee by visiting sweatshops and workers' homes and by taking photographs and conducting interviews. Armed with these facts, they demanded that the state's factory inspectors enforce the laws regulating child and woman labor. In 1899 and 1900 the Social Economics Club, which had confined its activities to discussions in the early years of the depression, brought several Milwaukee clubs together to form a consumers' league to boycott stores and products that exploited the labor of women and children.[83] The Child Study Society and the College Endowment Association undertook investigation of educational programs and proposed ways of making the Milwaukee public schools more responsive to the problems disclosed by the depression.[84]

Discussion groups in smaller cities also launched reform movements in diverse areas of civic life. At Appleton the Good Citizenship League worked to convince fraternal and social organizations of the need for consolidated schools and a modern hospital.[85] The Ladies' Literary Club of Wausau began a drive in 1898 to aid the city's working women,[86] and Madison's Contemporary Club led the movement for establishing municipal garbage collections.[87]

The new civic consciousness spread from discussion clubs and extension centers to other groups and organizations. Wherever one turned in the depression, one found previously antagonistic groups cooperating. Unsafe and unjust social divisions and local and immediate problems drove established groups to develop an outward focus and individual members to broaden their perspectives. Labor unions, which had long felt isolated from other groups, found new allies in organizations that began developing across the state. Local unions joined insurance companies in urging cities to hire electrical inspectors to prevent faulty wiring of buildings and thereby reduce the incidence of fires; at Superior in 1895 the entire Trades and Labor Assembly

83. For examples, see *Milwaukee Sentinel*, January 15, December 26, 27, 1897, October 9, 1899, June 19, August 2, 1900. *State Journal*, April 27, 1897. Labor Bureau, *9th Biennial Report, 1899–1900*, xxvi–xxvii.
84. *Milwaukee Sentinel*, November 6, December 16, 1896, August 24, 1899.
85. *Appleton Weekly Post*, February 6, July 2, 1896.
86. *Milwaukee Sentinel*, March 13, 1898.
87. *State Journal*, March 24, 1900.

endorsed the project.[88] The common problems of all residents of economically stagnant cities led unions to cooperate with businessmen in Oshkosh, Sheboygan, and Appleton to force city governments to employ industrial agents who would attract new industries to the area.[89] Labor groups at Milwaukee and Superior supported the demands of women's clubs to improve working conditions of women and children.[90] Indeed, the Superior Trades and Labor Assembly by 1895 had developed so many points of cooperation with that city's chamber of commerce that it paid the membership fee for one of its officials to join the chamber to discuss workers' problems with businessmen.[91] Even more important than cooperation between organizations was the support individual workers gave cross-class reform movements in their communities. While self-interest still played a large part in the motivation of groups' activities, workingmen and their organizations had obviously lost some of their stereotyped suspicions of clergymen, women's clubs, and even businessmen.

Workingmen and unions soon found that the developing civic consciousness brought them many more friends than they could have imagined in the days before the panic. Groups that had previously opposed them now supported them in strikes, when they most needed aid. This growing sympathy for workers was nowhere more evident than at Ashland, where members of that city's chamber in 1890 had served conspicuously as strikebreakers to demonstrate united business opposition to unions. By 1895 the chamber resolved during a strike on the ore docks to "extend their sympathy to the laborers who are trying to get at least a living wage for their work."[92] While the Pullman strike of 1894 was cause for great alarm among conservatives, Frank A. Woodward, president of the Superior Chamber of Commerce, warmly and publicly took the union's side.[93] The state's worst strike of the depression was that of Milwaukee streetcar workers in 1896, and nearly all Milwaukeeans—including businessmen—supported the workers. No fewer than 127

88. *Appleton Weekly Post,* August 6, 1896. Superior Trades and Labor Assembly, Minute Book, 115.

89. *Appleton Weekly Post,* July 15, 1897.

90. Superior Trades and Labor Assembly, Minute Book, 52. *Milwaukee Sentinel,* August 2, 1900.

91. Superior Trades and Labor Assembly, Minute Book, 66, 119.

92. *Ashland Weekly Press,* January 12, 1895.

93. *Milwaukee Sentinel,* July 3, 1894.

businessmen expressed their anger at the company by urging the city council to annul the company's franchise.[94] Workers gained support for their political goals among the new groups. Women's clubs assumed the role played by unions before the panic and supported enforcement of the state's factory inspection laws, and the state's women's clubs in 1899 joined the Wisconsin Federation of Labor in demanding stricter inspection laws.[95] Many workers—as well as their wives—deeply appreciated the successful crusades by women's clubs at Ashland and Madison to persuade merchants to close their stores by 6:00 or 7:00 P.M. so the women employees could spend their evenings at home.[96] Prejudices that had once circumscribed workers seemed to be receding, and many other Wisconsinites had come to believe that reforms were urgently needed to narrow the differences between rich and poor.

The state's farmers, who had long felt miles of social as well as geographical distance between themselves and townspeople, began during the depression to emerge from their isolation. They turned increasingly from their emphasis on education to aggressive political action. In 1894, for the first time in over fifteen years, the State Grange urged its local affiliates to enter political and legislative campaigns.[97] This decision to enter the world of politics meant choosing to work with others. The state's farm groups, which before the panic had confined their minimal interest in legislation to such narrow goals as the organization of farmers' institutes and the prohibition of oleomargarine production, turned during the depression to support legislation concerning trust-busting, abolition of railway passes, income and inheritance taxes, and school reforms, and for the first time since the mid-1870s, in which regulation of the railroads had been a public question, joined merchants in promoting regulatory laws.[98]

94. John A. Butler, "Street Railway Problem in Milwaukee," *Municipal Affairs*, 4 (March 1900), 213. Forrest McDonald, "Street Cars and Politics in Milwaukee, 1896–1901, Part I," *Wisconsin Magazine*, 39 (Spring 1956), 206–8.

95. Labor Bureau, *9th Biennial Report, 1899–1900*, xxv–xxvii. Minutes of Milwaukee Social Economics Club, 112.

96. *Ashland Daily News*, October 28, 1899. *Ashland Daily Press*, February 28, April 8, 1899. *State Journal*, January 4, 1897.

97. State Grange, *23rd Session, 1894*, 27–28. See also *Wood County Reporter*, July 12, 1894.

98. State Grange, *22nd Session, 1893*, 9; *23rd Session, 1894*, 12; *24th Session, 1895*, 7; *26th Session, 1897*, 26–27, 30–31; *28th Session, 1899*, 15;

The campaign that best revealed the farmers' growing willingness to cooperate with other groups was the movement for good roads. Bicyclists began an active campaign for good roads in Wisconsin about 1890, but the farmers initially opposed the "city dudes" and their drive. The farmers regarded the road proposal as one more area in which the city was infringing on the rural way of life, and they viewed the cyclists as examples of the decadence of city ways. Promotion of good roads was simply a drive to make farmers pay for cyclists' pleasure outings. By 1895 the cyclists had won the support of many of the state's commercial and manufacturing groups, an alliance cemented that year by the formation of the Wisconsin Good Roads League, which chose a leading Sheboygan furniture manufacturer as president.[99] When the Good Roads League began an aggressive campaign for the farmers' support that year, its leaders found that farmers were abandoning their old prejudices. Following the urgings of the Farmers Institutes and the *Wisconsin Agriculturalist* in 1895 and the Dairymen's Association in 1896, the state's agricultural groups began to support good roads until, by the end of 1896, the *Milwaukee Sentinel* announced that the Good Roads League had been very successful in "overcoming the prejudice at first evidenced among the farming classes." Farmers like F. J. Frost reflected the civic consciousness that was breaking down social barriers when they declared that good roads would break down "the isolation of the country." By 1899 farmers had become so sympathetic to the issue that the state's leading campaigner, a Milwaukee lawyer, could write dairy leader William D. Hoard of "the fact that we are 'getting together.'" Although the voters did not approve a constitutional amendment for state highway aid until 1908, the predominantly rural assembly passed state aid resolutions at each session between 1897 and 1901.[100] Not until after the panic did the state's farmers reject their social isolation and decide to

---

29th Session, 1900, 8. The Letter Books of William D. Hoard, Manuscripts Division, State Historical Society of Wisconsin, for these years are filled with accounts of farmers' interest in such programs.

99. *Milwaukee Sentinel,* April 1, 1894, January 23, 1895. Ballard Campbell, "The Good Roads Movement in Wisconsin, 1890–1911," *Wisconsin Magazine,* 49 (Summer 1966), 273–81.

100. *Milwaukee Sentinel,* February 11, March 8, 1895, March 11, November 27, 1896, July 27, September 14, October 25, 1899. *Appleton Weekly Post,* January 25, 1900. *Handbook,* bull. no. 9 (1895), 61, 72, 73, 178; (1896), 46–49, 203; (1897), 213. Otto Dorner to William D. Hoard, March 20, 28, 1899, Hoard Letter Books. Campbell, "Good Roads," 279–84.

cooperate with such other groups as cyclists and manufacturers. As businessmen, women's clubs, and clergymen had drawn workers closer to them, so cyclists and manufacturers drew farmers into closer alliance with other groups.

No movement was more revealing of the new civic consciousness than the growing cooperation between parents and teachers for improvement of schools. Not long before the panic parents and teachers were as mutually suspicious of each other as were bosses and workers or farmers and city dwellers. Women's clubs had confined their educational interests to campaigns that would impose on the schools such mugwumpish programs as instruction on the evils of liquor. Mothers and teachers did not communicate sympathetically; each regarded the other as the enemy who undid her own good works. As the growing civic consciousness convinced many people that the public school was one major institution that might lead in reforming the social order, both parents and teachers began to discover the dangerous communication gulf between them. Carrie E. Morgan, superintendent of Appleton schools, expressed the need to close the gulf in 1897: "The home life and the school life are inseparable. . . . For nine months in the year, the care of the average child is divided about equally between parent and teacher. How absolutely essential it is that the parent and teacher should co-operate!"[101] "Only by parents and teachers working together," declared the *Ashland Daily Press,* "can we expect the best results from our public schools."[102]

Out of this mutual concern were born such new practices as the formal conference between parents and teachers and the informal reception where parents and teachers met each other socially. By 1897 or 1898 these meetings were common in cities throughout the state.[103] Green Bay, under Supt. F. G. Kraege, pioneered in cooperation between home and school; after Green Bay's parents and teachers had established a number of ways of helping each other to reach their children, they branched out to lead attacks on such community-wide problems as poverty and

101. *Handbook,* bull. no. 11 (1897), 147, 149.

102. *Ashland Daily Press,* April 11, 1898.

103. *Ibid. Ashland Daily News,* April 28, 1900. *Superior Evening Telegram,* August 1, 1898. *Appleton Weekly Post,* July 2, 1896, July 7, 1898. *Madison Schools, 1897–1898,* 38; *1899–1900,* 47, 58. *State Journal,* January 15, 26, 1900. *Biennial Report of the State Superintendent . . . 1895–1896,* 50, 73, hereinafter cited as *Superintendent's Report.*

truancy. Several religious and educational journals urged other communities to copy Green Bay's example.[104]

The new civic consciousness, the desire to cross social divisions in campaigns to solve common problems, derived its vitality from its local and immediate focus. Because the depression touched everyone, it forced every citizen to examine the ways that the new industrialism had transformed lives and communities. The crisis gave urgency to campaigns to change habits and institutions. In the face of such widespread deprivation and questioning a great many Wisconsinites discovered that they had a stake in the lives of fellow citizens who had previously been strangers. Common local and immediate problems transcended social backgrounds and revealed that many old ideas and institutions were only hollow shells that bore no relationship to industrial realities. Since nothing could be worse than present conditions, many citizens seemed to believe, they hastily began scrapping old ideas and building new institutions.

III

Behind these movements to bridge social gaps was an emerging ideology that sought, in the words of an editor in Superior, to "save our social system from destruction into the vortex of which it is fast traveling."[105] This ideology was an attempt to develop and apply new social yardsticks to the differences between the rich and the poor. The first gropings toward achieving new yardsticks appeared in the arbitration movement, which many Wisconsinites hoped would assert their interest in struggles that had not previously seemed so immediately relevant. By 1895 nearly everyone agreed with Horace Rublee that "society, as a whole, is vitally concerned to delimit the area within which this strife can be carried on by insisting that its own rights shall be respected by both sides to the struggle." As a result, Gov. William Upham had no trouble securing passage of his pet project: a State Board of Arbitration and Conciliation.[106] Industrial arbitration assumed near-panacea proportions

104. *Superintendent's Report, 1897–1898*, 178–79. *Our Church Life*, 5 (September–October, 1899, supplement), 3. Form letter from Charles E. Vrooman, May 14, 1900, Ely Papers.

105. *Superior Sunday Forum*, July 14, 1895.

106. *Milwaukee Sentinel*, January 25, February 22, May 27, 29, 1895. *Appleton Weekly Post*, July 19, 1894, February 7, 1895. Wisconsin, *Laws*

as eager citizens felt they had found a way to limit class conflict and assert the public's rights in labor struggles.

The arbitration movement, whose limitations became evident less than a year later when the new board proved unable to end the street railway strike at Milwaukee,[107] represented the beginnings of a new approach to bridging the gulf between rich and poor. Since the whole thrust of the new civic consciousness was to prevent any further widening of the gulf, men and women increasingly evaluated the activities of all groups in terms of whether they widened that gap. Those actions that further fragmented society were labeled by citizens as selfish and arrogant. The urgent hope, declared an Appleton editor, was to "minimize the selfish and aggrandizing characteristics of each and establish a relationship, in which the theoretical and true conditions of mutuality will be practically recognized."[108]

Armed with the new criteria of "selfishness" and "arrogance," a great many Wisconsinites felt increasingly capable of responding to industrial and class conflict. They could now define what it was that had been bothering them about the changes in their communities. They had a new ideology to supplant their shattered faith in equal opportunity and the self-made man, and they set out to apply that ideology.

The first result was the feeling that most of the selfish and arrogant actions were committed by the rich. Newspapers with no radical leanings believed that such activities of the new monopolies identified by the papers as "extorting" high prices from consumers, driving out smaller businessmen, using "improper" political influence, and paying their workers and stockholders too little were arrogant acts that had to be halted. They "could only unreasonably benefit the few at the expense of the many" and "would tend to disturb the whole social fabric." By 1899 even Edward Scofield, the state's conservative governor, found much to fear when "great aggregations of capital may be tempted to exercise that power outside of its legitimate province."[109] By 1897 a restless citizenry had at last developed ways

---

(1895), chaps. 258, 364. Donald J. Berthrong, "Social Legislation in Wisconsin, 1836–1900" (Ph.D. diss., University of Wisconsin, 1951), 257–61. Records of State Board of Arbitration, Box 1, Wisconsin State Archival Series 1/1/8–9.

107. *Biennial Report of the State Board of Arbitration and Conciliation, 1895–1896,* 11–12, 16, 19, 23, 206–7, hereinafter cited as *Arbitration Report.*

108. *Appleton Weekly Post,* July 19, 1894.

109. *Milwaukee Sentinel,* April 30, September 20, 1894, February 26,

of evaluating the merger movements they began to confront in the 1880s.

The second feeling of Wisconsinites was that workers were generally the victims of corporate arrogance, and they found few examples of what they deemed selfish or arrogant behavior by workers. In fact, the *Appleton Weekly Post* stated, "The opinion largely obtains that labor has not had its proper share" of the fruits of industrialism.[110] Since they were not widening the social divisions, workers either received sympathy or indifference when Wisconsinites applied the new yardsticks.

These feelings reflected an urgent yearning to heal the raw wounds that industrialism had created and the depression exposed. If an individual or group was arrogant, it was a threat not to any particular class so much as to everyone in the community; the new yardsticks provided a means of binding together the rest of a society whose members urgently demanded reintegration. An Appleton editor expressed the new ideology: "We are men and brethren, not groups, not classes. We live in common wealth or common suffering. The maintenance of our heritage centers in the unity of our action when danger threatens."[111] A Congregationalist magazine commented: "By the great truth of social solidarity we are made to understand that there is no such thing as individual protection dissociated from mutual protection."[112]

The new ideology of social solidarity was rooted in common experiences. There were several bonds that united residents of a community across social barriers. The most important of these bonds was that all men and women are, after all, consumers—of high prices, defective products, and unresponsive politicians; their roles as consumers forced them to make common cause.[113] A second source of cooperation was a new and social conception of religion. The rapid spread of the social gospel among Catholic and Protestant clergymen during the depression gave religious sanction to the quest for social solidarity. "The Golden

1899, February 18, 1900. *Appleton Weekly Post*, August 23, 1894, February 7, May 30, June 20, 1895, December 10, 17, 24, 1896, March 2, April 13, August 10, 1899. *Wausau Daily Record*, April 1, 1899. *State Journal*, February 8, 1897. *Madison Old Dane*, October 1, 1897. *The Madison State*, September 15, 1899. *Handbook*, bull. no. 9 (1895), 138.

110. *Appleton Weekly Post*, August 23, 1894.

111. *Ibid.*, November 21, 1895.

112. *Our Church Life*, 1 (March 1895), 59.

113. *State Journal*, February 8, 1897. *Appleton Weekly Post*, February 11, 1897.

Rule is the Rule of Love, and as such is the very opposite of that which calls forth hatred and jealousy and bigotry and . . . heedlessness of others' interests and forgetfulness of their crying need."[114] The popular social scientists provided a third and intellectual basis for the new ideology. They taught that society was naturally evolving from competition toward cooperation and, in the state where Ely's influence was greatest, they called for a "golden mean of social reform" that would further the evolution of society and unify all classes.[115] A fourth reason for cooperation was geographical. Men developed social solidarity by working together against a common enemy. After the citizens of Grand Rapids had successfully defied the hated Bell telephone monopoly, one participant observed that "the greatest point gained in the struggle for independence was the building up of a local patriotism, an *esprit de corps,* that has united our people to such a degree that we can protect ourselves against *any* monopoly that oppresses us."[116] The voluntary associations that sprang to life as a result of the new civic consciousness— discussion clubs, extension centers, parents and teachers associations, and dozens of others—provided another root for the new ideology. "By so enriching a city with associations, activities and interests in which rich and poor alike feel a mutual stake," declared a Madison editor, "they will not tolerate invasion of their city any more than of their home."[117] The common impulse of patriotism that accompanied the Spanish-American War drew groups more closely together. "Whatever previous relations have been," wrote an Appleton editor, the war "has brought people—neighbors—nearer together."[118]

Although some observers would subsequently maintain that this organicist ideology was romantic and fruitless, it was precisely this ideology, however hazily perceived, that inspired the reform movements born of the new civic consciousness. Practical results of the ideology could be seen in the growing cooperation among a community's residents and between businessmen

114. *Our Church Life,* 4 (September 1898), 164.
115. For examples, see *Milwaukee Sentinel,* June 8, August 17, 1896. Rader, *Influence of Ely,* chaps. 3, 4.
116. Gaynor, "Wisconsin Valley Plan," in *Municipal Monopolies,* ed. Edward W. Bemis (New York: Thomas Y. Crowell, 1899), 361.
117. *State Journal,* April 12, 1899. Editors after 1893 emphasized how fairs broke down class lines. See *Milwaukee Sentinel,* October 20, 1895, July 1, 1899. *The State,* June 30, 1899. *Sheboygan Herald,* October 14, 1893.
118. *Appleton Weekly Post,* June 30, 1898.

and workers, farmers and city dwellers, parents and teachers. According to Lawrence University's economist Jerome H. Raymond, at a time when "the very air of this closing decade of our old century is burdened with sociological thought,"[119] the new organicism also fostered social justice movements to assist the victims of the social order.

The greatest impact of the new ideology was probably on the political habits of Wisconsinites. Rejecting the stale national formulas of the past, Wisconsinites demanded that politicians listen to the new concerns of the grass roots of society. The civic consciousness was fundamentally a new kind of citizenship. "There never was a time when citizenship means as much as it does today," pronounced the Fond du Lac school superintendent in 1896. "Public opinion . . . is rapidly becoming more potent than the will of princes, and, what is more significant, every member of the body politic has a share in making this opinion."[120] The new political mood was evident everywhere. "The year 1894 will pass down into history as a year remarkable for its revival of civic patriotism," reported a Milwaukee Methodist preacher.[121] Bound together by the new ideology and driven by a sense of urgency, the aroused communities forced politicians to obey their commands or lose their jobs.

The new spirit of reform began on the local level where desperate men and women came together to build bridges over valleys they had discovered only when the panic hit their communities. The feelings of doubt and anger engendered by the failure of established institutions and beliefs cut across the earlier social barriers. The new moralistic and psychological yardsticks for measuring individual and group activities—selfishness and arrogance—were, after all, yardsticks that all men could use together. From them came a dichotomy that was central to all subsequent movements—the dichotomy between "selfish interests" and "the public interest." The will of the public, of the united community, was to reign in the future society. Reflecting this new approach, an Appleton editor proclaimed: "No man, however wealthy, can be independent of public opinion in matters appertaining to the public interest."[122] It was this concept of a transcendent public interest, of a united commun-

119. *Ibid.,* June 7, 1894.
120. *Handbook,* bull. no. 10 (1896), 131.
121. *Wood County Reporter,* January 10, 1895.
122. *Appleton Weekly Post,* December 24, 1896.

ity solving common problems and resisting common enemies—
a concept so alien to Gilded Age Wisconsin—that served to join
men and women of varied backgrounds as they set out to remake the institutions of the state.

FOUNDATIONS OF SOCIAL PROGRESSIVISM: THE "NEW WOMAN" AND THE "NEW RELIGION"

The new civic consciousness forced each social institution to apply the new ideology to its own practices. As clubwomen and clergymen pursued their familiar philanthropic activities, they were staggered by the new dimensions of poverty and shaken by the failure of their institutions to narrow the divisions between rich and poor, men and women, home and school, worker and church. They hastily devised programs that would reunite a divided society, programs whose basic new features were participation by the poor themselves and belief that the individual is a product of his environment, not of his nature. Bewildered by the rapid transformation of both the character and programs of these groups, feature writers after 1895 wrote about the "New Woman" and the "New Religion." No other adjectives so well described the phenomena the writers only dimly understood.

I

The New Woman movement that blossomed during the depression resulted from a combination of old tendencies and new departures. For more than a generation before the Panic of 1893 the state's women had joined groups. Suffragettes had formed the Wisconsin Woman Suffrage Association in 1867 and reorganized it in 1885;[1] they had been joined in 1874 by the Woman's Christian Temperance Union (WCTU); the state's first secular woman's club, Clio, had been formed at Sparta in 1871.[2] The process of organization was well under way by 1893. In addition, women had won some acceptance into what had been a man's world. Organizations like the Grange and the Knights of Labor had admitted women as members, and the legislature had granted women equal property rights (1877), the right to practice law (1877), and suffrage in certain elections (1885).[3]

1. Theodora W. Youmans, "How Wisconsin Women Won the Ballot," *Wisconsin Magazine of History*, 5 (September 1921), 8. Sarah A. Powers to Mrs. Laura James, March 14, 1884. WWSA Proceedings, 1885, 1–6, Ada James Papers, Box 36, Manuscripts Division, State Historical Society of Wisconsin.

2. Jane C. Croly, *The History of the Woman's Club Movement in America* (New York: H. G. Allen, 1898), 1151, 1158–59.

3. Donald J. Berthrong, "Social Legislation in Wisconsin, 1836–1900"

Before the mid-1890s, however, the literary, suffragette, temperance, and religious organizations had been essentially mugwumpish. Believing that their comfortable social and economic positions had resulted from superior virtue, industry, and character, the organizations had confined their projects to those which emphasized the individualistic techniques of education and moral suasion. The various clubs had reinforced the members' elitism and had isolated themselves from other women; they had found no reason to listen to the voices of the inferior poor. Accepting the existing social structure, they had acted as philanthropists from the comfort of their suburban and avenue homes. Mrs. Laura James, wife of a wealthy Richland Center merchant, typified these Gilded Age women. Bored by her superfluous role in her comfortable home, she had turned for amusement to the romantic intrigues and foreign travels of her family and friends and to the state woman suffrage association, which she had served as secretary since 1885. Such suffragettes and their WCTU allies—all eighty WCTU members in Marathon County had been suffragettes—had been repelled by the life styles of the poor immigrants who had recently come to central Wisconsin. Their "reforms" had consisted of support of temperance, restriction of immigration, and limitations on the immigrants' right to vote; their attitudes toward the poor had been thoroughly nativist and elitist. They had tried to preserve their Yankee, upper-middle-class homes from the onslaughts of what were in their eyes dirty, drinking, ignorant foreigners.[4] As late as the mid-1890s the leader of Milwaukee's Jewish philanthropic women had to tell her colleagues that the "dirty alleys," "rickety stairs," "dark damp basements," and "unique atmosphere" of the Russian Jewish ghetto were only a few "paces" from their husbands' downtown offices.[5] Believing that their superior character divorced them from any contact with the poor, Wisconsin's women's organizations had reinforced the social divisions through mugwumpish ideas and had been, as a result, nothing new for the feature writers.

This elitist and mugwump pattern did not completely disap-

(Ph.D. diss., University of Wisconsin, 1951), 281–82, 291–307.

4. See James Papers, particularly Sarah A. Powers to Mrs. Laura James, March 14, 1884, undated note ca. 1895, Box 2, and WWSA Proceedings, 1885, 1–6; (1886), 26; (1887), 40; (1888), 45; (1890), 65; (1891), 79, 88; (1892), 106; (1895), 2: 82.

5. Unidentified speech, Lizzie Black Kander, ca. 1897, Kander Papers, Manuscripts Division, State Historical Society of Wisconsin.

pear during the depression. As late as 1897 perhaps three-fourths of the local clubs continued to discuss classical literature.[6] Many clubs persevered in their efforts to regulate morals by crusading for the enforcement of blue laws, by securing curfews, and by banning the sale of obscene literature, and they continued to collect and sew clothes for the poor in their own homes.[7]

Many of the state's women's clubs, however, were substantially altered by the depression, and the resultant changes produced the New Woman. Women came to believe that it was no longer safe or just for them to perpetuate the social isolation and mugwumpish programs that they had previously followed, and they formulated a unique role in developing the emerging civic consciousness. One cause for their position was that they had ample time to discuss and study the new social discoveries that had accompanied the depression. Mrs. Ellen M. Henrotin perceptively observed that "the woman's club movement represents a part of the great popular educational movement which is sweeping like a tidal wave over the country."[8] The women's quest for understanding of the new problems led them to become prominent sponsors of university extension courses, discussion clubs, and church lecture series. Their central importance in the popular education movement came to be appreciated by the director of the University of Wisconsin's extension courses when correspondents repeatedly told him that the local woman's club "would be the proper and best parties" for sponsoring classes in the community.[9] The members of such groups as the Kenosha Woman's Club, the Baraboo Woman's Club, the Stevens Point Woman's Club, and, in Milwaukee, the West Side Literary Club, Social Economics Club, and College Endowment Association profited so greatly from such courses that an editor was probably correct when he observed that "the known results of this current topic study have placed

6. Croly, *Woman's Club Movement,* 1152.

7. *Ashland Daily News,* October 31, 1895. *Superior Evening Telegram,* March 2, 1896. *Superior Leader,* April 3, 1897. *Milwaukee Sentinel,* November 10, 1895, July 3, November 16, December 18, 1898. *Appleton Weekly Post,* September 17, 1896. Wisconsin, Petition 563A, 1897 Legislature, Box 59, Petitions to the Legislature, Wisconsin State Archival Series 2/3/1/5–7.

8. Croly, *Woman's Club Movement,* x.

9. J. R. McDowell to J. H. Raymond, May 26, 1897, J. H. Raymond File, Papers of the University of Wisconsin Extension Division, University of Wisconsin Archival Series 18/1/1–4.

Ashland women on the same level with their husbands in the discussion of every phase of the situation." Women learned that more than defects of character separated them from poor women, that social divisions were dangerous, and that structural reforms were essential.[10]

As clubwomen pursued their ordinary charitable activities their firsthand experiences confirmed their studies. The depression forced them into direct contacts with the poor, in particular with poor women, and those contacts led them to emerge from the comfort of their homes, values, associations, and traditions, and to modify their class assumptions. Following the panic charitable women decided that they must at least determine the extent of the suffering and do more than sew a few garments to help relieve it. As a result, new groups like Superior's East End Women's Relief Corps, Madison's Benevolent Society, and Milwaukee's West Side Catholic Relief Corps visited the homes of their community's poor. The poor, on their part, came to the charitable women at such institutions as Milwaukee's Free Hospital, House of Mercy, and Catholic Girls Home.[11] Even more jolting to the clubwomen was that many young, poor, and working women wanted to join their clubs. By 1895 mothers from Milwaukee's poor South Side had begun to play a major role in reorienting women's educational reforms in the city. A group of seventy-two workingwomen in Appleton sought a voice in the state federation of women's clubs.[12] As a result of these contacts many clubs lost the social exclusiveness and elitism that had characterized them in the past. "We gladly welcome all who will join us with the same spirit and purpose," declared a Milwaukee club.[13]

Their direct contacts with all classes and their study of the problems resulting from gaps across social classes led the new women of the depression to develop the feeling that woman-

10. Letters to University Extension Office from Dr. May Cleo Smith, January 23, 1895; Mrs. Charles Gorst, August 13, 1897; Mrs. E. N. Kimball, December 2, 1897; Extension Division Papers. *Ashland Daily News,* February 2, 1895, November 1, 1899. *Milwaukee Sentinel,* November 17, 1895, August 30, December 27, 1897, February 25, 1898, August 24, 1899, April 15, 1900.

11. *Ashland Weekly Press,* February 16, 1895. *State Journal,* January 19, 1895. *Superior Evening Telegram,* November 7, 1895. *Milwaukee Sentinel,* July 14, 1895, May 30, 1897. *Milwaukee Catholic Citizen,* November 11, 1893, January 9, 1897.

12. *Milwaukee Sentinel,* May 19, 1896, February 21, 1897, October 16, 1898, March 19, 1899.

13. *Ibid.,* December 27, 1897.

hood transcended all other social divisions. This strong sense of the common identity of womanhood was stimulated by the powerful feeling that their husbands and fathers had failed to comprehend and solve the new problems of industrialization and urbanization. Since womanness came to transcend social class as a primary allegiance, the new women were less interested in perpetuating their social position than in confronting the new problems. Shedding her earlier elitism, Olympia Brown, president of the Wisconsin Woman Suffrage Association, proclaimed in 1897 that suffragettes suffered whenever a working-woman was oppressed.[14] Convinced that men were too preoccupied with their roles as producers of goods to understand the new problems, women determined to take the lead themselves. "The despised rib has become the heart, the vitalizing force," declared a speaker to the state federation in 1896.[15] Whether they saw themselves as the heart or as consumers of an unjust social order, the new women set out to unite the members of their sex in a common assault on the evils the depression had revealed.

The first need, as they saw it, was simply to form more women's groups of all kinds. The depression's New Woman movement vastly accelerated the process of organization that had begun a generation earlier. Thirty-seven of the sixty-nine clubs that came together to form the State Federation of Women's Clubs in 1896 had been founded since 1893.[16] By 1900, "owing to the multiplicity of women's organizations," one club in Ashland substituted biweekly for weekly meetings so its members could attend all their other club meetings.[17]

The New Woman, now burning with the special mission of her sex, became increasingly militant in her demands for integration into a man's world. After long campaigns women won appointment to the Milwaukee School Board in 1895 for the first time, and two years later they secured a state law that permitted members of their sex to serve on school boards in smaller cities.[18] In 1897 Angie Sanborn, an Oshkosh garmentworker,

14. WWSA Proceedings, 1897, 2:97–98.
15. *Milwaukee Sentinel,* October 21, 1896.
16. *Directory of the Founders of the Wisconsin State Federation of Women's Clubs,* January 1897, lists the member clubs and their formation dates.
17. *Ashland Daily Press,* May 26, 1900.
18. *Milwaukee Sentinel,* April 8, 1894, March 5, April 1, 1896. Wisconsin, Petition 61A, 1897 Legislature, Box 58, Petitions to Legislature. *Superior Leader,* May 13, 1897.

became the first woman delegate to an annual convention of the Wisconsin Federation of Labor.[19] Women first received the right to attend Beloit College in 1895.[20] The greatest victories for women came in their battles to integrate the churches. In 1895, stated the *Fond du Lac Commonwealth*, "the women, who have been doing the greater part of the work of the Methodist Church for years," were permitted to become delegates to the conventions of the Wisconsin Conference of Methodists.[21] Feeling the pressures of the militant new women, other churches hastily followed the Methodists. When the Milwaukee Episcopal Council waited until 1899 to permit women to vote at parish meetings, the *Sentinel* gently chided them for their hesitation "to fall in line with the spirit of the age and to admit women to the ecclesiastical franchise."[22] The rapid acceleration of organization and integration after 1893 reflected the growing militancy of the new women as they sought to bridge dangerous social gulfs. Alarmed by this militancy, male editors could only complain that "the 'new woman' . . . is a little too radical, too much of a man and too little of a woman, to suit the average taste."[23]

The new groups and the new-found militancy confirmed the women's sense that women of all classes had unique and forceful roles to play in changing society. As they became increasingly self-conscious, they turned their discussions from men's literary creations to such topics as "Woman's Work," "Woman's Influence in Municipal Reform," and "Woman's New Place in the Home, in Business, and in Society."[24] At the same time they began to use local newspapers to trumpet their new mission. Beginning with a fifty-page edition of the *Milwaukee Journal* in 1895, women's clubs persuaded editors to let them publish issues describing the past and potential contributions of women to the schools, charities, and arts of the community, and they

19. *Appleton Weekly Post,* June 10, 1897.

20. *Congregational Minutes,* 55th Meeting, 1895, 21. *Milwaukee Sentinel,* January 17, 1895.

21. *Fond du Lac Commonwealth,* in *Appleton Weekly Post,* October 17, 1895. *Methodist Minutes,* 1895, 26. See also *Appleton Weekly Post,* October 8, 1896.

22. *Milwaukee Sentinel,* September 21, 1899. For recognition of women's political power, see *Congregational Minutes,* 54th Meeting, 1894, 22–23.

23. *State Journal,* June 1, 1895.

24. 1896–1897 program of Milwaukee Social Economics Club, Milwaukee County Historical Society. *Milwaukee Sentinel,* October 23, 1896. *Ashland Daily News,* April 9, 1896.

donated the proceeds from these special women's editions to local charities to dramatize their growing determination to benefit their communities. Special editions of the *La Crosse Press,* the *Superior Leader,* the *Appleton Post,* and the *Milwaukee Sentinel* united local women's clubs and served as evidence that "the 'coming woman' is surely coming" at the same time that they reflected the new belief that womanhood was more important than social origins.[25]

After announcing that they had a new mission, the women's groups began to devise programs that would reintegrate the fragmented industrial society. Discussion groups and university extension lectures convinced them that adult education movements of all kinds were crucial and that others should share their discovery of the new problems the depression had revealed. They seized on the public library as a place where all classes could mingle and find answers to the new questions; therefore, women's clubs throughout the state promoted establishment of new libraries. Wisconsin had established twenty-seven public libraries in the forty years before the Panic of 1893, but in the five years between 1894 and 1899, when women's clubs began their campaigns, thirty-seven public libraries were created in cities as widely separated as Kenosha, Ashland, Appleton, and Wausau.[26] More interested in breaking down social isolation than in displaying impressive shelves of books, the women worked especially hard to establish "traveling libraries." The idea was to fill a carton with fifty volumes of popular fiction and essays on industrial problems and to circulate the carton among people whose social or geographical isolation cut them off from other sources of adult education. The campaigns of groups like Green Bay's Shakespeare Club, Ashland's Monday Club, Eau Claire's Woman's Club, Wausau's Literary Club, and Milwaukee's Association of Collegiate Alumnae were so successful that by 1898 Wisconsin, without any state aid, ranked second only to New York in the number of traveling libraries.[27] Such libraries

25. *Superior Leader,* March 12, April 9, 1895. *State Journal,* February 23, 1895. *Milwaukee Sentinel,* April 19, 1896. *Appleton Weekly Post,* April 19, 1900.

26. *Ashland Weekly Press,* January 12, 1895. *Appleton Weekly Post,* March 19, 1896. *Milwaukee Sentinel,* January 23, 1898, May 13, 1900. *Blue Book,* 1901, 560–61. Kathryn Saucerman, "A Study of the Wisconsin Library Movement, 1850–1900" (M.A. thesis, University of Wisconsin, 1944), 30–64.

27. *Ashland Daily Press,* February 16, 1898. *Superior Evening Telegram,*

helped to break down the separation of poor from rich and farmer from city dweller.

Most of the depression's new women believed that the public school was their best instrument for remaking the social order. Before the panic they had rarely doubted that the school's main function was to teach classical skills, basic principles, and moral precepts, but, as the depression challenged the safety and justice of the social order that supported formalistic education, women began to question the validity of those skills, principles, and precepts. Their new educational thrust was toward making the schools more relevant for the poor. Formalistic traditions and practices defied the urgent spirit of change that motivated the new women to seek reform. Discovering the need for parent-teacher cooperation, the women envisioned the school as a community center where rich and poor parents could work with teachers to solve the common problems of educating children for an industrial society.

The impact of the depression on women's educational activities was typified by the development of the Wisconsin Woman's School Alliance. Its origins reached back to 1891, when the Athenaeum, composed of the wives of Milwaukee's most influential men, invited other women's clubs to discuss the schools. From 1891 until 1893 these clubs confined their campaigns to establishing better janitorial methods of tidying school buildings, but, when the depression struck, they organized the School Alliance and opened their membership to all interested mothers. By 1895 mothers from the poorer wards on the city's South Side had joined the alliance and had taught the older clubwomen about the urgent connections between poverty and education. While their husbands, books, fears, and consciences may have all contributed to pointing out new goals for them to achieve, their new and poor colleagues probably made the greatest impact. At any rate, the School Alliance launched a massive crusade to open the schools to poor children. They learned that thousands of Milwaukee school children did not attend school because their parents were too poor to buy them clothes and too proud to ask for charity. As a result, the alliance began in 1893–1894 to collect clothes and then forced the city to hire truant officers whose function was to distribute clothes to all

February 16, 1898. *Ashland Daily News,* July 10, 1899. *Milwaukee Sentinel,* January 23, April 14, November 20, 1898, October 8, 1899, February 4, 12, 1900.

children who could not attend school for want of clothes. When women in Fond du Lac and Portage formed branches of the School Alliance, they too tried to clothe all needy children.[28] The second program of the alliance, won in 1895, was to force men on the school board to listen to the voice of the New Woman. They began to push for the creation of informal kindergartens as a first step toward uniting home and school and encouraged conferences between parents and teachers. After 1895 they devoted most of their energies toward forcing the schools to adopt manual training programs. Manual training, the alliance believed, would provide skills for poor children to qualify them for better jobs, would inject "real life" into the curriculum for all children, and would teach rich children a respect for manual labor. This evolution from elitist concerns with temperance and sanitation to more democratic concerns with making schools relevant for poor children and uniting parents and teachers reflected the transformation of the alliance from an upper-class group into one that included a broad, relatively classless spectrum of Milwaukee's mothers.[29]

Other women's clubs followed the pattern of the alliance. Coming to believe that children were products of their environment, not their characters, Milwaukee's women's clubs began in 1897 to improve the physical appearance of classrooms.[30] The Jewish women's clubs began in 1896 to offer manual training classes.[31] But the project hailed by the *Sentinel* as "one of the most successful experiments in latter day altruism" was the vacation school that began in 1899. Attacking the "cut and dried atmosphere of the average public school," all of Milwaukee's women's clubs united in the effort to create this school, which took 400 of the city's poorest children during the summer and, in a less formal atmosphere, provided weekly excursions to

28. Croly, *Woman's Club Movement,* 1157. *Milwaukee Sentinel,* February 22, September 24, 1895, March 5, November 29, 1896, January 17, February 21, March 14, 1897, May 28, October 16, 1898.

29. *Milwaukee Sentinel,* May 19, November 29, 1896, May 28, October 16, 1898. Memo, November 25, 1898, Kander Papers.

30. Milwaukee Social Economics Club, Minute Book, Milwaukee County Historical Society, 97. *Milwaukee Sentinel,* March 6, 1898.

31. Mrs. Simon Kander to Mrs. C. S. Benjamin, October 23, 1896, undated address to Ladies Relief Sewing Society, ca. 1896, and Cooking School Memo Book, 1898, Lizzie Kander Third Annual Report, June 9, 1899, Kander Papers. See Ann Shirley Waligorski, "Social Action and Women: The Experience of Lizzie Black Kander" (M.A. thesis, University of Wisconsin, 1969), 64–75.

neighboring lakes and farms and classes in manual training, art, music, and nature study. During the winter the clubs raised the necessary thousands of dollars to finance the popular program. The clubwomen believed that the vacation school offered poor children special opportunities that would ultimately narrow the gap between rich and poor. They believed the school provided a model for undermining educational formalism that the public schools would soon copy, as it demonstrated that relaxed environments could also be stimulating.[32]

The New Woman's educational reforms were not confined to the state's metropolis. At Madison the women's clubs opened a kindergarten in 1895 for the children of factory workers. In 1897 Madison's women forced the school superintendent to introduce manual training classes into the schools, and they led the movement that resulted in parent-teacher conferences.[33] As manual training came increasingly to seem a panacea for the ills within the social order, women's clubs at Superior, Eau Claire, Oconomowoc, Menasha, Fond du Lac, and other communities headed movements for instituting such classes.[34]

Wisconsin's new women were the vitalizing force in the New Education. Their campaigns to make the schools responsive to the new problems won the support of editors and professional educators who had also discovered the need for changes. The women thus formulated programs that appealed across the class lines that had once been so important to them.

If the New Education represented a major transformation in women's long-standing interest in schools, their other major activity was a complete innovation, based on the awareness that came with the depression. Before the financial panic, women's clubs had ignored the plight of working women and children. Their new-found concern for working women and children had tangled roots. For some, the face-to-face contact with poor women was the spark that ignited them; for others, issues raised in discussion clubs like Milwaukee's Social Economics Club or Madison's Woman's Club were the inspiration.[35] Other wealthy

32. *Milwaukee Sentinel,* June 4, August 6, 1899, April 13, July 6, 1900. *Publications of the Association of Collegiate Alumnae,* Series 3 (February 1900), 94. *Milwaukee Catholic Citizen,* July 25, 1896.

33. *State Journal,* February 6, April 20, 1895, January 12, 21, 1897, March 2, 14, 1899, January 15, 16, 26, March 6, 1900. *Public Schools,* 1904–1905, 30.

34. *Superior Leader,* June 7, 1895. *Milwaukee Sentinel,* April 9, October 8, November 12, December 10, 1899.

35. *State Journal,* April 27, 1897. *Milwaukee Sentinel,* October 9, 1899.

women who blamed social oppression for their roles as super-fluous members of society probably identified with oppressed poor women.[36] Whatever the immediate cause, the result in the depression was the profound sense that status as a woman was enough to bridge all other social barriers. Rich and poor, they were sisters in common suffering and common hope, and all women should unite to fight the problems of oppressed mothers and women.[37]

The exact character of the problems was little known when the state's new women began their crusades against child and woman labor. In 1890 the state labor commissioner had reported that almost no children were employed in factories.[38] Editors and manufacturers denounced as lies the 1895 charge of a special agent for the United States Labor Department that the exploitation of children and women was worse in Wisconsin than in any other state.[39] In such a charged atmosphere women's clubs decided that their first job should be to examine the situation themselves. In 1897 alone both the Milwaukee Ethical Society and the Sociological Club investigated the city's factories.[40]

Armed with firsthand knowledge and a sense of urgency, the state's new women began their crusades against exploitation of women and children in industry. The workingwomen with whom wealthy women had most direct contact were store clerks, and the earliest movements were aimed at improving their conditions. "True women," declared Appleton's women's clubs, would not tolerate the harsh conditions of their sisters. Women's clubs in Appleton, Wausau, Madison, and Ashland cooperated with fledgling clerks' unions to close stores at night.[41] The Milwaukee Social Economics Club had broader goals. In 1899 it began to organize the city's women's clubs into the Consumers' League, which boycotted stores that sold products made by exploited women and children. Less than two months after the league's creation it persuaded the city's Federated Trades

36. Waligorski, "Lizzie Black Kander," 36–37.
37. For example, see WWSA Proceedings, 1897, 2:97–98.
38. *Milwaukee Sentinel,* July 2, 1890.
39. *Ibid.,* June 16, 17, 1895.
40. *State Journal,* April 27, 1897. *Milwaukee Sentinel,* December 26, 1897.
41. *Appleton Weekly Post,* January 2, April 2, 1896. *Wausau Daily Record,* January 3, April 26, 1899. *Milwaukee Sentinel,* March 13, 1898. *State Journal,* January 4, 1897. *Ashland Daily Press,* February 28, April 8, 1899.

Council to urge wives of union members to shop only at stores on the league's "white list."[42] Other women's clubs provided places where workingwomen could meet other women, and some sponsored free summer trips to enable workingwomen to escape temporarily their factory and the city.[43]

The clubwomen's most common approach was to report their discoveries to the state labor commission and to demand that the inspectors enforce the state's labor laws. By 1898 women had forced one inspector to become a zealot, and by 1899 another inspector at Sheboygan and Racine had made things uncomfortable for violators. The state labor commissioner recognized this vital new role of the women's clubs. "When it is remembered that no law can be successfully enforced that is not backed up by a healthy public sentiment, the value and influence of the Woman's Clubs becomes fully apparent." He proposed that the legislature sanction this assistance by appointing clubwomen "honorary factory inspectors."[44]

Not content with enforcing existing laws, the new women pushed for additional legislation. Led by the Woman's Club of Madison, they worked diligently for the Wisconsin Federation of Labor's strict factory inspection bills of 1899, and their support helped to bring the first effective factory inspection to the state in 1899. Reflecting the pressure of women's clubs in this achievement, one new law forced employers to provide seats for all workingwomen.[45] When dozens of women's clubs congregated at Eau Claire in October, 1899, to map the State Federation's war on child and woman labor, the *Sentinel* could truly find the meeting "remarkable for the frank and outspoken stand which the clubwomen took on the industrial question as it relates to women and child labor and the sweat-shop."[46]

Wisconsin's new women did not stop with labor and education. At Ashland, Madison, and Milwaukee they led successful movements to segregate imprisoned women and children from male criminals by creating special wards, matrons, and a juve-

42. Milwaukee Social Economics Club, Minute Book, 112, 114, 120. *Milwaukee Sentinel,* October 9, 26, 1899, June 11, 19, July 8, August 2, 1900.

43. *Milwaukee Sentinel,* July 25, December 13, 1897, March 19, June 11, 1899.

44. *Ibid.,* November 5, 1898, May 14, September 1, October 11, 26, 1899. Labor Bureau, *9th Biennial Report, 1899–1900,* xxv–xxvii.

45. Milwaukee Social Economics Club, Minute Book, 112. Wisconsin, *Laws* (1899), chap. 77.

46. *Milwaukee Sentinel,* October 26, 1899.

nile court.[47] In 1896 Milwaukee women established the state's first settlement house to mount a concerted attack on all the problems of urban poverty.[48] Believing that an attractive environment stimulated civic consciousness among all classes, they directed campaigns at Wausau, Madison, Ashland, and Milwaukee to improve their cities' physical appearances.[49] At Milwaukee they joined movements for municipal ownership and home rule, and at Madison they led a drive for municipal garbage collections.[50] Everywhere they created clubs and playgrounds where children could escape the premature horrors of urban poverty.

The process through which the depression converted the progressive New Woman from the Gilded Age mugwump was most dramatically revealed in the new activities of the old clubs. In 1894 the Wisconsin Woman Suffrage Association began to advocate the establishment of kindergartens and to show sympathy for workingwomen for the first time.[51] Even more striking was the progressive drift of the WCTU, an organization that for two decades had rarely strayed from measures to control vice. By 1896 even the WCTU seemed to believe that vice resulted not from individual failings, but from the environment. "Industrial conditions," declared the state WCTU president in 1896, "drove women" to sin. The next year the state WCTU passed resolutions denouncing child and woman labor; at Ashland and Milwaukee they sponsored recreational clubs for poor boys.[52] The Green County WCTU outfitted traveling libraries, while the Ashland chapter sponsored lectures on municipal reform, led the fight to segregate women and children in the county jail, and crusaded for a louder female voice in church policies.[53] The Madison WCTU was one of the first groups in that city to discuss manual training in the schools.[54] Members

47. *Ashland Daily News*, May 9, 12, 1895. *Milwaukee Sentinel*, February 18, 27, 1900. *State Journal*, March 3, 1900.

48. *Milwaukee Sentinel*, February 7, 1897.

49. *State Journal*, January 19, 1900. *Ashland Daily News*, November 1, 1899. *Milwaukee Sentinel*, February 24, April 22, 1900.

50. Milwaukee Social Economics Club, Minute Book, 102, 113. *State Journal*, March 17, 1900.

51. WWSA Proceedings, 1894, 2:73; 1897, 2:97–98.

52. *Milwaukee Sentinel*, October 17, November 21, 1896, April 17, 1898, March 10, 1899. *Ashland Daily Press*, March 11, 1898.

53. *Milwaukee Sentinel*, November 20, 1898. *Ashland Daily News*, May 9, 12, 1895. *Ashland Weekly Press*, February 16, 1895. *Ashland Daily Press*, March 5, 1898.

54. *State Journal*, February 6, 1895.

of the Milwaukee WCTU left their homes to form circles for child study in the poorer neighborhoods.[55] While some local chapters continued to fight vice, they were remarkably less noisy now because they, too, had discovered that the chasm between rich and poor needed filling before souls could be saved from sin.

By 1897 Wisconsin men were no longer so shocked by their new women. One editor breezily noted of a meeting of the State Civil Service Reform League that "the ladies were in the majority, as they always are, whenever a movement is made for the betterment of society."[56] And the Green Bay school superintendent announced: "Reformatory work accomplished by woman's clubs has greatly improved social order."[57] Perhaps because no other loyalties restrained her, the state's New Woman revealed most clearly how the depression's social unrest had generated discoveries leading to a new spirit of reform that sought to breathe new life into old institutions. Having lost their elitist and nativist biases, women's clubs began to attract women of the working classes in an assault on problems that transcended the rigid class lines that had marked earlier reform movements supported by women's clubs. In the process of trying to liberate the school and the factory, the New Woman liberated herself.

II

The major function of the New Religion was to give Wisconsin churchgoers a new ideology to aid in coping with the discoveries they made during the depression. Clergymen in 1893 already had a considerable body of social gospel and institutional church writings to use in their efforts to adapt their ideas and practices to an industrial society. Their parishioners, however, were isolated from that heritage. Those who went to church for any other purpose than to fulfill a social obligation could not have dreamed that the church could offer social salvation. When clergymen during the depression merged the new social gospel with the expanded civic crusades, many churchgoers concluded that the churches had found an answer to the troubling problem of how to unite a society whose new-found divisions threatened conscience and order.

55. *Milwaukee Sentinel,* August 1, 29, 1899.
56. *State Journal,* February 5, 1897.
57. *Appleton Weekly Post,* April 13, 1899.

Before the panic most Wisconsin churches expressed a theological mission that harmonized with the mugwumpery of the larger society. That mission was to save individual souls. Since the individual was a product of his soul, not of his environment, the proper ways to reach him were by the individualistic techniques of revivals and moral suasion. Exercise of such virtues as hard work, right thinking, and moral behavior was the surest road to salvation, and ministers believed their primary social obligation was to remove the temptations that diverted individuals from that road. Indeed, the only social topics discussed at the state's ministerial councils in the decade before the panic were the assorted vices that menaced the parishioners. Like the mugwumpery of the larger society, that of the churches had become entrenched behind rigid class lines. The centuries-old alliance of Protestantism and capitalism, tightened by an American environment that offered unequalled opportunities for the individual to advance economically and morally, had by the Gilded Age turned a great many churches into defenders of the existing social class relations. As industrialization increasingly limited individual opportunities and bred a collectivist orientation, workers understandably quit listening to a theology that seemed cruel, outdated, and deaf to their needs. By 1891 even Horace Rublee felt that the churches were irrelevant. "If the services were what they should be, there would be no repugnance—Sunday newspapers or tennis could not lure anybody who could be benefited by religious services away from them."[58] Few clergymen paid any attention to the handful of dissenters who, like Milwaukee Methodist Sabin Halsey, blasted "a religion . . . that is satisfied to sit down at the feet of worldly aristocracy and minister solely to them while hundreds and thousands are crying for the bread of life."[59]

This individualistic orientation did not die suddenly with the panic. Ministers continued to save individuals through revivals, and the depression's social unrest probably increased the success of the revivalists as men and women sought salvation from an oppressive social order and saw no other alternatives.[60] Other clergymen merely expanded earlier programs they had devised to make churches more responsive to the poor. In 1887

58. *Milwaukee Sentinel*, August 12, 1891.
59. *Ibid.*, July 25, 1892.
60. Revivals were most popular between 1894 and 1895. *Congregational Minutes*, 55th Meeting, 1895, 18. *Milwaukee Sentinel*, May 6, June 17, December 2, 1894. *State Journal*, June 21, 1895.

Judson Titsworth had begun to earn his reputation as a western leader of the "institutional church" movement by developing programs at his Plymouth Congregational Church in Milwaukee that would extend the church's influence to all aspects of community life. Charging that most churches ignored their obligations to their communities and that the YMCA did better work than most of his colleagues, Titsworth used his own church for a boys' club, for manual training classes where girls learned sewing and boys such trades as carpentry and tailoring, and for adult education classes at the same time that he promoted the Milwaukee YMCA and an orphans' home.[61] A few other ministers, like Milwaukee Methodists E. G. Updike and Sabin Halsey, had taken workers' sides in labor disputes.[62]

These few pioneers labored virtually alone. No local ministerial council or state denominational convention gave serious consideration to either the institutional church or the social gospel before the panic, even though they had ample opportunities. In 1892 Richard T. Ely launched a strenuous campaign to convert the state's Protestant clergymen to the social gospel. He lectured to the Milwaukee Ministerial Council and the state Congregational convention on the need for clergymen to form clubs where ministers of all faiths could learn the responsibilities forced on the churches by the new social science. The ministers listened politely, then ignored his advice.[63] Not until the depression created a new sense of urgency would Ely's message strike a responsive note with more than a handful of Wisconsin's clergymen.

The depression forced a great many clergymen to reappraise their practices and turn toward preaching of the social gospel. As they pursued their customary philanthropic activities among their parishioners, they could not escape the staggering proportions of suffering. Clergymen were the only people who could relieve distress for many poor people and, perhaps because they

61. *Milwaukee Sentinel,* September 19, October 5, 1891, November 27, 1892, January 5, June 18, 1893, January 6, 1894. Annabell Cook Whitcomb, *Report of the Boys' Busy Life Club* (Milwaukee: privately published, 1899). *State Journal,* May 13, 1903. Hugh H. Knapp, "The Social Gospel in Wisconsin, 1890–1912" (M.A. thesis, University of Wisconsin, 1968), 69–74.

62. *Milwaukee Sentinel,* September 24, November 14, 1887, July 8, 1889, May 4, 1891, May 9, July 11, 25, September 13, 1892.

63. "The Study of Social Science and the Christian Minister," Box 9, Richard T. Ely Papers, Manuscripts Division, State Historical Society of Wisconsin. *Congregational Minutes,* 52nd Meeting, 1892, 20–21.

could not escape it, the discovery of the chasm between rich and poor was a more shocking blow to them than to any other group. If a little bitterness toward businessmen crept into their rhetoric, the drain on the churches' resources partially explained it. As clergymen had to look into the eyes of their suffering neighbors and parishioners, they came to feel, as in Ashland, that "a man cannot become a Christian with an empty stomach."[64]

This feeling of desperation underscored a second factor that forced clergymen more than others to acknowledge the existence of the poor. The depression made clergymen realize the gap between the church and the workers. "How to bridge that gap so that sympathy and helpfulness may cross and recross it freely from one to the other is the question of the hour," cried a Milwaukee Methodist preacher. A Catholic editor urged the development of programs that would unite rich and poor members of that faith. As one clerical group after another grappled with this problem, they often concluded that "the church has . . . been making the mistake of seeking respectability among its adherents." "Individualistic evangelization" had estranged the workers.[65] The expanded charitable activities and the discovery that masses of people found churches cruel and irrelevant ignited in a great many clergymen a burning sense of a special mission, as a committee told the state Congregationalist convention in 1895, to "strive in every way to break down the partitions between rich and poor in church and social life."[66]

Wisconsin clergymen began to develop ways of bridging the social gap. Inspired by the popularity of cross-class discussion groups, a Milwaukee Methodist preacher, S. W. Naylor, formed the Church and Labor Social Union early in 1894, and less than two years later his Methodist colleague C. M. Starkweather created the more radical Christian Labor Union. Many workers reciprocated these overtures. The entire leadership of the Federated Trades Council attended the first meeting of Starkweather's union, and the Wisconsin Federation of Labor asked a Milwaukee minister to address its convention on "The

64. *Ashland Daily Press,* February 1, 1895.
65. *Congregational Minutes,* 55th Meeting, 1895, 24; 56th Meeting, 1896, 29. *Baptist Minutes,* 30th Meeting, 1894, 11. *Milwaukee Sentinel,* March 13, 1893, December 8, 13, 1895. *Our Church Life,* 1 (March 1895), 59 and (September 1895), 157. *Milwaukee Catholic Citizen,* June 24, 1893, March 9, 1895.
66. *Congregational Minutes,* 55th Meeting, 1895, 25.

Church and the Labor Problem."[67] From these contacts came a new-found sympathy. Where only a handful of Wisconsin clergymen had defended workers before the panic, dozens began taking the workers' side during the depression. They denounced the "inhumanity" and "hard soul" of employers and adopted resolutions to prohibit church members from patronizing unjust employers.[68] No Catholic reformer in the United States was more outspoken in his pleas for helping the urban masses than Milwaukee's Catholic editor Humphrey Desmond.[69] A far greater number followed the advice of the state's Congregationalists that "the right aspirations and demands of labor be as often voiced in the pulpit as the errors of 'socialists and anarchists' are denounced."[70]

The second response of clergymen was to expand social service activities. They hastily sponsored the setting up of restaurants, soup kitchens, rescue missions, hospitals, and homes for dependent women and children.[71] Clergymen began to take a greater interest in education, creating manual training classes at their churches and synagogues and leading movements, as at Eagle River, to improve public schools.[72] They breathed new life into the YMCA. In 1894 alone, clergymen helped to establish six new local YMCAs in the state for providing restaurants for the poor and night classes for those who worked during the day. By 1897 Milwaukee employers allowed "Y" workers to bring their extension services for men and women into the factories.[73] Taking an interest in cooperatives for the first time, clergymen worked with socialists to open a cooperative store in

67. *Milwaukee Sentinel,* June 9, 1893, January 2, February 3, March 2, May 5, 1894, December 8, 13, 1895. *Appleton Weekly Post,* December 19, 1895. *Milwaukee Daily News,* March 1, 1894.

68. For examples, see *Ashland Daily News,* January 13, 1895. *Milwaukee Sentinel,* April 23, 1894, May 15, August 17, 31, 1896, November 29, 1897, December 4, 1899, July 23, 1900.

69. Aaron I. Abell, *American Catholicism and Social Action: A Search for Social Justice, 1865–1950* (Garden City, 1960), 131–32.

70. *Congregational Minutes,* 55th Meeting, 1895, 26.

71. For examples, see *Milwaukee Catholic Citizen,* December 16, 30, 1893, February 17, 1894. *Milwaukee Sentinel,* June 9, November 17, 1895, January 6, 1896, November 14, 1897.

72. For examples, see *Milwaukee Sentinel,* April 15, 1900. Milwaukee Hanover Street Congregational Church, Minute Book, 189, Wisconsin Congregational Church Papers, Manuscripts Division, State Historical Society of Wisconsin. Mrs. Simon Kander to Mrs. C. S. Benjamin, October 23, 1896, Kander Papers. *Our Church Life,* 5 (September–October 1899), 174.

73. *Milwaukee Sentinel,* October 17, 1894, June 9, 1895, October 16,

Milwaukee and with Grangers to operate a cooperative factory in a small town.[74] They organized an 1896 state-wide convention to develop more humane ways for helping the thousands of "tramps" who roamed the state after losing their jobs.[75] At the rate churches were expanding their services, prophesied an Ashland minister in 1895, the twentieth century would be the century of Applied Christianity. By 1900 clergymen had indeed widened their horizons so far beyond the church walls that a Madison editor could correctly observe that there was "less Bible reading, less 'personal experience' " than in the past, but that the state's spiritual life "shows itself equally well in other ways—in ethical movements, in benevolence, in expressions of genuine brotherhood."[76] These attempts to break out of earlier social isolation and to win workers back to the churches constituted one important feature of the New Religion.

While some churchgoers participated in these activities, more were interested in a second feature of the New Religion. By the end of the depression they would hear from the pulpits an ideology that combined social-gospel sympathy for the poor with the demand for a new citizenship that had resulted from the depression's impact on the earlier vice crusades. It was the convergence of the new benevolence with the expanded crusades that influenced parishioners so powerfully.

The depression led the vice crusaders to expand their programs in several directions. The urgent necessity of change made many clergymen demand "something besides effervescent resolutions."[77] They extended the doctrine of Applied Christianity to mean that their congregations had to practice during the week what they heard on Sunday. Thus, they had to promote not only Sunday-closing movements but, in the words of a Marinette Baptist preacher, "all matters of reform."[78]

Even more important, the crusaders, who had previously regarded the poor as dirty people whose vices had to be controlled

1897. Adolf Gerd Korman, "A Social History of Industrial Growth and Immigrants: A Study with Particular Reference to Milwaukee, 1880–1920" (Ph.D. diss., University of Wisconsin, 1959) , 163.

74. Otto Fairfield Humphreys to Richard T. Ely, May 18, 1899, Ely Papers. State Grange, *27th Session, 1898,* 18.

75. *Milwaukee Sentinel,* February 26, 1896.

76. *Ashland Weekly Press,* October 26, 1895. *State Journal,* February 2, 1900.

77. *Congregational Minutes,* 54th Meeting, 1894, 20. *Presbyterian Minutes,* 1896, 41.

78. *Baptist Union Minutes,* 31st Meeting, 1895, 14.

from afar by rigid enforcement of blue laws, now recognized the nature of the gap between themselves and the poor. "Study the heart of the laboring classes," declared the state's Congregationalists. "Come into touch with them that you may be able to help them. Then patiently, perseveringly educate them" to the need for wiping out vice.[79] The crusaders were as interested in the votes of the poor as they were in their souls, and in order to expand their crusades enough to topple political machines they needed a broader voting base. "If too great power seems to be placed by democracy in the hands of the lower classes, then the Church must go down where they are, win their confidence, and teach them how to use it. It is the responsibility of the hour."[80] Shedding some of their elitism and manifesting an interest in poor people as persons, the vice crusaders won support from a number of appreciative labor groups for the Sunday-rest movement which the crusaders began in 1895.[81]

The new concern with the condition of the poor and the expanded doctrine of Applied Christianity were parts of what became the major thrust of the vice crusaders during the depression. In 1893 and 1894 the state's crusaders were learning that vice was hopelessly interlaced in the entire social and political fabric; to abolish it they would have to broaden their attack to include all facets of political corruption. The new strategy was to isolate the merchants of vice and their political allies from the rest of the community. "By cultivating a high moral sentiment in the community; by letting principle be above party and by taking a stand for the right and purity in politics," as a Milwaukee Methodist preacher put it, the new crusaders could rid their communities of all the "open and powerful enemies of righteousness." The alderman who tolerated immorality, stated a Catholic editor, was a "moral leper." Reflecting the broadening of the crusades, one group of clergymen after another declared its intention to overthrow local politicians who were more responsive to the needs of merchants of vice than to the pleas of the religious voter. The majority of moralistic citizens could no longer tolerate such politicians, and they began to champion such political reforms as corrupt practices acts, civil service reform, and nonpartisan local elec-

79. *Congregational Minutes,* 56th Meeting, 1896, 29.
80. *Our Church Life,* 1 (March 1895), 59.
81. *Congregational Minutes,* 56th Meeting, 1896, 29. *Our Church Life,* 4 (December 1897), 24.

tions as weapons to attract better candidates and weaken the power of the bosses.[82]

As clergymen throughout the state launched their campaigns to topple corrupt politicians, they revealed that the old prejudice between Catholics and Protestants was ebbing as both groups faced a common enemy. Many Catholics, who before the panic had shunned the vice crusades as thinly veiled Protestant efforts to control Catholics, now sensed a new tolerance among Protestant clergymen that would permit a united movement. They appreciated attacks by the state's leading social gospeler, Protestant clergyman Judson Titsworth, on the American Protective Association. In an abrupt about-face, the *Milwaukee Catholic Citizen* began to urge Wisconsin's Catholics to support the new campaigns.[83] In 1894, 1895, and 1896, Milwaukee's Protestant, Jewish, and Catholic clergymen formed several committees to "federate the moral forces of the city" against immoral politicians.[84] United clergymen began similar drives at Green Bay, Racine, and Sheboygan in 1894, Madison, Ashland, Superior, and Fond du Lac in 1895, and Racine again in 1896 to replace partisan politicians with more righteous nonpartisans. Nor was anyone surprised that many Protestant churchgoers flocked to a crusade originated by a Catholic priest in 1897 at El Paso, a small town in Pierce County.[85] Because they had

82. *Milwaukee Catholic Citizen,* July 22, August 12, 26, September 2, 1893, May 11, 1895. *Milwaukee Sentinel,* February 26, 1894, March 9, 1896, October 28, November 28, 1898. *Baptist Minutes,* 51st Meeting, 1895, 63. *Congregational Minutes,* 54th Meeting, 1894, 13; 56th Meeting, 1896, 19–20. *Presbyterian Minutes,* 1896, 42. *Methodist Minutes,* 1895, 68–69. *Our Church Life,* 2 (November 1895), 8 and (May 1896), 110. *Charities Review,* 8 (February 1899), 538–39. *State Journal,* June 4, 1895. *Milwaukee Sentinel,* February 2, 1895. *Our Church Life,* 1 (April 1895), 79. *Proceedings of the First Annual Meeting of the National Municipal League* (Philadelphia, 1895), 519, hereinafter cited as *National League. Milwaukee Catholic Citizen,* June 1, 1895. *Methodist Minutes,* 1895, 42-43, and *Congregational Minutes,* 55th Meeting, 1895, 45, are the first endorsements of civil service reform by those sects.

83. See *Milwaukee Catholic Citizen,* December 16, 1893, March 31, December 15, 29, 1894, July 6, November 23, 1895, November 21, 1896, January 1, 1898, for examples.

84. *Ibid.,* June 8, July 6, November 23, 1895. *Milwaukee Sentinel,* March 1, 1894, April 30, May 6, 21, June 17, July 16, August 30, 1895, February 25, March 19, 1896. *Our Church Life,* 1 (May 1895), 98.

85. *State Journal,* January 15, 17, 19, 1895. *Ashland Daily News,* October 21, 23, 1895. *Ashland Weekly Press,* October 26, 1895. *Superior Leader,* August 20, 1895. *Superior Evening Telegram,* August 12, 1895. *Milwaukee Sentinel,* May 9, 1895, March 9, 1896. *Milwaukee Catholic Citizen,* December 29, 1894, August 14, 1897.

broadened the scope of their attacks from the saloon to the politician, the vice crusaders struck a responsive chord in a great many of their neighbors who by 1895 had come to oppose partisan politicians for other reasons. By 1895 a Congregationalist magazine could accurately proclaim that "municipal purging is in the air."[86]

These broadened crusades had great importance in preparing churchgoers for the new interpretation of social relations that was to change reform patterns in Wisconsin. In the first place, vice crusaders now tried to unite the local community, including its poorer residents, in a common fight against corrupt politicians and in so doing nurtured new conceptions of citizenship. Parishioners came to agree with their efforts "to organize the public conscience," as the Milwaukee Civic Federation described it.[87] "That the church is to work specifically for a Christian citizenship is coming more and more to be recognized," declared the state's Congregationalists.[88] This good citizenship movement began as a few isolated fires in 1893 and, by 1895, had become a raging blaze that swept across the state.

In the second place, the new crusaders argued that it was not enough to save individuals, that society itself needed regeneration. "We should awake to the axiom," said a Superior minister, "that city governments as well as individuals must give an account to God, and the path of history is strewn with wrecked, ruined cities which disregarded that truth."[89] "God is calling the churches to work for the regeneration of the state as well as the individual," proclaimed the state's Congregationalists.[90] After hearing the crusaders preach the need for unifying the community and emphasize the regeneration of society over that of the individual, parishioners, motivated by their urgent sense that society had to be reintegrated, eagerly adopted the vision of a good society that they began to hear from the pulpits after 1895.

The basic problem that prevented clergymen from uniting their communities in wars against politicians, clergymen increasingly maintained, was the unchecked individualism that buttressed the social chasms that so profoundly threatened efforts to strengthen order, conscience, and the church. Be-

86. *Our Church Life,* 1 (May 1895), 98.
87. *Milwaukee Catholic Citizen,* July 6, 1895.
88. *Congregational Minutes,* 56th Meeting, 1896, 19.
89. *Superior Leader,* March 12, 1895.
90. *Congregational Minutes,* 54th Meeting, 1894, 18.

lieving in competition as "the regulating principle," Americans in the Gilded Age had encouraged each man and group to accumulate as much money as possible, and the result, to a Milwaukee Methodist preacher, was "a form of war, and not much more merciful than battles with gun and saber." This individualism, in turn, had produced "the greed for riches," in a Catholic editor's phrase, and the resulting materialism had long offended clergymen: "The Christian ideal is not the worldly ideal." By paying their workers the lowest possible wages, greedy capitalists had reinforced materialism, created the gap between rich and poor, forced workers to organize unions out of self-defense, and built an "earthly civilization of organized selfishness." Both to destroy materialism and to bridge the chasms of society the crusaders felt a special mission to develop a new message that would minimize the ethic of competition and replace individualistic theology.[91]

In developing this message clergymen felt with special force the appeal of the new social scientists that so many other Wisconsinites had discovered during the depression. Clergymen who before the depression had ignored Ely's evangelism now begged social scientists to lecture them and formed their own study clubs. The state's Congregationalists created a permanent committee on sociology in 1893, and the Pastors' Union of Appleton, Kaukauna, Neenah, and Menasha studied sociology in its biweekly discussions. Armed with "the right of sociology to demand that theology be ethicized," many clergymen evolved the ethicized theology: "It is a change from regarding man as an individual, to regarding man as a member of society." Men were no longer products of their own characters; clergymen now stressed "the importance of reaching the individual through [his] environment."[92] The most significant legacy of the social

91. For examples, see *Milwaukee Sentinel*, August 17, 1896. *Appleton Weekly Post*, February 21, 1895. *Our Church Life*, 2 (May 1896), 116, 4 (September 1898), 164, and 5 (March 1899), 76. *Milwaukee Catholic Citizen*, July 20, August 10, 1895, September 19, December 26, 1896.

92. For information on the influence of social science, see *Appleton Weekly Post*, February 22, 1894, October 3, 1895, March 11, 1897, August 17, 1899. *Congregational Minutes*, 53rd Meeting, 1893, 32; 54th Meeting, 1894, 34–36; 55th Meeting, 1895, 24–26. Madison Convention of Congregational Churches and Ministers, Minute Book, 1896, and Milwaukee District Congregational Convention, Minute Book, 213, 217, Wisconsin Congregational Church Papers. *Baptist Union Minutes*, 30th Meeting, 1894, 11–12. *Charities Review*, 4 (December 1894), 57–64. *Milwaukee Sentinel*, November 20, 1894, August 30, 1897, July 13, 1898, December

scientists, nonetheless, was the burning passion to reintegrate society. Few clergymen could resist the sermon of the new social scientists: Society was evolving from a competitive jungle into a cooperative commonwealth, from individualism toward socialism, from class war to class peace, from division to unity. Inspired by this new concept of evolution, the clergy proclaimed a trend toward social cooperation. "In the new society toward which we are now tending," declared an Appleton Presbyterian minister, "men will cease to compete against each other, and the better to compete against Nature will co-operate with one another to make common cause, burying their mutual differences before a common foe."[93]

The clergymen, searching the Bible for support in applying this new mission, did not have to look beyond "the teachings of the great founder of Christianity." Jesus was "a man of sorrows," a "wanderer," a "tried and convicted malefactor" who wanted his followers to help the poor. Even more important was His "golden rule" that all men should be good neighbors and that society should be one big neighborhood.[94] Clergymen were to "hold up Christ as the inspirer of all that is best in modern social movements." His associations with the poor and His doctrine of social integration fitted perfectly with the new social science. "The best book for social guidance is the New Testament; the best commentaries are the works of scientific sociology," announced a committee to the 1895 Congregational convention.[95] Although one did not ordinarily associate the word "Christian" with a scientific discipline, said a Milwaukee minister, "as Christianity is interwoven with all this phenomena and perhaps is the cause of much of it, it does not seem far out of the way to speak of Christian sociology."[96] Clergymen at last had

18, 1899. Judson Titsworth to Richard T. Ely, January 10, 1895, Graham Taylor to Richard T. Ely, January 24, 1899, Ely Papers. *Our Church Life,* 4 (November 1897), 11; (December 1897), 23; 5 (July 1899), 133; (September–October 1899), 165; 6 (September–October 1900), 164. *State Journal,* February 26, 1900. *Milwaukee Catholic Citizen,* November 24, 1894.

93. *Appleton Weekly Post,* February 21, 1895.

94. For examples, see *Milwaukee Sentinel,* November 20, 1894, December 13, 1895. *Our Church Life,* 4 (December 1897), 23; (September 1898), 164; 6 (September–October 1900), 164. *Milwaukee Catholic Citizen,* September 19, 1896.

95. *Appleton Weekly Post,* October 3, 1895.

96. Quoted in Aaron I. Abell, *The Urban Impact on American Protestantism, 1865–1900* (Cambridge: Harvard University Press, 1943), 83. *Our Church Life,* 4 (December 1897), 23.

a message for churchgoers who were searching for a way to reintegrate a divided society.

Believing that "the church is the only disinterested organ" because it "has a free platform under commission from Jesus Christ" and was not beholden to any interest group, Wisconsin's clergymen urgently wanted to use the new gospel to build a fresh community spirit. "The Christian spirit is the only hope of a redeemed, unified and lovable human society," declared a Madison minister. Other ministers were more evangelical in their insistence that "men shall not learn the gospel aright until they bear in mind the fact that it is intended to teach men to be good citizens of earth as well as of Heaven. We are to put into operation down here the principles of the Kingdom up yonder."[97]

These clergymen believed that the golden rule was not merely an abstraction to be preached on the Sabbath, but that it was also a realistic doctrine to govern men's activities. "In all this great work the Golden Rule is wonderfully practical and far reaching beyond all human conception," editorialized a Congregationalist magazine.[98] It led the churches to repeatedly employ and defend the yardstick of "public interest" against "selfishness." "Selfish" behavior prevented reintegration of society and defied the golden rule. Methodist, Congregational, Catholic, Presbyterian, Episcopal, and Jewish clergymen in Milwaukee repeatedly scored acts of political arrogance as sinful. Arguing that "laborers and employers are servants of the common welfare, and controversies between them must be settled so that the public interest shall be cared for," the clergymen promoted the industrial arbitration movement as an application of the golden rule. They maintained that "the great mission now before the church is to revolutionize men's notions of the rights of property as against those of mankind"; many sponsored plans for "the righteous distribution of wealth"; and a few became socialists. A far greater number attacked as selfish behavior the bribery by which the wealthy escaped regulation and thereby widened the social chasms. By 1900 Milwaukee's Catholic priests had nearly unanimously agreed that Pope Leo's social

97. *Our Church Life,* 4 (May 1898), 101; (September 1898), 164; (October 1898), 179; 5 (June 1899), 116. *Milwaukee Sentinel,* March 13, 1893. *Appleton Weekly Post,* February 21, 1895.
98. *Our Church Life,* 4 (September 1898), 164.

justice encyclical, *Rerum Novarum,* should serve as a guide to their activities.[99]

Applied Christianity was the message Wisconsin churchgoers had been waiting for. It fitted perfectly their new needs, discoveries, and experiences. Unlike the politicians, clergymen were discussing the structural divisions that so deeply troubled them; their churches now encouraged them to seek ways of cooperating with others across previously unbridgeable valleys by adopting such actions as part of their religious obligation. The vice crusaders' increasing emphasis on social instead of individual regeneration matched churchgoers' growing rejection of political and economic individualism and prepared them for the social gospel. From vice crusaders and social gospelers alike churchgoers heard the message of an aroused, united community in which men were brothers in the common battle against arrogant enemies. The golden rule became the religious magnet that drew and held together previously isolated men and groups. If they did not go so far as the La Crosse woman who declared that "the giving up of self for the good of another lies at the foundation of a regenerated society,"[100] many Wisconsin churchgoers were at least willing to submerge their class and interest loyalties in seeking answers to common problems and fighting wars against common foes. More than other institutions, the churches showed Wisconsinites that they shared problems and enemies and helped to gain acceptance for the concept of "the public interest."

III

As products of the depression, the New Woman and the New Religion profoundly altered the patterns of reform in Wisconsin. They reflected and hastened the process by which Wisconsinites scrapped individualism and mugwumpery for cooperation and progressivism. They left the familiar confines of the

99. *Appleton Weekly Post,* February 21, October 3, 1895. *Milwaukee Sentinel,* April 23, 30, 1894, June 22, 1895, May 18, June 8, August 17, 1896, November 29, 1897, December 19, 1898, January 2, December 4, 1899, June 21, July 23, 1900. Madison Churches and Ministers, Minute Book, 224. *Congregational Minutes,* 55th Meeting, 1895, 24; 56th Meeting, 1896, 20. *Our Church Life,* 1 (March 1895), 59; 2 (June 1896), 127; 3 (August 1897), 184; 4 (September 1898), 164; (October 1898), 183; 5 (March 1899), 76; (June 1899), 116.

100. Annette J. Shaw, "Methods of Dealing with Mothers and Their Infants," *Charities Review,* 5 (June 1893), 413.

parlor and church for the unfamiliar surroundings of the tenement and union hall and tried to understand and help their new-found neighbors. They revealed how the depression's social unrest and civic consciousness broke down social partitions that had divided men and drove them to work together. And women and clergymen helped to teach their husbands and parishioners the same lesson. Their proposals for manual training in the schools, settlement houses, consumers' leagues, factory regulation, their skepticism toward politicians who subordinated the community to the party, and their attacks on corporations and individuals whose arrogant acts corrupted the political process widened social gulfs and violated the golden rule; above all, their campaigns to build a united community made good sense to a troubled people.

Wisconsin's poor and workers were the chief beneficiaries of the changes that had occurred in women's clubs and churches. While these victims of the depression received public support in the forms of welfare payments and public works, the heaviest responsibility in the new crisis rested with private groups. The sheer magnitude of the depression forced private charity workers to listen to the poor and thereby to formulate new attitudes and programs for social justice. By the end of the depression many private charities had by necessity shifted their principles and practices from mugwumpery to progressivism.

I

Private charity before the Panic of 1893 came from two sources. Philanthropy was one motive, as communities applauded wealthy citizens who donated some money to the less fortunate. A Milwaukee banker subsidized an old people's home and a restaurant where the poor could buy meals for five cents.[1] More prominent than the wealthy men were their wives, who, motivated by conscience, status, or boredom, contributed time and money to the charities. For the wealthiest, like Mrs. E. P. Allis or Mrs. Alexander Mitchell, education was their favorite charity. Mrs. Allis donated a school to train nurses, and Mrs. Mitchell sponsored mission kindergartens.[2] Women of means also devoted time and money to the collection and mending of clothes for the underclad, to the distribution of flowers in hospitals, to the sponsorship of a boardinghouse, and to women's exchanges in cities like Oshkosh and Milwaukee, where women could sell handwork and products of their kitchens.[3]

Religion was the second wellspring of charity in the Gilded Age. Many churches had some provision—if only a visit from the

1. *Ashland Daily News,* March 8, 1890. *Milwaukee Sentinel,* December 29, 1888, October 6, 1889, January 12, 1891.

2. *Milwaukee Sentinel,* October 22, November 3, 1888, July 26, 1891.

3. *Ibid.,* August 21, 22, October 21, November 21, 1887, August 30, 1888, May 12, October 7, 1889, June 21, 1891, January 3, February 21, July 12, October 6, 1892, January 6, 12, 1893. Labor Bureau, *First Biennial Report, 1883–1884,* 113–14. Milwaukee Woman's Industrial Exchange, Minute Books, Milwaukee County Historical Society.

pastor—for the unfortunate members of their congregations, and denominational groups operated institutions for their members. The Hebrew Relief Society paid rents and found jobs for Milwaukee's destitute Jews.[4] Such institutions as Milwaukee's Protestant Home for the Aged and the WCTU's home for unwed mothers at Eau Claire were only two among dozens of similar facilities supported by Protestant churchgoers.[5]

Inspired by religious and philanthropic motives, private charities had multiplied rapidly in Gilded Age Wisconsin as a process of revolt against the formalistic public system of poor relief, which they believed created a permanent pauper class. By 1882 Milwaukee had so many private charities overlapping in their efforts to help the poor that they united to form the Associated Charities. The staff of this organization acted as brokers and investigators, referring each applicant to the appropriate charity and checking so no one received "indiscriminate almsgiving that only promotes pauperism." The Associated Charities, financed by donations of nearly $7,000 from businessmen, directed some poor people to their churches for relief, others to the Soldiers Relief Society, still others to the women who distributed clothing, and reprimanded a large number for begging.[6]

Through such wide-ranging private charities of the 1880s and early 1890s still ran the single, dominant theme of mugwumpery. There was never any question that men and women reached the point where they needed charity because of some individual failing of character, health, training, or parentage. The root causes of distress, reported the director of Milwaukee's Associated Charities in 1891, were the individual problems of intemperance, illness, and "inability" to find a job.[7] Criminals were regarded simply as "morally defective persons."[8] Charity workers rarely hid their elitism while dealing with the under-

4. *Milwaukee Sentinel,* October 5, 1888, January 9, 1889, November 20, 1892.

5. *Ibid.,* December 10, 1888. A. O. Wright investigation of Wisconsin Woman's Christian Temperance Union Home, undated [1895 or 1896], "Investigation of Charges, Surveys, Relief, Disasters, and Social Unrest," Box 6, Wisconsin State Archival Series 1/1/8–1.

6. *Milwaukee Sentinel,* December 26, 1887, February 21, 1890, January 23, June 21, 1891, January 22, 1892, January 20, December 17, 1893. American Association of Societies for Organizing Charity, *Directory of Charity Organization Societies . . .* 1917, 11.

7. *Milwaukee Sentinel,* January 22, 1892.

8. *Ibid.,* April 18, 1887.

privileged; a charity-minded Milwaukee Catholic editor referred to the poor as "barbarian elements."[9] These charity workers firmly believed that there would be no more beggars if all beggars were sternly lectured and reprimanded. The solution to any distress was invariably to reform the individual or his children. One boys' club began as a Bible-reading class to prevent boys from being "irresistibly drawn into vice and crime" and to permit them a glimpse of "what is high and beautiful."[10] Very few of Wisconsin's charity workers believed that environmental factors were influential, that poor people had valid ideas, or that they themselves should leave their parsonages and comfortable homes.

There were, however, a few institutions emerging on the eve of the panic that, while substantially mugwumpish, pointed a different way. Two of the most prominent began in Wisconsin in 1890. The more noticeable of these was the Salvation Army, whose members lived in the slums of cities like Milwaukee and Green Bay and provided meals for hungry people. Placing total faith in the revivalist technique of individual conversion, the Salvation Army's soldiers, sympathetic with the problems of individual poor people, reportedly wept at the misfortunes of their clients and became truly elated when a ragged waif converted.[11] The second new institution was the Friendly Visitors' Home of the Milwaukee Associated Charities. From this "home" in the middle of the slum young women visited poor families to teach them hygienic habits of living, investigate applications for relief, teach women to make money by taking in washing, and generally show families "how not to make paupers." Although the Friendly Visitors emphasized individual regeneration through education and moral suasion and imposed solutions from above, they, like the members of the Salvation Army, lived in poor neighborhoods.[12]

II

The sudden, cruel depression vastly hastened the erosion of mugwumpery. The changes did not come overnight, of course, and a number of charitable groups continued their old practices

9. *Milwaukee Catholic Citizen,* July 21, 1888.

10. *Milwaukee Sentinel,* June 18, 1893.

11. *Ibid.,* May 24, 1891, January 26, June 20, December 23, 1892.

12. *Ibid.,* January 31, May 5, August 24, 1890, January 23, June 21, 1891, March 30, 1892.

and attitudes. Denominations continued to build institutions for their own needy members; humane societies still punished cruelty to both animals and children; and women continued to distribute clothes and flowers.[13] Women like Milwaukee's Mrs. James M. Pereles continued to boast that by visiting hospitals "we have done lots of good."[14] But as most charity workers confronted mass unemployment and poverty on an unparalleled scale, they realized that the sheer size of the problem forced them to discard old rules and rigidities. Old institutions bent practices to new pressures, and new institutions were hastily devised.

As soon as the depression hit the cities, private charities were swamped by huge numbers of hungry and unemployed men and women. When the depression began in the early summer of 1893, the Milwaukee Rescue Mission opened to give free meals and lodging to the poor. Each month of the depression the mission provided lodging for over 850 persons and 2,100 meals to men who chopped wood and women who mended clothes in exchange. Three Catholic-sponsored soup kitchens in Milwaukee served over 24,000 meals during two weeks in December of 1893.[15] The women of Superior operated a free restaurant for that city's poor.[16] Dozens of institutions, from local YMCAs to the La Crosse Associated Charities and the Milwaukee Seventh Day Adventist Rescue Mission, established employment bureaus where the unemployed could try to find jobs.[17] Labor unions held benefits for their unemployed or striking members.[18] During the four worst years of the depression the state's building and loan associations loaned their funds not so much for the

13. *Ibid.*, November 24, 1892, December 10, 1893, October 17, November 17, December 2, 1894, January 3, 1895, November 24, 1896, November 14, December 16, 1897, May 27, 1900. *Ashland Daily News*, May 29, 1895. *Superior Evening Telegram*, August 10, 1898. E. Clifford Nelson and Eugene L. Fevold, *The Lutheran Church Among Norwegian-Americans: A History of the Evangelical Lutheran Church*, 2 vols. (Minneapolis: Augsburg Publishing House, 1960), 1:291–92, 2:109–10.

14. *Milwaukee Sentinel*, October 17, 1894.

15. *Ibid.*, May 28, December 8, 10, 1893, March 21, June 17, October 8, 1894, November 17, 1895. *Milwaukee Catholic Citizen*, December 16, 30, 1893.

16. Albert Shaw, "Relief of the Unemployed in American Cities," *Review of Reviews*, 9 (January 1894), 187–88.

17. *Milwaukee Sentinel*, October 16, 1897, April 30, 1899.

18. Superior Trades and Labor Assembly, Minute Book, 72, Manuscripts Division, State Historical Society of Wisconsin. *Appleton Weekly Post*, February 11, 1897.

building of homes as simply to provide for sustenance.[19] Businessmen of cities like Milwaukee and Superior copied Detroit's "potato patch" scheme, which provided land for the unemployed to grow food.[20] The crisis forced old groups to develop new services at the same time that it encouraged formation of new groups.

The depression's major contribution to private charity was the confrontation it brought between charity workers and the poor. Whether they were members of religious, philanthropic, or woman's groups, the dispensers of charity were forced to leave their relatively comfortable surroundings and come into direct contact with the poor in order to make maximum use of their meager resources. Further, the depression's unparalleled suffering forced private charities in the smaller cities to unite in order to use their funds most efficiently. During 1893 and 1894 Associated Charities were formed at Janesville, Superior, Sheboygan, La Crosse, and Eau Claire to hire friendly visitors who would canvass the poor neighborhoods to make certain that some people were not being supported by several charities while others were starving in their homes.[21] The same motive prompted groups like the Grand Rapids Epworth League, the Madison Benevolent Society, and the Superior King's Daughters to visit poor people.[22] Some leaders, like Mrs. Simon Kander of Milwaukee's Jewish charities, offered a different reason when they urged charity workers to "become acquainted with at least one" poor family. "In this simple and available manner," argued Mrs. Kander, Jewish women could "create a bond of friendship between their brethren rich and poor and could strengthen the Brotherhood of Mankind."[23] Other religious leaders urged their charity workers to develop "the

19. *Appleton Weekly Post,* August 12, 1897.

20. *Milwaukee Sentinel,* April 24, 1895. *Superior Evening Telegram,* February 26, 1895. *Superior Leader,* April 12, 1895.

21. *Charities Review,* 2 (January 1893), 190; 3 (December 1893), 102; (April 1894), 316 (June 1894), 409–10. Carlos C. Closson, Jr., "The Unemployed in American Cities," *Quarterly Journal of Economics,* 8 (July 1894), 455. *Milwaukee Sentinel,* December 10, 1893. Kendall Birr, "Social Ideas of Superior Business Men, 1880–1898" (M.S. thesis, University of Wisconsin, 1948), 68–72.

22. *Superior Evening Telegram,* November 7, 11, 1895. Shaw, "Relief of the Unemployed," 187–88. *Grand Rapids Wood County Reporter,* November 23, 1893. *State Journal,* January 19, 1895.

23. Unidentified speech by Lizzie Black Kander, ca. 1897, Kander Papers, Manuscripts Division, State Historical Society of Wisconsin.

power of suffering love" that would carry them into direct contact with the poor.[24]

Whatever the original cause, the result of this confrontation was a profound shock for charity workers when, for the first time, they recognized the objects of their charity as human beings with ideas, values, and problems. "Once having pierced the outer husk of reserve," declared a Superior woman's club in 1895, "we find the poor, the sin-sick and the crime stained [to be] human like ourselves and possessed of powers for good as well as evil."[25]

This direct contact led charity workers to agree with other observers, who had also been staggered by the magnitude of the crisis, that men were poor not because of an individual failing but because of an unjust social order. "They are after all only what circumstances have made them, what we ourselves might have been, had we suffered the long oppressions, the bitter persecutions," observed Milwaukee's Mrs. Kander. Even beggars, she said, "surely have feelings of pride only they have to crush them when want stares them in the face."[26] From direct contacts the superintendent of the Milwaukee House of Mercy concluded that "the forces of society seem to make it impossible" to consider individuals apart from their environments.[27] Charity workers now believed that the poor were victims of a "condition of things" the depression had dramatized; pessimists, like a Fond du Lac editor, feared that in an urban society "to the many times will always be hard, while only to the few will prosperity be a reality."[28] With this new exposure to the poor came a new view of criminals. "The most effective way" for society "to protect itself from crime" was "by removing its most prolific cause—poverty."[29] From these direct experiences a great many charity workers in all fields concluded that they would have to scrap education and moral suasion in favor of the conviction that "the best system of charity is that which goes to

24. *State Journal,* March 19, 1895. *Baptist Union Minutes,* 30th Session, 1894, 11. *Charities Review,* 5 (June 1896), 413.

25. Woman's edition of *Superior Leader,* April 9, 1895.

26. Unidentified speech by Lizzie Black Kander, ca. 1897, and ca. 1896, Kander Papers.

27. *Milwaukee Sentinel,* November 2, 1896, December 13, 1897.

28. *Ibid.,* December 29, 1893. *Fond du Lac Reporter,* in *Appleton Weekly Post,* June 10, 1897.

29. *Appleton Weekly Post,* February 18, 1897.

the causes and sources of poverty and by removing these, succeeds in preventing so much misery and degradation."[30]

The courses of action seemed evident. "The economic problems of the day must be met and solved, and such a social order established that no one shall be crushed, but all have equal opportunity to supply their needs from the unlimited storehouse of the universe," proclaimed a conference of religious workers at Sharon.[31] Concluding that government had failed to protect the weak against the strong, an Appleton editor now announced: "The world does not owe a man a living but in a broad sense it does owe him the chance to earn one."[32] "We must place before *all* children an *equality of opportunity* for *right development*," declared the leader of a Milwaukee boys' club who had been an individualist before the panic.[33] The same consideration had led school alliances in cities like Fond du Lac, Portage, and Milwaukee to provide clothes for poor children so they would have an equal opportunity to attend schools.

Spearheaded by the New Woman and social-gospel clergymen, charity workers began applying their environmentalist assumptions to provide more opportunities to the slum dweller. Above all, they demanded that the conditions under which men, women, and children labored be made healthful, safe, and reasonable. The climax of a strenuous campaign by women, clergymen, and unions came in 1899 when the legislature passed a number of labor laws and allocated six new inspectors to the state labor commission to enforce the labor laws. By 1899 Wisconsin had taken long steps toward improving the working environment. Workshops, factories, and mines could not employ children under fourteen, and no child under sixteen could work longer than a sixty-hour week at a hazardous job. To minimize the frightful number of cruel industrial accidents, the state now required employers to provide adequate safeguards around such machines and equipment as railway switches,

---

30. *Milwaukee Catholic Citizen,* January 29, 1898. Madison Literary Club, Record Book, 2:171–72, Manuscripts Division, State Historical Society of Wisconsin. *Congregational Minutes,* 54th Meeting, 1894, 34–36; 55th Meeting, 1895, 24–26.

31. *Our Church Life,* 4 (October 1898), 183.

32. *Appleton Weekly Post,* February 8, August 23, 1894, December 10, 1898, May 24, 1900.

33. Annabell Cook Whitcomb, *Report of the Boys' Busy Life Club: Story of the Boys' Club and the Boy Problem* (Milwaukee: privately published, 1899), 29.

elevators, bull-wheels, flywheels, tumbling rods, and boiling vats. While the courts frequently upheld employers' common law defenses against liability for such accidents, the reformers secured legislation that stripped the railroads of those defenses, and by 1898 the courts were finding for other types of workers. Reformers persuaded many employers by the turn of the century to contribute large amounts to the workers' benevolent societies that compensated workers for accidents. The state also provided other protections of the working environment: buildings had to have fire escapes, outward-swinging doors, metal balconies and stairs, and other structural devices to prevent injury or loss of life in case of fires. As a sweeping reform, unsanitary sweatshops for clothing and cigar workers were outlawed. Employers were required to pay wages in cash and at weekly or biweekly intervals. The state regulated employment bureaus and offered an arbitration service for strikes. Many charity workers came to agree with workers that labor unions were the best instrument to improve their working environment, and by 1899 unions had considerable legal protection. Employers could not blacklist union members, hire armed guards like Pinkertons, fire workers who joined unions, or intimidate workers in their votes, and workers were allowed to apply the union label to their product.[34]

Although some of the reform laws had passed before the panic, they had resulted from campaigns by unions fighting alone. Because of a lack of inspectors, enforcement of the laws was in effect the responsibility of the unions instead of the state. By 1899 this pattern had changed. Workers now received strong support from women's clubs, clergymen, and editors, and a great many people had come to believe that conscience and safety demanded that the community alleviate the hardships of workers' environments. The new charity workers and their en-

34. Wisconsin, *Laws* (1883), chap. 135; (1885), chap. 50; (1887), chaps. 46, 349, 427, 453, 549; (1889), chaps. 123, 304, 438, 474; (1891), chaps. 226, 280, 430; (1893), chaps. 14, 163; (1895), chaps. 151, 240, 279, 355, 364; (1899), chaps. 79, 152, 158, 189, 213, 221, 232, 274, 330, 332. Railroad Commissioner, *2nd Report, 1886*, xvi–xvii. Labor Bureau, *9th Biennial Report, 1899-1900*, 125. *Milwaukee Sentinel*, May 1, October 8, 1899. *Ashland Daily Press*, January 29, 1900. *State Journal*, January 16, 1900. Adolf Gerd Korman, "A Social History of Industrial Growth and Immigrants: A Study with Particular Reference to Milwaukee, 1880–1920" (Ph.D. diss., University of Wisconsin, 1959), 149–55. Donald J. Berthrong, "Social Legislation in Wisconsin, 1836–1900" (Ph.D. diss., University of Wisconsin, 1951), 325–37.

vironmentalist principles had converted state factory regulation from isolated political concessions made to unions into a major public effort to remake the environment. The new charity workers believed that they had conducted such an effective publicity campaign that large numbers of citizens would support a consumers' league in Milwaukee by 1900. That league had been predicated on the belief that consumers were so disturbed by the exploitation of workers that they would refuse to buy the products of employers who were unfair to their workers.

Many more charity workers were interested in ameliorating the living as well as the working environment of the poor. This meant establishment of parks, playgrounds, night schools, labor unions, classes in sewing and cooking, boys' clubs, juvenile courts, hospitals, potato patches, penny savings banks for children, truancy procedures, kindergartens, parent-teacher associations, neighborhood clubs, settlement houses—and toward such ends charity workers now labored. Working with union organizers to establish a cooperative store in a poor neighborhood as a "co-partnership of the small consumers," a Milwaukee minister called the project "an entirely new propagandum, one that is socialistic in its form, but which I hope will redound to the benefit of the individual in its results."[35] The Reverend Mr. Humphreys was simply stating the new mission of the charity workers: to create greater opportunity for individuals by reforming a cruel environment. Environmentalism was the depression's first contribution to the breakdown of the isolation and mugwumpish individualism that had dominated charity programs before the panic.

III

The depression's second major impact on charity work was to accelerate and fundamentally redirect the thrust toward what subsequent historians would describe as professionalization. During the depression the state's charities began exhibiting many of the outward appearances of professionalism: city-wide organizations; revolts against interference by politicians; better-trained workers; groups to discuss and plan programs; and even a lobby at Madison.[36] Mass distress certainly quickened the

35. Otto Fairfield Humphreys to Richard T. Ely, May 18, 1899, Ely Papers, Manuscripts Division, State Historical Society of Wisconsin.
36. Richard T. Ely to Robert C. Spencer, March 6, 1895, Ely Papers.

pressures for "professionalism" from inside the existing charities, and the new Associated Charities federations outside Milwaukee were evidences of such internal demands.

But the crucial impact of the depression toward the "professionalization" of charities came from people who had taken
only a minor interest in charities before the panic. As these
newly concerned groups became interested in charities during
the depression, they forced the established organizations to
listen to new voices and to develop new programs at the same
time that the new groups recruited the people who would there-
after staff the charities. The pressures for withdrawing charities
from politics, for example, came as much from citizen groups
as from the professional charities. No one was surprised when
officials like the principal of the State Industrial School for Boys
and the Dane County Poor Commissioner protested, as they had
for a generation, that politicians meddled in their jobs.[37] But it
was other new groups, like retrenchment-minded taxpayers'
leagues and the nonpartisan Wisconsin Federation of Labor
and State Federation of Woman's Clubs—groups that opposed
politicians for other reasons—that led the new drive to free
charitable and educational institutions from political domination. Political interference was too expensive for hard-pressed
taxpayers in the depression.

The drive for more professional training of charity workers
and the motives for the new people who received that training
also originated outside the charities. It was the ambitious zeal
and empire-building of Richard T. Ely, not demands of charity
officials, that led charitable institutions increasingly to employ
trained workers. Ely mounted a tireless campaign of correspondence and public appearances to persuade charity officials that
trained workers were effective and that the officials should support his department.[38] Ely's students, who increasingly domi-

Milwaukee Sentinel, December 27, 1897, May 30, 1899. *State Journal,*
April 27, 1897. Memo from Lizzie Black Kander, November 25, 1898,
Kander Papers. *Milwaukee Conference for Good City Government* (Phila-
delphia: National Municipal League, 1900) , 59, hereinafter cited as *Good
City Conference,* Milwaukee. One result of lobbying by charities is Wiscon-
sin, *Laws* (1895) , chap. 290.

37. Ira W. Bird to Richard T. Ely, February 11, 1895, F. G. Kraege to
Richard T. Ely, October 7, 1896, Ely Papers. *Milwaukee Sentinel,* June
9, 1893.

38. Richard T. Ely to Robert C. Spencer, March 6, 1895, Lynn S. Pease
to Ely, January 3, 1895, Fred Wilkins to Ely, January 6, 1895, Ely Papers.
Richard T. Ely, "Schools and Churches in their Relation to Charities and

nated the state's charities during the depression, were almost completely lacking in "professional" motives. They were, in fact, students whose depression-inspired zeal to reform a troubled society had been focused by their classes in social science. What they brought to their new jobs after graduation was less a professional consciousness and concern with techniques and processes than a strong motivation to remake the harsh environments of the poor.[39] This was not surprising, for the training students received at the University of Wisconsin pointed them less toward professionalism than toward cooperation with the poor to root out injustices. The method of teaching charity workers at the university was aimed at showing "the complexity and interdependence of social problems." This approach, what educators termed the "excursion method," thrust students into poor neighborhoods to learn "truly scientific humbleness (particularly important, perhaps, for youthful reformers)" so that they could see how people actually lived and worked and would realize that they could not transplant programs from the classroom. The purpose was to educate reformers who would be less likely to impose their own values on their clients than to derive the programs from the needs of the poor.[40] It is no wonder, then, that the new "professionals" were more distinguished by their reforming zeal and eagerness to learn from the poor than by any traits they developed from within the groups of established charities.

The depression forced charity workers to interact with other people who had discovered the urgency of the problems of poverty. Prior to the annual 1894 meeting, charity officials who comprised the Wisconsin Conference on Charities and Corrections had emphasized individual salvation as the key for protecting society against the dangerous impulses of poor clients. At the 1894 meeting several other social groups, led by a philosophy professor from Beloit College, redirected the conference along the lines it was to follow for the rest of the decade. They stated that social justice reforms rather than individual

Correction," *Charities Review*, 4 (December 1894), 57–64. *Milwaukee Sentinel*, December 6, 1896. Benjamin G. Rader, *The Academic Mind and Reform: The Influence of Richard T. Ely in American Life* (Lexington: University of Kentucky Press, 1966), 122–24.

39. For examples, see Irma Reel to Richard T. Ely, March 8, 1900, Annie Ulaine to Ely, June 6, 1896, Ely Papers.

40. Edward D. Jones, "Methods of Teaching Charities and Correction at the University of Wisconsin," *Charities Review*, 5 (April 1896), 289–93.

reform were the first step; and the initiative for the conference's new environmentalism came from outside the charities "profession."[41] At Superior in 1895 established charity workers could only acquiesce when an editor and the local chamber of commerce instituted a system of potato patches as a substitute for traditional forms of charity.[42] Such external pressures broadened the perspectives of older charity workers.

Now geared to the actual needs and circumstances of the poor, the aims of the profession of charity work became increasingly integrated with the concerns of journalists, women, clergymen, and the larger society in general. Direct confrontation with the poor, whether in journalists' columns, college charity classes, or relief surveys, drove the broader society to encourage charity workers in their emerging tendencies to shun their earlier elitism and individualism in favor of what they believed was the more professional approach of letting programs derive from needs and using charity work to promote social reforms that would remake environments. A Lawrence University social scientist was so impressed by this new popular interest in social reforms that he believed "this universal awakening of thought on social reform, may yet be recognized as the characteristic of our generation."[43] The new order was reciprocal. Charity workers learned that they could count on significant new allies for their programs; the allies learned that they could influence charity programs; and charity workers learned that they could expect journalists to promote their new plans. As the basis for their growing interest in theoretical and applied sociology, the charity workers were reacting more to developments in the outside world than to those within their own institutions.

IV

The ways that environmentalism and professionalism transformed charity were well illustrated in the changing treatment of tramps and vagrants. Products of industrial dislocation, "tramps" were unemployed men who rode freight trains from place to place in search of sympathetic communities. Since law enforcement officers earned their salaries on the basis of the

41. Hugh H. Knapp, "The Social Gospel in Wisconsin, 1890–1912" (M.A. thesis, University of Wisconsin, 1968), 88–97.
42. *Superior Leader,* April 12, 1895.
43. *Appleton Weekly Post,* June 7, 1894.

number of their prisoners and the meals they provided in the jails, they often tried to lure tramps with promises of women, liquor, cigarettes, and money. Before the financial panic most Wisconsinites applauded this system because they believed tramps to be depraved souls who belonged in prison, but as the depression drove greater numbers of men to vagrancy, citizens held mass meetings throughout the state to devise new ways to deal with these homeless men. In the winter of 1895–1896 the problem became acute, and 500 people from all types of charities gathered at Fond du Lac for a state-wide convention to consider methods for reform. Casting aside the earlier view that tramps were depraved individuals and that all such persons should be jailed, the participants came to believe that tramps were products of industrialism. They therefore turned their criticism against the greedy agents of the law who exploited these unfortunates. With taxpayers "groaning under the burden" of subsidizing sheriffs, the Fond du Lac convention urged abolition of the system of paying these officers by the number of their prisoners and proposed the creation of county workhouses "or some other judicious system of labor for all prisoners." In addition, charity workers should try to prevent tramps from becoming vagrants by copying the policy of the Milwaukee Rescue Mission, which provided meals and lodging in exchange for such work as cutting wood.[44] Charity workers had become sufficiently environmentalist in their views to recognize that the lack of jobs had caused men to become tramps. Conscious of the unbearable tax burdens the old system placed on citizens, they insisted that responsibility for the tramps be taken away from political law enforcement officers and be given to such charities as the rescue missions. The pressure for professionalism in this matter came from taxpayers, not charity workers.

While such changes dealt with the transient poor, the greatest interest of the new charity workers was in those people who could not escape their environments. The apex of the community structure developed by the new progressive charity was the settlement house. It was at once the ultimate in the acceptance of environmentalism—the assumption that men could be changed by manipulating the environment through

44. *Milwaukee Sentinel,* February 14, 1892, January 21, 1894, May 9, 1895, February 26, 1896, January 31, 1897. *Appleton Weekly Post,* November 19, 1891, November 28, 1895, February 13, March 5, 1896, January 14, 1897. Wisconsin, *Laws* (1895), chap. 290.

programs derived from the neighborhood—and the rejection of philanthropy's elitism, isolation, and fixed principles in favor of the "professional" dedication to pragmatic experiments to reform society. Because of the proximity to Chicago, Wisconsinites were frequently exposed to the ideas and practices of the settlement pioneers through lectures by Jane Addams, Florence Kelley, and Graham Taylor, through reports from the hundreds of annual visitors to Hull House and Chicago Commons, and through frequent features in the Wisconsin press. Reflecting the new humanitarianism and antiformalism, a visitor to Hull House wrote the *Appleton Post:* "I wish all could see the genuine good humanity back of all this work. We read so much and hear so many theories that we are apt to forget that there are men and women whose lives are devoted to the actual working out of these theories."[45]

The first Wisconsin settlement house to win national recognition was Milwaukee's Happy Home. The steps that led its head resident Mrs. M. Isabell Carpenter to found the settlement typified the impact of the depression on charity work. Mrs. Carpenter, for seven years before the panic, had worked in mission kindergartens, becoming superintendent of the city's work in that area. In 1894 she became principal of the Wisconsin Free Kindergarten, which she operated in her home. Finally, in 1896, she decided that kindergarten work was only part of the broader necessity to change the whole environment of the poor, and, announcing that "to share the life of the neighborhood was the predominant motive," she established the Happy Home Settlement House and moved in, letting the needs of the neighborhood dictate the programs. She naturally began with the community's youngest residents; sixty-eight children attended the settlement's kindergarten which removed the children from tenement walls while it freed their parents from the responsibility to watch their children at all times. The Happy Home's classes in cooking and housekeeping injected an informal approach into the educational experiences of children while they relieved neighborhood mothers of some of their burdens. The home also housed a boys' club. The challenge of ameliorating the environment produced alternating enthusiasm and frustration for the charity workers. "As we become familiar with the neighborhood types," wrote Mrs. Carpenter, "we

45. *Appleton Weekly Post,* July 27, 1893. See also *Milwaukee Catholic Citizen,* November 10, 1894.

realize the true value of settlement work." Mrs. Carpenter's metamorphosis from kindergarten teacher to settlement resident was an accurate reflection of the new directions in charity work.[46]

Settlement houses sometimes evolved even more directly from existing charities. Milwaukee's most distinctive and prominent early settlement house was a product of the evolution of the city's Jewish charities from mugwumpery to progressivism. Representing the city's wealthy and established German Jews, the original charity workers had hoped to uplift the characters of the newly arrived, ghetto-ridden Jews from Eastern Europe whose presence undercut acceptance by gentiles of the established Jews. The workers' method had been to collect and sew clothes in the comfort of their homes, but the depression exposed them to the suffering of the new immigrants and taught them the importance of environment. As a result, Mrs. Simon Kander, leader of the Jewish charities, announced in 1895 that the Ladies Relief Sewing Society was outmoded and that poverty was too widespread and complex to be relieved through the society's established methods. Inspired by her direct contacts with the poor as a truant officer, she headed the Keep Clean Mission that year at Temple Emanu-El, which by 1898 occupied three rooms and was named the Milwaukee Jewish Mission. A major purpose of the mission was to bring charity workers into direct contact with Jews of the ghetto. Classes in wood carving and clay modeling for boys and in knitting for girls attracted hundreds of children from poor families. Finally, as the charity workers came to understand the total life of the neighborhood from their newly begun friendly visiting of poor homes and from their work at the mission, they decided to open a settlement house in the midst of the ghetto where they could become still better integrated into ghetto life. In May of 1900 they moved into a two-story house on Fifth Street, which they called simply "The Settlement," where they offered manual training classes for boys and girls, a cooking school, night classes for adults, public baths, ethical and literary clubs for young and

46. *Milwaukee Sentinel,* February 7, 1897. John Palmer Gavit, *Bibliography of College, Social, and University Settlements* (Cambridge: College Settlement Association, 1896), 48. *Charities Review,* 7 (February 1898), 1043. I am indebted to John O. Holzhueter, Research Division, State Historical Society of Wisconsin, for an unidentified clipping, July 15, 1893, in the Milwaukee County Historical Society, and information from city directories on Mrs. Carpenter.

old, and a circulating library. Ten or fifteen volunteers at a time tried to make old programs effective and to devise new ones. As they adapted their programs to the neighborhood, the settlement workers demonstrated the rejection of their earlier isolation and elitism. Among the new programs was the teaching of Hebrew, the common heritage of Russian and German Jews, regardless of social standing. While the charity women did not keep kosher kitchens themselves, they organized their cooking lessons "on the 'kosher' plan" in deference to the orthodoxy of their students. The settlement workers and neighborhood parents worked closely with the local public school teachers, winning the teachers' enthusiastic support and encouragement for The Settlement. By 1900 Milwaukee's Jewish charity workers had overcome nationality and class prejudices to emphasize a common heritage, had let the needs of their new neighborhoods dictate their programs, and had abandoned individualism for environmentalism. In a very short time the depression had forced charity workers to travel a long way from the Ladies Relief Sewing Society, and the rush of poor immigrants to The Settlement suggested that they had found an effective approach.[47]

Such settlement houses were the best reflections of the new mood of egalitarianism that the depression had generated in charity work. The missionary religious zeal that had once fired the YMCA was transformed into an equally zealous enthusiasm for social service.[48] The sheer magnitude of the problems of charity and the social unrest of the depression had led workers to lose their fear of contact with the poor; indeed, many believed that conscience as well as public safety required that they build as many bridges as possible between classes. They learned that the poor were prisoners of their environments, not of their characters, and with considerable support from previously indifferent sources they set out to remake those environments.

47. Mrs. Simon Kander's addresses to Ladies Relief Sewing Society, ca. 1896 and 1897, Annual Reports of Milwaukee Jewish Mission, 1899, 1900, Mrs. Simon Kander to Mrs. C. S. Benjamin, October 23, 1896, report of The Settlement, March 27, 1901, Kander Papers. *Milwaukee Sentinel*, April 15, 1900. *The Settlement Cook Book*, 1965 ed. (New York: Simon and Schuster), 1–2. Ann Shirley Waligorski, "Social Action and Women: The Experience of Lizzie Black Kander" (M.A. thesis, University of Wisconsin, 1969), 40–42, 60–81.

48. *Milwaukee Sentinel*, July 25, 1897. Korman, "Industrial Growth and Immigrants," 163.

At heart this shift in attitude was the essential change from mugwumpery to progressivism. By contending that men and women had complete control over their lives, mugwumpery had been a mood and approach that reinforced social divisions and encouraged social isolation. Because there was something inherently evil, diseased, lazy, or immoral in people who had not reached the middle-class social level, a great many Wisconsinites could admit no reason for communication with their inferiors and indeed viewed reform as a means of social control to maintain existing divisions and to reassure citizens of the stability of their own social positions. This basic attitude not only meant that charity workers were patronizing toward—and rejected by—their objects, but it also made it very difficult for groups to find common denominators on which to base programs for improvement and relief. The depression significantly changed this situation. Economic adversity planted a seed of doubt in everyone from unskilled workers to bank presidents. Men and women were forced to build bridges over the social chasms in order to survive. In the process, parents found new allies in teachers, farmers in cyclists, workers in clergymen, and the poor in many charity workers. What was most novel in progressivism was not so much environmentalism as the spirit of cooperation across class lines to solve problems that were being seen for the first time as mutual problems. However much self-interest and long-standing suspicions hedged this new spirit, they could not prevent its application as the central mechanism for social progressivism. While the New Woman, New Religion, New Education, and new forms of charity reflected the changes, it was in the political arena that men and women felt most acutely the shift from mugwumpery to progressivism.

III | THE ROOTS OF POLITICAL PROGRESSIVISM, 1893–1900

The depression brought to Wisconsin's cities a variety of problems—enough to overwhelm the city fathers at the same time that it drove many Wisconsinites to turn their attention from the unresponsive national arena to problems in their own communities. The result was that groups arose in one community after another to diagnose and cure one sickness or another. Some of these groups lasted only a few weeks, others for more than a decade. Some cities united to support a program that other cities rallied to ridicule. A program that businessmen organized in one community was sponsored by workers in another. But the important point was that large numbers of individuals and groups wanted to reform city governments: reform was in the air. By 1894 the reformers had become so militant that the National Municipal League could accurately label them "a new force in American politics, a new Grand Army of the Republic."[1]

Through this generalized spirit of reform and the variety of individuals and groups seeking to reform their cities emerges an outline. In the thrust of their motivation and programs these groups essentially comprised two municipal reform movements. The first, rooted in the 1880s, represented the initial response of a frightened and confused people to the depression, and it might well be labeled mugwumpery. For these reformers the politician was evil incarnate, a sticky-fingered, partisan incompetent whose closest allies were the merchants of vice.

After reformers had experimented with the mugwumps' solutions, about 1895, they began to feel that the mugwumps had somehow not identified the basic sources of the city's and their own ills; and so was born a second group of reform organizations, which reacted partially to the failure of mugwumpery and partially to a series of new problems that were themselves products of the depression. The programs and rhetoric of these organizations identified them as progressives. Locating the

1. Herbert Welsh, "Municipal Leagues and Good Government Clubs," *Proceedings of the 2nd National Conference for Good City Government, 1894* (Philadelphia: National Municipal League, 1895), 153, hereinafter cited as *Good City Conference.*

basic civic evils in corporate arrogance, tax dodging, and unresponsive and undemocratic political machinery, the Progressives advocated a number of devices to regulate and tax corporations, to equalize the tax burden, and to make the political process more democratic. For the Progressives, politicians were evil only to the extent that they succumbed to the blandishments of corporations or wealthy individuals.

In practice, of course, the distinctions between the movements often blurred. Both favored corrupt practices acts and civil service reform, and both worried considerably about the tax burden; both movements received widespread popular support, and many organizations shifted easily from mugwumpery to progressivism as they discovered the failure of mugwumpish solutions to meet new problems. However hazy were the limits of both movements, the distinction between them was important for Wisconsin's new groups of municipal reformers.

The cityward trek of ambitious, discouraged, or bored farmers and the arrival of immigrants during the Gilded Age were especially pronounced in Wisconsin. More than three-fourths of the state's unmarried farm workers told a state official that they would rather move to a city than remain on a farm. Between 1880 and 1900 the state's total population increased 57.5 per cent; its population in cities over 4,000 increased 162 per cent. In 1880, 20.8 per cent of the state's residents lived in its 20 cities with over 4,000 people; by 1900, 34.7 per cent of its population lived in the 37 cities of that size. Indeed, the urban population grew more than four times faster than the farm population. Few cities anywhere matched the rise of Superior from a village of 655 people in 1880 to the state's second-largest city in 1900, with 31,091 residents. Towering over all Wisconsin cities in 1900 as in 1880, and boasting one-seventh of the state's residents, was Milwaukee, which had grown from 115,587 in 1880 to 285,315 in 1900.[1]

With their political attention focused on the national arena and their interest in the community confined mainly to economic opportunities generated by its rapid growth, most Wisconsinites during the 1880s and early 1890s ignored the staggering obstacles that confronted the men who had to govern their communities. They cared little about the great opportunities for graft that followed the hurried creation of municipal services to keep pace with the cities' rapid growth and worried even less that the state legislature possessed a virtual stranglehold on the real authority to handle urban problems. Until 1889 the legislature could order individual cities to buy certain lots or pave certain streets, and even after a constitutional amendment in 1892, which prohibited special municipal incorporation laws, the state still determined the local tax rate, collected taxes from most corporations, decided how such services as the police department or poor relief would be adminis-

1. Arthur M. Schlesinger, *The Rise of the City, 1878–1898* (New York: Macmillan, 1933), 53–80. Labor Bureau, *7th Biennial Report, 1895–1896,* 108. U.S. Department of Commerce, Bureau of the Census, *Tenth Census of the United States: Population, 1880,* 456, 853. *Twelfth Census of the United States: Population, 1900,* 1: 645–46. *Twelfth Census of the United States: Occupations,* 414–18.

tered, and held the general power to make all important policy decisions.[2] As they discovered the urgent necessity for reform in the management of their cities, the new reformers frequently concluded that their greatest problem was the legislature's death grip on their destinies. They learned that municipal reform would continue to be extremely difficult unless they first gained control of the state legislature.

During the days before the financial panic city administrators were thwarted in their efforts for improvement by public apathy toward civic problems. The overlapping jurisdictional boundaries between county and city governments meant that the city and county frequently pursued diametrically opposed policies in the areas of taxation, prosecution of criminals, and poor relief.[3] Further, local officials lacked the accumulated and shared experience necessary to cope with such problems in the prevailing atmosphere of popular indifference.

Before the panic, in fact, most Wisconsin urban residents expected only one thing from their elected officials: that they pursue policies that would guarantee a splendid future for their cities. As a community grew faster than the wildest dreams of its inhabitants, Wisconsinites in each town developed the buoyant faith that their city could outpace its rivals in the mad race to become the future Chicago. These were the halcyon days of the urban promoters, when city officials and journalists vied with merchants in booming the future metropolis. They boasted that their city offered more business opportunities and better jobs than any other.[4] When Superior announced that it was

2. Wisconsin, *Laws* (1889), chap. 326. Wisconsin, *Constitution*, art. 4, sec. 31. Herbert P. Secher, "The Law and Practice of Municipal Home Rule in Wisconsin Under the Constitutional Home Rule Amendment of 1924" (M.A. thesis, University of Wisconsin, 1949), 20ff. *Milwaukee Sentinel*, December 9, 1888, July 4, 1889, April 26, 1895, August 17, 1897. *State Journal*, February 28, 1895. Wisconsin, Legislative Petitions 760S and 1210A, 1897 Legislature, Box 57, Wisconsin State Archival Series 2/3/1/5–7.

3. For information on overlapping jurisdictions, see *Milwaukee Sentinel*, November 12, 1896, October 20, 1897. *Superior Leader*, May 19, 1895. On county government problems, see F. C. Winkler, "Municipal Government of Milwaukee," *2nd Good City Conference, 1894*, 123–24. *Milwaukee Sentinel*, September 15, 1889, March 29, 1892, May 10, 23, September 5, 14, 1894, November 24, 1895, January 13, 1897, March 26, 1899. *Ashland Daily News*, October 24, 1895.

4. For example, see Quartermaster Gen. M. Griffin to Gov. William D. Hoard, July 25, 1889, "Strikes and Riots," Box 1, Wisconsin State Archival Series 1/1/8–9.

"The City of Destiny," Ashland replied that it was "The City of Certainty." The motto of the *Superior Leader* typified the spirit of urban rivalries: "Superior, may she always be right; but right or wrong, Superior." The phenomenal growth of cities led residents to face the future with confidence.[5]

The boosters of each city believed that the best way to guarantee prosperity in the future was to create the state's smoothest streets, fastest transportation system, most efficient garbage removal, biggest schools, and best fire and police protection. All agreed that "the enterprise of every city is estimated by the character and magnitude of its public improvements."[6] As earlier Wisconsin villages had bonded themselves for the railroads that would prevent them from becoming backwater eddies,[7] so now, in the late eighties and early nineties, as competition increased for the growing numbers of city-bound farmers and immigrants, Wisconsin cities hurriedly created improvements to make them more attractive. They granted franchises and contracts to any and all seekers, as when they paved streets where few houses stood.[8] Within two years Milwaukee spent over $1 million to purchase and improve land for new parks.[9] Cities fought each other fiercely to be selected as the site for new state charitable and educational institutions; Superior had to sell $65,000 in tax certificates to win the new normal school.[10]

In the promising days before the panic few men had the courage to warn of possible dangers in the mad scramble for

5. *Superior Leader,* April 3, 1897. *Appleton Weekly Post,* October 13, 1892. For examples of urban promotion, see *Ashland Daily News,* February 23, 1890. Kendall Birr, "Social Ideas of Superior Business Men, 1880–1898" (M.S. thesis, University of Wisconsin, 1948), 107–60.

6. *Appleton Weekly Post,* August 18, 1892.

7. See William F. Whyte, "The Watertown Railway Bond Fight," *Proceedings of the State Historical Society of Wisconsin,* 64 (1917), 268–307, for an example. On efforts to lure railroads, see Frederick Merk, *Economic History of Wisconsin During the Civil War Decade* (Madison: State Historical Society of Wisconsin, 1916), 238–70.

8. For example, see *Milwaukee Sentinel,* August 31, 1887, September 24, 1889. *Ashland Daily News,* February 27, 1890. *Superior Evening Telegram,* April 4, 1896.

9. Milwaukee Chamber of Commerce, *34th Annual Report of the Trade and Commerce of Milwaukee,* 1892, 44–45.

10. *Superior Evening Telegram,* August 3, 1893. For information on rivalries for selection as normal school sites. see *Grand Rapids Wood County Reporter,* May 18, 1893. William H. Herrmann, "The Rise of the Public Normal School in Wisconsin" (Ph.D. diss., University of Wisconsin, 1953), 196–208.

public improvements. It was almost impossible to challenge the boosters' infectious optimism. To cranks and critics who warned of mounting municipal debts the boosters replied that, by the time the interest and principal for the bonds came due, their city would have grown so much that no taxpayer would feel a pinch.[11] With the clarity of hindsight an editor recalled the frenetic pace of municipal spending: "Property owners were anxious for improvement. They wanted pavement, they wanted water, they wanted sewers. If more conservative men tried to prevent this breakneck rush for public improvement and municipal bankruptcy, they were at once accused of being obstructionists. . . . [The mayor's] life would have been a burden to him if he had attempted to stay the folly of those boom days."[12] The greatest possible misfortune to befall a city at this time was to be "subjected to the devouring cankers of deep-seated parsimony," warned an Appleton editor.[13] In the four years between 1889 and 1893 the bonded indebtedness of the state's local governments—primarily of the cities—skyrocketed from $5,726,590 to $11,287,884.[14] Wisconsin cities were so confident of the future that they felt no qualms in doubling their bonded indebtedness in four years. No one could have guessed that a depression would soon strike down that optimistic mood and generate such anger among taxpayers that they would create municipal reform movements all over the state.

I

The mugwump impulse of Gilded Age Wisconsin was fundamentally altered and broadened by the sudden urgency of tax problems. The most prominent mugwumps, who confined their expressions before the panic to attacks on politicians for pandering to the forces of vice and sin and who shrouded themselves in nativist and elitist exclusivism, were notable mainly for their isolation from mass support. The legacy of Gilded Age mugwumpery to the new reform groups was the identification of the partisan politician as the basic wrecker of moral and efficient government.

11. Norman S. Gilson, "Municipal Debts, Expenditures, and Taxation," *Municipality*, 1 (June 1900) , 1–14.

12. *Superior Evening Telegram,* April 4, 1896.

13. *Appleton Weekly Post,* February 19, 1891.

14. *Biennial Report of the Secretary of State, 1890,* 221–26; *Biennial Report, 1894,* 224–51, hereinafter cited as Secretary, *Biennial Report.*

The most significant influence of the predepression years toward the broadening of mugwumpery was not due to the activities of a handful of reformers but to the staggering debts. Even without the new demands placed on city governments by the depression the debts would have been hard to repay, but the depression forced cities to spend more public funds in order to support poor relief and public works, and the bank failures wiped out sizable sums from many city treasuries. In the six years before the panic the problems of local taxation had sparked a major campaign in only one Wisconsin city;[15] after the panic no community escaped such campaigns. Taxation gave the thrust that broadened mugwumpery's appeal.

The reason for this sudden interest in taxes was not hard to find. "In a time of business depression the wail of high taxes is always raised; not because the taxes are disproportionately high but because the taxpayer does not have the sources of income he would have under ordinary circumstances," declared Appleton's Mayor Herman Erb. Not only did the loss of customers and jobs deprive Wisconsinites of the income needed to pay taxes, but the value of taxable property also declined markedly during the depression. At Superior one citizen paid the same amount of tax on his property in 1897 as in 1892, but the market value of his property had shriveled from $22,000 to $3,200.[16] Unable to pay their taxes, Wisconsinites from all social backgrounds demanded relief and appealed to their county boards for lower assessments. They sped to the courts to prevent local officials from collecting their taxes or simply refused to pay. The protests came from the owners of thousands of acres of timberland and from poor workers who rented their homes.[17] Wisconsinites tried frantically to find "some plan that would relieve the burdens of taxation for improvements that

15. *Milwaukee Sentinel*, February 21, 1892.

16. *Appleton Weekly Post*, April 22, 1897. *Superior Evening Telegram*, October 20, 1897. Helen M. Wolner, "The History of Superior, Wisconsin to 1900" (M.A. thesis, University of Wisconsin, 1939), 113–43, provides information on declining property values in that city.

17. For examples, see K. K. Kennan to Richard T. Ely, June 5, 12, 1895, Ely Papers, Manuscripts Division, State Historical Society of Wisconsin. *Superior Leader*, April 13, August 25, 1895, April 21, 1897. *Superior Evening Telegram*, August 26, 1895, April 7, 1896. *Ashland Weekly Press*, February 16, March 9, 16, 1895. *Ashland Daily News*, February 13, 1895. *Appleton Weekly Post*, January 18, 1894, February 22, 1900.

were made when the future seemed rosy-hued and the day of reckoning far off."[18]

The first response of taxpayers was to demand that local politicians cut the community's operating budget. "It is the right and the duty of the people to insist that economies which are forced upon them by the stringency of the times in their private affairs, shall be practiced with equal care in the conduct of public affairs," proclaimed the *Wisconsin State Journal*.[19] The enemy of the taxpayers became the local official who, they now believed, increased tax bills by looting the public till, by creating sinecures for loyal friends, and by rewarding contributors with public works contracts. Typical of the dozens of groups that now demanded retrenchment was the Ashland Civic Federation whose "primary object . . . is to prevent if possible the confiscation of property, real and personal through high taxation."[20] The Wisconsin Federation of Labor in a similar vein blasted the politicians' reckless spending.[21]

Soon after the panic struck, groups of taxpayers from widely scattered backgrounds successfully forced local politicians to afford them immediate relief through spending cuts. Superior businessmen forced the city to adopt a stringent retrenchment program that reduced the tax bill from $1,230,000 in 1893 to $847,000 by 1895.[22] What businessmen and Republican officials accomplished at Superior was performed by workers and Populist officials at La Crosse, where the Populist mayor led a retrenchment campaign that drove local taxes from $373,000 in 1893 to $276,000 in 1895.[23] A man's occupation, political affiliation, or religious background made little difference in his attitude toward tax rates; city dwellers of all classes and parties demanded that politicians cease their profligate ways. Ashland officials slashed the costs of local administration from $445,000 in 1893 to $334,000 in 1895. In Oneida County, dominated by

18. *Superior Leader,* April 13, 1895.

19. *State Journal,* January 21, 1897.

20. *Ashland Daily News,* November 15, 1895.

21. Joseph Dana Miller in *Official Wisconsin State Federation of Labor Directory,* 1896–1897, 101, 103.

22. *Superior Leader,* June 13, 29, July 6, 9, 13, 1893, April 13, 1895. *Superior Evening Telegram,* June 29, July 13, 1893. J. A. Monger in *2nd Good City Conference, 1894,* 12–14. Secretary, *Biennial Report, 1894,* 238; *Biennial Report, 1896,* 353.

23. *Milwaukee Sentinel,* November 2, 1894. Secretary, *Biennial Report, 1894,* 238; *Biennial Report, 1896,* 353.

the city of Rhinelander, advocates of retrenchment cut local taxes from $114,000 in 1893 to $72,000 two years later.[24]

While the difficulty of meeting tax bills in the depression was one urban residents shared with farmers, retrenchment was primarily an urban movement. Of the 11 urban counties where more than half of the inhabitants lived in one or two cities, 7 cut their taxes between 1893 and 1895, 1 retained its 1893 tax rate and 3 raised their taxes during the depression's first two years. By contrast, of the state's 59 rural counties, only 18 lowered their taxes between 1893 and 1895, 5 retained the same rate, and 36 raised their taxes.[25] Nearly three-quarters of the urban counties adopted retrenchment campaigns while fewer than one-third of the rural ones did. For reasons ranging from the greater ease of reducing such municipal services as police protection and street paving, the fact of higher taxes, and the earlier effect of depressed conditions on the farm, to the existence of more mugwumps in cities, the greater political sensitivity of city dwellers and their politicians, and, above all, the greater ease of organizing urban residents into a movement, retrenchment remained primarily urban.

These retrenchment campaigns created the mass constituency for the broadening of mugwumpery. Angry taxpayers, who believed they had discovered a devil in the politician, tried to convert the retrenchment drives into a permanent system to maintain low taxes. They developed an analogy that became the bedrock of mugwump movements in Wisconsin cities after the panic. Fired by steep tax bills and imbued with the ideal of the self-made man, these men compared city governments to business establishments and city officials to merchants. The trouble with the cities, they reasoned, was that they were not managed under the same principles as businesses. "Is there not waste, or worse than waste, in our city government that no private corporation would stand?" asked a member of the Milwaukee Municipal League.[26] A leader of the Madison Civic

24. Secretary, *Biennial Report, 1894,* 238–39; *Biennial Report, 1896,* 353–54.

25. While the counties of Ashland, Brown, Douglas, Eau Claire, La Crosse, Lincoln, Marinette, Milwaukee, Oneida, Racine, and Winnebago did not include all the state's large cities, their 1895 populations were dominated by one or two cities. *Blue Book, 1899,* 441–80. Secretary, *Biennial Report, 1894,* 238–39; *Biennial Report, 1896,* 353–54. Fluctuations of less than $1,500 were considered to represent no significant change.

26. *Milwaukee Sentinel,* February 2, 1895.

Federation defined the problem as "a mere question of business. . . . We often entrust city affairs to men whom we would not entrust with the smallest of our private affairs."[27] Business-like officials would confine budgets to the limitations of income and would not permit reckless spending that forced citizens to mount continual retrenchment campaigns.

From this analogy stemmed the mugwumps' polarization of men into "businessmen" and "politicians." "What the city wants," declared Madison's mugwump journalist Amos P. Wilder, "is a business, and not a political administration of its affairs."[28] The basic difference between the businessman and the politician was a difference in loyalties. For the mugwump the businessman was intelligent, honest, experienced, public-spirited, and he naturally gravitated toward "whatever in our midst makes for a higher, purer, healthier life." His loyalties were to his customers and hence to the best interests of the city. The competitive world of business bred for talent, integrity, and common sense.[29] By contrast, claimed a Milwaukee reformer in the *Sentinel*, the politician "places party service above efficiency."[30] To be successful in business a man had to be intelligent, thrifty, and honest; to be successful in politics he had only to be loyal. As angry taxpayers began to measure politicians against the yardstick of the idealized businessman, they cataloged five sins for which they blamed the politicians.

The first evil that taxpayers blamed on partisanship had long been a favorite target of mugwumps: the patronage system—the cement that held parties together. "Needless offices have been created almost without number for their support of partisan parasites," the Ashland Citizens' League pointed out, and the president of the Milwaukee Municipal League agreed that partisanship led politicians to promote "the littering up of municipal offices."[31] Mugwumps at Madison and Superior charged that policemen and firemen halted protection of citizens during the spring elections so they could protect their jobs

27. *State Journal,* January 22, 1895.
28. *Ibid.,* March 19, 1897.
29. This assumption is crucial to every mugwump group in Wisconsin. See, for example, *Milwaukee Sentinel,* March 15, 1893, November 16, 1894. *State Journal,* March 20, 1895. *Ashland Weekly Press,* March 23, 1895.
30. *Milwaukee Sentinel,* February 5, 1897.
31. *Ashland Daily News,* April 2, 1896. *Milwaukee Sentinel,* December 28, 1895.

by campaigning for their benefactors.[32] As irate taxpayers concluded that the patronage system was too expensive a luxury for hard-pressed city treasuries in the depression, they agreed with C. K. Adams, University of Wisconsin president, that "the spoils system spoils everything."[33]

Because party loyalty was the sole criterion for office, city officials were hopelessly incompetent in the eyes of their accusers. Here was the second sin in the mugwump catalog. "It required a mighty effort, with much tribulation and gnashing of teeth," stated Ashland mugwumps, "to remove any officer, however inefficient, provided he had political pull—and that class of men, as a rule, were generally put in as policemen."[34]

Since city officials had only to prove their loyalty to the party, mugwumps argued, there were no limits to their corruptibility —the third sin. The party, in fact, encouraged them to accept bribes from the faithful. Embezzlement by officials of funds belonging to the Milwaukee Public Library and the La Crosse Board of Public Works was the impetus toward formation of municipal reform leagues in those cities.[35]

The fourth evil—alliance between partisan politicians and the merchants of vice—long a concern of mugwumps, acquired special urgency during the depression as reformers broadened their retrenchment campaigns into full-scale attacks on politicians. No longer as concerned with saloonkeepers and their clients as earlier mugwumps had been, reformers now concentrated on reaching the politician. Politicians deprived their cities of significant revenues when they took saloonkeepers' votes in exchange for allowing the annual license fee on their saloons to remain unpaid. Such deals, in addition, demoralized the local community. Madison's leading mugwump, Amos P. Wilder, declared that corruption was less important than politicians' "neglect in prosecutions, eternal pigeon-holing of indictments for grave offenses, and even systematic collusion with crime. These things have to do with the moral conditions that underlie all community life; and, these undermined, not only is municipal government a failure in the generic use of that expression, but crime is encouraged, the safety of the home and individual is imperilled, and conditions ripen apace for the

32. *State Journal*, April 22, 1897. *Superior Evening Telegram*, March 15, 1898.
33. *State Journal*, February 2, 1895.
34. *Ashland Daily News*, in *Milwaukee Sentinel*, May 17, 1897.
35. *Milwaukee Sentinel*, July 19, 1892, May 19, 1895.

rearing of a generation of 'toughs.' "[36] Inspired by the 1894 victory of New York mugwumps over Tammany Hall, Wisconsin's reformers formed nonpartisan reform organizations. Although a majority of the state's mugwumps believed that the ties between politicians and traffickers in vice were a major evil that resulted from partisanship, the strength of that belief varied considerably from that in Racine and Beloit, where it was the paramount consideration, to that in La Crosse and Milwaukee, where the main reform groups ignored vice.[37]

Over all, the worst sin, a result of the others, was that the cost of partisan politics was too expensive for taxpayers to maintain in a depression. Most of the mugwumps' supporters had come to them by way of the retrenchment campaigns, and it was from the demand for economical city administrations that they had generalized their hatred of partisan politics. The demand for lower taxes remained the driving force behind the mugwumps' municipal reform movements.[38]

The root of these evils was partisanship. Partisan national issues and personalities, declared the Ashland Civic Federation, formed "the screen behind which the systematic plundering of the city is accomplished."[39] The only way reformers could persuade voters to demand that political candidates measure up to the yardsticks of thrift, honesty, and ability—virtues that they associated with businessmen—was to force local elections to be fought solely on local issues and personalities. From Wausau, where reformers were notably successful in maintaining nonpartisan local elections, came the declaration that "there is no way in which questions that divide parties in national and state elections can enter into our municipal elections. We have here a municipal corporation, a business enterprise, which is purely local in its aims and business character."[40]

36. Wilder, "The Citizen and the Law and Order Movement," *Lend a Hand,* 12 (June 1894), 437–41.

37. For information on the degree of strength of mugwumps' beliefs in various cities, see *Milwaukee Sentinel,* January 22, 1893, February 9, March 27, December 16, 1894, May 19, 1895. *State Journal,* January 22, February 2, 1895. *Ashland Daily News,* February 10, 16, November 15, 1895. *Superior Leader,* August 20, 24, 27, 1895. *Superior Evening Telegram,* August 13, 21, 26, 1895.

38. For example, see *Ashland Daily News,* November 15, 1895. *The [Milwaukee] Municipal League Bulletin,* 1 (February 19, 1898), Reference Collections, Milwaukee Public Library, hereinafter cited as *League Bulletin.*

39. *Ashland Daily News,* February 9, 1895.

40. *Wausau Daily Record,* March 18, 1899.

The reformers' unanimity in defining the problem of city government vanished when they tried to solve it. As amateurs drawn into the world of politics by their opposition to unbearable taxes, mugwump reform groups differed on the best method for securing the nonpartisan local elections that would bring economical government. One approach, that of the powerful Milwaukee Municipal League, was for its members to attend party caucuses and conventions to force the existing parties, in the words of President John A. Butler, "to bid up to its standards in the capacity, integrity, and non-political character of their candidates."[41] Prior to each election between 1893 and 1900 the league distributed thousands of copies of a circular listing the reforms it desired and held mass meetings to convince voters of the need for the reforms. The league tried to force the parties to include the desired programs in their platforms and entered the caucuses to nominate men who were sympathetic to their causes. This strategy President Butler called "heckling" the major parties.[42]

A second stratagem of nonpartisanship was to endorse the best candidates of the major parties. Typified by the Madison Civic Federation of 1895, the Appleton Independents of 1894, and the Ashland Citizens' League of 1898, these reformers reminded the parties before the caucuses that "there is enough of that independent spirit abroad to make it perilous to saddle unworthy men on any ticket," and after the caucuses they endorsed the candidates who best reflected their views. When Madison's Democratic candidate, Jabe Alford, answered affirmatively all the questions placed by the Civic Federation to all nominees, while Republican William T. Fish refused even to answer the questions, the federation advised its members to support Alford, and that support was enough to swing the close election to Alford.[43]

In cities where party lines were less rigid or taxes especially

41. *Milwaukee Sentinel,* January 31, 1894.
42. For examples, see *ibid.,* January 22, 24, 25, February 7, 9, 17, March 15, May 21, June 20, December 15, 1893, January 14, 1895, February 11, 1896. Clinton Rogers Woodruff, "The Advance of the Movement for Municipal Reform," *Good City Conference,* Indianapolis, 1898, 104–5. John A. Butler in *3rd Good City Conference, 1895,* 194–98. William Howe Tolman, *Municipal Reform Movements in the United States* (New York: Fleming H. Revell, 1895), 113.
43. *State Journal,* January 26, February 23, March 2, 12, 20, April 1, 1895. *Madison Democrat,* March 31, 1895. *Ashland Daily Press,* March 22, 1898. *Appleton Weekly Post,* April 12, 1894.

steep, reformers persuaded partisan leaders to accept a third approach. As practiced at Green Bay in every election after 1895, at Columbus in 1894, at Manitowoc in 1899, and at Grand Rapids in 1895, the cities held joint meetings of Republicans, Democrats, and Populists to choose a Citizens' ticket that would pledge honest and economical government. This method of selection was especially popular in smaller towns where citizens knew each other and where parties did not fill as important an institutional need. Indeed, by 1900, more than twenty small communities, such as Fennimore, Thorp, Lodi, Boyd, Brodhead, Merrill, and Kewaunee, had elected Citizens' tickets.[44]

By far the most radical stratagem was to create an independent party. Such nonpartisanship was rare in Wisconsin,[45] but it revealed the extent to which many citizens had become disaffected from partisan politicians.

Nonpartisan election campaigns were only one form of action taken as the result of the swelling distrust of partisan politicians that accompanied the disruptions of civic life in the early years of the depression. Lecturers like Amos P. Wilder toured the state proclaiming mugwumpery to be what the university's President C. K. Adams called "the lesson of the hour." The popularity of lectures on municipal issues revealed that men everywhere were dissatisfied with partisan politicians.[46] In May of 1894 the state had two municipal reform leagues; one year later it had nine; by May of 1896 twelve of the state's cities boasted reform groups. Although Wisconsin's population ranked it fourteenth among the states, it ranked sixth in the number of cities with reform leagues in 1895 and 1896.[47]

The history of one of the reform organizations reflects the diffuse nature of the mugwump spirit. The Madison Civic

44. *Milwaukee Sentinel,* March 18, 1894, February 20, March 29, 1896. *Appleton Weekly Post,* March 30, 1899. *Wood County Reporter,* March 7, 28, 1895. *Wausau Daily Record,* March 27, 1900. *The Madison State,* April 8, 1898, April 6, 1900.

45. *Ashland Daily News,* February 9, 16, 19, March 26, 1895. *Ashland Weekly Press,* February 16, March 16, April 6, 1895.

46. *Milwaukee Sentinel,* December 21, 28, 1895. *Appleton Weekly Post,* October 31, November 7, 1895. Amos P. Wilder, *The Government of Cities* (University of Wisconsin Extension Division Syllabus No. 41, 1895). Anna E. Anderson to J. H. Raymond, Raymond File, Papers of the University of Wisconsin Extension Division, University of Wisconsin Archival Series 18/1/1–4.

47. Clinton Rogers Woodruff, "The Progress of Municipal Reform, 1894–1895," *National League,* 1895, 305–6. Woodruff, "A Year's Work for Municipal Reform," *3rd Good City Conference, 1895,* 64.

Federation had begun as a protest against the action of the city council for repealing the midnight-closing ordinance so that legislators and lobbyists could relax. Hundreds of members were attracted when the federation announced that "good government" was its purpose. Members, reacting mainly to the vague feeling that it was right to favor good government, could develop no concrete proposals. Possessed mainly of the sense that partisan politicians were evil, gradually the less active federation soon declined into a lecture forum.[48]

While the Madison group was reacting to the mugwump spirit, most citizens' organizations knew exactly which evils they wanted abolished. Civil service reform, which before the depression had been the aim of a few elitists and Milwaukee unions, now became a major goal for many of the new groups who wanted to cut the costs of local government. Influenced by such new organizations as Superior's Good Government Club and Taxpayers' League and the Milwaukee Municipal League, civil service reform by 1895 had won support from religious groups, such as the Congregationalists, Catholics, and Methodists, from the Wisconsin Federation of Labor, and they even converted administrators, such as the mayors of Appleton, Chippewa Falls, Fond du Lac, Janesville, Eau Claire, Sheboygan, and Beloit.[49] So great was mugwump pressure that the legislature in 1895 removed all of Milwaukee's jobs from the patronage rolls and in 1897 extended civil service reform to police and fire departments outside Milwaukee.

What stung the politicians most painfully and demonstrated the popularity of mugwumpery most effectively was the transformation of the vice crusades. While a few of the new mugwumps championed the old practice of using Sunday-closing movements as a way of controlling the community's shiftless members, most of the new reformers gave the crusades a new twist by using alliances between politicians and vice lords as weapons to attack the politicians. The new mugwumps, in addition, were less interested in perpetuating the ideal of the re-

48. *State Journal,* January 22, February 25, March 1, April 23, 27, 1895. See also January 15, 16, 17, 19, 22, 26, February 2, 23, March 1, 2, 20, April 1, May 3, June 3, 1895. *Madison Democrat,* March 31, 1895. *Milwaukee Sentinel,* February 27, May 19, 1895.

49. *Congregational Minutes,* 55th Meeting, 1895, 45. *Methodist Minutes,* 1895, 42–43. *Milwaukee Sentinel,* June 9, 1893. *League Bulletin,* 12 (January 28, 1899). *Superior Leader,* April 13, 1895. *Superior Evening Telegram,* March 7, 1895. *Milwaukee Catholic Citizen,* June 1, 1895.

ligious Sabbath than in abolishing what were in their eyes such secular evils as gambling and prostitution.[50] The impeachment of Superior's popular mayor, Charles S. Starkweather, in 1895 revealed that most people now blamed the politicians, not gamblers, madames, or saloonkeepers, for the existence of vice.[51] By 1895 the older vice crusaders were swept along by the broader current of reform through the condemnation of partisan politicians.

Mugwumpery provided the initial direction for taxpayers' demands for reform in the depression. The new mugwumps, so eager for reform that they easily shed the earlier mugwumps' emphasis on education, moral suasion, and fear of politicians, accepted aid wherever they could find it—in courts and major party caucuses, as well as in churches and schools. They only wanted the extravagant, partisan politicians to follow the practices of the successful businessman.

II

Most historians subsequently described mugwumpery as a movement by a narrow segment of social, economic, and religious elitists to assume supremacy over the lower and middle classes who were running and ruining their cities. While this appraisal fitted Wisconsin mugwumpery before the Panic of 1893, it would have been incomprehensible to the state's mugwumps who labored during the depression, when the economic and secular turn of reform brought recruits from all social backgrounds.

Wisconsin's mugwumps after 1893 would have had a hard time recognizing themselves in the historians' portrait. They had too often smarted under criticism from their cities' genuine conservatives and elitists. Editors frequently ignored local mugwump groups as they echoed the lament that "the crying need of our system" was to lure "the good citizen" into reform movements that were led by others.[52] An elitist Madison editor expressed his opinion of the moral character of his city's mugwumps when he snarled that "members of the Reform league in coming out of [the saloons] should be careful not to

50. *Ashland Daily News,* October 21, 23, 31, November 2, 1895. *Ashland Weekly Press,* October 26, 1895.
51. See chap. 9, sec. II.
52. *Superior Evening Telegram,* March 6, 1896.

get hurt in the crush."[53] Thirty-nine of Superior's leading businessmen opposed the impeachment of the immoral and patronage-minded mayor because it had brought unfavorable publicity to the city.[54] In fact, only two of the state's leading businessmen contributed to the new mugwumpery. William W. Allis, president of the million-dollar Edward P. Allis Company, was a member of the Milwaukee Municipal League's governing Committee of One Hundred. The company had long occupied a distinctive place in the state's reform movements, since its founder had led the Greenback movement in the mid-1870s and had pioneered in paternalistic programs for his employees.[55] The other wealthy mugwump was John A. Johnson, president of the Gisholt machine works, who served as president of the Madison Civic Federation at the same time that he developed paternalistic programs for his workers.[56] Allis and Johnson were exceptional among the state's business leaders not only for their enlightened labor policies, but also for their mugwumpery.

The one social group that was conspicuously absent from the new mugwump organizations was the business elite, as in Milwaukee, where none of that city's thirty-three wealthiest men participated in any reform campaigns.[57] The story was the same in smaller cities. Reform groups frequently blasted their wealthiest inhabitants, men like Ashland's Col. John H. Knight, and wealthiest corporations, like Superior's Land and River Improvement Company, for their refusal to pay taxes.[58] The reasons for lack of interest by the business elite were not

53. *State Journal*, April 22, 1895.

54. *Superior Evening Telegram*, July 23, 1895.

55. Graham A. Cosmas, "The Democracy in Search of Issues: The Wisconsin Reform Party, 1873–1877," *Wisconsin Magazine of History*, 46 (Winter 1962–1963), 107. Ellis Baker Usher, *Wisconsin: Its Story and Biography* (Chicago: Lewis, 1910), 3: 548–52. Adolf Gerd Korman, "A Social History of Industrial Growth and Immigrants: A Study with Particular Reference to Milwaukee, 1880–1920" (Ph.D. diss., University of Wisconsin, 1959), 149–55. Thomas W. Gavett, "The Development of the Labor Movement in Milwaukee" (Ph.D. diss., University of Wisconsin, 1957), 84–85.

56. *State Journal*, January 22, February 2, 23, 1895, January 16, March 6, 1900.

57. *Milwaukee Sentinel*, September 30, 1894.

58. *Ashland Daily News*, February 9, 10, 19, March 26, 28, 30, 1895. *Ashland Weekly Press*, April 6, 1895. *Ashland Daily Press*, March 13, 15, 1899. *Superior Leader*, August 27, 1895, July 22, 1897. *Superior Evening Telegram*, August 26, 1895. *Milwaukee Catholic Citizen*, December 29, 1894, June 8, 1895.

hard to find. First, they had achieved their economic pre-eminence by devoting their energies to business affairs; it made little difference to them whether the city was adminis-tered by patronage employees or civil servants. Second, they had the resources to create their own retrenchment programs —they hired lawyers to set aside their tax assessments. Third, the officers of some of the largest corporations, particularly the utilities, were often the leading financial and organiza-tional contributors to the political machines the mugwumps were trying to destroy; in effect, they sponsored the bosses. Finally, as the *Superior Leader* observed, "Nothing will so thoroughly frighten the average business man in any city . . . as visions of a Puritanical government."[59]

Although the state's business elite generally avoided mug-wump organizations, many less prominent businessmen became active reformers. The leading businessmen in the Milwaukee Municipal League were the head of a lubricant company, a bank vice-president, the vice-president of a cabinet company, a bank messenger, a commission merchant and his assistant, an assistant in a bank, and an official of a leather company.[60] The executive committee of the La Crosse Civic Federation in-cluded a banker, several lumberyard owners, a few real estate and insurance salesmen, two manufacturers, a clerk, and a utility president.[61] The Madison Civic Federation featured among its leaders eight owners of small businesses, four bankers, two salesmen, two manufacturers, and an accountant.[62] Among Ashland Republicans who bolted their party's nominee in 1899 to support a mugwump Democrat were twenty shopkeepers, fifteen accountants and agents, four bankers and four manu-facturers.[63] With the possible exception of the bankers, those

59. *Superior Leader,* July 24, 1895.
60. The activities of E. K. West, Robert Hill, Charles W. Norris, Robert Camp, Henry S. Eskuche, Jeremiah Quinn, G. H. D. Johnson, and Edward P. Bacon are reported in *Milwaukee Sentinel,* January 25, May 11, 1893, December 6, 16, 1894, January 14, February 2, 1895, April 8, 1896, June 3, 1897. *Superior Evening Telegram,* March 6, 1897. *2nd Good City Con-ference, 1894,* 174. *3rd Good City Conference, 1895,* 536. I relied on *Wright's Directory of Milwaukee* for occupations of reformers. Various city directories established occupations for reformers of other cities men-tioned in this discussion.
61. *La Crosse Chronicle,* February 22, March 1, 1895. *La Crosse City Directory for 1895.*
62. *State Journal,* March 2, 1895. *Madison, Wisconsin, City Directory, 1894–1895.*
63. *Ashland Daily Press,* March 25, 1899. *Ashland City Directory, 1897.*

businessmen who led the state's mugwump groups tended to be either proprietors of small businesses or lower-echelon corporation officials.

Businessmen had a number of reasons for joining reform groups. First, they felt the sting of high taxes in a depression more than did other citizens because their dwindling business deprived them of the funds needed to pay taxes. Second, businessmen were the members of the community toward whom reformers were looking for leadership in the wars against partisan politicians, and some of them eagerly answered a call to reform the cities that was only partly of their own initiative. Businessmen were, at least in theory, the citizens most acutely aware of how far local politicians fell short of the business ideal exalted by mugwumps. Third, businessmen had traditionally assumed a major role in formulating local fiscal policies. They had led demands for municipal improvements in the years before the panic, and it was natural that they should continue their parental concern for municipal expenditures. They rated a city's standing by its ability to meet its debts and obligations. Chambers of commerce across Wisconsin carefully scrutinized their cities' fiscal policies.[64]

Professional men in the 1890s embraced new mugmump groups with the same enthusiasm that they have traditionally shown for most social and political movements. The representation of each profession varied widely from one organization and city to the next, depending on the organization's activities and the city's power structure. At Madison, where educators were relatively more numerous than in other Wisconsin cities, they took the lead in the Civic Federation,[65] whereas teachers shunned the Milwaukee Municipal League and Superior Good Government Club. These latter two organizations had no doctors as leaders, but doctors eagerly participated in the Republicans-for-Bardon movement at Ashland in 1899 and the Madison Civic Federation. Clergymen played major roles in mugwump groups at Racine, Beloit, Sheboygan, and Madison in 1895 and were the only prominent citizens in the Milwaukee Civic Federation of 1895, but they completely ignored the Milwaukee Municipal League, the 1899 Ashland Republicans for Bardon

64. *Superior Evening Telegram*, June 29, July 13, 1893. Milwaukee chamber, *40th Annual Report*, 1898, 40–41.
65. *State Journal*, March 2, 1895. *Madison Directory, 1894–1895.*

organization, and the Superior Good Government Club.[66] These clergymen hoped to convert the popularity of mugwump attacks on politicians into larger movements to regulate vice.

The participation of lawyers and journalists depended on the thrust and activities of each group. The Milwaukee Municipal League, which mainly scrutinized the legal business of the city council and county board and drafted reform ordinances and bills, was dominated by lawyers like John A. Butler, John F. Burke, James A. Mallory, Frederick W. von Cotzhausen, Joshua Stark, Charles E. Monroe, and Charles E. Estabrook.[67] Lawyers ignored the formation of the Ashland Civic Federation until the group decided that the only way to curtail expenses was to bring injunctions against politicians, and then lawyer A. E. Dixon emerged as its spokesman.[68] At Beloit, Racine, and Madison, where mugwump organizations concentrated on educational campaigns and expanded vice crusades, lawyers ignored mugwumpery.[69] Journalists exploited mugwumpery for partisan ends. Where they thought nonpartisanship offered the best way to defeat the incumbent opposition party, as at Superior in 1896, they eagerly embraced—even led—mugwump groups,[70] but where editors feared that mugwump groups would support nonpartisan candidates who could not be manipulated, as at La Crosse, Ashland, and Madison in 1895, they shunned the reform organizations.[71]

The remarkable feature of mugwumpery after 1893 was not the participation of business and professional men, who had

66. *State Journal*, January 17, 22, March 2, 1895. *Milwaukee Sentinel*, May 19, 1895. *Milwaukee Catholic Citizen*, December 29, 1894, June 8, November 23, 1895.

67. Reports of some of their activities can be found in *Milwaukee Sentinel*, January 25, 31, April 7, 1893, February 24, March 13, December 6, 16, 1894, January 14, 20, February 2, 1895, June 3, 1897. *Superior Evening Telegram*, March 6, 1897. *League Bulletin*, 1 (February 19, 1898). *2nd Good City Conference, 1894*, 174. *National League*, First Meeting, 1895, 536. Winkler, "Municipal Government," 119–24. John A. Butler, "A Single or a Double Council?" *National League*, 2nd Meeting, 1896, 252–62. Butler, "The Place of the Council and the Mayor in the Organization of Municipal Government," *Good City Conference*, Indianapolis, 1898, 167–73.

68. *Ashland Daily News*, August 2, 14, 15, September 4, October 4, 24, November 15, December 20, 1895, March 4, 1896.

69. *Milwaukee Sentinel*, May 19, 1895. *State Journal*, January 2, 15, 16, 17, 19, 22, February 2, 1895.

70. *Superior Evening Telegram*, March 14, 1896.

71. *La Crosse Chronicle*, March 1, 1895. *State Journal*, March 2, 1895. *Ashland Daily News*, March 2, 1895.

traditionally led such movements, but the enthusiasm with which workers, immigrants, and Populists contributed to the new cause. While some workers had sympathized with mugwump programs before the panic, they had never been able to bridge the social divisions between them and more prominent local residents. The depression brought about the first union of workers and businessmen in the same organizations. Workers were among the leaders of the Ashland Civic Federation, easily the most successful of the four civic federations formed in 1895. James Anderson, a member of the Wisconsin Federation of Labor's executive board, was one of the dozen Ashlanders who organized the Civic Federation, and Mike Cannon a longshoreman, union organizer, and Populist leader, was one of the group's vice-presidents. One-fourth of the federation's policymaking Committee of forty-five were laborers.[72] Workers continued to take a strong interest in Ashland's mugwump groups after 1895, forming one-sixth of the governing Committee of Thirty of the 1896 Citizens' League and one-fifth of the 1899 Republicans for Bardon.[73] Workers and Populists were equally prominent in the Superior Civic Federation of 1895, and two of the eleven speakers at that group's mass meeting of 1,000 Superiorites were both workers and Populists. Andrew J. Newberg, a cooper, and Angus McQueen, a plasterer, were both Populist aldermen.[74]

Two prominent Populists and labor spokesmen played major roles in directing the powerful Milwaukee Municipal League. Robert Schilling, former organizer for the Knights of Labor, current state leader of the People's party, and editor of the *Advance and Reformer,* was a prominent early leader of the Milwaukee league. Schilling was one of the three-man Committee of Special Inquiry whose report in May, 1893, determined the league's course for the next several years. Schilling was joined by Henry Smith, a laborite congressman in the late 1880s before becoming a Populist alderman, in serving on the policymaking Committee of One Hundred.[75]

72. *Ashland Daily News,* February 10, March 2, 1895. *Milwaukee Sentinel,* June 9, 1893. *Ashland Weekly Press,* February 23, 1895. *Ashland City Directory, 1895.*
73. *Ashland Daily News,* February 10, 1896. *Ashland Daily Press,* March 25, 1899. *Ashland City Directory, 1895,* and *1897.*
74. *Superior Evening Telegram,* August 26, 1895. *Superior Leader,* August 27, 1895. *City of Superior Directory, 1894,* and *1896.*
75. *Milwaukee Sentinel,* January 25, 31, February 8, 15, March 10, 15, April 7, May 11, 1893.

A great many workers who did not serve as leaders still were attracted to the new mugwump groups. Reports of the proceedings of reform meetings were testimony to the appeal of mugwumpery to workers in the depression. The organizational meeting of the Madison Civic Federation "was very largely made up of workingmen, with a fair sprinkling of professional and business men."[76] Workers were equally prominent in forming civic federations at Ashland and Superior.[77]

Workers and Populists reinforced their attendance at reform meetings with their votes for mugwump candidates for public office. Indeed, the local Populist parties were consistently more friendly to mugwump principles and candidates than were either Democrats or Republicans. Milwaukee Populists in 1893 tried to persuade John A. Butler, Municipal League president, to be their mayoral candidate because "the interest which he has displayed in the reform movement" made him "a strong man with all classes."[78] In the same vein, workers who formed the Unity Club of the Madison Populists wanted to nominate insurance salesman W. H. Rogers, a prominent mugwump, for mayor in 1895.[79] When the Ashland Civic Federation nominated Republican lawyer A. E. Dixon on a nonpartisan platform in 1895, the only support he received was from the Populists, a large number of whom wanted to show their sympathy for the federation.[80] Superior's Populists in 1896 endorsed the Good Government Club's candidates for every city office except mayor.[81]

Workers had a number of grievances with partisan politicians that led them to embrace mugwump groups and candidates enthusiastically. Above all, the burdens of taxation rested almost as heavily on workers as on businessmen. At a time when most workers' wages were reduced and many had lost their jobs, they were incapable of paying high taxes. This applied equally to the renters, who paid taxes in the form of rents, and the many Wisconsin workers who owned their own homes. They demanded relief. "The taxpayers of the city are being robbed by

76. *State Journal,* February 2, 1895.

77. *Ashland Daily News,* March 2, 1895. *Superior Evening Telegram,* August 26, 1895. *Superior Leader,* August 27, 1895.

78. *Milwaukee Sentinel,* March 6, 1893.

79. *State Journal,* March 4, 1895.

80. *Ashland Daily News,* March 9, 10, 12, 14, 1895. *Ashland Weekly Press,* March 9, 16, 1895.

81. *Superior Evening Telegram,* March 16, 31, 1896.

extravagant and unnecessary taxation," proclaimed Superior's Populists in 1895 and 1896, "and we therefore advocate an honest and economical administration of public affairs."[82] Ashland Populists in 1895 attacked "the incapacity or criminal neglect of preceding administrations" that had brought on "fast accumulation of indebtedness."[83] Pinched by taxation, La Crosse Populists in 1895 demanded "that the affairs of this city be conducted upon good, sound and businesslike principles."[84]

Sharing the mugwump approach, workers found partisan politics an intolerably expensive burden and demanded reforms that would replace extravagant politicians with community-minded, tightfisted officials. "We can't work with the present ward heeler, ward bummer system," objected Robert Schilling.[85] A great many workers came to agree with the 1895 La Crosse Populist convention that "national and state politics should be eliminated from municipal affairs" and that delegates to all party conventions "should rise above all party prejudices and select such men as have the confidence of the people and will prove good and faithful servants."[86] At Wausau the Populists led the drive for nonpartisan local elections.[87]

Workers were also attracted to mugwump groups because they found that many of the business and professional men in those groups were sympathetic to their side in labor disputes. During the Pullman strike, when businessmen throughout the state denounced the union, Superior's leading mugwump businessman, Frank A. Woodward, vehemently defended the railway workers.[88] Ashland's mugwump business and professional men showed even more significant friendship toward local workers. When a strike erupted in Ashland's sawmills in 1895, John F. Scott, a prominent businessman and Civic Federation leader, joined two union officials in presenting the workers' demands to the mill owners.[89] In the election of 1896 Republicans tried to defeat Mayor Bardon, darling of retrenchment-minded mugwumps, by charging that he had joined other Ashland businessmen in trying to break a longshoremen's strike in 1893.

82. *Superior Leader,* March 14, 1895, March 15, 1896.
83. *Ashland Daily News,* March 12, 1895.
84. *La Crosse Chronicle,* March 10, 1895.
85. *Milwaukee Sentinel,* February 8, 1893.
86. *La Crosse Chronicle,* March 10, 1895.
87. *Wausau Daily Record,* March 18, 1900.
88. *Milwaukee Sentinel,* July 3, 1894.
89. *Ashland Weekly Press,* August 31, October 19, 1895.

Workers apparently considered Bardon a friend because no one came forward to claim the fifty dollars he had promised to every church in the city if the Republican charge could be substantiated. The backfiring of the Republican tactic only proved that Bardon was more sympathetic to workers than were any other Ashland businessmen.[90] Those Wisconsin businessmen who campaigned for a corrupt practices act to limit candidates' expenses were explicitly trying to make it easier for poorer men to seek public office. The bill's author, Charles N. Gregory, announced that his objective was "the equality of the poor man with the rich man at the polls."[91] Believing that incompetence was a by-product of partisanship, mugwumps of all types hoped that the bill would allow a poor man to seek office without having to rely on the financial support of a faction or party to which he would later be indebted.

Members of all religious and ethnic groups were as eager to join the new mugwump groups as were the representatives of various occupations. As early as 1880 Wisconsin had a greater proportion of immigrant voters to native-born voters than any other state, a fact that alarmed eastern mugwumps,[92] but one that also led Wisconsinites to expect that immigrants would participate in political movements. Religious affiliation was so unimportant to mugwumps after 1893 that it is nearly impossible to determine the churches attended by their members. Catholic priests headed reform movements at Milwaukee, Madison, and Green Bay.[93] Humphrey Desmond, a Catholic editor in Milwaukee, urged that city's Democrats to nominate Butler, the league's president, for mayor in 1894.[94] Urging Catholic voters to reject their "sectarian prejudices" against Republicans for earlier alliances with nativists, Desmond found evidence in the elections of the mid-1890s that "the once despised doctrine of 'Mugwumpery' is now subscribed to with remarkable ease." Catholics were increasingly voting for men and measures, and many, said the *Milwaukee Catholic Citizen*, "no longer care

90. *Ashland Daily News*, April 1, 3, 1896.
91. *Milwaukee Sentinel*, February 2, 1895.
92. For example, see *New York Post*, quoted in *State Journal*, March 16, 1887.
93. *State Journal*, January 17, March 2, 1895. *Milwaukee Sentinel*, March 7, August 28, 1893, December 16, 1894. *Wright's Directory of Milwaukee, 1893*. *Milwaukee Catholic Citizen*, December 29, 1894, July 6, 1895.
94. *Milwaukee Catholic Citizen*, March 17, 1894.

for mere party names and watchwords."[95] From such evidence it seems probable that a sizable number of Wisconsin's mugwumps attended Catholic services on Sundays.

Mugwumpery was apparently just as congenial for the state's Jews. Rabbi Sigmund Hecht was a prominent early member of the Milwaukee Municipal League, and such leading Milwaukee Jews as Bernard Goldsmith, Isaac Adler, Bernard Gross, Emmanuel Adler, and A. W. Rich participated, to one degree or another, in the league.[96] The vice-president of the La Crosse Civic Federation, Albert Hirsheimer, described himself as "a moderate Democrat and a moderate Jew."[97]

National origins apparently made little difference to Wisconsin mugwumps after 1893. The names of the state's reformers demonstrated that the movement was by no measure characterized by members' names: Strohmeyer, Niederman, von Cotzhausen, Winkler, Krackowizer, Magdeburg, Kraege, Graebner, Eskuche, Anderson, Keogh, McLenegan, Koch, Rauschenberger, Shea, Haggerty, Kiehle, O'Carroll, Romadka, Murphy, and Hanson.

Most of Wisconsin's mugwumps would probably have scoffed at this attention to their religious and nationality affiliations. While an occasional reformer continued to sound nativist at times,[98] most of them proved their tolerance of differences by aiming their campaigns against nativist politicians. The Ashland Civic Federation directed most of its energies toward impeaching the partisan Republican mayor, C. M. E. McClintock. Had they been confirmed nativists they would have hesitated, for McClintock was also a rabid spokesman for and later statewide president of the nativist American Protective Association.[99] At Superior in 1896 immigrants formed an Equal Rights Club to force the city's partisan politicians to give them a more effective role in politics, but the only group to sympathize with them was the Good Government Club.[100]

95. *Ibid.*, November 10, 1894, September 5, October 31, November 14, 1896.

96. *Milwaukee Sentinel*, February 8, March 7, 10, April 7, 1893, March 1, 1894, April 10, 1896.

97. *La Crosse Chronicle*, February 22, 1895. *Milwaukee Sentinel*, May 19, 1895.

98. *2nd Good City Conference*, 1894, 12–14. *State Journal*, January 21, 1895.

99. *Ashland Daily News*, August 15, 16, September 27, 1895, February 15, 1896.

100. *Superior Evening Telegram*, March 21, 1896.

Wisconsin mugwumpery after 1893 paralleled other social and political movements because, with leaders and supporters from every social background, mugwump programs were capable of affecting all classes. Relief from unbearable taxes, as much the demand of workers as bosses and of immigrants as native-born, was the basic motivation. The feeling that partisan politicians served a very small constituency in local governments was another cause for unity. Incompetence and corruption infuriated workers and Populists as much as merchants and Democrats. Through such specific grievances ran the vague sense that good government should somehow be their watchword, a feeling well expressed by a Portage Baptist preacher: "You call me a 'Mugwump,' but I have concluded that I must be if I want to be a decent man."[101]

III

Mugwumpery was the first political response of urban residents to the depression, but this new force was largely unfocused in the months immediately after the financial panic. Angry taxpayers at first took up any cudgels they could find against their local politicians. The only existing state-wide organizations that harbored significant numbers of mugwumps before the panic were the Yankee Protestant annual conventions, which were not oriented toward the new economic and secular turn of mugwumpery in the depression. Most mugwump groups after 1893 felt an acute need to share experiences with reformers in other cities in order to discover what tactics would dethrone the ruling politicians. Ultimately, the group that emerged to build the morale and give direction to the programs of Wisconsin's mugwumps was the Milwaukee Municipal League.

101. Adam Fawcett in *Baptist Union Minutes,* 32nd Meeting, 1896, 14–15.

Taxes, as an issue in the depression, had created enough dissatisfaction to enable mugwumps to win significant victories in
their communities. On the local level, groups of taxpayers could
force city officials to cut taxes by staging mass meetings, by conducting educational campaigns through the press, by indicating
places where tax dollars were wasted, by proposing respected
and tightfisted candidates for office, and by securing injunctions
against extravagant programs. Politicians, in their turn, could
retain power by promoting economies in government.

The situation was entirely different at the state level. As reformers broadened their mugwumpery from retrenchment of
expenditures into programs to weaken the power of partisan
politicians, they discovered that the state legislature held
virtually total control over the structure of their local governments. If they wanted to alter their mill rate, set aside special
assessments, remove the privilege of patronage from city officials
by introducing civil service reform, or restrict activities of
partisan politicians in the nomination or election of city
officials, reformers had to go to Madison. There, the vote of a
legislator whose constituency was hundreds of miles distant was
as important in their local affairs as the votes of their own
representatives. Clearly, to be effective, reformers would need
to create a state-wide reform movement, and they soon learned
that this was much harder than reform at home.

The first hurdle for reformers was the realization that partisanship played a much more important role at the state level
than at the local. Candidates for the state legislature ran on
partisan, not local, issues, and they ran on tickets headed by
candidates for state and national offices, so that partisan loyalties
were more important in the November elections than in the
April elections for local offices. Voters expected legislators to
follow their party's position on state matters. This attitude
within the electorate lent proportionately greater influence to
party leaders over state legislation, and reformers soon learned
that party leaders were reluctant to surrender the structural
tools of their trade.

The second major hurdle was the difficulty of arousing state-
wide sentiment over issues that grew out of problems in one

community. Legislators from one city rarely understood why voters in another were so aroused over a particular problem. As a result, they followed the lead of their party's representatives from the community in which reformers were seeking change. Further, differences in local political traditions, practices, reform groups, and power structures sometimes made a program that was necessary and popular in one city unnecessary and unpopular in another. The reformers' legislative proposals did not promise the immediate political results that lower taxes offered incumbents in local elections. The issue of high taxes that first undergirded mugwumpery in the cities was not as immediately potent at the state level because state taxes were relatively low and were levied, in the main, on a few corporations.

The third hurdle was the brevity of the legislative sessions, contrasted to continuously meeting city councils. In the cities reformers had numerous opportunities to mount campaigns and force city officials to confront their issues—aldermen and mayors could not dodge them forever—and they could be held immediately accountable. The state legislature, however, met for less than four months every two years, and most significant legislation was passed or defeated in a wild flurry during the last week of the session. A reform bill could easily be killed in committee in either the Senate or the Assembly or, as more often happened, could be emasculated by amendment in the frantic confusion of the last week or two. This manner of dealing with legislation placed disproportionate power in the hands of the ablest parliamentarians, who could manipulate the legislative machinery, take advantage of the inexperience of most legislators, and capitalize on the hectic pace of legislation at the end of each session. The legislative process, in the hands of experienced politicians, gave them a tremendous advantage over the inexperienced reformers, who came to Madison armed with an intangible and unreliable weapon—an aroused public opinion—to achieve their goals. Once defeated, reformers could only go home and mourn their losses for two years, while the politicians knew that editors and the reformers themselves would probably forget their votes on a particular bill by the time they came up for re-election nearly two years later.

Politicians and municipal reformers alike understood these hurdles. By 1897 both groups showed their respect for the Milwaukee Municipal League, which had built and coordinated

157

such a successful state-wide reform movement that in two years it had brought about enactment of most of its programs. Reform groups in other cities and states copied its programs and tactics, and the National Municipal League pronounced the Milwaukee group the most successful mugwump organization in the country. They knew how far the league had come since its formation in 1893 as a group concerned only with affairs in Milwaukee. Some of them realized that the Milwaukee Municipal League was more effective because the event that sparked its creation had forced its members to ask different questions from those raised by most mugwump groups.

I

K. August Linderfelt, Milwaukee's public librarian, was one of the city's most respected and cultured citizens. In 1891 he was elected president of the National Library Association in recognition of his personal charm and hard work over the preceding dozen years in building the Milwaukee library into a major institution. Milwaukeeans were understandably stunned and shocked on April 29, 1892, when the city treasurer reported that Linderfelt had embezzled over $9,000 of the library's funds. Many citizens would not believe the treasurer's evidence, and the trustees of the library board demonstrated their faith in their librarian by refusing to fire him and by reimbursing the city out of their own pockets. When a jury convicted Linderfelt the judge suspended his sentence.[1]

The actions by officials angered many Milwaukeeans; they felt that the city's leaders were shielding a thief. Led by the *Sentinel*'s editor Horace Rublee and Populist leader Henry Smith, 1,000 people gathered at a July protest meeting at the West Side Turn Hall. Declaring that the existing system of law should be abolished "if wealth or social influence exerted on behalf of a convicted man can shield him," the meeting passed resolutions demanding the imprisonment of Linderfelt and the resignation of the library trustees. Their meeting was too late, for Linderfelt escaped to Europe just as Milwaukee officials arrived in Boston to rearrest him.[2]

1. *Milwaukee Sentinel,* October 17, 1888, April 29, 30, May 2, 6–26, July 2, 14, 17, 19, 1892, December 25, 1894.
2. *Ibid.,* May 11, July 14, 19, 1892.

The librarian's embezzlement and the protest meeting set the pattern for action by the Milwaukee Municipal League. As a wide variety of Milwaukeeans met during the first months of 1893 to form the league and develop its programs, they showed how the Linderfelt incident had shaped their thinking. They could not accept the popular mugwump shibboleth that "the only way to get good government is to get good men." Linderfelt had been a good man—and a crook. "If a man of his apparent character is not proof against temptation," Rublee had asked, "whom can we trust?" In the process of answering this question, the Milwaukee league attacked the system that corrupted even the best of men. The league's president, John Butler, announced that the group's strategy would be "to make it unprofitable for bad men" to hold public office: "We do not aim to have any quarrel with individuals; we are at war with the system in Milwaukee." From January until May of 1893 the league's members debated the best programs for changing that system.[3]

During these debates it became clear that the league appealed to a wide variety of Milwaukeeans, from Populists to conservative businessmen, and that each group had a different idea of what was wrong with the system that had produced Linderfelt. Ultimately, the league was captured by the men who felt that the worst evil in city government was the high tax burden that extravagant and incompetent politicians had foisted onto the taxpayers. The league took this direction because the Populist newspaper, suspicious of any organization that attracted prominent businessmen, hinted that radicals who participated in the league were traitors and because the panic suddenly made the issue of high taxes a burning one. The league decided in May that the best way to reduce taxes was to extend civil service reform beyond the fire and police departments, which had been taken out of politics in 1885, to include every city office or job except those for which men were directly elected. Without the attraction of the spoils, the league reasoned, partisan incompetents would not seek city offices, and the new city officials would have no reason to create unnecessary jobs to reward the party faithful. The new city officials would operate the city in a busi-

3. *2nd Good City Conference, 1894,* 60–61. *National League,* First Meeting, 1895, 195–97; Second Meeting, 1896, 300–302. *Milwaukee Sentinel,* April 30, 1892, January 22, 25, 31, February 15, March 7, 10, 15, May 11, 21, 1893.

nesslike and economical way and would thus bring tax relief. While a few Populists like Robert Schilling supported civil service reform, the league's program was essentially a victory for business and professional men like merchants E. P. Mathews, T. W. Buell, and A. W. Rich, bankers James K. Ilsey and William Plankinton, clergymen Judson Titsworth and Henry T. Secrist, and lawyers John A. Butler, Frederick W. von Cotzhausen, and James Mallory, who had issued the call in January for organization of the new group.[4]

The league, standing squarely in the mugwump tradition, drew criticism from other members and from outsiders alike. The critics charged that the worst corrupters of the system were not the politicians, but the quasi-public corporations whose lucrative franchises offered great opportunities for boodling aldermen. They were to argue over the next several years that the league was so concerned with obtaining tax relief for its wealthy members, who paid the city's largest tax bills, that it had "no regard for the robbery of the people by monopolies." The critics hinted that the presence of lawyers for the utilities in the league prevented it from sticking to such projects as its early and disastrous lobbying efforts to secure repeal of the Milwaukee Gas Company's exclusive franchise. As late as 1897, after the league had shifted its attacks from partisan politicians to corporations, the critics still protested that the league's major objective was to secure tax relief for wealthy Milwaukeeans.[5] While this criticism of the league's activities was fairly accurate until 1895, it ignored the organization's obvious appeal to poorer taxpayers—who also wanted relief—and to Populists like Robert Schilling and Henry Smith who supported the league's campaigns for honest government.

Before the league could begin in 1893 to implement its decision to work for civil service reform it faced a new challenge: Milwaukee's mayor resigned to take a seat in Congress, and the city had to elect a new mayor at the end of June, 1893. While some members, notably Von Cotzhausen and Smith, wanted to run an independent candidate, the league's majority decided to

4. *Milwaukee Sentinel*, January 31, February 15, May 11, 21, 1893. *2nd Good City Conference, 1894*, 60–61. *National League*, First Meeting, 1895, 195–96. *Milwaukee Daily News*, June 22, 1893, April 2, 1896.

5. *Milwaukee Catholic Citizen*, January 28, 1893. *Milwaukee Daily News*, June 22, 1893, March 30, 1894, December 9, 1895, January 4, February 11, March 13, April 2, 3, 1896, February 13, 20, 1897. *Milwaukee Sentinel*, February 9, April 7, 1893.

persuade the existing parties to nominate an honest, apolitical businessman. The Republicans chose John C. Koch, a wealthy merchant and political neophyte, who pledged to "administer the city in a businesslike way." The league was delighted with Koch's candidacy, and its members campaigned actively for him. Koch's subsequent victory showed the party managers that the new league was a potent force and also gave the league's members confidence.[6]

The Koch campaign was only a diversion from the real work of reform, although it had served to dramatize the importance of Butler, who had emerged as the league's spokesman over the previous three months and was to serve as its president for the rest of the decade. Son of one of the city's most prominent early lawyers, Butler was a Yale-educated, wealthy lawyer who voted Democratic in national elections. But, as events were to show, his background was less important than his personality. An informal person with few rigid ideas and no prejudices against workers or political radicals, Butler impressed even the league's worst enemies as an honest, earnest, and "well-meaning" man who cared only for the city's welfare. While occasionally belittled by critics as too impractical and a bit absent-minded, he was far more popular with workers and Populists than with either Democrats or Republicans. He consistently tried to persuade other league members that the group should represent the interests of all Milwaukeeans. No small part of the league's successes derived from its earnest and open-minded president.[7]

After Koch's election in June, Butler and the league mounted a campaign of popular education and political pressure for a program of civil service reform. The objective was to persuade the 1895 legislature to bring all of Milwaukee's city employees under civil service. In March of 1894 the league, announcing that it was going to force every candidate and party to take a position on the civil service issue in the forthcoming municipal elections, distributed 10,000 circulars among voters, urging them that the best way to lower taxes was to nominate in the

6. *Milwaukee Sentinel,* May 21, June 7, 9, 20, 25, 1893. *Milwaukee Daily News,* June 12, 26, 1893.

7. *National Cyclopedia of American Biography* (New York, 1931), 21: 55–56. *Milwaukee Daily News,* February 11, 1896, February 20, 1897. Amos P. Wilder to J. H. Raymond, November 17, 1895, J. H. Raymond File, Papers of the University of Wisconsin Extension Division, University of Wisconsin Archival Series 18/1/1–4. *Milwaukee Sentinel,* February 15, March 6, 15, 1893. *Milwaukee Journal,* June 17, 1922, in "Wisconsin Necrology," 20:75, State Historical Society of Wisconsin. Charles K. Lush,

caucuses candidates who would support repeal of the patronage system. Members read the league's demand at every ward caucus of all three parties, and, after the nominations had been made, the league asked each candidate whether he supported its program. Even the league's enemies conceded that it had forced the issue; "a majority" of candidates supported the league and all three mayoral candidates endorsed the principle. The league was so successful, in fact, that many Milwaukeeans forgot its concern with issues instead of men and urged it to endorse candidates. When Republican Koch won re-election and Republicans carried the Common Council, the league was confident of extending its victory to the state legislature, for that body had traditionally passed any measure endorsed by both the mayor and aldermen of the city.[8]

The league soon learned that a politician's love for his patronage was greater than for any campaign promise. Barely a month after the election the Common Council refused to pass a resolution urging the legislature to enact civil service reform, and the aldermen were unimpressed by the league's mass protest meeting of 400 Milwaukeeans.[9] In August the Common Council once again refused to pass the resolution and, in addition, directed the city health commissioner to name all Democrats on his staff so they could be replaced by Republicans. Amid cheers from the league, Mayor Koch vetoed this ordinance aimed at the health commissioner.[10] Over the next several months the aldermen refused to pass the resolution that would be needed to direct the state legislators to support civil service reform. By early December, with the legislature to convene in a month, the league had become angry and desperate. It blasted the "effrontery" of the aldermen "in opposing a great public measure when drunk with the wine of partisan politics and infatuated with the doubtful glories of machine tyranny." The league held protest meetings in all parts of the city in hopes of igniting a popular brushfire that legislators, if not aldermen, would heed. When the Common Council still refused to endorse the civil service resolutions, the league began to bring

The Autocrats: A Novel (New York: Doubleday, Page, 1901), 259. Milwaukee Catholic Citizen, March 17, 1894.

8. Milwaukee Sentinel, February 9, March 13, 30, 1894. National League, First Meeting, 1895, 195–96. 2nd Good City Conference, 1894, 121–22. Milwaukee Daily News, March 6, 24, 30, 31, 1894.

9. Milwaukee Daily News, May 5, 1894.

10. Milwaukee Sentinel, August 17, 30, 1894.

direct pressure on legislators. It repeatedly sent delegations to Madison, and its leading members testified before committees of the legislature. To support the lobbying campaign the league sponsored a petition drive among all segments of Milwaukee society. Mayor Koch signed the first petition, and he was followed by two German *Turnvereine,* many leading Populists, bankers like F. G. Bigelow and John Johnston, merchants like A. W. Rich, Cassius M. Paine, and Edward P. Bacon, and doctors like Lewis Sherman. The 1,325 signatures showed that the league had won broad support for its bill. Impressed, Gov. William H. Upham endorsed the Milwaukee civil service bill in his inaugural speech.[11]

Probably the most important petition was the one signed by Henry C. Payne, the man who pulled the strings of city and state Republican politics. Payne believed that the basic function of the elected politician was to make policy—preferably favorable to Payne's corporations—and policy interested him more than did patronage. He believed that he might even be able to tighten his hold over the aldermen if the city spoils were removed, because his corporations could then provide jobs for faithful party workers. Payne knew what the ward heelers did not, that Horace Rublee was right when he declared that "unless these petty schemes for demoralizing the public service are discontinued, the people, at their first opportunity, will smash the machine." The league had captured public opinion in Milwaukee by exposing the aldermen's greedy quest for the spoils of office. Payne's best stratagem was to concede the lesser point of patronage—even to champion civil service reform—in order to retain the more important fact of Republican ascendancy. Thus, the legislator who promoted the league's bill most vigorously was Sen. William H. Austin, a corporation lawyer and close associate of Payne in the top echelons of the Milwaukee Republican machine.[12]

The newspapers considered the 1895 law a major victory for the league, even if the reformers had needed Payne's assistance. The league had secured its pet bill over the opposition of the aldermen, "a circumstance never known before, so far as I am

11. *Ibid.,* December 6, 1894, January 14, February 2, 1895. *State Journal,* January 26, 1895. *National League,* First Meeting, 1895, 195–98. Wisconsin, *Senate Journal,* 1895, 234, 275, 276–77, 312. *Milwaukee Daily News,* March 22, April 11, 1895.

12. *Senate Journal,* 1895, 179, 279, 497. *Milwaukee Sentinel,* August 17, 1894.

aware in the history of Milwaukee legislation," said Butler. On July 1, 1895, nearly every employee of the Milwaukee city government came under the control of the new City Service Commission.[13] The league perfected the workings of civil service reform in 1897 when it won laws that prohibited parties from soliciting civil servants for campaign contributions and that extended civil service reform to the employees of Milwaukee County.[14]

At the same time that it was promoting civil service reform in the state legislature the league was active in local elections. When politicians betrayed their promises after the 1894 elections, the league modified its strategy for 1896. Four months before the election its members created Good Government Clubs in each ward, governed by committees that included one man from each party and intended to recruit candidates for the Common Council who were "unqualified champions of measures that lead to permanent reform" and not "mortgaged body and soul to the mere politician." The clubs then promoted their candidates at the caucuses of the three parties and sometimes endorsed the best of the aldermanic nominees. The upper-class seventh ward and the lower-middle-class and German sixteenth and nineteenth wards generated the most activity among the clubs. Although Rublee called it "injudicious and arrogant" for the league to dictate its wishes to the ward caucuses, the league was pleased with the results. In the campaign that followed, the Democrats ran on national issues while the Republicans, styling themselves "the Supreme Good Government club," devoted their campaign to league issues. The Republicans won, proving to the league, at least, that parties could win elections when they confined their campaigns to local issues. Even the grumpy Rublee conceded that the results offered "good reason for gratification to all advocates of better municipal government."[15]

In addition to its fights for civil service laws and nonpartisan elections, the Milwaukee Municipal League continued to oppose any measures that would raise the city's taxes. Perhaps its

13. *Milwaukee Sentinel*, April 21, July 1, August 1, 1895. *National League*, First Meeting, 1895, 196–98. Wisconsin, *Laws* (1895), chap. 313.
14. *Milwaukee Sentinel*, February 11, September 13, 1896, April 29, 1897. Wisconsin, *Laws* (1897), chaps. 218 and 342.
15. *Milwaukee Sentinel*, December 14, 1895, February 11, 13, March 4, 17, 25, April 4, 8, 1896. *Milwaukee Daily News*, February 13, March 13, 22, April 3, 1896. Clinton Rogers Woodruff, "The Advance of the Movement for Municipal Reform," *Good City Conference*, Indianapolis, 1898, 104–5.

most strenuous battle came in 1897 when the Common Council asked the legislature to raise Milwaukee's tax rate from 14 to 16 mills. The league's mass protest meeting was one of the most successful in its history, and it appointed a delegation of fifty representative Milwaukeeans to lobby in Madison against the increase in the mill rate. These retrenchment advocates succeeded, and the mill rate remained unchanged.[16]

Between 1895 and 1897 the league was equally alert for any municipal expenditures that seemed extravagant or corrupt. It blocked the county board's purchase of a stone quarry "at a price many times too high" and prevented a "hideous and needlessly expensive" alteration of the courthouse.[17] More significant were the protest meetings it organized in 1897 to blast aldermen for purchasing an expensive and unwanted piece of real estate as a site for a school. Rallying support from the Republican *Sentinel* and the Populist *Daily News,* which for once did not attack the league for its preoccupation with high taxes, the reformers persuaded Mayor William Rauschenberger to veto acquisition of the unwanted school site.[18]

The league persistently attacked the aldermen whenever they substituted partisanship for business principles in the operations of city government. In 1894 it unsuccessfully protested the Republicans' dismissal of a competent Democratic public works commissioner and persuaded Mayor Koch to veto an ordinance that would have turned the city health office into a patronage trough.[19] In 1895 it lambasted aldermen for impeaching the health commissioner, Walter Kempster, who refused to accede to Republican patronage demands.[20]

The Milwaukee Municipal League was one of the nation's most successful municipal reform organizations even before it turned its attention to local corporations. As early as 1895, following the victory for civil service reform, the National Municipal League announced that Milwaukeeans "have perhaps

16. *Milwaukee Sentinel,* February 18, 21, June 3, 1897. *Milwaukee Daily News,* February 17, 1897. *Proceedings of the Louisville Conference for Good City Government* (Philadelphia: National Municipal League, 1897), 54–55, hereinafter cited as *Good City Conference,* Louisville, 1897.

17. *Milwaukee Sentinel,* February 12, 1896. *Milwaukee Daily News,* April 3, 1896.

18. *Milwaukee Daily News,* March 2, 1897. *Milwaukee Sentinel,* March 3, 16, 1897.

19. *Milwaukee Sentinel,* May 5, August 30, 1894.

20. *Ibid.,* February 22, 1895. The state supreme court ultimately ruled that the aldermen had acted unconstitutionally.

met with more success during the past year than . . . any other single reform organization."[21] The root of the league's success was its ability to isolate partisan politicians from the rest of the community, from businessmen, *Turnvereine,* clergymen, and others who otherwise might have led the reform drive. Focusing on the system instead of personalities, the league waited until the politicians made some obvious patronage maneuver and then, when the whole community was aroused, it called protest meetings that drew a large constituency to demand fundamental changes. Had Milwaukee's politicians been more subtle in their methods or more responsive to community sentiment, the league would probably have failed. But, as Butler said, "the recent conduct of the spoilsmen," played a major part in the league's effectiveness.[22]

II

The favorable reputation of the Milwaukee Municipal League was based even more solidly on its state-wide than on its local activities. Successful at home, the league was soon able to organize effectively the mugwump movements that were emerging all over the state. The decision to extend its activities beyond the city's limits was a simple matter of self-interest. The longer the league's members studied Milwaukee's problems, the more they became convinced that fundamental changes required action at Madison, not Milwaukee. In this era before home rule a legislator from Superior, over 400 miles distant, could vote as effectively on Milwaukee's business as a legislator from the city. The Milwaukee Municipal League, its members understood, must become the first state-wide political reform organization, and its constituents must include all Wisconsin voters.

The league's initial plans for a state-wide movement stemmed from its attempts to resolve local problems in Milwaukee. When the Common Council in the fall of 1894 refused to endorse the extension of civil service reform—a traditional prerequisite for action by the legislature—the angry league members had to overcome this opposition at home by finding support from the rest of the state. They needed some way to promote and direct

21. Clinton R. Woodruff, "The Progress of Municipal Reform, 1894–1895," *National League,* First Meeting, 1895, 309.
22. *Ibid.,* 194–95.

mugwump sentiment in the state's smaller cities. The league turned to its friend, Professor Charles Noble Gregory of the University of Wisconsin's School of Law, who had written its civil service bill and was now promoting a corrupt practices bill, which the league now added to its legislative demands. As part of the emphasis on throwing "such checks and balances about the machinery of government that all who are concerned in it are removed from serious temptation on every side," the bill would deprive politicians of their chance to trade drinks or money for votes and would thereby help to purify the climate of local elections.[23]

This sudden sponsorship of corrupt practices legislation was to encourage other reformers to look to the Milwaukee league for leadership and in turn to support its civil service program. The league members had several reasons to buttress their faith that this proposal would be popular. First, the idea of reporting campaign expenses, while not enacted by any state until 1890, when New York had taken the lead, was neither new nor radical; a quarter of a century earlier Horace Rublee, as chairman of the Republican State Central Committee, had published reports of the party's income and expenditures.[24] Second, the financial panic spurred interest in Gregory's crusade to end the purchase of political offices. Finally, as La Crosse's John J. Esch said, "The theory of reform was in the air, and the end had not been reached" with earlier secret ballot laws. A corrupt practices act was an obvious second step in the fight for a pure ballot and the adjustment of voting practices in an urban society.[25]

At any rate, the Milwaukee league assumed leadership of the state's municipal reformers in November of 1894 when it sent hundreds of circulars to influential citizens in every Wisconsin community, seeking support in a united campaign in the 1895 legislature for a corrupt practices act, for the application of civil service reform to fire and police departments in smaller cities, and, most importantly, for the extension of civil service regulation to all city employees in Milwaukee. The league soon dis-

23. *Ibid.*, 196. Charles Noble Gregory, *The Corrupt Use of Money in Politics and Laws for Its Prevention* (Madison: Historical and Political Science Association of the University of Wisconsin, 1893). *Milwaukee Sentinel,* December 16, 1894, January 14, February 2, 1895.

24. Gregory, *Corrupt Use of Money*, 12. George L. Fox, "Corrupt Practices and Election Laws in the United States Since 1890," *Proceedings of the American Political Science Association,* 2 (1906), 171–86.

25. *Milwaukee Sentinel,* March 15, 1895.

covered that mugwumpery was more popular than it had imagined. Reformers in cities like Ashland, Superior, Madison, Appleton, La Crosse, Racine, Oshkosh, and Beloit were organizing their own clubs and eagerly responded to the Milwaukeeans' overtures. Editors joined the *Appleton Post* in urging their readers to develop local support for the Milwaukee league's proposal and to join the Milwaukeeans' lobby. Beginning in January the league fed favorable replies to a sympathetic Rublee, who in turn printed them. The league also sent representatives wherever reformers wanted to learn how to organize clubs.[26]

By February 1, 1895, President Butler reported that "we have not only the city, but the whole state behind us." He had received "the most earnest and intelligent endorsement of our proposed measures of relief" from "the leading men" of forty-two Wisconsin cities.[27] The circular had not only won statewide support for the Milwaukee league's position as leader in defining the issues, but it had encouraged citizens elsewhere to organize reform groups. At Ashland and Superior in the north, at Beloit, Racine, and Madison in the south, at Appleton in the east and La Crosse in the west municipal leagues sprouted; the spring of 1895 was the high point of Wisconsin mugwumpery. While the Milwaukee league's subsequent claim of full credit for the creation of the new clubs was much too extravagant, Milwaukeeans clearly helped spark them and directed the statewide lobbying campaign.[28]

The league and its new allies set out to convert the legislature. From the beginning they believed that their only hope to change the politicians' traditional practices was to create an aroused public opinion. They were trying to build a new political style in which mass pressure—protest meetings, petition campaigns, newspapers—would break through the old political practices of patronage, caucuses, and established partisan leadership. They could counter their lack of experience and ability in traditional political techniques with their abilities in mobilizing public opinion and persuade politicians that their

26. *Ibid.*, November 16, 1894, January 14, February 2, 1895. *State Journal*, January 26, 1895. *Appleton Weekly Post*, January 17, 1895. *National League*, First Meeting, 1895, 195–98. *Milwaukee Daily News*, February 1, 1895.

27. *Milwaukee Daily News*, February 1, 1895.

28. *Milwaukee Sentinel*, May 19, 1895. *National League*, First Meeting, 1895, 195–98, 309.

constituents were now interested in scrutinizing and purifying the electoral and legislative process.

The first step in the campaign of mass pressure was to bury the legislature under an avalanche of petitions. More than 2,600 citizens in twenty cities signed petitions to the Senate alone, accounting for more than one-seventh of all the petitions received by that body at its 1895 session. They came from Wisconsinites of all backgrounds and from such enemies of Demon Rum as Beloit's Second Congregational Church and such enemies of prohibition as two Milwaukee *Turnvereine*.[29]

The second step was to mobilize the press. Many editors warned their legislators that the sudden creation of civic federations reflected the mounting disgust with the corruption that surrounded the polls. The *Sentinel* found "a well-defined opinion that money should not play the part that it does in elections," and the *Appleton Post* declared that "the unlimited use of money in elections and the corrupt results which inevitably follow, is undoubtedly the greatest evil in our politics." Editors at Madison, Superior, Waukesha, Fond du Lac, Hudson, Beloit, and other cities informed their legislators of the popular demand for a corrupt practices act. Some editors quoted particular politicians to remind legislators that it was in their own interest to be spared the increasingly expensive costs of elections. Morality and self-interest, declared editors, demanded that legislators support the corrupt practices bill.[30]

The legislative battle over the corrupt practices act opened the ideological split that was to splinter the Republican party in the state. Where the machine and Payne had assisted the reformers earlier by nominating Koch and supporting civil service reform, they now adamantly opposed the corrupt practices bill. Payne declared that "the law is too radical." He probably did not want voters, especially in Milwaukee, to know how much money certain corporations had contributed to the party. Ranged against Payne in 1895 were Republican reformers like Senators Thomas B. Mills of Superior, James H. Stout of Menomonie, and James J. McGillivray of Black River Falls,

29. *Senate Journal*, 1895, 158, 234, 273–79, 305, 312, 361, 373, 374, 398–99, 423, 445, 565.

30. *Milwaukee Sentinel*, February 2, 22, March 15, 18, 19, 23, 1895. *State Journal*, January 21, February 27, 1895. *Appleton Weekly Post*, November 29, 1894, February 21, April 11, 1895. Wisconsin, *Senate Bills*, 1895, 60S. Nils P. Haugen, *Pioneer and Political Reminiscences* (Madison: State Historical Society of Wisconsin, ca. 1930), 110.

and Assemblyman Albert R. Hall of Dunn County. More issue-oriented than men like Payne, they were popular enough not to need the machine's support, and disclosure of how they spent money in their elections could not hurt them.

The differences in the styles of these two political approaches could be observed in the hearings on the bill. Butler led several delegations of reformers in public appearances before legislative committees. Opponents of the bill said nothing in public hearings; they practiced the old politics, which was not concerned with public opinion. Most legislators were committed to neither the machine nor the reformers in this highly charged and bitterly contested battle and apparently voted on the basis of how the bill would affect their own elections. The legislature eventually passed a compromise law that provided no enforcement machinery; strong advocates of the Milwaukee league's bill voted against it.[31]

Passage of the compromise measure disappointed the reformers bitterly. They were less disturbed by the defeat of the bill that would have brought civil service reform to police and fire departments in smaller cities. Sensing that popular opinion outside Milwaukee was more receptive to a corrupt practices act, which only politicians opposed, than to civil service reform for police departments, toward which voters were more ambivalent, the Milwaukee league largely ignored this bill. The league hoped that out-state legislators would be more willing to pass the Milwaukee civil service law if their own spoils were left untouched. With the Milwaukeeans on the sidelines, the main support for the bill came from such mugwump groups as the Superior Taxpayers' League and from police chiefs in Oshkosh, La Crosse, Sheboygan, and Racine who wanted continuity and competence in their expanding departments. Unlike the fight over the corrupt practices bill, where opponents dared not speak without appearing to support corruption in public office, the debate over the civil service bill drew round denunciations. Officeholders, particularly sheriffs in the northern counties, attacked it, and at scattered mass meetings the civil service reform bill was charged with depriving voters of control over

---

31. *Milwaukee Sentinel,* March 3, 12, 19, April 16, 18, 1895. *Milwaukee Daily News,* March 15, April 6, 1895. *Appleton Weekly Post,* April 25, 1895.

their local policemen. Feeling no coordinated pressure from reformers, the legislators killed the bill.[32]

The 1895 legislature hardened the preconceptions of the Milwaukee league and its new allies. Politicians would surrender the tools of their trade—money and patronage—only when they could not escape the wrath of public opinion. Led by the league, the reformers began almost immediately after the legislature adjourned to build a broader foundation for public support in the 1897 legislative session. John A. Butler and Charles N. Gregory lectured on the need for a corrupt practices act to any discussion club or woman's club that would invite them.[33] They fed the columns of such sympathetic papers as the *Milwaukee Sentinel* and *Superior Evening Telegram* with descriptions of the successful operation of Missouri's 1893 act, on which their bill was patterned.[34]

Even more important were the state-wide reform conferences that the Milwaukee league began to sponsor in December of 1895. Speakers at the first conference came from "almost every large city," and they demanded that the 1897 legislature enact the unfinished portion of the league's 1895 program. By this point it was clear the Milwaukee league was shaping Wisconsin mugwumpery on the state level.[35]

The strategy was the one used by the league in its 1894 civil service fight with the aldermen. The basic idea was to commit politicians publicly to the cause and then, if they violated their pledges, to isolate them from public support. Butler illustrated this faith in publicity a few months after the defeat in 1895 of the corrupt practices bill when he announced: "We have placed the legislature on record as a foe to popular government and the earnest wishes of the people."[36] Demanding the selection of

32. *Superior Evening Telegram,* March 7, 1895. *Superior Leader,* March 3, 1895. *State Journal,* February 28, 1895. Wisconsin, Legislative Petitions 453A and 446A, 1895 Legislature, Box 57, Wisconsin State Archival Series 2/3/1/5–7. Kendall Birr, "Social Ideas of Superior Business Men, 1880–1898" (M.S. thesis, University of Wisconsin, 1948), 191–92. *Milwaukee Daily News,* March 6, 1895.

33. *State Journal,* May 11, 1895. Madison Literary Club, Record Book, 2:114–15, Manuscripts Division, State Historical Society of Wisconsin. 1895–1896 program of Milwaukee Social Economics Club, Milwaukee County Historical Society.

34. *Milwaukee Sentinel,* February 23, 1895. *Superior Evening Telegram,* March 6, 1897.

35. *Milwaukee Sentinel,* December 28, 1895. *Milwaukee Daily News,* December 28, 1895.

36. *National League,* First Meeting, 1895, 196–98.

candidates "who are above a mere electioneering pledge," the league in 1896 asked all candidates to state publicly whether they would support a corrupt practices act in 1897. The members felt that their publicity campaign was succeeding when William A. Fricke, secretary of the Milwaukee County Republican Committee, voluntarily published an account of the party's expenditures in 1896.[37] In its home base the league had forced politicians to make specific pledges, and Fricke's action encouraged the belief that politicians were now sensitive to the type of outcry that greeted the betrayal of pledges by the faithless Milwaukee aldermen in 1894 and the inconstant legislators in 1895.

By 1897 the reformers had secured the nearly unanimous backing of the state's editors. Such support was crucial if they were to effectively threaten the politicians with isolation for defiance of their wishes. The skepticism toward reformers, which had led editors before the panic to attack advocates of change, began to disappear during the depression. The editors felt acutely the sting of high taxes that reformers blamed on partisan politicians. Such reform leaders as Butler, banker John Johnston, or Edward P. Bacon, former president of the Milwaukee Chamber of Commerce, were obviously not "impractical" or "cranks" and could not be dismissed as easily as the pre-depression reformers. Many editors, in addition, were awed by the league's accomplishments and by the support the league's program received from prominent men throughout the state. They began to sense that politicians who defied the mugwumps would weaken the party ticket. Whatever the cause, the state's editors by 1895 or 1896 argued that the alienated people—the cranks, one might say—were the politicians, not the reformers. The politicians were the outcasts. Edgar T. Wheelock, whose *Wausau Record* had opposed all reformers before the panic, reflected this conversion when he declared late in 1895 that "there are too many professional politicians for the good of the parties."[38] By 1897 the Madison *State Journal,* long haunted by the specter of crank reformers, demonstrated the results of the league's efforts to turn public opinion against the politicians when it warned incoming legislators: "The people want reform,

37. *Milwaukee Sentinel,* December 14, 1895, February 11, 13, March 4, 17, 25, April 4, 18, 22, 1896. *Good City Conference,* Indianapolis, 1898, 104–5.

38. Quoted in *Milwaukee Sentinel,* November 27, 1895.

and they want it to be thorough, practical and efficient. They do not want promises made to the ear, and broken to the hope. They want the too free use of money in politics . . . prohibited by stringent law."[39] When Sen. William H. Austin, spokesman for the Milwaukee machine, tried to bury the corrupt practices bill in 1897 by rekindling old prejudices against reformers, the *Sentinel* rebuked him: "There are thousands of people in Wisconsin who favor the passage of this measure and not merely 'a half dozen men with heads full of theories,' " as Austin had charged.[40] By the time the legislature convened in 1897, Butler could accurately boast, as he had prematurely in late 1895, that the Milwaukee league was "in possession of the public opinion, not only of the city, but of the state at large."[41] Reformers and editors, it became clear, would hold legislators responsible for the passage of the league's program.

The league developed a more systematic lobby for the 1897 session. Its leaders met frequently with such legislative reformers as Senators Stout and Julius E. Roehr of Milwaukee and Assemblymen William A. Jones of Mineral Point and Herman C. Whipperman of Grand Rapids. They testified before committees and urged out-state mugwumps to bring pressure to bear on their representatives. Senator Roehr and the editors reminded legislators that Milwaukee Republicans had pledged in their platform to enact a corrupt practices act and that the fate of the party depended on its willingness to fulfill its promises. The long fight further intensified the polarization of Republicans between the reformers and the Payne machine. As a result, the league emerged from the fray with a weakened act. While it was "relatively rudimentary," according to a national observer, it embodied the reformers' main demand that campaign receipts and expenditures be reported.[42]

The legislators most friendly to the bill were the urban Republicans toward whom the league and its allies had aimed their two-year campaign. Of the twelve senators living in cities

39. *State Journal,* January 28, 1897.
40. *Milwaukee Sentinel,* April 10, 1897.
41. *National League,* First Meeting, 1895, 196–98.
42. *Milwaukee Sentinel,* April 10, 21, 1897. *State Journal,* January 28, April 8, 1897. *Superior Evening Telegram,* April 6, 1897. Wisconsin, *General Assembly Journal,* 1897, 1225–26. Wisconsin, *Senate Journal,* 1897, 795, 985. Wisconsin, *Laws* (1897), chap. 358. E. Dana Durand, "Political and Municipal Legislation in 1897," *Annals of the American Academy of Political and Social Science,* 11 (March 1898), 43.

of over 10,000 inhabitants, nine favored the strong bill while only three wanted a weak one; of the twelve senators from communities of less than 10,000, five favored a strong bill and seven wanted a weak one; of the five small-town advocates of pure elections, four had previously developed such hatred of the Payne machine that they would have supported the bill even without a state-wide campaign. In addition, the league and its allies showed their ability to mold public opinion on this issue in the next election, when three times as many advocates of the strong bill were re-elected as were its opponents.[43] Not surprisingly, the machine was strongest in those areas most remote from the reformers and weakest among urban Republicans who were most affected by the league's campaign.

The Milwaukee league's campaign was so effective that the legislature also enacted the other 1895 demand—civil service reform for police and fire departments outside Milwaukee. The 1897 fight was significantly different from what it had been in 1895 as a result of the actions of reformers. In both years office-holders and doctrinaire democrats opposed civil service, but in 1897 the reformers, guided by the league, could portray it as a needed reform and could picture its enemies as mere politicians—an argument made meaningful by the opposition of politicians to a corrupt practices act. To oppose the bill would be to run the risk of losing public opinion again. Politicians of all persuasions had come to respect the league's abilities.[44]

III

The Milwaukee Municipal League was the jewel of municipal reform in Wisconsin. By the influence of its members, the importance of its city in the state's life, the relevance of its proposals to the needs of cities in a depressed economy, and the energy and brilliance of its state-wide campaigns, the league had overcome some of the seemingly impossible obstacles that stood in the way of state-wide reform. Between 1894 and 1897 it had created a favorable climate in the press for reform, developed a state-wide program, built a movement where before there had been only individual interest, and, above all, severed public opinion from the politicians. The Chicago Civic Federation

43. See *Senate Journal,* 1897, 751, 795, 985, for roll calls.
44. *Milwaukee Sentinel,* December 28, 1895, September 13, 1896, April 22, 1897. *Appleton Weekly Post,* February 20, 1896.

copied the Milwaukee league's successful strategy in its campaigns for civil service reform.[45] The secretary of the National Municipal League repeatedly credited the Milwaukee league with more successes than most other mugwump groups.[46] In 1897 the national league paid the Milwaukeeans further tribute by electing John A. Butler to its executive committee.[47]

The Milwaukee league deserved these plaudits. It had molded Wisconsin mugwumpery into a concerted, state-wide movement at a time when mugwumpery in other states had supported only a series of scattered, local campaigns. In 1897, however, at the peak of its success, with major victories over the patronage system and corruption at the polls to its credit, the Milwaukee league began to shift its ground. As municipal reformers discovered new evils at the roots of urban problems, they began to alter their programs until, by 1899, the mugwump thrust was no longer recognizable. Since the experiences that led the league down new paths would be repeated in most communities, reformers would again follow the Milwaukeeans.

45. *Milwaukee Sentinel,* December 27, 1894.
46. For examples, see Woodruff, "Progress of Municipal Reform," 309. Woodruff, "The Progress of Municipal Reform," in *Good City Conference,* Louisville, 1897, 54–55.
47. *Good City Conference,* Louisville, 1897, 6. John G. Gregory, *History of Milwaukee, Wisconsin* (Chicago: S. J. Clarke Publishing Co., 1931), 4:171.

A casual visitor to Ashland and Superior in the mid-1890s would have been struck by the social and economic similarities of the two cities. Stimulated by the mining boom that hit the Lake Superior region in the 1880s, both had exploded from small villages in 1880 to important manufacturing and shipping cities. As frontier boom towns, both experienced the wild, schizophrenic swings between exaggerated lawlessness and exaggerated respectability. Their phenomenal growth had infected both with an especially virulent form of the urban promotion spirit in the years before the panic and, as a result, the residents of both cities were among the most heavily taxed in the state. Although Superior's 1895 population of 26,168 made it twice as large as its neighbor fifty miles to the east, the people who settled there were remarkably similar to Ashlanders; about three-fifths were native-born, and the predominant immigrant group was Scandinavian. Further, both cities generally returned Republican majorities in national elections.[1]

If demographic, social, economic, partisan, or geographic character determine patterns of municipal reform, no two Wisconsin cities should have been more alike than Ashland and Superior. In reality, however, Ashland and Superior developed strikingly different reform movements and political moods. Mugwumpery persisted as the dominant political mood of Ashland into the twentieth century. The issues in local elections and city council debates never strayed far from retrenchment and nonpartisanship. While similar concerns dominated Superior politics until 1895, that city, unable to sustain mugwumpery beyond 1896, moved early toward progressivism. By 1896 politics in Superior pivoted on issues of popular control over local corporations, equalization of the tax burden, and new devices to restrict the activities of bosses within the major parties. A comparison of the patterns of reform in these two cities reveals the forces and experiences that sustained the mugwump and progressive impulses.

1. *Ashland Weekly Press,* January 12, 1895. *Pen and Sunlight Sketches of Duluth, Superior, and Ashland* (Chicago: Phoenix, 1892). *Blue Book, 1899,* 258–59, 271. *Census Enumeration . . . of the State of Wisconsin, 1895,* 60–61, 71.

I

During the first two years of the depression Ashland experienced a wide variety of sporadic reform movements. Vice crusaders continued to press city officials to enforce blue laws in this wild boom town and continued to achieve little permanent success.[2] Other reformers tried to force the Ashland Water Company to provide healthful water to local residents, but in 1895 the quality of the drinking water was steadily deteriorating and the company had refused to pay taxes.[3] A third group, heirs of the 1890 movement, were doctrinaire champions of nonpartisan local government who by 1895 could only lament the continuing reign of partisan politicians.[4]

The reason that these early reformers had failed to make any major impact on conditions in their city was that they had ignored the fundamental problem created by the depression: the unbearable tax burden. Not only had Ashland been extravagant in its civic improvements in the boom days before the panic—a problem that other Wisconsin cities had begun to attack with retrenchment campaigns in 1893—but also a large number of wealthy citizens had refused to pay their taxes after 1893. Indeed, so many rich Ashlanders had hired lawyers to set aside their assessments that, in 1894, taxes were paid on only 57 per cent of the city's taxable property.

Because Ashland's wealthiest citizens were the most notorious for their tax-evasion, the issue of high taxation had a particularly democratic appeal.[5] Infuriated by the failure of city officials to relieve their tax burden, Ashlanders from all walks of life came together in February of 1895 to form the Ashland Civic Federation, destined to become the most democratic and successful of the many local reform groups formed throughout Wisconsin in 1895. The new Civic Federation elected as president Mrs. E. E. Vaughn, a wealthy and philanthropic widow who typified the New Woman, and it chose a longshoreman, a

2. *Ashland Weekly Press,* January 5, 1895. *Ashland Daily News,* January 5, 1895.

3. *Ashland Daily News,* January 9, February 19, 21, 1895. *Ashland Weekly Press,* January 19, April 13, 20, 1895. "The Ashland Water Pollution Case," *Engineering Record,* 39 (December 14, 1898), 67–68.

4. *Ashland Weekly Press,* January 12, 26, 1895. *Ashland Daily News,* February 9, 1895.

5. *Ashland Daily News,* January 18, February 6, 13, 1895. *Ashland Weekly Press,* January 26, March 16, 1895.

lawyer, the wife of a building contractor, and a traveling salesman as vice-presidents. The group's secretary, Jessie Haggerty, was another typical New Woman who led the Ashland WCTU along charitable and feminist paths. The federation's governing Committee of Forty-Five included, among others, eleven laborers, three of them unskilled, seven small merchants, six clerks and salesmen, three lawyers, three doctors, three women, two manufacturers, two bankers, one railroad superintendent, and one Swedish Lutheran minister.[6] Reflecting its broad base and the popularity of economy-minded mugwumpery, the group's constitution declared its support for enforcement of blue laws, nonpartisan local elections, civil service reform, government by "the best men," and, above all, tax relief.[7]

While most members believed that electing a nonpartisan ticket in 1895 was the best means to achieve economical government, they represented such a broad constituency that they were unable to agree on campaign strategy and candidates. When only the Populists showed any interest in the project, the federation decided to wait until after the elections before launching its reform campaigns.[8] From the debate that developed over the group's participation in the election it was clear that its reform campaigns would need to appeal to the wide variety of members.

Following the election, Mayor C. M. Everett McClintock soon committed enough sins to reunite the federation's members and to rekindle their zeal. A staunch member of the Baptist church, former vice crusader, notorious nativist, and tax dodger, McClintock emerged almost immediately after assuming office as the worst type of partisan politician. He granted immunity to all saloonkeepers, prostitutes, and gamblers who had contributed to his campaign fund, and he retained only those policemen and street workers who donated five dollars or more. He ignored the water company's abuses, and, finally, he increased the tax burden by creating city jobs for loyal Republi-

6. *Ashland Weekly Press,* January 12, February 16, 23, April 27, June 8, July 13, 1895. *Ashland Daily News,* March 10, May 31, 1895, January 8, 1896. *Ashland City Directory, 1895.*

7. *Ashland Daily News,* February 9, 16, 19, 1895. *Ashland Weekly Press,* February 16, 1895.

8. *Ashland Daily News,* March 9, 10, 12, 14, 26, 28, 30, 1895. *Ashland Weekly Press,* March 9, 16, April 6, 1895. David P. Thelen, "The Social and Political Origins of Wisconsin Progressivism, 1885–1900" (Ph.D. diss., University of Wisconsin, 1967), 101–3.

cans while failing to collect any taxes from the tax dodgers. If a mugwump-minded Ashlander had any doubts about the need for action, Mayor McClintock soon dispelled them.[9]

In June the federation struck the McClintock administration on several fronts. To lower their taxes, reformers enjoined the city from hiring unneeded clerks for the offices of the city attorney and city clerk and threatened to close the twenty-two saloons that the mayor had permitted to operate although they had not paid their $500 license fees. In an appeal to more traditional mugwumps, the federation swore out warrants against two "notorious houses in the hollow" and drove the prostitutes out of town.[10] By August the federation was closing in on the mayor himself. When one of the raids revealed Police Chief John Boyd in bed with a prostitute (on the pretense of fulfilling McClintock's orders to regulate the brothels), the editor of the Republican paper joined the reformers. After appointing a committee to manage impeachment proceedings against McClintock, the federation charged him with extorting money from city employees, "oppressing" a policeman who provided tips to the reformers, and neglecting to enforce the blue laws. But the Ashland Common Council served as the jury, and the aldermen acquitted their boss in September. Everyone recognized that the politicians had stood by one of their own; a Superior editor who was visiting Ashland called the trial "the greatest side-splitting farce ever put on the boards." Besides its comic aspects, the trial had other merits; the aldermen's defiance of the mounting popular hatred for McClintock immeasurably enhanced the federation's growing prestige.[11]

Since the aldermen were to be unresponsive to citizen demands, the federation decided to work through the courts. While it was preparing its cases, the city's religious organizations, inspired by Theodore Roosevelt's prosecutions in New York and capitalizing on the federation's work, launched a Sunday-closing campaign. Recognizing a new weapon to discredit McClintock, the federation joined the clergymen's crusade. A

9. For examples, see *Ashland Daily News*, June 8, 14, 30, August 2, 7, 8, 10, 14–17, 28, September 4, October 4, 24, November 15, 1895. *Ashland Weekly Press*, June 8, 1895.

10. *Ashland Daily News*, June 8, 11, 30, August 8, 18, 1895. *Ashland Weekly Press*, June 8, 1895.

11. *Ashland Daily News*, August 8, 15, 16, 18, 28, September 1, 7, 11, 17, 20, 27, October 1, 1895. *Ashland Weekly Press*, August 17, 31, September 7, 14, 1895.

frightened McClintock suddenly discovered in November that he had "business" in Canada and, just before leaving Ashland, promised to enforce the Sunday-closing ordinance if the Civic Federation would pledge not to arrest him for malfeasance in office. Acting Mayor Claude Faude promptly ordered the saloons to remain open on Sunday; the federation just as promptly arrested Faude for breaking the law. No, no, pleaded Faude; he had meant that the police should arrest saloonkeepers only under the state law, not under the city ordinance: "I meant that no arrests were to be made under the city ordinance, but my grammar didn't reach far enough." His contrite attitude and conversion to more familiar forms of syntax spared Faude. The federation wanted McClintock, and when McClintock returned, he kept his pledge to the federation.[12]

However spectacular these prosecutions, the federation had intended them as tactical weapons to defeat the partisan and extravagant mayor. On November 15, 1895, the reformers reminded Ashlanders: "The primary object of the Civic Federation . . . is to prevent if possible the confiscation of property . . . through high taxation . . . which is brought about by the useless and extravagant expenditure of the city and county funds."[13] High taxes were still the city's worst evil. From August of 1895 until McClintock's retirement in March of 1896 the federation mounted a major retrenchment campaign. It secured injunctions restraining county supervisors from drawing pay for more than twenty meetings a year, blocked the city from ever hiring assistants for city officials, and annulled an ordinance that proposed spending public money on the county fair. Its members persuaded various people to cancel their bills against the city, and they used any means available to lower taxes by cutting local spending.[14]

The federation's members apparently realized that the technical and legalistic weapons they were using to attain the popular goal of lower taxes were boring to a large number of people who might prefer action on other popular issues. To retain public support for their principal program, the federation championed causes with wider appeal. At the peak of the

12. *Ashland Weekly Press,* September 14, October 26, November 9, 1895. *Ashland Daily News,* September 18, October 12, 16, 21, 23, 31, November 2, 4, 5, 9, 11, 12, 15, 1895, January 17, 1896.

13. *Ashland Daily News,* November 15, 1895.

14. *Ibid.,* August 2, 14, 15, September 4, October 4, 24, December 20, 1895, March 4, 1896.

retrenchment campaign, two of the federation's leading members won the gratitude of the city's workers by representing the striking sawmill workers in their efforts to gain concessions from the owners.[15]

The federation's most popular accomplishment was the compromise it engineered between the city and the Ashland Water Company. Ashland's reformers realized what mugwumps elsewhere learned too late: they could retain support for their goal of nonpartisan and economical government only so long as they also confronted the utilities' arrogance. The dispute that the federation now entered had roots reaching back to 1891. In the winter of 1891-1892 a series of annual and successively worse typhoid fever epidemics broke out in Ashland because the water company had refused to extend its intake mains beyond the polluted waters of Chequamegon Bay into the pure waters of Lake Superior. The company, in addition, had failed to provide sufficient pressure to extinguish major fires in 1892 and 1894, resulting in higher fire insurance rates for the city. The fight warmed up in 1894 when the State Board of Health condemned the water in Chequamegon Bay and the company refused to pay any taxes to the city. By the summer of 1895 Mayor McClintock had virtually conceded his inability to force responsible actions from the company.

At this point the federation's lawyer A. E. Dixon worked out a compromise, which the city council ratified on August 1. In exchange for the city's payment of back hydrant rentals and for excusing the company from its delinquent taxes, the company promised to extend its intake mains, to furnish water for such municipal services as flushing and fire hydrants at no cost, to resume paying taxes, and to lower its rates by 20 to 25 per cent. While the compromise brought only a temporary truce in the war, most Ashlanders were pleased that someone had finally won something from the company. They were gratified by the lower water rates, by the lower city taxes that resulted from the payment of delinquent taxes by a major withholder, from the annual savings of $7,000 on hydrant rentals, and by the new filtration plant that provided them with water pure enough to satisfy the State Board of Health for the first time in years.[16]

15. *Ashland Weekly Press,* October 19, 1895.
16. Fearing that the company's concessions would aid incumbent Republicans, Democratic politicians were the only critics of the compromise. *Ashland Daily News,* January 9, February 19, 21, August 2, 6, 11, October

The Ashland Civic Federation's activities of 1895 and 1896 set the city's political tone for the rest of the decade. Mugwumps learned that they could keep power so long as they embraced other issues that troubled their city. As the elections of 1896 approached, many reformers hoped that they could achieve more permanent results if they elected a friend as mayor. Advocating the fundamental mugwump tenet that economical government could best be achieved by nonpartisan candidates and elections, they formed the Citizens' League. The continuing popularity of this program was attested to by the men who composed the league's policymaking committee, including twelve merchants, six clerks and salesmen, five laborers, two manufacturers, one banker, one lawyer, and one minister. The league then nominated for mayor I., C. Wilmarth, long-time darling of the minority mugwumps within the city's Republican party.[17]

Sensing that the reformers had already proved the popularity of their approach, the Democrats decided to nominate an equally attractive independent businessman. On a platform pledging "the most rigid economy" of expenditures, enforcement of vice laws, and ultimate municipal ownership of utilities, they nominated Thomas Bardon. Though his long beard gave Bardon something of an otherworldly appearance, the Democratic nominee was the city's most successful businessman—president of the national bank, owner of a general store, and head of an insurance and real estate office. Charging that Ashland was nearly bankrupt, Bardon echoed the federation in blasting the "blackmailing of social evils" and the creation of needless offices "for the support of partisan parasites."[18]

Bardon's nomination flustered the mugwumps. Many believed that he would be as capable as Wilmarth and left the Citizens' League to support him openly. The remaining mugwumps, primarily Republicans, decided to vote for Wilmarth in the hope of punishing their party for its nomination of a partisan nonentity. They rejected urgent pleas from the Republican city committee that they withdraw from the race. Wil-

12, November 29, 1895, January 24, March 16, 20, 1896. *Ashland Weekly Press,* January 19, March 9, 16, 30, April 13, 20, August 8, 1895. "Ashland Pollution Case," 67–68.

17. *Ashland Daily News,* February 3, 7, 10, 15, 24, 26, 29, March 13, 30, 1896. *Ashland City Directory, 1895.*

18. *Ashland Daily News,* March 16, 23, 1896. *Ashland City Directory, 1895.*

marth's 234 votes threw the election to Bardon, who polled 49.5 per cent of the vote.[19]

Bardon's administrations followed the pattern laid out by the federation, and he was re-elected annually until 1901. Although not as rigorous as the federation had been in enforcing blue laws, Bardon did raid gambling houses and force saloonkeepers to pay their licenses.[20] He did not need to use the issue of vice, as had the federation, to embarrass the incumbent. Bardon's major crusade was for tax relief. Better than any other Wisconsin mayor, he fulfilled the mugwumps' dream of economical government. By cutting the graft from contracts, abolishing political sinecures, and making a minimum of sidewalk and street repairs, Bardon slashed McClintock's operating budget of $95,000 to $56,000 by 1898. By using the police to force propertyholders to pay their delinquent taxes and threatening to sell the property of tax dodgers, Bardon cut the delinquent tax roll from 43 per cent of the city's property in 1895 to 20 per cent in 1899.[21] As early as 1898 even the Republican editor was awed: "A few more economical administrations, and the city will see daylight through the financial fog that has so long obscured the light of day." Republicans put up only token opposition to Bardon in 1898.[22]

Bardon's re-election to a fourth term in 1899 revealed the popularity of his program of low taxes and his ability to isolate the politicians from public opinion. By 1899 Democratic politicians realized that they could get neither jobs nor contracts from Bardon, and they endorsed the Republican mayoral nominee. Reflecting the fluid state of political partisanship that Bardon had capitalized on in 1895 and nurtured as mayor, a large group of Democrats refused to follow the party regulars and nominated Bardon instead, and a large group of Republicans formed a Republicans for Bardon Club. "The head center of the opposition to Bardon is composed of a gang of office seekers," these Democratic and Republican mugwumps charged. Bardon's appeal to Republicans cut across occupational lines. Those who led the Republicans for Bardon numbered twenty

19. *Ashland Daily News,* March 25, April 2, 8, 1896.
20. *Ibid.,* May 25, June 4, 1896. *Ashland Daily Press,* March 31, April 1, 1898, March 27, 1899, January 26, 27, 1900, for examples.
21. *Ashland Weekly Press,* March 16, 1895. *Ashland Daily Press,* March 16, 25, 1899, January 8, 1900. *Ashland Daily News,* February 13, 1895, August 14, 1896.
22. *Ashland Daily Press,* March 11, 21, 22, 24, April 6, 1898.

merchants, fifteen clerks and salesmen, thirteen laborers, seven lawyers, four bankers, four manufacturers, four journalists, and one architect.[23]

Bardon knew that the best way to secure such widespread support for retrenchment and nonpartisanship was to champion the popular side in disputes with the quasi-public corporations. In 1898 he led a drive to annul the water company's franchise for its refusal to provide water and fire protection to residents in the newer parts of the city. He made the water company the main enemy again in his 1900 campaign for a fifth term. Charging that the company had violated city orders and had disobeyed the terms of its franchises, he urged the city attorney to take such drastic measures "against this company that they would know for the first time in their official existence that someone was after them." The reason that this mugwump now became the city's leading opponent of the utilities was simple: "They defy the city and citizens."[24]

The pattern of reform at Ashland was exceptional. Thomas Bardon was assisted in his successful efforts to create nonpartisan local government by the city's long tradition of weak party ties. The Ashland mugwumps—Bardon and the Civic Federation— succeeded in their primary goal of retrenchment and lower taxes because they built broad constituencies and incorporated all social groups, no matter how diverse, who held grievances about city politics. They avoided the Sunday-closing campaigns that wrecked their counterparts in other Wisconsin cities and shunned the nativist and elitist tone of earlier vice crusaders. Their emphasis on low taxes retained popular allegiance in the depression. They recognized the growing popularity of the emerging progressive attacks on wealthy tax evaders and defiant corporations. To prevent the rise of the kind of progressive politicians who were gaining support in other Wisconsin cities— and who were usually confirmed partisans and not much worried about local spending—they took the popular side of these progressive issues. Indeed, the shift in Bardon's rhetoric from a primary concern with high taxes in 1896 to an emphasis on corporate arrogance by 1900 reflected his political sagacity. Still, he was repeatedly re-elected primarily because he was remarkably successful in solving the pressing problems of taxation.

23. *Ibid.*, March 20, 24, 25, 27, 1899. *Ashland City Directory, 1897.*
24. *Ashland Daily Press,* March 9, 1898, May 10, 1900.

II

Superior's mugwumps lacked the will and the ability to build the kind of popular movement that had been so successful in Ashland and, as a result, lost control of local politics by 1895. When the panic first hit Superior, the city's leading businessmen promptly developed a retrenchment program whose narrow focus and implementation appealed to no other groups. In June of 1893, after the aldermen voted themselves a salary for the first time, the chamber of commerce called a mass meeting to appoint a committee of businessmen that would recommend to the city council the best places to slash municipal expenditures. Soon named the Superior Taxpayers' League, these business-men, who described themselves as "the best blood in the com-munity, and our most successful businessmen," had little trou-ble persuading the aldermen of the various places to use the pruning shears. This informal process of control by the business-men was formalized in 1894 when Superiorites, responding to popular demands for tax relief, elected Frank A. Woodward, president of the Superior Chamber of Commerce, as the next mayor. Woodward gave quasi-official status to the Taxpayers' League and its recommendations. In his 1895 farewell address Woodward could boast that this system of retrenchment had brought results and had allowed the city to cut its tax assess-ment from $333,000 to $216,000 and its tax rate from 2.74 per cent to 2.07 per cent. The businessmen succeeded in their re-trenchment campaigns of the depression's first two years because they had been the first to propose relief after the panic struck and because they enjoyed a privileged position in the city government.[25]

As events were to show, the businessmen had committed fatal errors in not making efforts to involve other groups in their movement or to convince any other citizens that they, too, had a stake in retrenchment. The businessmen's government had been disastrous for the politicians, unresponsive to the growing demands for stricter regulation of utilities, and boring for the majority of Superiorites who could only watch the busi-nessmen reform the city. The election of 1895 revealed the cost of exclusive pursuit of the dull, efficient mugwump programs

25. *Superior Leader,* June 13, 29, July 6, 9, 13, 1893, April 13, July 21, 1895. *Superior Evening Telegram,* June 29, July 13, 1893, March 7, 1895. *2nd Good City Conference, 1894,* 12–14.

of economy-minded businessmen. Many workers, blocked by the businessmen, decided to find relief from the utilities on their own initiative, so they formed Workingmen's Republican Clubs and seized control of the Populist party.[26] On March 8 representatives of many different groups of Superiorites held a mass meeting at which they denounced the recent proposal of the Taxpayers' League for civil service reform in the city departments.[27]

The dissatisfaction of such diverse groups failed to focus clearly, however, because it was rooted in the vague feeling that they had been denied the excitement of political participation. This widespread discontent created a political void that was soon to be filled by the most remarkable man to hold public office in Wisconsin in the 1890s. It was at the mass meeting to denounce civil service reform that Superiorites first considered turning over their city to an Episcopal priest named Charles S. Starkweather. The clergyman denounced the reform bill as a threat to democratic government and an affront by businessmen to the Populists.[28] Strange words, these, from an Episcopal clergyman.

Superior was to hear even stranger words from this man. Living in one of the city's finest houses, wearing a silk hat, smoking expensive cigars, riding around town with a Negro coachman holding the reins of his team of Kentucky thoroughbreds, Starkweather commanded attention wherever he went as "the most aristocratic man in town." But Starkweather was no elitist; in fact, he was happy only when surrounded by people. He befriended the boys in his choir and took them camping and converted a room in his Church of the Redeemer into a clubroom for the city's transients, but most of all, he loved to join the boys in a long beer at the saloons.[29]

It was natural for a man of Starkweather's temperament to ignore his clerical collar and aristocratic position, traditional symbols of a politician's enemies, and plunge into the political arena. He was elected Republican alderman in 1893 and widely

26. *Superior Evening Telegram,* March 7, 1895. *Superior Leader,* March 14, 1895. *Superior Sunday Forum,* March 31, 1895.

27. *Superior Evening Telegram,* March 9, 1895. *Superior Leader,* March 9, 1895.

28. *Superior Leader,* March 9, 1895.

29. *Milwaukee Sentinel,* July 14, 23, 1895. *Superior Sunday Forum,* March 31, 1895, April 10, 1898. *Superior Leader,* April 6, 1895. *Superior Evening Telegram,* March 14, 1895, March 1, 1897.

called "the weather cock of the council [able] to take three positions on an important question and be for it, against it, and neutral." Starkweather, in truth, possessed no political convictions. His "warm sympathies and generous impulses" were precisely that and nothing more—he loved people. Years of experience proved the accuracy of a subsequent appraisal of the man: "Vanity is the key note of his character. The shout of the mob is as music to his ears, and the applause of the gallery is wine to his palate. He cares not for what the applause is given; he is content if he be the cause. . . . He understands human nature and knows every stop and key of that wonderful instrument. . . . He is a locomotive, well built and with a full head of steam, but with no engineer to guide, nor regular track on which to run." About all that was predictable about Starkweather was that he would be wherever people were.[30]

First to convene in 1895 were the Populists, who appreciated Starkweather's tribute to them at the anti–civil service meeting. With nothing to lose they nominated him for mayor; ten days later the Democrats also chose him. He regarded these nominations as "the voice of the people," sensing that "the people" had grown tired of businessman governments. As part of his campaign of telling people only what they wanted to hear, he solemnly announced to a group of Norwegians that his own ancestry was Norwegian, and that many centuries back his name had been Starkodder. Standing in striking contrast to the dull efficiency of the businessmen, the colorful Starkweather was elected mayor by the greatest margin any Superiorite had ever won for that office.[31]

The new mayor, as might have been predicted, set out to administer the city with no regard for the political context of his election. He eagerly began appointing his friends to office, ignoring their partisan affiliations. The politicians on the Common Council felt betrayed and angry. Although they had ended the rule of nonpartisan businessmen and had beaten the Republicans, the Democratic and Populist politicians received none of the spoils. From the outset Mayor Starkweather alienated the professional politicians.[32]

More important, the mayor and the city's editors hated each

30. *Superior Sunday Forum*, April 10, 1898. See also March 31, 1895.
31. *Superior Evening Telegram*, March 14, 1895. *Superior Leader*, March 14, 24, 31, April 6, August 5, 1895.
32. *Superior Leader*, April 26, May 8, June 1, 9, 1895, for examples.

other from the beginning. When none of the editors supported his campaign, he viciously denounced them.[33] As a result, the editors—particularly those of the sensationalist *Leader* and the radical *Forum*—were poised to strike him. They wanted to turn their talents for yellow journalism, bred in Superior through intense newspaper competition, toward the city hall, which for too long had been occupied by men who offered no excitement and sold no newspapers.

The mounting tension between Starkweather on the one hand and the politicians and editors on the other created a highly charged political atmosphere. No group sensed this more acutely than the saloonkeepers and gamblers, whose existence always rested upon an accurate appraisal of local politics. When the mayor began to order them to obey the blue ordinances and pay their licenses, the merchants of vice decided to attack. They told the eager journalists that the mayor had promised to leave them alone if they would contribute to his campaign fund. The newspapers in turn told daily stories of how Starkweather was "as corrupt as damnation itself"; the *Forum* disclosed that firemen and policemen had to pay him to retain their jobs.[34] And so a major scandal began to unfold.

The saloonkeepers, yellow journalists, and partisan politicians appropriated the rhetoric of mugwumpery to accomplish their respective purposes of the nonenforcement of blue ordinances, the sale of newspapers, and the impeachment of Starkweather. Although seven aldermen urged the city to follow Chicago's example of using a grand jury for investigations into boodling, Superior's editors won their demand that the trial of Starkweather, which would hopefully produce his impeachment, be handled by his enemies—the politicians on the city council. The remaining eleven aldermen proceeded to try Starkweather for malfeasance in office. During the month of July the city was treated to a fascinating parade of witnesses uncovered by the *Leader* and *Forum*—prostitutes, gamblers, saloonkeepers, firemen, and policemen—who substantiated, in essence, the charge that the mayor and his police chief used their appointing and enforcement powers to enrich themselves. In his summation, the prosecuting attorney George C. Cooper warmed to the case:

33. See *Milwaukee Sentinel,* July 14, 1895. *Superior Leader,* June 11, 1895, for examples.
34. *Superior Leader,* April 30, May 8, 11, 22, 23, 30, June 11, 12, 13, 16, 1895. *Superior Sunday Forum,* July 7, 1895.

"The first time we knew him as a man of the world of politics," he cried, "is in a saloon kept by a colored prostitute. . . . There is no case in the history of the country . . . that has a parallel to this. There is no clergyman who would sell Sunday."

"Impeached!" screamed the *Leader*'s headline on August 2: "Superior is Purged of Her Moral Monstrosity/Justice Reigns and Octopus Starkweather Rules no Longer." Editors all over the country jested at Superior's plight; the *Minneapolis Penny Press* offered a jingle:

> Out in a Wisconsin town
> They chose a preacher for mayor
> And now they are vexed because
> The clergyman proved a preyer.[35]

Starkweather had been elected—and impeached—because Superior's more typical mugwumps were paralyzed by the inability to create programs and organizations that could surmount social barriers. Saloonkeepers, journalists, and politicians could successfully manipulate reform rhetoric because the reformers were divided into at least three camps. In the months that followed Starkweather's trial these reformers tried again to launch campaigns, but once again their internal divisions permitted saloonkeepers to undermine their goals.

Less than a month after Starkweather's impeachment, on August 25, more than 1,000 Superiorites jammed the Grand Opera House to form a Civic Federation that would give reformers a larger role in local politics. While most of the speakers agreed that Starkweather had been the victim of a sinister cabal, they could not agree on the direction for future action. Clergymen like Methodist preacher W. J. Johnson wanted the new group to punish the merchants of vice who had, after all, bribed Starkweather's officials, and they urged a frontal attack on saloonkeepers, gamblers, and prostitutes.[36] Denouncing the

35. *Superior Leader*, June 21, 26, 30, July 3, 4, 6, 7, 9–15, 19, 20, 27, August 2, 1895. *Superior Evening Telegram*, July 15, August 4, 1895. *Superior Sunday Forum*, July 7, August 11, 1895. *Milwaukee Sentinel*, July 14, 23, August 2, 1895. *Ashland Weekly Press*, August 3, 1895. Kendall Birr, "Social Ideas of Superior Business Men, 1880–1898" (M.S. thesis, University of Wisconsin, 1948), 189–91. Starkweather lost his appeal to the state supreme court. *Ashland Weekly Press*, September 28, 1895.

36. *Superior Leader*, June 21, July 5, 9, 13, August 2, 3, 5, 12–14, 20, 24, 26, 27, 31, 1895. *Superior Evening Telegram*, July 9, 10, 17, 24, August 1, 2, 12, 13, 21, 24, 26, 1895, March 13, 1896. *Superior Sunday Forum*, August 11, 1895.

vice crusaders as seekers of "cheap notoriety," in the words of a realtor, the businessmen formed a second group and demanded a return to the efficient retrenchment campaigns that had ended with Mayor Woodward's term. Spectacular movements such as vice crusades or impeachments harmed the city's reputation and were bad for business.[37] While spokesmen for the workers shared the businessmen's enthusiasm for retrenchment and their hostility toward vice crusades, this third group maintained that the local quasi-public corporations were the city's worst menace.[38]

After the meeting adjourned, the officers of the new Civic Federation hoped to keep the fragile alliance together by promoting economical government, which potentially had the largest constituency. When they persuaded the aldermen to reduce firemen's salaries by five dollars a month, their troubles began. A number of businessmen opposed the reformers' first step, charging that it would weaken the protection of their businesses against fire.[39] Before the federation could reply to this attack, they were forced to confront a more immediate challenge from the saloonkeepers. Alarmed that circumspect city officials were enforcing the Sunday-closing law, the saloonkeepers once again clothed themselves in mugwumpery and formed a Law and Order League with the announced objective of prosecuting anyone who violated the Sunday law. On the first Sunday in September they arrested streetcar employees, druggists, candy-store and cigar-store owners, newsboys, and anyone else they could find engaging in business. In retaliation, the Civic Federation collected evidence of any violations of ordinances and laws by the saloonkeepers. A few days later the enemies reached a tacit compromise. The saloonkeepers would not prosecute other businesses if they were permitted to violate the Sunday-closing law.[40]

Infuriated at the merchants of vice for having imposed their wishes on the city twice in the same summer and both times by

37. *Superior Leader,* June 16, July 23, 24, August 26, 27, 31, 1895. *Superior Sunday Forum,* July 7, August 11, 1895. *Superior Evening Telegram,* July 6, 9, 23, August 26, 1895.
38. *Superior Leader,* August 26, 27, 1895. *Superior Evening Telegram,* August 26, 1895.
39. *Superior Leader,* August 30, 31, 1895. *Superior Evening Telegram,* August 29, 1895.
40. *Superior Leader,* August 25, 27, 28, 1895. *Superior Evening Telegram,* August 24, 26, 27, 31, September 3, 4, 9, 1895.

perverting mugwump principles, the Civic Federation now directed its energies against the saloonkeepers and gamblers. Over the next few weeks the federation failed in its campaign to make the saloonkeepers pay $11,625 in delinquent license fees, but it did succeed in forcing Starkweather's successor, Albion Howe, to suppress gambling.[41] In truth, however, the federation failed to become a significant political force when it let the arrogance of the saloonkeepers divert its attention from retrenchment campaigns that might have developed a broad following. The reformers soon learned that Superiorites were confused and tired by months of controversies surrounding the saloons. They had seen editors, politicians, and saloonkeepers use reform rhetoric to impeach the beloved Starkweather and to prevent them from riding streetcars, hiring buggies, or buying cigars. When some of the city's ministers actually supported the saloonkeepers' Law and Order League,[42] Superiorites could hardly be blamed for souring on mugwumpery.

The narrow perspective of Superior's mugwumps was further demonstrated in the elections of 1896. Yearning for a return to economical government by businessmen, the Commercial Club and the Business Men's Club formed a Good Government Club, whose executive committee followed the Superior tradition of including only businessmen. The new club hoped to persuade the major parties to nominate nonpartisan businessmen. Its members soon discovered that the Populists and workers were their only potential constituents. While the Populists emphasized regulation of local corporations in their platform, they also advocated "an honest and economical administration of public affairs," and they endorsed the Good Government Club's candidates for every office except mayor.[43]

The businessmen of the Good Government Club were too conditioned by their domination of politics between 1893 and 1895 to exploit this potentially large following. In the first place, some of its members were such pure nonpartisans that they were ineffective. When the club endorsed L. J. Moss as a delegate from the seventh ward caucus to the Democratic city

41. *Superior Evening Telegram,* August 31, September 11, 17, November 20, 1895. *Superior Leader,* March 24, 1896. *Ashland Daily News,* October 10, 1895.

42. *Superior Leader,* August 27, 1895.

43. *Superior Evening Telegram,* February 26, 28, March 6, 7, 13, 14, 16, 31, 1896. *Superior Leader,* March 15, 17, 1896. *City of Superior Directory, 1896.*

convention, Moss refused to attend the convention, saying that it would violate his principles to participate in a partisan gathering. Such pristine scruples drove a number of members back to their original parties. In the second place, the Democrats tried to use the club to elect their ticket. Democratic club members called a secret meeting, endorsed Democratic mayoralty candidate Carl Wilson, and then declared it an "official" club meeting. Only 83 of the club's 522 members had been invited, and only two of them had voted for Republican candidate Martin Pattison. Enraged by the "snap" meeting and its actions, Republican club members returned to their party.[44] As a result of the splintering of the reformers, politicians paid little heed to the club. If the fate of the Civic Federation had not already established the fact, the failure of the Good Government Club finally proved that mugwumpery was dead in Superior.

The Republicans sensed the subtle shift of popular interest from mugwumpery to progressivism. Their platform ignored the favorite mugwump shibboleth of retrenchment; they reasoned that the confusion and hypocrisy of the past year had killed its appeal. Flouting the Good Government Club and nonpartisanship, the Republicans proclaimed that "the panacea for all our political and industrial evils . . . is a speedy return to republican management." Where in earlier years they would not have dared attack the businessmen, they ridiculed the club in 1896 as the "Goo Goos, the Hoo Hoos and the Boo Boos." Such rampant partisanship was, of course, precisely what the mugwumps hated most about municipal politics, but the Republicans sensed the unpopularity of the club's austere nonpartisanship.

The Republicans also knew that a growing number of voters were deeply troubled by bossism and corruption within the parties. The best way to prevent bossism, the Republicans argued, was not to abolish political parties, as the mugwumps desired, but to regulate them. As a result, the Republicans transformed their caucuses to eliminate the flagrant abuses of the bosses. Before 1896 all interested Republicans of a ward had congregated at the appointed hour, listened to the names proposed by the wardheelers, and vocally nominated the bosses' choices. The politicians knew exactly who opposed them. In 1896 the Republicans allowed anyone to place his name in contention for any office on a "ballot," and then, on caucus day,

44. *Superior Evening Telegram*, March 18, 19, April 3, 1896.

192

provided secret "ballots" to every Republican and left these "polls" open for several hours so that anyone could vote. The man with the most votes was that ward's Republican candidate.

Republicans showed their faith in regulated partisanship in other ways. Their leading speaker was state Sen. Thomas B. Mills, widely known as the champion of a corrupt practices bill that sought to prevent the corrupt use of money in caucuses and elections.[45] The party was a popular institution, and partisanship could be regulated. Recognizing these realities of politics, Republicans confronted the evils of bossism with regulation instead of abolition.

The real differences between mugwumpery and progressivism were not over such tactical problems as nonpartisanship or regulated partisanship, but over programs, and it was here the Superior Republicans showed their conversion best. Their platform revealed their acceptance of a local editor's observation: "The issues are beginning to be clearly outlined. Though the general lack of efficiency, economy and honesty in the works of city administration will be considered by the people in the coming contest, yet the prime issue will be a demand by the masses of people that corporations which have received donations of franchises from the city shall either live up to the condition of those franchises or forfeit them and that right speedily."[46] Superior Republicans saw that voters were interested less in retrenchment than in regulating the increasingly defiant corporations.

Since August of 1895 the city had been locked in battle with its two leading corporations. Much as the Ashland Water Company had done, the Superior Water, Light and Power Company had, despite repeated orders from the city, refused to supply clean water, to pay its taxes, or to lower its rates. Taxpayers resented the company's flagrant tax dodging, and the city's polluted water had caused epidemics of disease and consequent death, which forced the schools to buy bottled spring water. Superior Republicans in 1896 blasted the company in several resolutions. Republicans were equally unsympathetic to the street railway, which, since August of 1895, had defied a city order to issue free transfers from one line to another. Knowing that the city's workers were especially eager for a system of free

45. *Ibid.*, March 19, 31, 1896. *Milwaukee Sentinel*, March 12, 1895, reports the views of Mills on the corrupt practices bill.
46. *Superior Sunday Forum*, February 23, 1896.

transfers, the Republicans pledged to make the company obey the seven-month-old ordinance. Their platform summed up Superior's frustrations through the arrogance of its quasi-public corporations by demanding that "all public franchises granted by our city should be under the control and government of our city."[47] In their preference for regulated partisanship over non-partisanship, for municipal regulation and ownership of utilities over retrenchment, Superior Republicans sensed that the direction of municipal reform had shifted, with the frustrations of the city, from mugwumpery to progressivism. They swept the elections, their candidate Martin Pattison outpolling the combined vote of his Democratic and Populist opponents.[48]

The Republican rhetoric and activities in 1896 set the pattern for municipal reform at Superior for the rest of the century. Most Superiorites opposed such mugwump programs as civil service reform, retrenchment, and nonpartisanship. When reformers in other cities secured a law in 1897 that placed fire and police departments on a civil service basis, Superior's mayor and aldermen bitterly resisted. Indeed, in June of 1897, Superior had two police departments, one based on patronage and the other on civil service. Only a succession of court orders forced the mayor to obey the civil service law.[49] Superiorites tolerated the politicians' defiance of civil service reform only because their previous experiences with mugwumpery had been so bitter.

The thrust of reform was now against the quasi-public corporations. Martin Pattison became the first mayor in the city's history to force quasi-public corporations to fulfill their obligations. Not only did he force the street railway to obey part of the 1895 ordinance for free transfers, but he also made the Water, Light and Power Company lower its water rates by 20 per cent and construct a new filtration plant for pure water. Many of Superior's Republicans thought these triumphs entitled Pattison to a second term in 1897, but the utilities, and

47. *Superior Evening Telegram,* August 14, September 4, 11, October 23, 1895, March 12, 16, 18, 20, 28, April 18, 21, 1896. *Superior Leader,* August 15, 28, 1895, March 15, 1896. *Superior Sunday Forum,* July 14, 1895, February 16, 1896. Superior Trades and Labor Assembly, Minute Book, 102, 119, 143, 144, Manuscripts Division, State Historical Society of Wisconsin.

48. *Superior Evening Telegram,* August 8, 1896.

49. *Superior Leader,* April 30, May 4, 25, June 2, 3, 5, 22, July 14, 28, August 6, 10, 1897. *Milwaukee Sentinel,* August 8, 1897.

especially the water and light company, desperately wanted to defeat him. After an extraordinarily hard-fought battle, in which Pattison's friends charged that the water and light company used money liberally to sustain the machine it had created within the Superior Republican party, Pattison was defeated for renomination. Driven out of their party in search of effective regulation of utilities, Pattison's followers could not support the Republican nominee, so they looked for another candidate.[50]

That candidate was none other than Charles S. Starkweather. Defying "all the records of impudence for a parallel," Starkweather ignored the three existing parties and ran as an independent. He denounced politicians and leading citizens alike, admitted that he had extorted money in 1895, but charged that he had been the victim of a conspiracy. A typical campaign meeting began when a fife-and-drum corps met Starkweather as he alighted from a streetcar and marched ahead of him to the hall, to which two buxom young ladies clasped his arms "confidingly" and escorted him. Representing the "will of the people" that had been "defeated in the conventions," Starkweather then made his customary attacks on civil service reform. He closed each meeting by giving candy to everyone present: "Yes, candy; for they know I distribute that which does not bring ruin and devastation, starvation, degradation to their homes but that which brings happiness, and the only smiles from the lips of the wife and mother that the father has ever had during a political campaign before." Gathering 54 per cent of the vote in a three-way race, the "Old Cuss" proved anew his enormous popularity. But this time he had needed the votes of the progressive Republicans who had supported Pattison. This alliance was cemented at his victory celebration when Pattison mounted the platform not to applaud Starkweather but to denounce the Superior Water, Light and Power Company's creation of a Republican machine to ensure it against regulation by the party's progressives.[51]

Progressive Republicans and Populists set the tone for Starkweather's second administration in much the same way that

50. *Superior Evening Telegram,* March 23, 1897. *Superior Leader,* April 7, 18, May 19, 1897.

51. *Superior Evening Telegram,* March 23, April 1, 3, 5, 6, 1897. *Superior Leader,* April 1, 2, 3, 6, 7, 18, 1897. *State Journal,* April 7, 1897. *Milwaukee Sentinel,* April 7, 1897.

mugwump rhetoric had dominated his first term. For the next year the city conducted little business that was not aimed at controlling the utilities. Health Commissioner William E. Ground shocked Superiorites in May when he announced that water passing through the company's new filtration plant contained "unmistakable evidence of sewage contamination." When Mayor Starkweather replied by attacking Ground, progressives received their first indication that their support of the Old Cuss might have been misplaced. As evidence that the water was indeed polluted, a typhoid fever epidemic spread through the city, and in July the desperate Common Council annulled the company's water franchise. Starkweather vetoed the annulment resolution. Now Pattison's followers knew certainly they had erred. In February of 1898 the mayor once again vetoed an annulment resolution, but this time Superiorites were so angry that the city council overrode the veto. The aldermen began to collect evidence for quo warranto proceedings to dissolve the company's water franchise. Realizing that its existence was at stake, the company on two occasions in March secured injunctions prohibiting the city from testing whether it was providing sufficient pressure to extinguish fires. The city counterattacked. Led by the city engineer and the influential Dr. R. C. Oglivie, progressives condemned the company's lighting franchise. Arguing that Superiorites paid twice as much for lighting as residents in cities of comparable size, they persuaded the Common Council in March to advertise for bids for a municipal electric lighting plant. Dr. Oglivie sensed the prevailing mood when he warned city officials not to abandon citizens "to the tender mercies of this robber corporation (for their extortionate charges are little less than robbery)" if they sought re-election. Months of mounting frustration with corporate arrogance—which cost Superiorites dearly in disease and death, as well as high water and light rates—set the stage for the 1898 election.[52]

First to enter the ring was the irrepressible Starkweather, and the Democrats, hungry for office, nominated him. Starkweather

52. *Superior Leader,* April 18, May 19, 21, July 2, 7, 30, 1897, February 24, March 26, 1898. *Superior Evening Telegram,* December 14, 1897, January 19, 26, February 2, 16, 24, 25, March 5, 9, 16, 19, 23, 30, 1898. Superior, in fact, paid more for street lights than twenty-two other cities its size. Edward W. Bemis, "The Latest Electric Light Reports," in *Municipal Monopolies,* ed. Bemis (New York: Thomas Y. Crowell, 1899), 255.

ran a characteristically unconventional and demagogic campaign,[53] but circumstances were different this time. His failure to assess at its full strength the popular hatred of the Superior Water, Light and Power Company and his deaf ear toward his progressive Republican allies doomed him. Superiorites could not laugh at typhoid fever as they once had at Starkweather's quixotic crusades against civil service reform. His vetoes of the annulment resolutions transformed him from an unbeatable, charismatic incumbent into a merely vulnerable politician. "Now, when the city is trying to shake off the grasping tentacles of the water devil-fish," cried one editor, "this man interposes his individuality against a unanimous vote of the people who elected him. . . . It will take many a barrel of popcorn and candy to obliterate from the mind the memory of this act of treachery." Even during his impeachment proceedings in 1895 he had never heard such talk from so many directions. "He got what he never got before; the cold and clammy hand of silent public disapproval. This master of demogoguery saw that he had blundered." The aldermen, who voted with only two exceptions to override his veto and thus bring "a decided victory for the people against corporate insolence," saw Starkweather's blunder too.[54]

The Populists and Republicans had a better ear for public opinion than did the Democrats. On a platform that blasted the utilities company for "a crime against humanity in furnishing the City of Superior the vile, contaminated and impure water," the Populists nominated Gordon French for mayor. French was a day laborer who, as alderman, was the city's leading critic of the company. He had teamed with Mayor Pattison in 1896 to force the water company to lower its rates and had led the February, 1898, fight to override Starkweather's vetoes.[55]

In this atmosphere the Republican progressives had little trouble recapturing their party. After blasting the company in their platform, the Republicans nominated neophyte lawyer Hervey Dietrich for mayor. Dietrich ran his campaign as though his opponent were not Starkweather, but the hated utility, which he darkly hinted was supporting the incumbent.

53. *Superior Evening Telegram*, March 23, 24, 31, April 1, 1898. *Superior Sunday Forum*, February 20, 1898.
54. *Superior Sunday Forum*, February 6, 20, 27, 1898. *Superior Evening Telegram*, February 2, March 30, 31, 1898.
55. *Superior Evening Telegram*, February 2, April 1, 1898. *Superior Leader*, March 27, 1898.

"I went to a faucet . . . and drew a cup of the filthiest slime I ever saw," cried Dietrich. "If you would go to the most stagnant pool of water that can be found in Superior in the hottest days of summer you could not find slime that would equal it." Dietrich demanded "water first that is pure and second that is cheap, almost as cheap as air." The Republican theme was that Starkweather had proved his inability and unwillingness to cope with the city's quasi-public corporations.[56] The campaign became so bitter and the Populists were so eager for relief that French withdrew and announced his support for Dietrich a few days before the election. The fight then narrowed to an anti-corporation fusion of Populists and progressive Republicans against an extraordinarily popular man who was currently a nominal Democrat.[57]

Dietrich won. Superior had at last found a program and a coalition that could sustain widespread popular backing. For the first time since the panic, Superiorites from all classes could agree on a direction for the city government. By rejecting the popular Starkweather, they had decided that the issues of polluted water and high utility rates were more important than personalities or social backgrounds. They further showed how desperate were the events that had created progressivism and its popularity. They demonstrated the depth of their acceptance of progressivism a few months later in a direct test of strength between progressives and retrenchment-minded mugwumps. Determined to rescue the city from the Superior Water, Light and Power Company, the Dietrich administration announced its plans to construct a municipal lighting plant. When, late in May, the company refused to submit a street lighting bid lower than $115 per light—when Minneapolis paid half that amount —the city began plans for municipal lighting. At this point the mugwumps entered the fight. Hoping that a Republican city government would be as pliable as it had been between 1893 and 1895, sixty businessmen ordered the city on May 26 to accept the company's proposed contract. Superior, they said, could not afford a municipal lighting plant, and some of them hinted that they would not pay taxes for such a project.[58]

Although Populists and workers denounced this attitude of

56. *Superior Evening Telegram,* March 29–31, 1898.
57. *Superior Sunday Forum,* April 1, 1898. Gates Clough, *Superior: An Outline of History* (Superior: Evening Telegram Co., 1954), 21.
58. *Superior Evening Telegram,* May 18, 27, June 1, 9, 1898.

the businessmen, the aldermen heeded the mugwumps' pressure and extended the company's lighting contract for an additional month at $115 per light. The outcry was fierce; even the conservative *Telegram* called the contract exorbitant. Sensing that Superiorites in their present mood were capable of extreme action, the company now tried to buy time to cool tempers and offered a three-year contract at $110 per light. On July 6 the Common Council approved it. Mayor Dietrich stingingly rebuked the aldermen for defying public opinion and, to keep the progressive coalition together, he vetoed the contract. Three years was too long and $110 was too much. Realizing that the mayor had more accurately gauged public feeling than had the aldermen, and that the mugwumps had long since proved their inability to win mass support from Superiorites, the aldermen sustained Dietrich's veto by a 12 to 3 vote. The company then tried to extend its contract unilaterally by refusing to turn off the lights and charging the city for their use, but city officials refused to be blackmailed and accepted the consequences. They ordered the company to extinguish the lights and, on July 13, 1898, the streets of Superior were plunged into darkness.[59]

Failing as always to understand popular hatred of corporations, the mugwumps now begged city officials to restore the lights. No one was shopping at night in the shrouded city, but the progressive city officials ignored protests and ordered the company to dismantle its street lights. On August 25 the Common Council tentatively accepted a bid of seventy-five dollars per light by a firm that would use gas for lighting. At this point, apparently for the first time, the water and light company realized that the merchants had no influence in the city council. It then submitted a bid of eighty dollars per light and proportionately lower rates for private consumers. This offer the city accepted on August 31.[60]

This victory of progressivism over mugwumpery spurred the progressives into other battles with the utility company. Dietrich retaliated against its refusal to provide pure water or adequate fire protection and against its $200,000 tax debt by ignoring the company's bills for hydrant rentals and instituting proceedings to annul the company's water franchise. Early in 1899 the company began to fear that the city was as serious about building a municipal waterworks as it had demonstrated

59. *Ibid.*, June 1, 9, July 6, 12, 13, 1898.
60. *Ibid.*, July 20, 22, August 20, 25, 31, 1898.

a few months earlier when it plunged the city into darkness, and in May it agreed to compromise all of its disputes. In exchange for the city's concessions of paying future hydrant rentals and ending annulment proceedings the company was forced to pay its taxes, to reduce commercial and residential rates by 8 per cent with progressive reductions as Superior grew, and to build a filtration plant that would meet the health board's approval by December 1, 1899.[61]

Encouraged by their triumphs over the light and water utility, the progressives now turned their guns on the street railway company. When the company persistently refused to issue free transfers, to repair streets and snow fences, or to pay taxes, the aldermen in 1900 annulled its franchise.[62] Desperate events had made moderate men desperate and impatient. Superiorites had seen their corporations defy city orders and taxes too long. The summary actions toward the arrogant utility companies had been long in shaping, but once determined, they were applied with finality.

III

The experiences of Ashland and Superior reveal the origins of mugwumpery and progressivism at the grass-roots level and suggest that municipal reformers could significantly modify their local governments if they successfully solved three interrelated problems. First, they had to consider the type of political leadership that existed in their cities. Proposals for nonpartisan local government or civil service reform were clearly more appealing in cities like Ashland, with traditions of fluid party lines and weak partisan leadership, than in more firmly organized communities. Second, reformers had to recognize that the depression had thawed the icy hostility that had earlier divided class and status groups. Many people from all social backgrounds wanted to reform their cities. One economic group could not hope to impose its political will on the city for very long, as Superior's businessmen discovered. Reformers whose programs and tactics incorporated this democratization of poli-

61. *Ibid.*, August 3, 20, 1898. *Milwaukee Sentinel*, May 19, 1899. *The Madison State*, November 25, 1898. *Charter and Principal Ordinances of the City of Superior* (Superior, 1908 ed.), 123–28.

62. *Superior Leader*, June 26, August 28, 1895, April 18, 1897. *Superior Sunday Forum*, February 16, 1896, January 30, November 28, 1897. *Superior Evening Telegram*, December 15, 1897. *Municipality*, 1 (October 1900), 44.

tics would enjoy greater success than those who continued to assume that the predepression political isolation between social groups still existed. Third, reformers had to confront directly two new problems that the depression had created for Wisconsin cities. The first, which began immediately after the panic, was unbearable taxes, and the second, which began as corporations sought ways of saving money in the depression, was corporate arrogance. To ignore either problem was to kill a reform movement. In the end, Superior's experience was more typical of the experiences in the rest of the state. Events were producing a general shift in public interest about 1895, from issues of high taxes to those of corporate arrogance, from mugwumpery to progressivism.

The 1897 corrupt practices and civil service laws represented the final full breath of mugwumpery. Although the legislature did not bring state employees under the protection of civil service reform until 1905,[1] reformers in the cities had long since abandoned this cause and turned to new goals. Indeed, even as the legislators were enacting these two laws in 1897, municipal reformers were changing their approaches to urban problems. The experiences of Superior, not those of Ashland, were repeated in most Wisconsin cities between 1895 and 1897.

I

The most obvious area of mugwump failure was one that, despite its deep roots in Gilded Age Wisconsin, was ancillary to the main thrust of mugwumpery after 1893. This was the vice crusade, and particularly the Sunday-closing campaign. Mugwumps learned that most Wisconsinites resented reforms that, in effect, dried up their opportunities for drinking beer with their friends at their favorite saloons. Experience soon taught reformers the truth of friendly editors' repeated warnings that "social restrictions should not be in advance of clearly defined public sentiment."[2] In addition to those citizens who rejected Sunday closing because they liked their beer, many businessmen who joined and led mugwumpery after 1893 believed that such "Puritanical" restrictions marked their cities as regressive, as trying to repeal the secular spirit of the age.[3] Perhaps the most devastating fact was the failure of the crusades; no city stayed reformed for long. In urging reformers to shun vice crusades, one sympathetic editor warned that they were "seeking to enforce restrictions which never were nor never can be totally enforceable."[4]

The state's most effective mugwumps had recognized this truth almost from the beginning. The most successful mug-

1. Robert S. Maxwell, *La Follette and the Rise of the Progressives in Wisconsin* (Madison: State Historical Society of Wisconsin, 1956), 81–82.
2. *State Journal*, February 2, 1895. *Superior Leader*, July 23, 1895.
3. See *Superior Leader*, April 3, 1897, for example.
4. *The Madison State*, April 7, 1899.

wump mayors of the 1890s—Thomas Bardon of Ashland and John C. Koch of Milwaukee—realized that they would lose popular support for their more important fights—the battles for retrenchment and civil service reform—if they too eagerly embraced the causes of the vice crusaders. So carefully did these two men avoid action to further the crusades that even the editors most friendly to Bardon and Koch complained that "much needed reform has not come" in the regulation of vice merchants.[5] Bardon and Koch were too eager to establish nonpartisan and economical government to be sidetracked by programs that would lose them important votes. Other reformers learned the same lesson.

II

Unlike the vice crusades, taxation continued as a central concern of the state's mugwumps after 1893, and it was this area that best illustrated how experience forced reformers to change their thinking. When the panic first struck, reformers had hit blindly at local expenditures, believing that the easiest way to lower unbearable taxes was simply to cut budgets. But retrenchment, reformers and city officials learned, could rarely be more than a temporary solution to tax burdens. The cityward march of immigrants and farmers continued during the depression, and with these newcomers came demands for streets and schools, and fire and police protection—pressures that could not be ignored indefinitely. In addition, many cities demonstrated a sense of obligation to their unemployed by hiring them as street sweepers and by undertaking larger public works projects that also required manpower. Consequently, reformers were unable to maintain the low tax rates they had achieved during the first two years of the depression. About 1896 the cities began again to build streets and schools and to employ the personnel necessary to meet the expanding needs of their growing populations. From 1893 to 1895, when reformers demanded mere retrenchment, only three of the state's eleven urban counties increased their budgets, but between 1895 and 1899, when reformers focused on other aspects of the tax burden, nine of the eleven urban counties increased their spending.[6] Reformers were will-

5. *Ashland Daily Press,* March 27, 1899. See also March 31, 1898. *Milwaukee Sentinel,* July 23, 1893, May 9, 1895.
6. Six of the eleven urban counties (Brown, La Crosse, Lincoln, Oneida,

ing to release their grip on local budgets not only because increased spending was as inevitable as the growth of their cities, but also because they had discovered new ways to lessen their tax burdens, ways that generated broader constituencies for reform.

From the experiences of the retrenchment campaigns came the insights and techniques that undergirded the most popular and powerful of the state's reform movements in the 1890s: the taxation crusade. If they could not lower taxes by curtailing local spending, Wisconsinites came to believe, the other way to secure lower taxes was to redistribute the burden. Few efforts had been made to equalize taxes before the panic. Legislators in 1873–1874, 1881, and 1891 had sponsored bills to force the railroads to pay more taxes and in 1878 had petitioned Congress for a federal income tax.[7] More recently, in 1889, K. K. Kennan had tried to secure a state tax commission, but it was not until the depression of the 1890s and the failure of the retrenchment programs that Wisconsin mounted a concerted drive against tax dodging. By 1899 even the state's most conservative governor in two decades enlisted in the war against tax evasion. The tax crusade had so completely eclipsed retrenchment that an editor accurately observed that "the tax question has really nothing to do with the amount of taxes to be raised, but with their assessment or distribution, the apportionment of the burdens."[8]

The taxation crusade had deeper roots in the depression than in the failure of retrenchment. First, the same inability to support expensive government programs that had led reformers to espouse retrenchment had led other men and corporations to refuse to pay their taxes; tax dodging did not become an acute problem until after 1893. Second, taxes almost inevitably became a focus for the depression's social unrest, and many citizens came to feel that the tax system, manipulated by the powerful,

---

Racine, Winnebago) had their lowest budgets in 1895; one (Eau Claire) spent least in 1896; three (Douglas, Marinette, Milwaukee) were lowest in 1897; one (Ashland) had its lowest budget in 1899. Secretary, *Biennial Report, 1896,* 353–54; *Biennial Report, 1898,* 311–12; *Biennial Report, 1900,* 314–15, 320–21.

7. Emanuel L. Philipp and Edgar T. Wheelock, *Political Reform in Wisconsin: A Historical Review of the Subjects of Primary Election, Taxation, and Railway Regulation* (Milwaukee: privately published, 1910), 109–14, 119–21. Railroad Commissioner, *4th Report, 1890,* 12. Wisconsin, *Laws* (1878), Memorial to Congress No. 6, 716.

8. *Milwaukee Journal,* quoted in *State Journal,* March 24, 1899.

widened the gap between the rich and the poor by thrusting the heaviest tax burdens onto the poor. "Much of the spirit of unrest among the masses is due to the suspicion—nay, to the moral certainty—that an undue proportion of the burdens of government rests upon them and too little upon the shoulders more able to bear it. And it should be borne in mind that un-equal taxation . . . has been the cause of more revolutions . . . against 'the powers that be' than any other single cause, if not more than all others combined," declared an Appleton editor.[9] Many reformers came to agree with Richard T. Ely and former President Benjamin Harrison that tax reform was possibly the best means to narrow the gap between rich and poor.[10] Finally, many Wisconsinites favored tax reform because the depression forced them to accept the realities of an urban and industrial society and the need for expanded and expensive government services to meet those realities. A reform of the tax system was clearly the first step toward providing necessary funds.[11]

While the depression's ferment caused angry taxpayers to develop new interest in such old programs as taxation of church property and the single tax,[12] the most important feature of the taxation crusade was the widespread agreement among all groups about which specific evils most urgently needed reform. The most obvious of these was outright delinquency. At cities like Ashland, where 43 per cent of the property tax was de-linquent, mugwumps like members of the Civic Federation and Mayor Thomas Bardon by 1895 directed their guns against the wealthy tax evader who paid "some shyster for helping him to avoid the payment of just debts" while he rode "over the paved streets and [enjoyed] the improvements made at the poor man's expense."[13] As late as 1898 the state tax commission reported that a number of northern counties were bankrupt because they could not collect delinquent taxes.[14] Since the courts sometimes

9. *Appleton Weekly Post*, September 14, 1899.
10. Frederick M. Rosentreter, *The Boundaries of the Campus: A History of the University of Wisconsin Extension Division* (Madison: University of Wisconsin Press, 1957), 35–36. *Appleton Weekly Post*, April 19, 1899. *Superior Evening Telegram*, February 22, 1898.
11. See *Wausau Daily Record*, March 28, 1899, for an example.
12. For examples, see *Grand Rapids Wood County Reporter*, February 7, 1895. *Appleton Weekly Post*, December 21, 1893.
13. *Ashland Daily News*, February 13, March 30, 1895. *Ashland Weekly Press*, February 16, March 16, 1895.
14. *Report of the Wisconsin State Tax Commission, 1898*, 104, herein-after cited as *Tax Report*.

upheld the evasions on technicalities,[15] reformers and city officials had no alternatives but to seize and sell the properties on
which taxes were unpaid, as they did in Forest and Rock counties,[16] or to settle out of court with the tax dodgers for a fraction,
usually from 20 to 60 per cent, of the actual taxes owed. Since
settlement on this minimal basis was the only way to collect any
tax at all, bitter taxpayers asked, as at Ashland: "Has the 60 per
cent anything to do with the lack of funds to run our schools?"[17]
As anger over the delinquent taxes mounted, many community
governments overcame their hesitancy to seize private property
when that appeared to be the only means to force the payment
of taxes. As they learned the difficulties that arose with the curtailment of only a few services in a retrenchment program,
many mugwumps came to believe that they could achieve their
goal of lower taxes by somehow compelling even a few of the
wealthiest tax dodgers to pay their civic debts.

The widespread tax delinquency among wealthy individuals
and corporations led Wisconsinites to suspect other forms of tax
dodging, and investigation confirmed this suspicion. The basic
difficulty lay with administration of the general property tax,
which had developed in Wisconsin's rural past when most
property was visible to the assessor. With the development of
an urban society other types of property—"intangible" personal
property—came into being, and under the existing system were
not being assessed. "Perhaps the most noticeable of all defects in
the administration of our tax laws," reported the state tax commission in 1898, was that holders of notes, bonds, mortgages,
securities, and other "hidden" assets did not report these forms
of personal property to the assessors.[18] K. K. Kennan estimated
in 1898 that $100,000,000 in hidden personal property in Mil-
waukee alone was missing from the city's assessment rolls.[19] By

15. In January of 1896 the state supreme court upheld the delinquents'
claim that special street, sewer, and sidewalk taxes were unconstitutional
as a means for paying off municipal improvement bonds. Twenty-eight
months later the court reversed this decision. *Superior Evening Telegram*, April 16, 1898.
16. *Janesville Gazette*, in *Milwaukee Sentinel*, May 18, 1894. *Appleton
Weekly Post*, February 27, 1896.
17. *Ashland Daily News*, August 2, 1895. For further information on
Ashland's 60 per cent settlement, see *Ashland Weekly Press*, February 23,
July 20, 1895. *Ashland Daily News*, January 18, 20, February 26, March 30,
1895.
18. *Tax Report, 1898*, 109–10.
19. *Milwaukee Sentinel*, February 8, 1898.

1898, as groups like the State Grange and the State Federation of Labor joined editors and reformers in denouncing this form of tax dodging, even the conservative Gov. Edward Scofield proclaimed the "notorious fact that in Wisconsin by far the greater part of personal property escapes taxation entirely."[20] The only problem was to find workable means to reach and assess these hidden assets and thus to equalize the amount paid by holders of real and personal property.

As angry taxpayers searched for effective means of equalizing taxes, they returned to K. K. Kennan's 1889 proposal for a state tax commission. City officials and reformers alike agreed that creation of the commission should be the first step toward tax reform. The 1897 legislature thereupon established it with powers to "thoroughly investigate all complaints which may be made to them of illegal, unjust or excessive taxation" and to propose reforms. The tax commission, which the 1899 legislature made a permanent state agency, served as the focus of power reformers had envisioned to implement the state-wide taxation crusade.[21]

The tax commission reported in 1898 that the most effective way to reach a man's hidden assets was through an inheritance tax, because at the time of his death a man's estate was publicly probated in the courts. On the commission's recommendation, the 1899 Republican legislature placed Wisconsin among the more than twenty states that used the inheritance tax to compel payment of taxes on personal property.[22]

The commission recommended other ways of equalizing per-

20. *Superior Evening Telegram*, March 10, 1898. *Wausau Daily Record*, January 12, May 4, 1899. *Appleton Weekly Post*, April 13, 1899. State Grange, *22nd Session, 1893*, 7; *24th Session, 1895*, 7; *25th Session, 1896*, 38–39; *26th Session, 1897*, 30. *Official Wisconsin State Federation of Labor Directory*, 1896–1897, 121.

21. Wisconsin, *Laws* (1897), chap. 340; (1899), chap. 322. K. K. Kennan to Richard T. Ely, November 20, 1895, May 20, 1897, Ely Papers, Manuscripts Division, State Historical Society of Wisconsin. Philipp and Wheelock, *Political Reform*, 104–14. Carroll Pollock Lahman, "Robert Marion La Follette as Public Speaker and Political Leader, 1855–1905" (Ph.D. diss., University of Wisconsin, 1939), 427–28. *Tax Report, 1898*, 5–7. *Tax Report, 1900*, 3–4. William D. Hoard to M. Griffin, May 3, 1899, Hoard Letter Books, 54: 588, Hoard Papers, Manuscripts Division, State Historical Society of Wisconsin.

22. *Tax Report, 1898*, 71–72, 161, 166. Wisconsin, *Laws* (1899), chap. 355. *Milwaukee Sentinel*, February 12, 1899. Maxwell, *La Follette and Progressives*, 89, 208n2. When the state supreme court declared the 1899 tax unconstitutional, the 1903 legislature passed another tax that the court upheld.

sonal with real property under the general property tax. The 1899 legislature authorized the commission to investigate all local assessments to make certain, among other things, that assessors included hidden assets. In response, mayors like Appleton's Herman Erb, Jr., ordered local assessors to include personal property in their assessments.[23] With the 1899 laws, reformers won state-wide support for their mounting demands that the wealthy pay their share of the burden under the general property tax.[24] Communities began to adjust the tax laws to reach the urban forms of wealth disclosed by conditions in the depression.

The most popular of the reformers' fights to equalize the tax burden was their attack on various forms of corporate tax dodging. The 1854 legislature had established the precedent that most disturbed Wisconsinites in the 1890s: a license fee system of taxation whereby the railroads paid the state a fixed percentage of their gross receipts in lieu of any other taxes. By 1893 subsequent legislatures had applied the license fee tax to such other businesses as telephone and telegraph companies, life insurance companies, and sleeping car and express companies.[25] When the depression hit in 1893, Wisconsinites, who had largely ignored the license fee system of taxation during its first forty years of operation, bitterly denounced it because it permitted certain favored corporations to lower their tax payments as their earnings declined. "No other property," reported the state tax commission, "enjoys the privilege of a scale of taxation so perfectly adjustable to earnings." Most taxpayers had to pay taxes at their predepression levels, even though their incomes had dwindled, while corporations like railroads could pay lower taxes as their earnings declined. As a reflection of their declining license fees, the railroads contributed 72 per cent of the state's revenues on the eve of the Panic in 1891–1892 and only 47 per cent by 1897. Wisconsinites were acutely aware of the added tax burden that lower railroad license fees transferred to them.[26]

23. *Tax Report, 1898*, 71–72, 181–83. *Milwaukee Sentinel*, May 11, 1899. *Appleton Weekly Post*, April 20, 1899. *Wausau Daily Record*, December 28, 1898. *2nd Tax Report, 1903*, 260–61.

24. The 1911 state income tax climaxed this campaign.

25. Guy E. Snider, "History of the Taxation of Railway Corporations in Wisconsin" (B. Lett. thesis, University of Wisconsin, 1901), 13–15, 24, 30–31, 66. *Milwaukee Sentinel*, April 29, 1894. *State Journal*, March 29, 1899. *Tax Report, 1898*, 139–41, 151–53. *Tax Report, 1900*, 5, 36–37.

26. *Tax Report, 1900*, 89. *Tax Report, 1898*, 134. Philipp and Wheelock,

Hatred of the license fee system mounted during the depression when other corporations, looking for tax relief, persuaded the legislature to bring them under this system. An angry, economy-minded Superior editor bitterly asked: "Why should corporations pay taxes when a few hundred dollars spent with a venal legislature will exempt them, with the payment of a small license fee, and throw the burden of taxation on the individual?"[27] Since evidence of political corruption always held popular interest, reformers drew widespread support whenever they linked corporate tax dodging to corporate lobbying. Not until the corporations "discard the lobby," warned one editor, will the "taxation and other crusades cease to be, as they now are, in large part, anti-corporation movements."[28] In 1895, after several utilities persuaded the legislature to bring them under the license fee system, the Milwaukee Municipal League began conversion of its program from retrenchment to reform. From 1896 onward the league headed the drive to repeal the 1895 act that street railways and electric lighting companies had "smuggled" through the legislature to exempt themselves from local taxation. Angry taxpayers and city officials supported the league's new campaign for lower taxes when it was aimed at the corporations.[29]

By the late nineties reformers had won significant victories against corporations that had been dodging their taxes under the license fee system. While the Milwaukee league and its allies failed to repeal the 1895 exemption act in 1897, they did succeed in trebling the taxes paid by utilities.[30] Demanding that "corporate property be placed upon the same plane that private

Political Reform, 138. Railroad Commissioner, *7th Report, 1896*, 7; *8th Report, 1898*, 11. *State Journal*, January 21, 1897. *Madison Old Dane*, October 1, 1897. *The State*, March 25, 1898, February 3, 1899. Kenneth C. Acrea, Jr., "Wisconsin Progressivism: Legislative Response to Social Change, 1891 to 1909" (Ph.D. diss., University of Wisconsin, 1968), 65. See also *Racine News*, June 3, 1905, and Albert R. Hall to Flower, November 13, 1894, in Hall Papers, Manuscripts Division, State Historical Society of Wisconsin.

27. *Superior Sunday Forum*, November 28, 1897.

28. *Vernon County Censor*, quoted in *Milwaukee Sentinel*, April 7, 1899.

29. *Milwaukee Sentinel*, February 6, 1896, December 21, 1897. *Milwaukee Daily News*, February 11, 1896. Wisconsin, *Laws* (1895), chap. 363.

30. *Milwaukee Sentinel*, February 11, March 4, 17, 25, April 4, 8, 22, 1896, March 3, 6, 10, 21, 1897. *League Bulletin*, 11 (December 20, 1898). Butler, "Street Railway Problem in Milwaukee," *Municipal Affairs*, 4 (March 1900), 212–13. *Milwaukee Daily News*, March 26, 1896, March 10, 1897.

property is placed," reformers and city officials prevented the 1897 legislature from granting the license fee to eager water companies.[31] That same year reformers persuaded the legislature to remove sleeping car, freight line, and equipment companies from the license system—only to see Governor Scofield veto the results of their efforts. His vetoes infuriated taxpayers to such an extent that the state Republican party in 1898 pledged to re-enact the laws, and the 1899 legislature subsequently repealed the license fee privilege for these corporations.[32]

From the standpoint of revenue, the greatest victory in 1899 was passage of the law that raised the license fee of life insurance companies. Assemblyman Philo H. Orton, who had underestimated the new tax crusade, was "much surprised" when Wisconsinites flocked to support his bill to soak insurance companies. His cry that the insurance lobby was "as smooth as razors dipped in oil and as sharp" helped win passage of a law that raised the taxes of Milwaukee's Northwestern Life Insurance Company alone from $35,000 to $224,000, a sum equal to the budget of the state university.[33] While the legislature did not repeal the license fee tax on railroads until 1903, reformers by 1899 had so completely paved the way for the 1903 law that it was only a question of time before those corporations were forced to pay taxes at the same rate as individuals.[34] Since the depression had forced individual taxpayers to shoulder much of the tax burden that certain corporations could shrug off as their revenues declined, reformers had little trouble finding public support for attacks on the license fee system.

Thus, in the area of taxation, a major concern of mugwumps, reformers altered their programs as experience and new threats

31. For examples, see Wisconsin, Legislative Petition 1210A, 1897 Legislature, Box 59, Wisconsin State Archival Series 2/3/1/5–7. *Superior Evening Telegram*, March 23, 1897. *Milwaukee Daily News*, April 21, 1897.
32. Wisconsin, *Laws* (1899), chaps. 111–14. *State Journal*, March 29, 1899. *Blue Book, 1899*, 711. *Tax Report, 1900*, 5, 36–37. Philipp and Wheelock, *Political Reform*, 115, 123–30. Albert O. Barton, *La Follette's Winning of Wisconsin, 1894–1904* (Des Moines: Homestead, 1922), 102–3. *Milwaukee Sentinel*, January 28, 1898.
33. Philo Orton to William D. Hoard, March 31, 1899, Hoard Papers. *State Journal*, March 29, 1899. John Johnston to Richard T. Ely, March 30, 1899, Ely Papers.
34. For examples, see Philipp and Wheelock, *Political Reform in Wisconsin*, 138–41. *The State*, February 3, 1899. *Tax Report, 1898*, 134. *Milwaukee Sentinel*, April 13, 1899. Nils P. Haugen, *Pioneer and Political Reminiscences* (Madison: State Historical Society of Wisconsin, ca. 1930), 130.

dictated. When the mounting demands for municipal improvements forced mugwumps to retreat from their earlier preoccupation with retrenchment, they changed their emphasis from the size to the distribution of the tax burden. After two years of seeking support for tax reforms, the Milwaukee Municipal League could report that most taxpayers possessed "a firm conviction that they are called upon to bear more than their fair share of the public burdens."[35] The shift in focus from retrenchment to reform brought special benefits, for, while retrenchment had appealed to many poor taxpayers and Populists, it had also come under question as a system of relief that mainly benefited wealthy taxpayers. When the reformers began to direct their attack against obviously wealthy tax dodgers, they stilled the previous criticism. Beginning in 1895 mugwumps joined such earlier tax reformers as the Populists in changing their taxation objectives from a mugwumpish concern with lower budgets—which had led them to attack politicians—to a progressive concern with the tax dodging of rich individuals and corporations—which led them to cooperate with politicians.

III

The second area in which experience drove reformers to modify their programs was that of political action. The mugwumps had believed that partisanship was the root evil that confronted men who wanted to elect honest, competent, and tightfisted officials; they had wanted elections to be as nonpartisan as possible.

As reformers became desperate for relief and preferred winning elections to maintaining their purity, however, they realized that party loyalty was a basic fact of political life. The siren call of the national party lured most voters even at local elections. However much reformers yearned to fight local elections on local issues, they soon learned that voters in local elections "want to hear what congress has done and will do; they want to get enthused about presidential candidates; they want to hurrah for Republicanism, pure and simple."[36] Even those editors who sympathized with some mugwump programs rallied to defend their parties in elections. The *Wisconsin State Journal,* which eulogized mugwumps at other times, warned

35. *League Bulletin,* 10 (October 15, 1898).
36. *Superior Evening Telegram,* March 31, 1896.

that "Republicans should stick together this spring as they did last fall, for the loosening of party lines will merely result in the strengthening of an opposition which is never ready to yield a point."[37] At a time when E. A. Strong of Ashland intended in 1900 to name his son McKinley Roosevelt Strong, a Wausau editor could accurately declare that "the public pulse . . . did not beat in harmony with the non-partisan movement."[38]

Even more threatening to reform ideals than party loyalty was the partisan politicians' exploitation of mugwumpery for their own ends. Mugwumps in 1897 had waged a hard fight to bring fire and police departments outside Milwaukee under civil service reform; but politicians had other motives. The 1897 Republican legislature passed the law because Democrats had won most of the municipal elections in early April. Civil service reform, in this case, allowed Republican policemen and firemen to retain jobs they would have lost under the patronage system when Democrats were inaugurated on May 1.[39] The ink was barely dry on the new law before politicians began fighting to control the new fire and police commissions. Mugwumps had anticipated these maneuvers by providing that no more than two members of the four-man commissions could be appointed from one party, but they failed, alas, in their estimates of the politicians' determination. At Marinette the outgoing Republican mayor maintained Republican control by appointing a Prohibitionist, and at Superior the mayor appointed a Populist.[40] Such not-so-nonpartisan commissions angered residents of Green Bay and Fond du Lac by firing popular police chiefs.[41] The policemen themselves showed their displeasure with the law by rioting in several cities.[42]

Throughout the state mugwumps watched partisan politicians exploit this law, their panacea for the spoils system. At Madison a Democrat was elected mayor largely because he had promised to fire the unpopular police department. When the outgoing Republican mayor tried to protect the policemen by hastily appointing a commission, the new Democratic mayor appointed his own. Not until the new Democratic city council

37. *State Journal*, March 28, 1895.
38. *Ashland Daily News*, June 28, 1900. *Wausau Daily Record*, April 4, 1900.
39. Burr W. Jones's analysis in *State Journal*, April 21, 1897.
40. *State Journal*, April 22, 1897. *Superior Leader*, April 30, 1897.
41. *The State*, February 10, 1899.
42. *Appleton Weekly Post*, May 6, 1897.

forced the incumbent policemen to resign by appropriating only twenty-five dollars to the whole police force did the politicians reach a compromise, with two members of each commission becoming the permanent police administrators.[43] At Superior, Mayor Starkweather predictably ignored two competing commissions and hired his friends as though the new reform law had never been passed. Not until the state supreme court ordered Starkweather to obey the law did Superior's fire and police commission set down its regulations—eight months after the law had passed.[44] Aware that such problems had made the 1897 law unpopular, the newer reformers urged repeal of this "silly and harmful" act.[45] Although their sacred principle of civil service reform ultimately triumphed, the mugwumps learned during these fights just how deeply partisanship was etched into Wisconsin's political fabric.

What hurt mugwumps more than open defiance of the civil service law, which they knew would ultimately be overcome, was the widespread popular scorn and hostility toward nonpartisanship. An Appleton editor wrote that his city's 1894 nonpartisan movement failed because of the popular "suspicion of 'star chamber' machinations" that surrounded it.[46] But a Racine editor best explained the general view: "Non-partisanship is colorless; it is insipid, and sterility itself. The man who is or claimed to be nonpartisan has a negative character; he is full of scruples and void of emotions. He is an industrious critic standing by the wayside to watch the processions pass by."[47] Election returns supported these views. In fact, lamented Horace Rublee, "It is only too apparent that nine out of ten of these reformers will vote their party ticket at the municipal elections."[48] With reformers helpless to loosen the grip of party loyalty on their own members, they could scarcely hope to elect nonpartisan candidates.

This popular hostility toward nonpartisanship led reformers to modify their views of partisan politics. Although they remained committed to civil service reform, they soon scrapped

43. *State Journal,* April 19–21, 23, 26, May 3, 10, 1897.

44. *Superior Leader,* May 4, 25, June 2, 3, 5, 22, July 14, 28, August 6, 10, 1897. *Superior Evening Telegram,* December 2, 1897. *Milwaukee Sentinel,* August 8, 1897.

45. *The State,* September 8, 1899. See also February 10, 1899.

46. *Appleton Weekly Post,* March 22, 1894.

47. *Racine Journal,* in *State Journal,* March 7, 1895.

48. *Milwaukee Sentinel,* April 4, 1896.

the mugwump practice of nominating independent candidates. Most groups by 1895 or 1896 adopted the strategy the Milwaukee Municipal League had used since the Koch campaign of 1893. Realizing that in the close elections of the 1890s the politicians needed all the votes they could find, the reformers believed their function was to be "a 'regulator,' to force good nominations" by the existing parties.[49] "We will hold the balance of power," proclaimed a member of the Madison Civic Federation, "and the old parties must nominate good men to hope for success."[50] Even with this approach reformers maintained their stance outside the major parties. They held themselves remote enough to choose impartially between the candidates of both parties. They were still nonpartisans, but, because they had learned to work within the partisan arena, they were clearly shedding some of their pristine mugwumpery.

Part of the reformers' willingness to reject the practice of nominating independent candidates stemmed from their belief that they were more effective when they tried to abolish the inducements that attracted partisan incompetents to politics, rather than when they tried to defeat individual politicians. They evolved to the position the Milwaukee league had maintained since 1894, when it had begun the fight for civil service reform.[51] As Milwaukeeans increasingly assumed command of the state-wide reform movement, most of the state's reform groups embraced their strategy of removing the lures for partisan politicians. In concentrating on alteration of the system, rather than on defeat of individual men, reformers devoted an increasing amount of their energies to state-wide reform measures and focused more closely on structural changes at Madison and less on their home cities.

The successes of these new strategies of endorsing the best candidates and attacking the system hastened the decline of non-partisanship. When they held the balance of power in close elections, reformers could convince editors that attack on naked

49. *Appleton Weekly Post,* March 16, 1895, used this language in explaining the failure of Appleton's civic federation in its first political campaign.

50. *State Journal,* January 26, 1895. See also March 20, April 1, 1895. *Madison Democrat,* March 31, 1895. *Superior Evening Telegram,* February 28, March 18, 19, April 3, 1896. *Milwaukee Sentinel,* January 31, 1894.

51. *2nd Good City Conference, 1894,* 60–61. *National League,* 2nd Meeting, 1896, 300–302. *Good City Conference,* Louisville, 1897, 23–24. *Superior Evening Telegram,* March 7, 1895.

political grabs was advantageous and could persuade politicians to avoid blatant partisanship. As a result, the politicians began to nominate men who were not blatant partisans and incompetents and to enact the reformers' structural changes in the political process. Whether the cause was the enactment of laws that made officeholding less appealing to party hacks, the growing "independent" spirit fostered by the mugwumps, the desperation of depression voters and the new civic consciousness, or the manifestly urgent pressures on city officials applied by tax dodgers and utility companies, the general level of mayoral, if not aldermanic, candidates improved greatly from 1892 to 1897. Energetic and able men like Thomas Bardon of Ashland, Hervey Dietrich of Superior, A. B. Ideson of Oshkosh, George O. Bergstrom of Neenah, John Koch and William Rauschenberger of Milwaukee, John Thoroughgood of Janesville, C. A. Born of Sheboygan, Charles E. Whelan of Madison, F. B. Hoskins of Fond du Lac, and James H. Elmore of Green Bay were all elected mayors, and they were a good deal less partisan and more competent than the men who had occupied their offices before the panic. Some, like Dietrich, Bardon, and Elmore, won widespread support from voters of the opposition party. There was little need for mugwumps when mayors like Milwaukee's William Rauschenberger claimed by 1896 that "the question of municipal taxes I regard as the most important one for the city government to consider."[52] By 1897 fiercely partisan newspapers like the *Milwaukee Daily News* contended that Milwaukee's representatives were incompetent because they had been elected on partisan, not local, issues.[53] The mugwumps had won part of the war. Indeed, by the late 1890s the mayors felt the obligations of their offices so keenly that they assumed some of the responsibilities of the position taken in the mid-1890s by the Milwaukee league in building the state-wide reform movement. Mayors joined mugwumps in forming the League of Wisconsin Municipalities to exchange experiences, recommend needed changes at Madison, and coordinate reformers throughout the state.

As politicians increasingly accepted the reformers' yardsticks, reformers felt more comfortable in the partisan political arena. As a consequence they developed two new strategies in the late 1890s that distinguished them from the mugwumps: They com-

52. *Milwaukee Daily News,* March 29, 1896.
53. *Ibid.,* April 26, 1897.

pletely abandoned nonpartisanship in any form and entered party caucuses and conventions. They came to believe that by attending the caucuses they could "do more for good government in one session than they can do by their so-called educational and reform movements in half a decade. The caucus is the drawbridge which must first be scaled before the castle of corruption and bad government can be captured."[54] Some, like E. F. McCausland of the Superior Good Government Club and James Mallory of the Milwaukee Municipal League, returned to the Democratic party.[55] But most of the reformers, if not Republicans before their mugwump adventure, were Republicans now. Even John A. Butler, a lifelong Democrat, found that, as president of the Milwaukee league, he was more often supporting Republican candidates and issues than those of his party.[56] As these former mugwumps discovered more support among Republican legislators for their bills on corrupt practices and civil service reform and appreciated the administrations of John C. Koch, the voluntary publication of campaign expenses by the party's county chairman, and the willingness to fight local elections on local issues, they came to feel that the Republican party was "by natural instinct the party of clean politics."[57]

When the mugwumps entered the party caucuses they did not lose their zeal for limiting bossism, which led to their second innovation in the late 1890s. Rejecting nonpartisanship, they joined the growing movement for regulated partisanship. Long interested in structural changes in party politics to weaken the ward heeler's power, they had always at least sympathized with the efforts to make the caucus and convention more responsive to majority sentiment. They had not actively championed the caucus reform laws of 1891–1895, however, because the partisan bosses had supported them. The Milwaukee direct primary of 1891 and the 1893 caucus law had come from Democratic politicians who could no longer manipulate the caucuses in the congested city. Similarly, William Fricke, Milwaukee

54. *Superior Evening Telegram,* March 4, 1896.
55. *Ibid.,* March 15, 1897. Graham A. Cosmas, "The Democracy in Search of Issues: The Wisconsin Reform Party, 1873–1877," *Wisconsin Magazine of History,* 46 (Winter 1962–1963), 107.
56. *National Cyclopedia of American Biography* (New York, 1931), 21: 55–56.
57. *Milwaukee Sentinel,* March 12, 1895.

Republican chairman, backed the 1895 caucus law to simplify the complicated paperwork required by the 1893 act.[58] Dedicated nonpartisans felt ambivalent toward these laws. However strongly they endorsed those features that minimized the influence of "heelers and disreputables," they suspected the laws because bosses had sponsored them and because they discouraged nonpartisan elections by forcing voters to commit themselves to one party.[59]

In the mid-1890s, as the mugwumps despaired of electing nonpartisan candidates and discovered more defects in the electoral process, they joined the caucus reform movement. They came to believe that if the caucus were conducted like a general election, with secret ballots instead of voice votes, reformers could campaign for issues and men with the mass techniques they best understood—education and publicity—without having to worry about the bosses' influence. The Milwaukee Municipal League, representing the only city to which the early caucus laws applied, soon discovered how to exploit the secret caucus to nominate such nonpolitical men as Koch and to force the parties to endorse its principles. Its leaders promoted efforts to regulate caucuses and conventions.[60] Such leaders of the Madison Civic Federation as Col. George W. Bird and C. K. Adams, president of the University of Wisconsin, argued that the most important political reform was the secret ballot at party caucuses.[61] An Appleton editor who sympathized with mugwump programs argued that with caucus reform bosses could no longer "get control of the party machinery, call caucuses without sufficient notice and often in places where no respectable man would be seen, pack them with their followers whom they persuade, bribe or otherwise corrupt to do their bidding."[62] Reflecting this conversion of municipal reformers to regulated partisanship, the League of Wisconsin Municipalities made caucus reform one of its major objectives.[63] Former mug-

58. Philipp and Wheelock, *Political Reform,* 10–14.

59. *Milwaukee Sentinel,* April 26, September 27, 1891, March 14, 1892, April 17, 22, 1893.

60. *Ibid.,* January 23, February 9, 18, 24, March 13, 30, 1894, December 14, 1895, February 11, 13, March 4, 17, 25, April 4, 8, 1896. *Good City Conference,* Indianapolis, 1898, 104–5.

61. *State Journal,* February 2, 1895.

62. *Appleton Weekly Post,* February 11, 1897.

63. *State Journal,* February 15, 1900. *Proceedings of the Milwaukee Conference for Good City Government* (Philadelphia: National Municipal

wumps generally worked hard for the Mills Law of 1897, which established state regulation of political party caucuses outside Milwaukee. State inspectors made certain that on primary day the parties provided election booths and secret ballots for all voters.[64]

Many former mugwumps had so completely rejected nonpartisanship in favor of regulating the parties that they supported the direct primary, which envisioned destruction of boss influence at the same time that it virtually destroyed nonpartisan movements. Amos P. Wilder and C. K. Adams, who lectured for nonpartisan elections in 1895, came to support the direct primary after the nonpartisan movements collapsed—Adams in 1897 and Wilder in 1900.[65] More important was the conversion of the Milwaukee Municipal League to this view. In 1898 Charles E. Monroe, speaking for the Milwaukeeans, tried to persuade the National Municipal League to support the direct primary instead of more moderate forms of regulated partisanship. In 1900 Butler told the same group that "any system of city government" that did not include the direct primary "would necessarily be bad."[66] But the direct primary was a hope for the future and, in the meantime, municipal reformers were willing to sacrifice it for an immediate secret ballot in local nominations, a reality they achieved in 1897. By the time reformers had come to support the direct primary, which discouraged nonpartisan candidates, the reformers' political programs had truly evolved from mugwumpery to progressivism. From this point on they had few fears of all partisan politicians.

IV

Behind this conversion from nonpartisanship to regulated partisanship and a secret caucus ballot was the reformers' growing feeling that the worst corrupters of city politics were not partisans or even politicians but the local quasi-public corporations. In their mugwump campaigns the reformers had received

League, 1900), 63, hereinafter cited as *Good City Conference*, Milwaukee, 1900.

64. *Wausau Daily Record*, July 7, 1898. *Appleton Weekly Post*, February 11, 1897.

65. *Good City Conference*, Milwaukee, 1900, 221–25. *Milwaukee Sentinel*, October 17, 1897.

66. *Good City Conference*, Milwaukee, 1900, 105. *League Bulletin*, 1 (February 19, 1898).

considerable support from city officials, who turned voluntarily toward retrenchment because their cities were bankrupt and because there was no other way to meet the new pressures of the depression. As those officials tried to perform their duties of collecting taxes or enforcing elementary considerations of health and safety upon the local utilities, they soon discovered that the utilities frequently controlled the campaign funds, if not also the votes, of their own parties.

Prior to 1895 the Wisconsin mugwumps had not paid much attention to the quasi-public corporations. When the utilities secured the 1895 act that exempted them from local and equal taxes, however, the corporations came under mugwump attack because they undercut the reformers' efforts to secure lower taxes and at the same time corrupted politics. The 1895 law was the shock that awakened mugwumps to this new menace. Not only had some corporation lobbyists used questionable means to influence legislators to pass the law, but, what was worse, the chief lobbyist was none other than Henry C. Payne, Wisconsin's Republican national committeeman. When Payne used his political power to exempt the state's more than twenty street railway and light companies from taxation, reformers immediately saw great perils to economical and honest government in this evidence that corporation managers were also political leaders. Boss Payne was at the same time an executive of such powerful corporations as the Milwaukee Electric Railway and Lighting Company, the Wisconsin Telephone Company, and the Milwaukee Railroad. The Milwaukee Municipal League now charged that the "disgraceful lobby, long maintained" of the trolley and light monopoly "has . . . greatly militated against it among conservative business men throughout the city and state."[67] John A. Butler maintained that the league enlisted in the battle against the monopoly because of "the close connection of an unscrupulous political machine . . . with the Milwaukee Street Railways . . . and other corporations."[68] By 1900 Milwaukee Leaguers like Butler and Edward P. Bacon cried that the majority of "men in all parties are the willing slaves of selfish political rings which are devoted solely to the interests of public service corporations."[69]

67. *League Bulletin*, 5 (May 16, 1898).
68. *Good City Conference*, Indianapolis, 1898, 173.
69. *Milwaukee Sentinel*, February 17, 1900. See also *Good City Conference*, Milwaukee, 1900, 157–63.

Once the 1895 exemption act drew public attention to the political power of quasi-public corporations, reformers discovered the long train of violated ordinances, bribed aldermen, tax evasion, domination over local political parties, poor service, and high rates that the Populists had long decried. The former mugwumps came to agree with the Superior editor who had earlier advocated only retrenchment and civil service reform but now championed municipal ownership of utilities as the only way to control the corporations that "employ threats, bribery, cajolery, misrepresentation, every device that cunning and dishonesty can conceive to retain their holds on the public funds. There is hope . . . that the people are waking to the fact that they are not obliged to suffer eternally."[70] Throughout the state desperate events were creating desperate men. By 1897 former mugwumps could agree with the Milwaukee Catholic editor who had once espoused mugwumpery but now maintained that "the true direction of municipal reform" was toward municipal ownership of utilities.[71]

By the end of the decade reformers and city officials alike had generally concluded that corporate arrogance—and particularly corporate domination over politics—was the greatest political menace in the cities. In 1899–1900 the "principal work" of the Milwaukee league consisted of its battles against the street railway monopoly.[72] Heirs of the Milwaukee league's earlier statewide campaigns—the reformers and mayors who attended the 1898 and 1899 meetings of the League of Wisconsin Municipalities, sponsored by the Milwaukee league—were "almost unanimous" in declaring that nothing short of municipal ownership of utilities would end political corruption and restore popular government to the cities.[73] The most important new crusade that former mugwumps adopted during the late 1890s was the campaign against the utilities.

The full extent of their fury with corporate control over politics was revealed in the active support reformers gave Robert M. La Follette in his campaigns against the Payne machine of the Republican party. While they may have some-

70. *Superior Sunday Forum,* March 13, 1898.
71. *Milwaukee Catholic Citizen,* August 21, 1897.
72. *Good City Conference,* Milwaukee, 1900, 83–84.
73. Samuel E. Sparling, "League of Wisconsin Municipalities," *Annals of the American Academy of Political and Social Science,* 14 (September 1899), 116–17. *Milwaukee Sentinel,* December 25, 1898. *League Bulletin,* 12 (January 28, 1899).

times questioned La Follette's late conversion to reform programs, they turned to him because he seemed to be the one man who could defeat the influence of Payne and the corporations over the majority party. In backing La Follette, reformers plunged eagerly into the world of partisan politics to support a politician whose main political reform was the direct primary, which they knew would make nonpartisan elections virtually impossible. By this point, however, purity was far less important than defeating the corporations. And so, from all sides, former mugwumps enlisted in the La Follette campaign. J. F. Miles, who had won an earlier reputation with the Ashland Civic Federation, wrote La Follette in 1900: "I know of no man in the State that I could more heartily support than yourself, not because you adhere to the g,o,p, [sic] but because you have the backbone to fight the spirit of evil that has dominated the party for Lo these many years."[74] State Tax Commissioner K. K. Kennan, the state's oldest champion of economical government, wrote to his new convert La Follette in 1897 "to express the hope that you will continue to use your talents and influence to call public attention to the urgent need of reform in our present antiquated and inequitable system of taxation."[75] Such prominent leaders of the Milwaukee Municipal League as Cassius M. Paine, A. G. Weissert, T. L. Mitchell, Henry Baumgaertner, Edward P. Bacon, and Frederick W. von Cotzhausen all worked hard to secure La Follette's nomination.[76] Their eagerness to weaken the corporations' control of the Republican party led them to cast aside any doubts they entertained about La Follette's sincerity as a reformer. They were more interested in curtailing the domination of men like Henry Payne than in electing La Follette.

While the mugwumps were hardly the first Wisconsinites to attack the utilities and their political control, their conversion was crucial for the developing reform movement. They had already developed the state-wide organization and had won the respect of conscientious city officials and partisan editors. When

74. J. F. Miles to Robert M. La Follette, May 23, 1900, La Follette Papers, Manuscripts Division, State Historical Society of Wisconsin.
75. K. K. Kennan to Robert M. La Follette, September 27, 1897, La Follette Papers.
76. Barton, *La Follette's Winning of Wisconsin*, 119. *Milwaukee Sentinel*, August 11, 1898, March 26, June 26, 1900. Robert C. Twombly, "The Reformer as Politician: Robert M. La Follette in the Election of 1900" (M.A. thesis, University of Wisconsin, 1964), 81.

they concluded that the political process was unresponsive be-cause corporations wanted it that way, Wisconsinites gave them the attention and support they had withheld from the Populists, who were tainted with the label of radicalism. If men whose only goals had been honest and economical government were now lambasting the utilities, something must indeed be funda-mentally wrong. As their anger mounted, the old mugwumps worked with their old enemies, the partisan politicians. Poli-ticians now were evil only to the extent that they succumbed to the blandishments of the quasi-public corporations. The con-version of the old mugwumps, many of whom had been con-servative businessmen, into crusaders against corporate arro-gance was the most spectacular development in the reform movements of the 1890s.

V

The progressivism of the late 1890s differed significantly from the mugwumpery of the middle of the decade; but progressives did not oppose mugwumps. In fact, progressivism grew out of the failures of mugwumpery. Both were concerned primarily with issues of taxation and the machinery of local politics that the depression had made urgent. Both retained the basic ob-jectives of economical and honest government. The major difference was that experience had taught them to reject the vice crusades, which had been such an important part of pre-depression mugwumpery, and to attack the growing arrogance of quasi-public corporations. When the corporations threatened the stability of honest and economical government, the mug-wumps rose to meet that new threat. And indeed they had no choice. Events throughout the state, and particularly in the proud and booming metropolis of Milwaukee, were raising the question of whether any city government had any power at all over its own affairs.

The struggle between the cities and their local quasi-public corporations was the most dramatic feature of Wisconsin's urban political scene during the last years of the decade. As the depression drove the corporations to inaugurate increasingly unpopular actions, the corporations drove voters to create new coalitions that would both regulate the companies' economic activities and destroy their political influence. "Corporations can ride the people part of the time," cried the *Oshkosh Times* in 1900, "but, sooner or later the order is reversed and the people rise and drive the corporations at a killing pace."[1] The order was reversed in the mid-1890s.

The resulting process of reversal was dramatic because it involved questions of broad social policy and forced Wisconsin-ites to confront an uncomfortable dilemma. The corporations provided services that were absolutely essential for the develop-ment and expansion of the cities—on this point corporate man-agers and reformers agreed. Further, most reformers believed deeply in the sanctity of private property. As a result, they were torn between the alternatives of violating their principles by attacking property rights in their challenges of companies that produced urban growth on the one hand, or allowing corpora-tions to continue their defiance of the public welfare on the other. This tension-ridden dilemma explains both the wide variety of solutions proposed by the reformers and the fury that often possessed them when acting in this area. It actually ap-peared that they resented these corporations, which intimately touched their lives, principally because they forced citizens to choose between frightening alternatives.

I

It had not always been so. In the years before the panic the cities had eagerly induced and enfranchised any capitalists who would spare the city budget by providing vital urban services out of their private pockets. Since a city's future depended in large part on its services, most city dwellers were delighted when private citizens assumed the costs of building generators and

1. Quoted in *Milwaukee Sentinel,* January 20, 1900.

stringing wires to illuminate homes and streets, of laying the tracks and operating the streetcars, or of building pumping stations and piping the water. As men measured their city's progress by the miles of pavement, so they believed that an optimistic future was assured if a city possessed the most modern utilities. The Milwaukee Chamber of Commerce proudly boasted that "one of the most notable events in the progress of Milwaukee" occurred in 1891 when an eastern syndicate of capitalists created a giant monopoly to electrify the utilities and "give Milwaukee the most complete and extensive system of rapid transit possessed by any city in the world in proportion to its size." As soon as some new invention pointed the way to a more modern service, the cities granted franchises to eager promoters. Since most of the important inventions—notably the electric light and street railway—became practical in the 1880s, that decade comprised the halcyon years when city government and quasi-public corporations courted each other in an atmosphere of which most city residents approved. If street railway promoters wanted new routes and faster streetcars to collect more fares and lure residents of the inner city to homesites in outlying parts of the city where the companies speculated in lands, workers and Populists could agree on the desirability of relieving congestion in the inner city and could support the promoters. City governments even turned their older waterworks over to private capitalists. The years between 1875 and 1890 reversed the earlier trend toward municipal ownership of waterworks as city officials in the 1880s sought promoters to shoulder the expense of enlarging and modernizing the local facilities. These were the days of the friendliest relations between the cities and the new quasi-public corporations.[2]

The cities in these years maintained control over any utility that seemed unresponsive to its needs by simply enfranchising a competitor. Before the panic competitors were readily available, since most promoters had little difficulty finding willing investors; quasi-public corporations were considered good risks. When Racine's electric lighting company raised its prices, when a Milwaukee lighting company meddled in city politics, when

2. *Municipal Monopolies*, ed. Edward W. Bemis (New York: Thomas Y. Crowell, 1899), v, 16–20, 509. Milwaukee Chamber of Commerce, *34th Annual Report of the Trade and Commerce of Milwaukee*, 1892, 41–42. Clay McShane, "The Growth of Electric Street Railways: Milwaukee, A Case Study, 1887–1900" (M.A. thesis, University of Wisconsin, 1970), 51–81.

an Eau Claire street railway disobeyed the city council, those cities did not try to regulate the existing corporations; they just granted franchises to competitors.[3] Possessing this alternative and being willing to tolerate the few inconveniences that resulted from hasty applications of new technology, city officials rarely had to confront their utility corporations.

Very few Wisconsinites heeded the handful of cranks who before 1893 had attacked this system. When the State Grange complained that "the granting of valuable franchises with too many privileges and too few restrictions" was unwise, most city residents disagreed.[4] The majority of Wisconsinites dismissed as "radicals" labor leaders like Milwaukee's Robert Schilling and groups like the Populists who supported municipal ownership of utilities in preference to ownership by private corporations. Even the Populists opposed municipal ownership of street railways.[5] Few people listened when economists like Richard T. Ely warned that these corporations "by virtue of their own inherent properties" were "natural monopolies" that the cities would ultimately be forced to regulate, if not operate as municipal services.[6] Since the cities wanted the promoters' services without spending a single tax dollar and since they could rely on the time-tested device of competition to regulate their new creations, most of the state's urban residents and city officials could ignore such warnings and find little to criticize in the relations between utilities and cities.

II

The depression radically changed this friendly pattern. Underlying the increasingly bitter fights between cities and corporations was a revolution in the internal development and organization of the utilities. The panic vastly accelerated what economists had called the "natural" thrust of utilities toward

3. For examples, see *Milwaukee Sentinel,* July 29, 1887, September 1, 24, 1889, May 24, 1891, June 26, 1892, March 19, 1893.

4. State Grange, *22nd Session, 1893,* 9.

5. Milton M. Small, "Biography of Robert Schilling" (M.A. thesis, University of Wisconsin, 1953), 255. McShane, "Milwaukee Street Railways," 83.

6. Richard T. Ely, "Natural Monopolies and Local Taxation," *Lend a Hand,* 4 (March 1889), 178–92. Ely, "Natural Monopolies and the Workingman: A Programme of Social Reform," *North American Review,* 158 (March 1894), 294–303.

monopoly. If such technological developments as the application of electricity made operation through mergers more efficient for the utilities, the panic provided the opportunity for such mergers. Prior to the panic most Wisconsin cities had one or more lighting companies and a separate electric-powered street railway. In a number of communities the depression forced one or all of these companies into bankruptcy or receivership, since their promoters had generally overcapitalized their properties when they bought out the older horse-drawn and gas-operated utilities. Typically, soon after the initial bankruptcies, the stronger company or the receiver merged the electric power facilities and the street railway into a single corporation. This new corporation then was strong enough to fight off any competitors the city might subsequently enfranchise.[7]

So rapidly did the consolidation movement develop during the early days of the depression that by the mid-1890s one, or at most two, companies provided all the fuel, transportation, lighting, power, and water services of most Wisconsin communities. Superior depended upon one company for its water, lights, and power, while Eau Claire derived its transportation, lights, and power from a single monopoly. Not content with a monopoly on the transportation and lighting needs of the state's metropolis, the Milwaukee Electric Railway and Light Company extended its operations 35 miles south to Kenosha, 25 miles west to Waukesha, and 7 miles north to Whitefish Bay. Whether the process was natural or not, the depression had left most cities dependent on one or two utility monopolies.[8]

The depression-bred consolidations produced three vitally important results that severely strained relations between cities and utilities. The most important result developed from the high costs the original promoters paid to create their monopolies. To buy out their competitors and modernize their power sources they had generally sold well-watered stocks and bonds, and the financial crisis caught them greatly overcapitalized. At the same time, the business conditions that accompanied the crisis sharply curtailed markets for their services; only half as many passengers rode the Milwaukee streetcars in 1894 as had

7. Forrest McDonald, *Let There Be Light: The Electric Utility Industry in Wisconsin, 1881–1955* (Madison: American History Research Center, 1957) , 94. For details on individual cities, see 34–90. McShane, "Milwaukee Street Railways," 93–96. *Appleton Weekly Post*, April 8, 1897.

8. *Milwaukee Sentinel*, June 26, 1892, April 7, 1893, March 4, 1894, May 25, 1899. "The Electric Railway System of Milwaukee and Eastern

before the panic, for example.[9] Further, the corporations found it increasingly difficult to borrow needed funds.[10] Squeezed between declining revenues and overcapitalized properties, they searched for ways to raise income and cut costs. The ways they chose were extremely unpopular. In the summer of 1894 the Milwaukee Street Railway raised its basic fare from four to five cents.[11] The hard-pressed street railway at Appleton, claiming that it was losing $120 per month, cut the number of cars in operation from four to two in February of 1894 and forced passengers to wait twice as long between cars on cold winter days.[12] At Ashland and Superior the bankrupt water companies could not afford to extend their intake mains into the pure waters of Lake Superior to prevent the incidence of typhoid fever epidemics in those cities.[13] As their financial straits forced quasi-public corporations to adopt unpopular economies, the city residents became critical of the new utilities.

A second result of the consolidation movement deprived cities of their traditional means for regulating utilities. Now, considerably fewer investors were seeking franchises to compete with a single powerful monopoly; the *Milwaukee Sentinel* could never again hope to find a realistic solution, as it had in 1887, by urging more people to enter the traction business.[14] But the old ways died hard. As late as 1896 many urban Wisconsinites continued to hope that competition was still possible, particularly in the case of street railways.[15] It came as a shock to learn that few investors were foolhardy enough to challenge an entrenched utility monopoly. Unable to play one company against another, the cities now had to confront the fact that their antagonists were monopolies. As a result, a city could only

Wisconsin," *Street Railway Journal,* 15 (June 1899), 339–52. Forrest McDonald, "Street Cars and Politics in Milwaukee, 1896–1901, Part I," *Wisconsin Magazine of History,* 39 (Spring 1956), 166–69.

9. McShane, "Milwaukee Street Railways," 94.

10. See *Milwaukee Daily News,* May 21, 1895, for example.

11. *Milwaukee Sentinel,* August 2, 1894. McDonald, "Street Cars, Part I," 166–69.

12. *Appleton Weekly Post,* February 15, 1894.

13. "The Ashland Water Pollution Case," *Engineering Record,* 39 (December 24, 1898), 67–68. *Ashland Daily News,* January 9, February 19, 21, April 17, May 1, 1895. *Ashland Weekly Press,* January 19, February 9, March 9, 16, 23, 30, April 20, May 11, 25, 1895. *Superior Leader,* May 25, August 14, 1895. *Superior Evening Telegram,* August 15, 1895.

14. *Milwaukee Sentinel,* August 31, 1887.

15. For example, see *Milwaukee Daily News,* December 2, 1895. *Milwaukee Sentinel,* March 5, 13, 19, 29, 1896.

voice its protest when the local monopoly raised prices or refused to obey city regulations. The new monopolies were quick to take advantage of their positions of power. In the spring of 1894, after they had defeated the competition and while they were trying to solve revenue crises, electric light companies at both Oshkosh and Milwaukee substantially raised charges for local street lights.[16]

This same need for revenues, thrust upon corporations by the depression, was also felt by city officials, and this mutual pressure shaped the collisions between cities and monopolies. Since the cities had bonded themselves to their constitutional limits in the years before the depression and since the powerful mugwump forces continued to demand retrenchment, the cities could not afford one obvious solution to their utility problems —public ownership. Although many cities had come increasingly to look with favor on municipal ownership as the only long-range solution to the problems surrounding utilities, few could command the necessary funds to buy or construct power plants, water facilities, or street railways.[17] At the same time that the cities could not finance municipally owned utilities, the companies raised water hydrant or street light rentals and secured laws to dodge their municipal taxes. City officials could not afford the increased rentals or decreased taxes, nor find competitors for the franchises, nor construct municipal plants. Reformers and politicians, therefore, could only inveigh against the quasi-public corporations in bitter rhetoric, but they were usually unable to resolve their fights with the utilities. Precisely because the cities were powerless in these conflicts, a profound resentment against quasi-public corporations developed. That resentment ran deep and its remnants outlived the depression, for it forced city residents to confront the dilemma of public versus private rights and responsibilities that prosperous times had allowed them to escape before 1893.

The depression inaugurated a major change in the relations between cities and corporations that had promoted their expansion and had provided them with modern services. In all six years between 1887 and 1892 only five cities had major

16. *Milwaukee Sentinel,* March 4, May 1, 2, 1894.
17. For examples of cities stymied by lack of funds from creating municipal utilities, see *Superior Evening Telegram,* March 28, 1896, August 31, 1898. *Milwaukee Sentinel,* August 7, September 2, 1894, May 14, 24, 25, July 20, 21, September 3, 1895, October 20, 1896, September 14, October 15, December 11, 1897, August 13, 1899.

quarrels with their utilities. During the twelve months of 1899 alone, by contrast, nineteen cities fought full-fledged battles with their utilities.

III

While the underlying dilemmas of the corporations and cities were the same throughout the state, the events that triggered the fights varied from city to city. In sum, however, they clustered around four groups of interrelated complaints: inadequate service and high costs, refusal to obey city orders, taxation, and political influence.

The area of inadequate service and high costs was exemplified during the single month of September, 1895, when four cities—Superior, Fond du Lac, Ashland, and Waukesha—battled their water companies for failure to provide pure and healthful water.[18] Wars began when the Appleton water company failed to provide sufficient pressure to extinguish several fires and when electric companies at Grand Rapids, South Milwaukee, and Appleton were unable to generate enough light without frequent power failures.[19] The Sheboygan city council became so irate with its street railway for not extending service to the newer parts of town that it ordered city employees to lay the tracks and billed the company.[20] After years of trying to force the street railway to restore service to predepression levels, one Appleton resident demanded that the company "either give us car service or give up the use of the streets which are now encumbered and obstructed by their useless ties and rails."[21]

The lack of funds was responsible not only for the corporations' refusals to provide an adequate quality and quantity of light, water, and transportation, but also for increases in service charges. The Oshkosh Electric Light and Power Company forced the city council to accept its increase in fees for street lights from forty-two dollars to seventy-five dollars by turning out the lights in five-sixths of the city.[22] City councils at Superior, Stevens Point, Appleton, and dozens of other cities blasted

18. *Superior Evening Telegram,* September 17, 1895.
19. *Appleton Weekly Post,* May 18, 25, September 21, December 21, 1893, February 22, 1894, September 3, 1896. *Milwaukee Sentinel,* December 13, 1897. *Grand Rapids Wood County Reporter,* February 21, 1895.
20. *Sheboygan Herald,* August 12, 1893.
21. *Appleton Weekly Post,* December 7, 14, 1893, August 8, 1895.
22. *Milwaukee Sentinel,* March 4, 1894.

their utilities for charging exorbitant rentals for street lights and fire hydrants.[23] City governments were not alone in feeling the pinch of increased charges; private consumers also complained about higher streetcar fares, lighting bills, and water and telephone charges.

The same pressures that forced utilities to curtail services and raise prices also led them to disobey city orders that sought to impose elementary considerations of health and safety and to force the companies to comply with their franchises and ordinances. When management of a new interurban line decided that it could secure more business by using Neenah's main street instead of the side street specified in the franchise and began to lay tracks, the entire police force was called out to restrain the workmen.[24] Appleton officials sped to the courts when a train killed another citizen at the unprotected College Avenue crossing where the city had ordered the railroad to erect guard gates two years earlier. Three years later the company had not installed the gates, so the aldermen ordered the city marshal to arrest the conductor of every train that passed through the city at a speed greater than the fifteen miles per hour stipulated by an antiquated state law.[25] Officials of Superior failed over several years to compel the street railway to obey ordinances that required free transfers and removal of snow that accumulated behind the company's snow fences and rendered sidewalks unpassable.[26]

Some city officials resorted to more forceful methods to compel corporate obedience. When its managers sensed that Sheboygan was going to enfranchise a competitor, the Wisconsin Telephone Company began feverishly to set telephone poles and string wires all over the city in an attempt to persuade the city to continue its franchise. This was not an unusual move. What was novel was Sheboygan's reaction. Protected by police, the superintendent of streets supervised city employees in chopping down all the newly erected poles.[27] City fathers in other Wisconsin communities exhibited the same angry spirit. The Ashland

23. For examples, see *ibid.*, January 9, December 11, 1898. *Superior Evening Telegram,* January 19, 1898. *Appleton Weekly Post,* September 21, 1893.

24. *Milwaukee Sentinel,* August 11, 1899.

25. *Appleton Weekly Post,* February 4, 11, 1897, January 11, 1900.

26. *Superior Evening Telegram,* October 14, December 15, 1897. *Superior Leader,* August 28, 1895.

27. *Milwaukee Sentinel,* January 15, 1893.

Board of Public Works ordered the Wisconsin Central Railroad to replace a rickety wooden bridge with a steel structure. When Public Works Commissioner George P. Rossman learned that the railroad was shoring up the wooden trestle with new timbers instead of steel, he used the cover of darkness on the night of October 16, 1895, to personally chop down the timbers.[28] Six weeks earlier policemen in Wausau had cut down the poles of the Wisconsin Telephone Company and arrested its construction superintendent for illegally extending its scope of operations.[29] Marshfield officials used the axe on the same company's poles when it violated its franchise.[30] Years of experience with the utilities had taught officials that the saw and the axe were often the only instruments of municipal authority that the companies respected. As corporations repeatedly refused to obey city orders, officials responded with whatever means they could command, within the financial limitations that prevented their buying and operating the utilities.

For hard-pressed city treasurers taxation became a third major area of grievances. Some corporations, such as the water companies of Ashland and Baraboo, blandly refused to pay their taxes.[31] Even those companies which paid their taxes (often discounted) were tainted in the minds of many Wisconsinites with evasion because their managers or most prominent stockholders refused to pay their individual taxes.[32]

Outright nonpayment was not the most common or disturbing form of tax dodging. As the depression forced city councils to cast about for new sources of revenue, a number decided to raise assessments of the undertaxed utilities. In 1894 Milwaukee's Tax Commissioner Thomas H. Brown more than doubled the assessment of the trolley and light monopoly from about 8 per cent of the value of its properties to 20 per cent.[33] The utility corporations could not afford such tax increases and,

28. *Ashland Daily News,* October 17, 1895.
29. *Milwaukee Sentinel,* August 30, 1895.
30. *Wausau Daily Record,* October 21, 1898.
31. *Ashland Daily News,* February 15, 21, 1895. *Ashland Weekly Press,* August 8, 1895. *Milwaukee Sentinel,* January 21, 1900.
32. For example, see *Ashland Daily News,* February 15, 1895.
33. The courts ultimately ruled that this increased assessment was an illegal "franchise tax." *Milwaukee Sentinel,* April 27, June 25, August 1, October 2, 1894, June 21, 1895. John A. Butler, "A General View of the New Municipal Program," *Proceedings of the Columbus Conference for Good City Government* (Philadelphia: National Municipal League, 1899), 92–94, hereinafter cited as *Good City Conference,* Columbus, 1899.

realizing that other officials would follow Brown's lead, lobbied a law through the 1895 legislature that cut in half the amount of taxes they owed their cities.[34] Aldermen at such cities as Milwaukee, Portage, and Superior begged the 1897 legislature to repeal this act, but the legislators only raised the license fee and refused to grant similar privileges to water companies.[35] As taxpayers and city officials raged against this form of tax dodging, the mayors of Oshkosh and Waupaca could accurately report in 1898 that the mounting demands for municipal ownership of utilities throughout the state were inspired mainly by the feeling that the corporations did "not pay an equal amount of tax with other property."[36]

Corporations varied their methods to meet the situation. The Racine Water Company told consumers it could not afford to charge lower rates because its properties were valued at over $300,000. When Racine officials promptly increased its assessment from $185,000 to $300,000 however, the company hired Wisconsin's U.S. Sen. Joseph V. Quarles to fight them. The League of Wisconsin Municipalities, representing city officials and reformers, declared that this case typified "the difficulty always involved in dealings with private monopolies in our municipalities. When such monopolies wish to defend exorbitant charges for the service supplied, they are able . . . to represent their plant at a high valuation. But when, on the other hand, they are attempting to escape their just contribution to a city's needs, it seems almost as easy for them to reduce their valuation to comparative insignificance" by employing "legal talent better than the city can usually feel itself justified in retaining."[37] The evasions and exemptions used by utilities to escape their taxes constituted perhaps the most frequent reason for collisions between cities and utilities. At the time the utilities argued that they could not afford to pay their taxes, city officials needed every tax penny they could get.

The 1895 exemption act was the most flagrant example of a fourth area of grievances. Reformers and city officials charged that the utilities too frequently circumvented the popular will by corrupting politicians and the whole political process. Cries

34. Wisconsin, Laws (1895), chap. 363.
35. Wisconsin, Legislative Petitions 1210A and 760S, 1897 Legislature, Box 59, Wisconsin State Archival Series 2/3/1/5–7. Superior Evening Telegram, March 23, 1897.
36. Milwaukee Sentinel, January 2, 1898.
37. Municipality, 1 (August 1900), 42–43.

of bribery by the companies grew louder as the financial straits of utilities and city fathers intensified. When a Milwaukee alderman announced that he had been offered $300 to vote in favor of continuing the city's garbage contract with the current franchise holder, the mayor and city council forced a grand jury investigation.[38] The Sheboygan city council annulled the electric company's franchise when an alderman declared that he had been bribed to vote for renewal of its franchise.[39] The conservative *Oshkosh Northwestern* warned the local street railway that it was unnecessarily creating hatred toward itself by using lobbyists and bribery instead of paying the same amounts publicly into the city treasury.[40]

Such devices came increasingly to form a pattern as the corporations sought immunity from public demands for lower rates, better service, and higher taxes by attempting to control local politics. By 1898 the mere suspicion that Superior's Mayor Starkweather had been "reached" by a corporation was enough to defeat him.[41] The Milwaukee trolley and light monopoly knew what it was doing when it made the state-wide Republican boss its manager, for his political influence protected the company not only at Milwaukee but also at Madison. Payne, defending his other utility, the Wisconsin Telephone Company, from effective competition by the independent companies, persuaded Republican legislators to defeat any bills that would have given the independents long-distance hookups. "The bigger the concerns, the safer they are at the hands of our lawmakers," lamented one editor after Payne had killed the long-distance bill in 1897.[42]

While Wisconsinites speculated freely and imaginatively about the utilities' secret means for controlling politicians, they fought tenaciously against the most obvious forms. How, they wondered, could a politician fairly represent his constituents' demands for regulation when he used the company's free passes on streetcars and trains? One Milwaukee editor repeatedly insisted that the city's failure to regulate its streetcars could be

38. *Milwaukee Sentinel,* August 10, 12, 14, September 8, October 15, 1897.
39. *Ibid.,* February 24, March 10, 1895.
40. Quoted *ibid.,* December 13, 1897.
41. *Superior Evening Telegram,* March 31, April 6, 1898.
42. *Madison Old Dane,* March 26, 1897. See also *State Journal,* March 10, 1897.

blamed primarily on the aldermen's free passes.[43] Suspicion concerning the great influence of what Milwaukee merchant Edward P. Bacon called the "powerful R. R. lobby" underlay the movement to abolish free railway passes to legislators. "With their pockets bulging with free passes," declared an Appleton editor, "legislators cannot be the independent and untrammeled men that they would otherwise be in dealing with railroad corporations in any way." Although Assemblyman Albert R. Hall had promoted a kind of referendum on the antipass bill at the 1895 town meetings—which resulted in 51,000 voters opposing use of the pass and 600 favoring it—the legislature delayed until 1899 to outlaw railway passes.[44] Abolition of the free pass yielded some comfort for reformers who had witnessed repeated failures of efforts toward regulation. How else could one explain such failures except through the corporations' political influence?

In areas where quasi-public corporations were actively involved in politics Wisconsin politicians had to choose between heeding the votes of the majority or the money of the corporations. Those who chose the former course were frequently defeated by those who chose the latter. By the end of the decade conscientious city officials were convinced that they could never perform their duties properly until the corporations were stripped of their political influence. As Wisconsinites developed the yardsticks of selfishness and arrogance to measure the activities of groups, they came to agree with an Appleton editor who denounced "the power which wealthy men [and corporations] secure in coming to the front when campaign funds are being raised. Their action is seldom unselfish. In consequence they often claim a mortgage on their party which claim is not always denied."[45] Wisconsinites were increasingly agreeing with those

43. *Milwaukee Daily News,* April 17, August 29, December 26, 1894, May 24, 1895, January 12, 1897, February 15, 1898, for example.
44. *Milwaukee Sentinel,* March 22, April 4, 20, 1895, April 17, June 20, 24, August 15, 1897, March 20, April 28, 1899. Edward P. Bacon to William Langon, March 21, 1900, Milwaukee Chamber of Commerce Papers, Milwaukee County Historical Society. *Appleton Weekly Post,* November 29, 1894, December 19, 1896, March 9, May 4, 1899. State Grange, *26th Session, 1897,* 30–31. *Wausau Daily Record,* March 20, 1899. *Wood County Reporter,* January 24, April 4, 1895. *Superior Evening Telegram,* March 27, 1895. *State Journal,* April 17, 1895. *Ashland Weekly Press,* January 26, 1895.
45. *Appleton Weekly Post,* June 20, 1895.

public officials who demanded that the utilities' political influence be terminated.

The utilities' managers, of course, viewed the political scene in a different light. Their biggest problem was the uncertainty of a regulatory and taxation process that, in the depression context, could produce endless new pressures on them. The democratization of politics and reform in the depression caused attacks from many directions. Henry C. Payne defended the tax exemption act of 1895 as a way to escape "the mercy of the assessors" who had arbitrarily raised the trolley and light company's assessment, and charged that the company had gone into receivership because of orders motivated by the "caprice and pleasure" of city officials.[46] It is difficult to accept such justifications for the utilities' manipulation of the political process. Most Wisconsin aldermen and reformers seemed afraid of alienating companies that provided needed services, and there is no evidence in any Wisconsin city of widespread aldermanic sandbagging of the utilities, as happened in Chicago.

A variety of sparks ignited these local fights. The underlying cause for inadequate service, high costs, tax dodging, and political influence was the dire financial condition of the utilities. But if this were the sole cause it did not completely explain the fury of the battles on both sides. Why, for example, did the utilities continue to disobey city orders, to seek lower taxes, and to retain their political influence after the return of prosperous times? Why did they claim to be solvent in some instances, as in their reports to stockholders, and to be bankrupt whenever the city tried to tax or regulate them? If they were bankrupt, how could they afford such expenses as free passes to politicians? These questions, of great concern to reformers, help explain why reformers were less sympathetic toward utilities than to other businesses that had also been affected adversely by the depression. The utilities seemed to be blatant liars whose excuse of poverty sounded hollow when they issued free passes, refused to open their books, and continued to oppose regulation after 1897. Reformers continually asked why they spent money to influence politicians when they needed it urgently for improvements and taxes.

The utilities had answers. First, their political alliances had not begun with the panic, and the companies expected the same cordiality from politicians when they adopted unpopular econ-

46. *Milwaukee Daily News*, May 21, 1895.

omies after 1893 that they had experienced when they had originated municipal services in earlier times. Therefore, the utilities continued to seek friendly politicians. More important- ly, the utilities had not been accustomed to significant local regulation before the panic, and they now feared that one major concession would open the door for reformers to enact almost any measure. For this reason they continued to oppose local regulation after 1897 and sought devices—regulation and taxa- tion by the state government or long-term, specific franchises— that would prevent unpredictable actions by local politicians.

IV

While Milwaukee's six-year fight for a municipal garbage plant had certain unique features, it was not significantly differ- ent from hundreds of similar skirmishes around the state. To follow such a battle is to trace from its sources the mounting sense of frustration and anger within the community that made quasi-public corporations the most hated institutions in the state by the end of the decade.

Before 1878 every Milwaukee household or business had dis- posed of its own garbage. That year, as the city's population exceeded 100,000, the city assumed responsibility by contracting with individuals to remove the community's garbage. The first contractors were farmers who carried the garbage to their farms, but eventually their wagons with their smelly loads passing along streets drew such protests that the city had to end that system. During the eighties and early nineties the city con- tracted with corporations that either burned the garbage or dumped it in rivers and Lake Michigan. In 1891 the city's Democratic bosses granted a full monopoly on garbage removal to a group of ward heelers and campaign contributors that called itself the Forrestal Garbage Consuming Company. Since this monopoly raised the cost of garbage removal from $25,000 to $85,000 and deprived Republicans of the chance to compete for this profitable business, a few people—Horace Rublee, for one—proposed that the city build a municipal garbage plant at that time.[47]

Over the next five years Republicans regained power and gave the exclusive garbage collection contract to the Wisconsin

---

47. Bayrd Still, *Milwaukee: The History of a City* (Madison: State Historical Society of Wisconsin, 1948), 364–65. *Milwaukee Sentinel*, June 22, October 1, November 7, 1891, February 18, 1892.

Rendering Company, owned by party members. Once this public service had become a political football, the movement for a municipal plant gained momentum. Doctrinaire advocates of municipal ownership, such as the Populist *Daily News,* were joined by economy-minded groups like the Merchants and Manufacturers Association, the Taxpayers' League, and the Milwaukee Municipal League, which all believed that Milwaukee's system of garbage removal was an outrageously lucrative political payoff. The Municipal League's first project to win unqualified praise from the *Daily News*—it had retreated from a preoccupation with low municipal expenditures—was its 1897 drive for a municipal garbage plant. Supported by Mayor William Rauschenberger, a Republican progressive, the reformers tried to get the 1897 legislature to authorize the city to sell bonds for the plant. Although no one spoke out against the reformers' bill, the law included the strange and extraordinary provision that three-fourths of the Common Council would have to approve the bond issue.[48]

Infuriated with the rendering company for this evidence of lobbying at Madison, reformers returned to Milwaukee determined to curb the company's power. They forced the Common Council to ignore the company's exclusive contract and to reopen competitive bidding. One company submitted a bid $22,500 lower than that of the rendering company, but then strange events occurred: companies with lower bids suddenly were unable to meet the council's specifications. With the rendering company's contract due to expire in August, it appeared that the old company would receive the contract by default. Reformers, taxpayers, city officials, and the *Sentinel* felt "more than a suspicion that the emergency is made to order."[49]

So far, the company had aroused only the reformers. But on August 10 Alderman Charles Elkert announced that the company had offered him $300 to renew its contract. Now there was concrete proof that the company was defeating the reformers with bribery. The Municipal League focused the growing mass support at a huge protest meeting. The *Sentinel,* reflecting public opinion, charged that the twenty-two aldermen who voted for the contract ranked "as employees of a private corporation first and as representatives of the people . . . only when

48. *Milwaukee Sentinel,* March 31, August 17, 1897. *Milwaukee Daily News,* March 29, 31, 1897.
49. *Milwaukee Sentinel,* April 10, June 3, July 28, 31, August 5, 1897.

the public interests do not come in conflict with the profits of legislative jobbery." The mounting cries of corporate arrogance and political treachery unified nearly all Milwaukeeans in favor of the municipal garbage plant.[50]

The reformers persuaded the legislature's special session in August to repeal the requirement that three-fourths of the aldermen had to approve the bonds,[51] and, on August 26, 1897, the city's health department began carting the garbage to a seventy-three-acre plot in suburban Wauwatosa. Although the rendering company mounted an energetic campaign to "embarrass the Health department" and "confuse the public" by claiming that its system was cheaper and more sanitary, the aldermen on September 14 voted 27 to 13 to sell bonds for a municipal plant. This "wise and progressive step," in the words of the *Catholic Citizen,* seemed to end the matter. In fact, however, the battle had only begun. Two months later the state supreme court ruled that the 1897 garbage law was unconstitutional because it was, in effect, "special legislation" forbidden in the Milwaukee charter.[52]

Sustained in the courtroom, the rendering company hastily organized a new firm under the name "Cooper and Burke" and applied for the garbage contract. The aldermen granted the contract in February, 1898, but the company had forgotten Mayor Rauschenberger. He vetoed the contract with a scathing message, in which he blasted the men "who make it a business and trade to influence legislation and shape it to their profitable ends, even at the expense of the welfare of the commonwealth and at the cost of the reputation of public officials." This latest piece of corporate arrogance prompted the *Catholic Citizen* to observe that Milwaukeeans preferred "a moderate and gradual course towards municipal ownership. But this hornswoggling double dealing is too much for public patience." Realizing their error, the aldermen sustained the mayor's veto by a 34 to 8 vote, and all three parties endorsed the municipal plant in the 1898 elections. For good measure Milwaukeeans turned out the Republican aldermen and replaced them with Democrats and Populists.[53]

50. *Ibid.,* August 10, 12, 14, September 8, 1897. *Milwaukee Catholic Citizen,* August 21, 1897.
51. *Milwaukee Sentinel,* August 17, 21, 1897.
52. *Ibid.,* August 27, September 14, October 15, November 11, December 11, 1897. *Milwaukee Catholic Citizen,* August 21, 1897.
53. *Milwaukee Sentinel,* February 1, 2, March 1, 12, 18, 1898. *League*

The rendering company never understood that its manipulation of the political process had assured its eventual defeat. Since the reformers were united and had captured the political process with their techniques of mass involvement, the company turned to the sympathetic courts. When it persuaded the supreme court in July, 1898, to restrain the city from issuing bonds, the city advertised for new bids with revenues from the current treasury. In October the company again enjoined the city—this time for exceeding its debt limit—but by 1899 the city was solvent and again advertised for bids. On September 26, 1899, Mayor David S. Rose signed the ordinance that permitted construction of the municipal plant. Ten minutes later William H. Austin, architect of the faulty 1897 law, enjoined the city once more, and a few months later the state supreme court again ruled in favor of the company. The legal tug of war began anew in February, 1900, and not until 1903 could the city finally complete its municipal garbage plant.[54]

Milwaukee's fight over municipal garbage disposal was not unusual among Wisconsin cities. A blatant act of corporate arrogance and political corruption—the bribery of an alderman —was required to unite reformers with disparate purposes and to rally public opinion to a single objective. Only when reformers could show concretely that the utility was a manifest menace to popular government could they use the techniques of mass pressure to defeat the older styles of city politics. With its propaganda deflated by the superior mass campaigns of reformers and its political force weakened by the politicians' recognition that their hopes for re-election lay in the voters' power, the rendering company had only the courts to defend it. The war had truly narrowed, as such struggles usually did, into a fight between the city and the arrogant "special interest" groups.

V

By about 1897 most Wisconsinites agreed that new techniques had to be developed to curtail the power of the quasi-public

Bulletin, 1 (February 19, 1898), and 2 (March 19, 1898), Reference Collections, Milwaukee Public Library. *Milwaukee Catholic Citizen*, February 19, 1898. *Milwaukee Daily News*, February 1, 15, March 12, 1898.

54. *Milwaukee Sentinel*, July 15, 19, December 4, 1898, May 9, September 26, 1899, February 3, 1900. Still, *Milwaukee*, 364–65.

corporations. The depression had eliminated forever the pre-1893 technique of enfranchising a competitor to force established companies to behave. Few investors cared to challenge what were now monopolies. But, with the return of prosperity, city governments and individuals had enough money available to fulfill the dreams they had developed in the lean depression years. Over the next several years they developed three important means to reassert popular control over services crucial for urban development.

The most obvious means was municipal ownership, which in the years before the panic, had been proposed only by a few doctrinaire radicals. Private ownership had appealed to the antigovernment and antipolitician prejudices of predepression reformers, and most urban residents had been eager for capitalists to spare them tax dollars by providing needed services. Few civic-minded individuals ever questioned the suitability of private ownership of public services. When cities had operated utilities, notably waterworks, it had been because no capitalist had come forward, and the cities' ownership entailed no battle against private owners. In such instances the label "municipal ownership" was considered as inappropriate for the waterworks as it would have been for streets or schools.[55]

The depression and its repercussions in public and private finances created the crusade for municipal ownership. Only *after* the private companies failed to provide safe and economical services did municipal ownership become a popular movement. When companies used political influence to defeat the demands of citizens for minor regulations, they drove their opponents into the radical camp, which sponsored municipal ownership. By the end of the decade the purpose of the crusade was as much to restore popular sovereignty over the cities as it was to secure better or cheaper services. To "break loose the grasp which [the] corporation has on the city's throat," in the words of Superior's Dr. R. C. Oglivie, cities increasingly followed Milwaukee's example in its settlement of the garbage controversy. The *Wausau Record,* a conservative paper, accurately reported in 1898 that "the large majority of citizens are growing more and more favorable to municipal control."[56] A

55. This applies mainly to waterworks. A total of 61 per cent of Wisconsin's waterworks were city-run in 1896. M. N. Baker, "Water-Works," in *Municipal Monopolies,* ed. Bemis, 25.

56. *Superior Evening Telegram,* February 25, 1898. *Wausau Record,* quoted *ibid.,* March 11, 1898.

Catholic paper in Milwaukee announced that "the political gales are blowing in the direction of municipal ownership."[57] The topic became standard fare at the new discussion clubs, and university extension lecturers made municipal ownership a nearly foolproof means for achieving honest local government.[58] By 1898 Mayor W. T. Hurd of Boscobel reported that every official who attended the monthly meetings of the state's mayors strongly favored municipal ownership.[59] Nearly all of Wisconsin's local political parties pledged municipal ownership of at least one local utility.

As voters' attitudes toward public ownership deepened and funds became available, one Wisconsin city after another turned to municipal operation of utilities. In 1899 "the spirit of municipal ownership made itself manifest" in the citizens of Oconomowoc, who voted $77,000 in bonds for a city water and light plant.[60] After overwhelming support in the 1899 elections, Wausau ended a long fight by purchasing and managing the electric company's plant. In 1896 Janesville began negotiations to buy the plant of its utility monopoly; Whitewater in 1899 and Sheboygan in 1900 created municipal waterworks; and Berlin, River Falls, and Plymouth began municipal lighting plants in 1900.[61] When four years of the "splendid success of the water works system" demonstrated to Columbus in 1899 "the great advantage of municipal ownership," that city built a lighting plant.[62] City officials welcomed the return of prosperity in 1897 because they could then, by managing the utilities themselves, eliminate the corporations.

While there were complaints about the rates and services of municipally owned utilities,[63] these complaints were surprising-

57. *Milwaukee Catholic Citizen,* May 6, 1899.
58. See 1898–1899 program of Milwaukee Social Economics Club, Milwaukee County Historical Society; *Wood County Reporter,* January 9, 1896, for examples.
59. *Milwaukee Sentinel,* December 25, 1898.
60. Gustav Meissner, "Electric Lighting Plant of the City of Oconomowoc," *Municipality,* 1 (October 1900), 15–18. *Milwaukee Sentinel,* March 26, April 23, May 21, 1899, January 7, February 11, 1900.
61. *Milwaukee Sentinel,* October 20, 1896, March 12, 1899, August 13, 1899, July 1, 1900. Karl Mathie to Richard T. Ely, January 3, 1899, Ely Papers, Manuscripts Division, State Historical Society of Wisconsin. *Municipality,* 1 (August 1900), 42, 44, and (October 1900), 44.
62. W. C. Leitsch, "Municipal Electric Lighting at Columbus," *Municipality,* 1 (April 1900), 32–36.
63. "Water Rates in Milwaukee," *Engineering Record,* 38 (July 30, 1898), 177–78. "The New Water Rates in Milwaukee," *ibid.,* 39 (Decem-

ly rare. Not a single local political party or reform league made an issue of the services or costs of a municipal utility. Charles E. Monroe, an official of the Milwaukee Municipal League, typified the average reformer's attitude when he reported to a statewide conference on Milwaukee's experience: "In contrast with the operation of public utilities by private corporations the success of our [municipally owned] water works system stands out in high relief."[64]

Some citizens were so angered by the poor service and high rates of their utilities that they could not wait for their city governments to create municipal plants and developed alternatives. Reflecting the depression's civic consciousness, the second means to reassert popular control was the consumer-owned-and-operated company. While private investors would not risk their capital on a new company to challenge a monopoly, consumers of the monopoly's service believed that they could provide better and cheaper service if they all banded together to form a competitive company. Profit was not their motive; service at low rates and responsible management were. The advocates of these companies persuaded the users of telephones or electric lights to cancel service from the local monopoly and to subscribe one share of stock each (usually fifty dollars) in the new cooperative company. No individual could buy more than one share, and each stockholder received telephone or electric light services in exchange for his investment.

Widely publicized as the "Wisconsin Valley Plan" because it originated in the Wisconsin River cities of Wausau, Grand Rapids, Merrill, and Marshfield, the cooperative movement began as a series of local revolts against the Wisconsin Telephone Company, which in 1894 had a monopoly in nearly every city in the state. Publicizing their viewpoint that local residents need no longer "slavishly submit to being robbed by a Bell dynasty as long as it chooses to sap at their vitals," the cooperative telephone companies of the valley had little trouble gaining subscribers. In 1895, when the Wisconsin Telephone Company was charging three dollars a month for residential telephones, the new cooperative Wood County Telephone Company soon

---

ber 31, 1898), 90. *Milwaukee Sentinel,* January 19, 30, July 12, 1898, January 31, 1899. *State Journal,* February 25, 27, March 6, 13, 1897. *Wood County Reporter,* November 4, 1898.

64. Monroe, "The Time to Deal with Corporations Asking Public Franchises," *Municipality,* 1 (August 1900), 13.

lured away three-fourths of the Bell monopoly's subscribers at Grand Rapids, and by 1896 it was charging its subscribers only fifty cents a month. Within a few months after its formation in 1895 the Wausau Telephone Company had won over all but one of the Wisconsin company's subscribers. Spreading out from the Wisconsin River Valley cities, these cooperative companies mushroomed until by 1900 there were over 100. Although the Bell monopoly tried to destroy these local competitors by slashing rates, by refusing to allow them long-distance connections, and by offering free telephone service, the cooperative companies gained strength as the decade wore on.[65]

The cooperative telephone companies offered such effective relief from the poor service, high rates, and general arrogance of the monopoly that a number of communities created similar companies to fight other utility monopolies. A Grand Rapids editor encouraged that city's Business Men's Association in its successful project, in 1897, to found the consumer-owned Twin Cities Electric Light and Power Company, and other cities, such as Fond du Lac, followed suit. Even more popular were local cooperative insurance companies in cities like Madison, and at Wausau, where the insurance company included a significant number of workers.[66]

These consumer-owned companies represented more than either traditional business competition or efforts to secure better service and rates. They revealed, above all, how the new

65. Albert H. Sanford, "A Co-operative Telephone System," *ibid.*, 1 (October 1900), 29–31. John Gaynor, "The Local Telephone System," *ibid.*, 1 (February 1901), 14–16. Gaynor, "Wisconsin Valley Plan," in *Municipal Monopolies*, ed. Bemis, 358–61. *Appleton Weekly Post*, March 16, August 24, 1893, January 10, October 10, November 14, 1895, February 13, July 2, 1896, February 22, 1900. *Wood County Reporter*, February 14, 28, March 28, May 2, 16, 30, September 12, October 31, November 7, 14, 28, December 26, 1895, June 18, 1896, September 30, October 14, 21, 28, November 11, 1897. *Ashland Daily News*, February 6, March 24, October 11, 1895. *State Journal*, May 13, 1895, March 20, 1900. *Old Dane*, March 12, August 27, 1897. *Ashland Daily Press*, March 2, 1899. *The Madison State*, October 13, 1899. *Wausau Daily Record*, February 8, 1899. Unidentified clipping dated July 9, 1897, Edward W. Bemis to Richard T. Ely, September 19, 1898, both in Ely Papers. *Municipality*, 1 (August 1900), 35. *Milwaukee Sentinel*, April 6, 1895, June 28, 1896, May 28, October 1, 1899. *Superior Leader*, July 17, 1897. *Milwaukee Daily News*, April 2, 1895. Frank Parsons, *The City for the People* (Philadelphia: C. F. Taylor, 1901), 119, 590.

66. *Wood County Reporter*, April 15, July 22, September 23, 1897. *Old Dane*, August 27, 1897. *Wausau Daily Record*, March 9, 17, 28, April 19, 1899. *Municipality*, 1 (February 1901), 46.

civic consciousness unified urban dwellers to act against an entrenched monopoly. John A. Gaynor, Irish-born businessman and politician at Grand Rapids, enthusiastically promoted the Wisconsin Valley Plan. "The greatest point gained in the struggle for independence" against the Wisconsin Telephone Company, he declared, "was the building up of a local patriotism, an *esprit de corps*, that has united our people to such a degree that we can protect ourselves against *any* monopoly that oppresses us. . . . So long as we can keep our people united there is no power that can crush us."[67] Arguing that "there is no worse slavery than that of selfishness," one editor urged local residents to boycott any businessman who undercut efforts of the cooperative company by accepting the Wisconsin company's free telephones.[68] The success of these aroused, united, local consumers was seen in the failure of the Wisconsin company's free telephone offers.

When they discovered obstacles in the paths of obtaining municipal and cooperative ownership, city residents sought relief through a third means—by appealing to the state legislature. Since they lacked legal power over most areas of regulation and taxation in their own communities, they were forced to secure help from the state government. Knowing that the utilities held great influence over the legislature, they expanded their economic demands for franchise limitations and referenda, permission to operate municipal utilities, and tax reform into political demands for local home rule, antilobbying laws, direct primaries, and the overthrow of the ruling state machine.

These state-wide campaigns revealed that by the late nineties reformers and city officials had concluded that corporate arrogance in its various forms was the greatest challenge to local government. Reformers and officials also realized that their problems were not unique, that other cities were also casting about for effective ways of controlling their utilities. In 1897 Mayor Schoetz of Menasha invited the mayors of three other Fox River Valley cities, Appleton, Neenah, and Kaukauna, to discuss the best ways of limiting franchises.[69] The best measure of how completely progressivism had supplanted mugwumpery was the new alliance that emerged to coordinate the state-wide

67. Gaynor, "Wisconsin Valley Plan," 361. *Wood County Reporter,* October 21, 1897. See also *Wausau Daily Record,* February 8, 1899.
68. *Wood County Reporter,* September 30, October 28, 1897.
69. *Appleton Weekly Post,* April 28, 1897.

conferences and lobbying campaigns. This alliance united former mugwumps with their old enemies, the politicians.

By 1898 members of the Milwaukee Municipal League believed that they were in dire need of the support of citizens in other cities. A basic transformation of the league's objectives since its formation reinforced the belief that Milwaukee's ills could be cured only at the state level. Through fights with the city's garbage, trolley, and light monopolies, the league's members by 1898 became convinced that the greatest menace to honest government was the quasi-public corporation. At the same time that the local battles made them eager to regulate utilities, league leaders had promised the National Municipal League that they would try to organize Wisconsin's cities to secure passage of the national league's model-city charter and the municipal corporations act. While these model bills looked toward closer centralization of executive authority in city governments, their primary appeals to the Milwaukee league were the provisions for home rule and utility regulation which would permit reformers to confront the utilities at Milwaukee instead of at Madison.

The local battles and the desire to apply the national model led the Milwaukee league to cast aside its old fear and hatred of politicians in the face of the greater menace of the utilities. City officials, on their side, were eager for some state-wide organization that would give them the necessary data to counter the elaborate statistics and impressive legal artillery of their local utilities and that would work for laws to liberate them from their corporations. Nearly all of the state's mayors—including those from Oshkosh, Fond du Lac, Waupaca, Janesville, Grand Rapids, and Neenah—told the *Milwaukee Sentinel* in 1897 that the greatest need of their cities was to find some way to force their utilities to obey city orders and pay their taxes, and most of the chief executives favored municipal ownership.[70]

When the Milwaukee Municipal League proposed formation of the League of Wisconsin Municipalities to exchange experiences and lobby in Madison, officials of various cities eagerly joined. Eleven mayors accepted the Milwaukee league's invitation for a preliminary meeting in 1898 to lay the groundwork for the League of Wisconsin Municipalities and elected Madison's Mayor Charles E. Whelan as president. This first conference established a bureau where cities could share experiences

70. *Milwaukee Sentinel,* January 2, 1898.

and set the stage for a larger meeting just prior to the 1899 legislative session.[71]

The January, 1899, conference at Milwaukee formally launched the League of Wisconsin Municipalities. The conference featured leaders of the National Municipal League like Clinton Rogers Woodruff, who promoted the new model-city charter and the municipal corporations act as the best ways for legislating home rule and municipal ownership. The national leaders had so much confidence in the Milwaukee league that they chose Wisconsin as the first state to try their model charter. In addition to most of Milwaukee's city officials, who wandered in and out of sessions that lasted for the better part of a week, mayors from twenty-seven Wisconsin cities formally endorsed the model bills and their provisions for utility regulation and home rule. They urged the 1899 legislature to adopt home rule and stricter taxation of utilities. At the conclusion of the conference, John A. Butler appointed a committee composed of Milwaukee leaguers John F. Burke, Charles E. Monroe, J. G. Flanders, Butler, the mayors of Madison, Columbus, and Hudson, and Samuel E. Sparling, professor at the University of Wisconsin and secretary of the League of Wisconsin Municipalities, to draft the needed bills.[72]

This committee directed the 1899 legislative strategy of the League of Wisconsin Municipalities and the Milwaukee Municipal League. When the committee introduced the model bills in the legislature they received support from several hundred leading Wisconsinites, including city officials, prominent businessmen, and the leader of the agrarian radicals, Assemblyman Hall. Aiming toward home rule to allow the cities to manage their own utilities, the league specifically promoted bills that would limit all franchises to twenty-one years, would force utilities to file financial statements that would be the bases for taxation and regulation, and would require referenda for consideration of such questions as franchises and municipal owner-

71. *Ibid.*, December 15, 1898. *Proceedings of the Convention Held at Fond du Lac, June 26–27, 1899,* bull. no. 3 (Madison: League of Wisconsin Municipalities, 1899), 3–5, 10–24. Ford H. MacGregor, *The League of Wisconsin Municipalities: Its History, Activities, and Accomplishments* (Madison: privately published, 1925), 2. *Milwaukee Daily News,* December 15, 1898.

72. *Milwaukee Sentinel,* December 15, 25, 1898, January 17, 1899. *State Journal,* January 6, 1899. *League Bulletin,* 12 (January 28, 1899). Woodruff, "A Year's Advance," *Good City Conference,* Columbus, 1899, 176. *Milwaukee Daily News,* January 5, 6, 1899.

ship. More significant in the history of the Milwaukee league was its support of the bill to eliminate the municipal debt limit for such investments as publicly owned utilities. The Milwaukee league, born in a revolt against municipal extravagance and haunted by the specter of the debt limit, now urged cities to forget this limit in order to bring about the municipal ownership that would free Milwaukee from its private utilities. While the reformers failed to secure most of the league's objectives, the new League of Wisconsin Municipalities was instrumental in enacting laws that forced utility lobbyists to register, required referenda on certain franchises, increased taxes of quasi-public corporations, and outlawed the granting of free passes.[73]

Despite these gains, the League of Wisconsin Municipalities was disappointed by the 1899 legislature, and it turned to the exchange of information for use in local fights. At its Fond du Lac convention in June, the secretary reported that "sentiment was almost unanimous" in favor of municipal ownership. At this meeting reformers and mayors were joined by other city officials and by the entire common councils of two cities. Denouncing mugwumpery and retrenchment as mere "pennywise enthusiasm" (in the words of John F. Young, mayor of Brodhead), they sought ways of finding enough money to buy their private utilities. To assist local officials the league expanded its information bureau and collected facts on the services, taxes, and franchises of Wisconsin cities. To disseminate these facts it established a magazine, *Municipality*, early in 1900.[74]

By 1900 the League of Wisconsin Municipalities had become a determined state-wide lobby that provided city officials with a potent weapon in their fights with corporations. By uniting politicians with their former enemies, the mugwumps, the league revealed how completely corporate arrogance and tax dodging had come to overshadow all other political issues. The secretary of the National Municipal League was so impressed

73. *Milwaukee Sentinel,* January 17, March 20, 22, 1899. Joshua Stark, "The New Municipal Program and Wisconsin Cities," *Good City Conference,* Milwaukee, 1900, 106–18. McShane, "Milwaukee Street Railways," 123–24.

74. *Proceedings of the Convention Held at Fond du Lac, 1899,* especially 31, 37. Samuel E. Sparling, "League of Wisconsin Municipalities," *Annals of the American Academy of Political and Social Science,* 14 (September 1899), 116–17. *Municipality,* 1 (April 1900), 30. *Milwaukee Daily News,* June 30, 1899.

with the activities in Wisconsin, "where the chosen officials of the cities show an intelligent and generous disposition to cooperate with public spirited citizens," that he declared he knew "of no state where the prospect is more hopeful" for enactment of the national league's bills.[75] In the meantime, Wisconsin's city dwellers would have the opportunity of going to the state level when municipal and cooperative ownership failed.

VI

The battles against the utilities forged a grass-roots coalition of consumers, taxpayers, and citizens. Older loyalties to interest groups, ethno-religious units, and national political parties, and pre-eminence of the rights of private property began to decline as city residents from all backgrounds discovered the far-reaching evils of corporate arrogance. As the corporations increasingly refused to obey city orders, the reform coalitions became larger and more determined to bring them under control. By the summer of 1894 Milwaukee officials felt themselves "powerless" to regulate the street railway company.[76] Sheboygan's three-year failure to regulate the Wisconsin Telephone Company raised "the vital question" of whether a city "has the control of its own streets, or whether any corporation can use them as it sees fit."[77] Ashlanders wondered whether "the streets of a city are public highways" or whether they belonged to the railroads.[78]

The emerging reform coalition would have had less popular appeal and would have been less firm in its resolve to curb the corporations had the political process responded to the pressures of city officials and reformers. But whenever the cities sought relief, reported the *Janesville Republican,* "it has been of no avail because of the powerful influences of wealth which the corporations have always at hand."[79] This discovery taught city residents that consumers and taxpayers could not expect relief until they developed political weapons for popular government and toppled the dominant machines.

75. Woodruff, "A Year's Municipal Development," *Good City Conference,* Milwaukee, 1900, 71.
76. *Milwaukee Sentinel,* August 25, 1894.
77. *Ibid.,* September 27, 1896.
78. *Ashland Daily Press,* December 15, 28, 1899. *Ashland Daily News,* December 15, 1899.
79. Quoted in *Superior Evening Telegram,* July 27, 1898.

The return of prosperity came too late to change the habits both sides had developed during the depression. Corporations still refused to make minor concessions because they feared what angry citizens would do, once they had established the principle of municipal regulation. The utilities sought political immunity in the forms of state regulation or long-term franchises. But political immunity was the one price angry citizens were least willing to pay.

These fights reinforced, when they did not create, the depression's new dichotomy between public and selfish interests. The body of aroused, angry consumers, united under the banner of "the public interest," became the core of the progressive political impulse. The most spectacular battle in this long war was fought at Milwaukee. After that battle city residents would not stop until the public interest was supreme in the political process.

He did not look like a villain. His bushy mustache and deep-set eyes gave him a slightly sinister cast, but he might have been the town barber or bartender. Nor did his personality mark him for the part. Known to a leading clergyman as "a liberal man, with large and generous ideas," he cared for an invalid wife for most of his adult life. For relaxation he loved whist and checkers and excelled at both. His engaging manners charmed a wide circle of friends that included men who were his political enemies. His friend Theodore Roosevelt called him "the sweetest, most lovable, and most trustful man" he had ever known.[1]

And yet, paradoxically, partly because of what Robert M. La Follette called "his genial personality," Henry Clay Payne was the most hated man in Wisconsin at the end of the century. In the prosperous days of urban promotion and political partisanship before the panic, humorist-politician George Peck observed that Wisconsinites had named their babies after Payne and his colleague Charles Pfister. After the depression had made them aware of the sinister power of corporations, parents were more apt to "frighten children when they are bad by telling them that if they don't look out, Payne and Pfister will get them."[2] The rise and fall of Henry C. Payne, his transformation from hero to villain in the public's judgment, was at once a major cause and a result of the origins of progressivism in Wisconsin.

Payne first attracted attention in 1872 when his Young Men's Republican Club stepped into a political vacuum left by the indifference of Milwaukee's Republican leaders toward President Ulysses S. Grant. Payne's group carried Milwaukee for Grant, and the grateful President offered him the Milwaukee postmastership, which Payne accepted in 1876 to prevent a rival faction from winning prestige. From his positions as postmaster and secretary of the Republican State Central Committee, which he occupied from 1876 until 1885, Payne converted Mil-

---

1. William W. Wight, *Henry Clay Payne: A Life* (Milwaukee: privately published, 1907), 12–13, 14–15, 20–21, 168, 170. George Nicholson to Richard T. Ely, March 13, 1894, Ely Papers, Manuscripts Division, State Historical Society of Wisconsin. *Milwaukee Journal*, October 5, 1895, in Wisconsin Biographical Collections, State Historical Society of Wisconsin.
2. La Follette in Wight, *Payne*, 170. *Peck's Sun*, in *Milwaukee Sentinel*, January 6, 1900.

waukee County from a predominantly Democratic into a leading Republican county in the state. His "superb ability as an organizer," in the words of Republican U.S. Sen. John C. Spooner, was "a marked natural aptitude," according to Democratic U.S. Sen. William F. Vilas. Because Payne possessed superior knowledge of what he called "the mathematics of organization and operation in practical politics," Republican National Chairman James S. Clarkson was delighted to have Payne represent Wisconsin on the Republican National Committee from 1880 to 1904. National politicians also demonstrated their profound respect for Payne's political acumen. Mark Hanna implored William McKinley to reward Payne for managing his 1896 western campaign with the postmaster generalship; Theodore Roosevelt, more impressed by Payne than McKinley had been, appointed the Milwaukeean postmaster general in 1901, a position Payne held until his death. Such national recognition naturally increased Payne's political power in Wisconsin. Republican legislators had early learned that their futures depended on following his lead. "Everybody," as La Follette said, "was taught to believe that Payne had some occult and mysterious power as a political manager," and consequently, "when he said a thing would happen in politics or legislation, it always did happen."[3]

Following Grover Cleveland's election in 1884 and Payne's forced retirement from the Milwaukee Post Office a year later, he turned his political influence and organizing talents to economic advantage. Before 1885 he had confined most of his business ventures to real-estate speculation, and his "fortune" was estimated at $15,000. In 1885 he turned to corporation management and within ten years was worth $500,000. In 1886 he was

3. The Clarkson, Spooner, and Vilas quotes are from Wight, *Payne*, 179, 37, 38. See also 24–44, 112, 114, 170, 175, 179, 183. Robert M. La Follette, *La Follette's Autobiography: A Personal Narrative of Political Experiences* (Madison: Robert M. La Follette Co., 1911, 1913), 74. Carroll Pollock Lahman, "Robert Marion La Follette as Public Speaker and Political Leader, 1855–1905" (Ph.D. diss., University of Wisconsin, 1939), 231–32, 346. Richard N. Current, *Pine Logs and Politics: A Life of Philetus Sawyer* (Madison: State Historical Society of Wisconsin, 1950), 237–38. *State Journal*, January 14, 1887. *Milwaukee Sentinel*, October 15, 1887, February 28, 1900. *Milwaukee Journal*, October 5, 1895, in Wisconsin Biographical Collections. Mark Hanna to H. C. Adams, February 5, 1896, Adams Papers, Manuscripts Division, State Historical Society of Wisconsin. H. Wayne Morgan, *William McKinley and His America* (Syracuse: Syracuse University Press, 1963), 262–63. John Morton Blum, *The Republican Roosevelt* (New York: Atheneum, 1962), 42–43, 69n.

made vice-president of the fledgling Wisconsin Telephone Company and in 1889 he became president of the corporation. In 1890, when he became a director of the First National Bank of Milwaukee, the Milwaukee Railroad made him president of its subsidiary, the Milwaukee and Northern Railroad. In 1894 he was appointed receiver of the Northern Pacific Railroad, which also operated the Wisconsin Central Railway, and in addition became president of the Fox River Valley Electric Railway. Most importantly, a prominent eastern syndicate of capitalists hired him in 1890 to consolidate Milwaukee's street railways and lighting companies into a single monopoly.[4]

The appeal of an unemployed postmaster to the stockholders of these large corporations was obvious. While Payne's brilliant managerial talents assisted corporate organization, his proven political influence was of enormous value to investors, whose quasi-public activities thrust them continually into politics. Payne became a corporation manager whose main qualification was his ability to influence every rank of politician from alderman to president; he was, in fact, one of the nation's most accomplished lobbyists before political bodies. Nothing, wrote one editor, could "compare with the mellifluous tones of Henry C. Payne . . . as he softly and sweetly pleads for 'vested rights' before a legislative committee. Henry is a 'sweet singer.' " A Milwaukee editor dubbed him "Hypnotizer" C. Payne in recognition of his uncanny legislative talents.[5]

When he began his career as a lobbyist in 1885, Payne could not have foreseen that as a result of such activities in behalf of Milwaukee's trolley and light monopoly, he would become Wisconsin's most hated man. But his lobbying in fact converted the state's mugwumps into progressives, transformed men from all backgrounds into his opponents, and produced a major revolt within the Republican party. Payne's activities served to define the issues of Wisconsin progressivism.

I

When Payne entered the Milwaukee traction business in 1890 Milwaukeeans had developed a fairly general consensus

4. Wight, *Payne,* 48–53, 56–59, 79–85. *Milwaukee Journal,* October 5, 1895, in Wisconsin Biographical Collections.

5. Wight, *Payne,* 51, 52. La Follette, *Autobiography,* 74–77. Nils P. Haugen, *Pioneer and Political Reminiscences* (Madison: State Historical Society of Wisconsin, ca. 1930) , 94. *State Journal,* March 24, 1897.

toward the need for companies that offered lighting and transportation services. Newspapers of all political shades urged electrification of the street railways to relieve congestion around the factories and extend the city's boundaries, and they were at least as enthusiastic about replacing gaslights with electric lamps.[6]

Milwaukeeans were more eager to obtain the services than to regulate the promoters. The city's street railway policy, declared the *Evening Wisconsin,* should be "to help build up and extend Milwaukee. Whatever antagonizes this one purpose is at least short-sighted, if not illegal."[7] Milwaukeeans thought they could secure regulation of service by encouraging competing companies and technologies. "The city needs rapid transit," proclaimed the *Sentinel* during an 1887 controversy over street railway service, "and if anybody is ready to provide it," the existing companies would "need to look out for themselves."[8] When the Badger Illuminating Company disobeyed city orders on the location of wires in 1889, the Common Council enfranchised a competitor, the Edison Illuminating Company.[9] By 1890 the policy of enfranchising competitors to secure better and more efficient service gave Milwaukee six street railways and an equal number of electric companies.[10]

By 1890 the policy of encouraging competition had begun to spawn opposition. Some people argued that the city could no longer evade its responsibility to regulate the existing companies. Following a ruling by City Attorney Eugene S. Elliott in 1887 that the city had the legal power to force street railways to obey its orders,[11] Republican Alderman Henry Baumgaertner began his long crusade against Milwaukee's private utilities. "If any company contrary to the plain provisions of its franchises . . . violates our ordinances," he cried in 1888, it "should in my opinion have its charter promptly revoked." But even Baumgaertner believed that the surest way to get better service was to

6. Clay McShane, "The Growth of Electric Street Railways: Milwaukee, A Case Study, 1887–1900" (M.A. thesis, University of Wisconsin, 1970), 61–64, 71–74.
7. Milwaukee *Evening Wisconsin,* September 13, 1887, in McShane, "Milwaukee Street Railways," 62.
8. *Milwaukee Sentinel,* August 31, 1887.
9. *Ibid.,* May 8, 1888, September 24, 1889.
10. Forrest McDonald, "Street Cars, Part I," *Wisconsin Magazine of History,* 39 (Spring 1956), 166–67.
11. *Milwaukee Sentinel,* June 7, 1887.

enfranchise competitors.[12]

Poor service drew fewer complaints in the partisan eighties than did relations between the companies and politicians. John Hinsey, the city's leading Democratic boss, managed not only the Badger Illuminating Company, which virtually monopolized electric power before 1889, but also two street railways. Politicians who had "control of the business of granting franchises," complained the Republican *Sentinel*, should not also manage the utilities.[13] But even this issue was more an expression of partisan differences than an attack on the political power of the utilities, and it, too, could be resolved by competition. By 1891 Republican electoral victories allowed the Common Council to strip Hinsey of his economic and political power by enfranchising Republican competitors.[14]

The rapid proliferation of franchises for transportation and lighting companies that accompanied the application of electricity in the late eighties bred a feeling that competition brought problems as well as benefits. All six electric companies served the same downtown area.[15] Late in 1889 the *Sentinel* questioned the Common Council's " 'go-as-you-please' [policy] for everybody who has chosen to string electric-light wires" because the "general crossing and mixing of electric-motor, electric-light, telephone and fire-alarm wires" had created a perilous fire hazard.[16] This competition further encouraged alliances between corporations and politicians. Companies realized that political advantages—such as immunity from the enforcement of ordinances, knowledge of competitors' bids, or friendship of public works commissioners—were good business. As early as 1887 one editor warned, "The danger grows that public interests may be overlooked in the sharp encounters of rival roads."[17] But Milwaukeeans seemed unable to develop any alternative to the policy of competition.

It was precisely this intense competition that attracted the interest of the fifty-million-dollar North American holding company syndicate. This syndicate, dominated by railroad magnate Henry Villard and inspired by Thomas Edison, saw

12. *Ibid.*, November 11, 1888.
13. *Ibid.*, August 15, 21, 1889.
14. *Ibid.*, August 2, September 24, 1889, January 12, 13, 17, 26, September 23, 1890, June 16, 1891.
15. McDonald, "Street Cars, Part I," 167.
16. *Milwaukee Sentinel*, December 5, 1889.
17. *Ibid.*, July 21, 1887.

in Milwaukee a great opportunity to create an electric central station, never before tried, that would provide power to operate the streetcars at the same time it lighted homes and businesses. In conceiving the first electric utility holding company, the Villard syndicate developed the principle of a "natural monopoly" to manage the power, lighting, and transportation needs of a major city. Milwaukee was also attractive because its residents had no prejudice against ownership of local enterprises by outside capitalists. ("It is only so much more capital brought to the city," the *Sentinel* had breezily declared in 1888 when some members of the Villard group had purchased a horsecar company.) Early in 1890 the Villard syndicate began to purchase the city's street railways and electric lighting companies, and, by 1893, they had bought out all their competitors. The cost had been so staggering—almost $14 million—that it was to drive the syndicate into receivership during the depression, but Milwaukee could boast of having the first monopoly of transportation and electric power in the nation.[18]

Most Milwaukeeans loudly applauded this development. Realizing the importance of local support, the Villard syndicate persuaded several prominent Milwaukeeans to invest in the enterprise and, more importantly, gave its two top executive positions to Henry C. Payne and Edward C. Wall, state-wide bosses of the Republican and Democratic parties. These efforts to win local support paid dividends. Rublee's *Sentinel* endorsed it by arguing that the monopoly would aid the "development of the city."[19] The Populist *Daily News* backed the monopoly because it controlled enough capital to extend streetcar lines and because the merger would guarantee transfers between the previously separate lines and equal fares.[20] Between 1891 and 1894 a few people complained about inadequacies of the streetcar service, and a few Republicans grumbled about Payne's control of the party,[21] but such complaints were rare. These were, in fact, the honeymoon years, when Milwaukeeans were generally happier with the Villard monopoly than they had

18. *Ibid.,* December 23, 1888, July 29, 1890, November 30, December 12, 1892. Wight, *Payne,* 56–59. McDonald, "Street Cars, Part I," 167–69. McShane, "Milwaukee Street Railways," 78–80.

19. *Milwaukee Sentinel,* November 1, 1891.

20. McShane, "Milwaukee Street Railways," 81.

21. *Milwaukee Sentinel,* September 18, 1891, November 30, December 12, 1892, February 12, March 3, 4, 1893. *Appleton Weekly Post,* February 13, 1896.

been with the competition of the late eighties, and when other cities were more troubled by their quasi-public corporations than was Milwaukee.

II

The depression year of 1894 abruptly terminated the honeymoon. The Villard syndicate had paid a high price to become the first such holding company. Its electrical equipment had cost three times its 1899 evaluation, and the existing companies had sold their equipment and franchises at exorbitant prices. The new monopoly was, in short, heavily overcapitalized; probably at least $5 million of its capitalization was water. When the panic struck in 1893, the Villard syndicate approached bankruptcy. Squeezed between its gross overcapitalization on the one hand and on the other by the declining demands for electric power and streetcar transportation in a community where factories were closing and workers were no longer traveling to jobs, the company began to search for ways of cutting costs and raising revenues.[22] Although the financial screws were tightening almost daily, there was hope for survival under the management of the politically influential Payne.

The company instituted its plan in the spring of 1894 with the announcement by its subsidiary, the Badger Illuminating Company, of higher rentals in the new street lighting contract with the city. Not only was it impossible for the city to pay the higher street light bill, but the company's demand came a week after the spectacular Davidson Theater fire, which killed nine firemen, and many Milwaukeeans blamed the Badger Company for the tragedy; its poor wiring had caused the fire. Following the advice of Mayor Koch and William Rauschenberger, president of the Common Council, the aldermen on May 1 created a committee that over the next several months investigated the costs of a municipal lighting plant. The city's editors warmly supported this movement.[23]

While the committee was meeting, Payne used his political power to kill a popular ordinance. Riding the crest of a national

22. McDonald, "Street Cars, Part I," 167–69. McShane, "Milwaukee Street Railways," 80, 93–96. Wight, *Payne*, 58–59. See *Milwaukee Sentinel*, September 18, 1891, for an early statement of the company's financial position.
23. *Milwaukee Sentinel*, April 11, 19, May 1, 2, September 27, 1894. *Milwaukee Catholic Citizen*, May 5, 1894.

wave of ordinances that were requiring companies to install smoke-consuming devices to curtail air pollution, Alderman Cornelius Corcoran introduced an antismoke ordinance in Milwaukee. The trolley and light monopoly—the city's worst polluter—could not afford the costs, and Payne persuaded the aldermen to kill Corcoran's proposal.[24]

This obviously was not the time for the company to make public its most unpopular decision. Nevertheless, on August 1 it announced that its impoverished condition forced it to raise streetcar fares. It abolished the commutation ("workingmen's") tickets that had permitted patrons to purchase twenty-five rides for one dollar and announced that every ride would henceforth cost a nickel. The outcry was deafening, since most patrons were as impoverished as the company. The next day, "war was declared by the Common Council upon the Milwaukee Street Railway company." As one threatening measure, the aldermen ordered the company to repave certain streets it had torn up, but Payne retorted that the company could not and would not obey the ordinance. Incensed by the company's attitude, Rauschenberger secured a resolution to the effect that, since a majority of Milwaukeeans favored municipal ownership, city officials should begin negotiations to buy all the properties of the Villard syndicate. When the officials reported that the cost was prohibitive, Rauschenberger suggested that the city build a competing street railway.[25]

Stymied by a bankrupt city treasury, Milwaukeeans spent the rest of the year grumbling at the Villard syndicate. As they debated what action to take, the city's reformers discovered two fundamental levels of discussion: the first concerned attitudes toward private property and the city's right to interfere in a company's internal management; the second concerned the kind of action to take—a discussion colored mainly by the ways the monopoly touched the debaters' lives. Workers and their Populist spokesman, the *Daily News,* demanded municipal ownership of electric lights and a system of low-rate, competitive street railways. Undisturbed by attitudes toward private property, they argued that lower fares would generate more traffic with reasonable profits, and that the city should enfranchise competitors who would guarantee a three-cent or four-cent fare. While many prominent union and Populist spokesmen would increasingly

24. *Milwaukee Sentinel,* June 17, July 14, 18, September 11, 1894.
25. *Ibid.,* August 2, 3, 5, 7, 25, September 2, 1894.

turn toward other solutions, these two demands continued as central points for the next three years.[26]

The other group of reformers, the Municipal League, was more widely divided in its purposes and attitudes. Its members among business and professional men disagreed on public invasion of private property and on the extent to which the city should interfere with a company's investments. It was not until 1897 that the league could unify sufficiently to declare the monopoly to be the major menace to honest government. Since its members did not worry about streetcar fares in their personal budgets, they were more concerned with securing lower taxes, which would come if the city could force the company to pay higher taxes and purchase its franchises.[27]

Most Milwaukeeans and their elected representatives approached the problems that originated in 1894 with ambivalent attitudes toward both issues. Crises and events, more than preconceptions, tended to shape their behavior. Just as Rauschenberger had freely vacillated between the solutions offered by municipal ownership and competition, citizens were more interested in practicality than in consistency. The increasingly anticompany position taken by Rublee's *Sentinel* after 1894 probably best reflected the emotional reactions of most Milwaukeeans, who strongly wanted popular sovereignty to be reasserted.[28] The most remarkable feature of the syndicate's economies was that they eventually unified all the different citizens' groups.

The only group that ignored the agitation in 1894 was the Municipal League, which was preoccupied with its attacks on high spending and partisan politics. While President Butler had mused as early as January of 1894 that the Villard monopoly was probably not paying its share of taxes,[29] that year's crusade to increase the company's assessment was led by city officials, not mugwumps. While searching for new tax revenues, City Tax Commissioner Thomas H. Brown and City Attorney Charles H. Hamilton raised the company's assessment in July of 1894 from $1,118,300 to $2,891,320, which most Milwaukeeans thought was fair, since it was common knowledge that the

26. See *Milwaukee Daily News*, August 16, 1894, March 9, December 2, 9, 1895, March 1, 15, 1898, for example.
27. *Ibid.*, December 9, 1895, January 4, March 5, 13, 1896, February 13, 1897.
28. *Milwaukee Sentinel*, November 10, December 22, 1894.
29. *Ibid.*, January 31, 1894.

syndicate had paid $14 million for its properties. Arguing that the new assessment was based on "the mere guess of the assessors," an infuriated Payne appealed the increase. The state supreme court agreed and ruled the increased assessment to be an illegal franchise tax.[30]

The stage was thus set for the event that brought the Municipal League over to the ranks of the opposition. Fearful that city officials would devise a legal method to increase the company's assessment, Payne steered through the 1895 legislature a law that exempted the company from all local and property taxes by the payment of a state license fee. A gleeful Payne understated the effect of the law when he wrote the monopoly's owners that the new law was "very advantageous."[31] Its attention distracted by efforts to further its civil service and corrupt practices proposals, the league failed to notice the tax exemption act until it had passed. "Un-American and wrong!" cried Butler of this law. He later recalled that if the company's 1894 fare increase was "sufficient cause for popular resentment [among] all classes of citizens," the 1895 law aroused "the people to a state of feeling bordering on revolution." Populists and Municipal Leaguers alike were furious with this act, which drove Milwaukee's mugwumps into their first opposition to the company.[32]

Payne's lobbying alienated the Municipal League, and it intensified opposition from the company's older foes. Not content with his tax victory, Payne emasculated a bill that was very popular among the company's patrons and workers. The occasion for consideration of the bill was a tragedy resulting from corporate economies on its streetcar system. One bitterly cold February night in 1895 motorman John Kennedy failed to hear the warnings of a bridge tender and plunged his streetcar through an open drawbridge into the icy Kinnickinnic River. Three men drowned and five were badly injured. The cause was obvious: in its efforts to economize the company was using its

30. *Ibid.*, April 27, June 25, October 2, 1894, February 23, June 21, 1895.
31. Minutes of Meeting of the Committee on Operations of the Milwaukee Street Railway Company, 4, 5, Wisconsin Electric Power Company, Milwaukee. Wisconsin, *Laws* (1895), chap. 363.
32. *Milwaukee Sentinel,* March 10, 1897. John A. Butler, "Street Railway Problem in Milwaukee," *Municipal Affairs,* 4 (March 1900), 212–13. Butler, "A General View of the New Municipal Program," *Good City Conference,* Columbus, 1899, 93. *League Bulletin,* 11 (December 20, 1898). *Milwaukee Daily News,* April 5, 17, 1895.

open-vestibule summer cars on raw winter nights and, unprotected from the cold, Kennedy's reflexes had slowed, and he had been unable to halt his car. Suddenly the Amalgamated Street Railway Employees Union was swamped with support for its old bill to prohibit the company from using summer cars in winter. So widespread was this support that Payne told the owners that he could not prevent the bill from passing, but that he could amend it to make it "less burdensome." This he did by gaining for the company two winters of grace before the law went into effect. Since these cars affected both workers and passengers, Milwaukeeans of all classes now blasted Payne for not only refusing, as manager of the company, to convert all the cars voluntarily, but also for his lobbying in the legislature for an additional delay.[33]

The company's older enemies seized this new opportunity. Between May and July, 1895, City Engineer George H. Benzenberg, City Comptroller Charles H. Fiebrantz, and a committee of the Common Council demanded municipal ownership of the electric lighting system, but again, as in 1894, the project died for want of funds.[34] At the same time, workers and Populists triggered a frequently bitter debate among the company's opponents that was not settled until after the 1896 municipal elections. They staged mass meetings throughout the city to win support for their project of enfranchising a competitor who would promise a four-cent fare.[35] On September 16 the Municipal League entered the local battle for the first time to oppose the Populists' plan and to champion municipal ownership. It charged that the Populist scheme would simply allow a few capitalists to obtain a franchise, which they would then sell to Payne at a good profit. City officials paid close attention to this statement, for its drafters included past presidents of the Milwaukee Chamber of Commerce and the Wisconsin Bar Association, as well as other influential citizens. Consequently, the city refused to grant the new franchise in the fall of 1895.[36]

33. *Milwaukee Sentinel*, February 5, 1895. *Milwaukee Daily News*, February 4, April 13, 1895. *Appleton Weekly Post*, February 21, 1895. Minutes of the Committee on Operations of the Milwaukee Street Railway Company, 3–4. Wisconsin, *Laws* (1895), chap. 279. Butler, "Street Railway Problem," 213. Thomas W. Gavett, "The Development of the Labor Movement in Milwaukee" (Ph.D. diss., University of Wisconsin, 1957), 176–77.

34. *Milwaukee Sentinel*, May 14, 24, 25, July 20, 21, September 3, 1895.

35. *Ibid.*, August 13, 15, 18, 19, September 16, October 22, 1895.

36. *Ibid.*, August 15, September 16, 19, 21, 1895.

A few weeks later, though, when a group of capitalists came forward with enough money to challenge Payne and with the promise of a four-cent fare, the issue continued as a force through the 1896 elections. The Populists and their political arm, the hastily formed Citizens' League, charged that the Municipal League opposed competition because it was dominated by corporation lawyers friendly to the monopoly, because its members rode carriages instead of streetcars and thus the fare was irrelevant for them, and because its preoccupation with low taxes made it insist on a large payment to the city treasury, which weakened the attraction of a competing franchise to other capitalists.

There was some truth to the Populists' charges, and the Municipal League debated acceptance of the competing franchise. President Butler urged the league to support the Populists on the desirability of the four-cent fare, but he was countered by a faction led by the Reverend Charles S. Lester, whose Saint Paul's Episcopal Church was attended—and supported—by Payne. The league's 1896 address to Milwaukee voters revealed the strength of both factions; it called for a reduction in fares, but it also urged that the city insist on compensation for future franchises. Taxation was still a vital concern for the league, which demanded repeal of the 1895 exemption act and more equitable assessment of the monopoly.

Reform-minded city officials shared the league's confusion. Republicans and Democrats promised repeal of the exemption act and favored competing franchises only if the city's "interests" would be protected. The Republicans nominated William Rauschenberger for mayor, and this sturdy enemy of the company vacillated between support of competition and municipal ownership. One notable feature of the campaign was a series of mass meetings at which Butler and Republican Tax Commissioner Brown demanded repeal of the exemption act. These joint appearances typified the growing cooperation, which had begun with the exemption act, between the Municipal League and its old enemies, the politicians. The league had traveled a long way since 1894 when it had supported the wealthy nonpartisan and tightfisted Koch. In supporting the victorious Rauschenberger it backed a poor man and loyal Republican whose main political appeal was his long-standing opposition to the monopoly. The alliance between the Municipal League and progressive Republican politicians, cemented in the 1896 elections, remained the heart of Milwaukee's crusades against quasi-public corporations for the rest of the decade.[37]

III

While the company's enemies were organizing, the company itself was reorganizing. All its unpopular measures—higher lighting rates and streetcar fares, disobedience of city ordinances, tax evasion—could not prevent the depression from overtaking it. Driven into receivership in 1895 by what Payne called a hostile political climate and what Milwaukee newspapers called its "heavily watered" stock, the North American syndicate reorganized its monopoly in friendly hands into The Milwaukee Electric Railway and Light Company—TMER&L. While revealing the company's financial straits, this reorganization caused little change in its political stance, since Henry Payne, Charles Pfister, and F. G. Bigelow remained as its managers in Milwaukee.[38]

The last thing the newly formed company needed was labor troubles, but, by the time it resolved the strike and boycott of 1896, TMER&L welded most Milwaukeeans into a single alliance whose agreed aim was to undertake any measure to terminate its power. On April 30, 1896, TMER&L rejected demands of the Amalgamated Street Railway Employees Union for shorter hours, higher pay, and union recognition and began to import strikebreakers. The strike and boycott that followed the company's refusal to negotiate with the workers was, according to Samuel Gompers, "without parallel in the labor world." On May 4, the date set for the strike, only twelve of TMER&L's 750 motormen and conductors reported for work. The workers hoped that by taking a determined stand against Payne and

37. *Ibid.*, February 6, 11, 18, March 4, 5, 13, 17, 19, 25, 26, 29, April 3, 4, 8, 22, 1896. Butler, "A General View," 92–93. Clinton Rogers Woodruff, "The Advance of the Movement for Municipal Reform," *Good City Conference*, Indianapolis, 1898, 104–5. E. Dana Durand, "Political and Municipal Legislation in 1897," *Annals of the American Academy of Political and Social Science*, 11 (March 1898), 43. *Milwaukee Daily News*, December 9, 1895, January 4, February 11, March 4, April 2, 3, 1896.

38. *Appleton Weekly Post*, May 23, 1895. Executive and Financial Committee of The Milwaukee Electric Railway and Light Company, Minute Book, 3. Minutes of the Board of Directors of The Milwaukee Electric Railway and Light Company, 4–27, 64, 69–70, 101, 109, 111–12, 131–32, 163, both in Wisconsin Electric Power Company, Milwaukee. McShane, "Milwaukee Street Railways," 93–96.

TMER&L they could capitalize on "a strong sentiment of hostility toward the Street Railway company [that] has grown up among the people of this city."[39]

Payne set out to crush the strike with strikebreakers. The regular workers reacted by forming mobs that stoned the scabs, their police guards, and the windows of their dormitories. By refusing even to talk with the union's officers, by adamantly rejecting the suggestions of several businessmen, city officials, and the State Board of Arbitration that he submit the dispute to voluntary arbitration, Payne made most Milwaukeeans sympathetic to the workers' cause. "Arbitrate?" snorted Payne. "The company has nothing to arbitrate." Few could accept his argument that to arbitrate the dispute was to "yield the ultimate right of deciding for ourselves all questions as to the executive management and policy of the company." "The company seems to lose sight altogether of its responsibilities to and dependence on the public, based on its franchises and the services it has to render," warned the *Milwaukee Journal*. "It seems infatuated to make enemies where it should have only friends. It rushes on toward the end of which is legal action to terminate its existence."[40]

In the strike's second week, as TMER&L had managed to restore nearly full service with strikebreakers, Milwaukeeans spontaneously released their pent-up hatred of Payne and the company. They joined the workers in boycotting streetcars. Horse-drawn jitneys and omnibuses began to appear and, by the end of the boycott's second week, three times as many of these ancient vehicles traveled the streets as did streetcars. A woman wrote her family about the city's mood in the spring of 1896:

> I have yet to hear an expression of sympathy for the Street Car Company. There are a few cars running on some of the lines today; but it is wonderful to note the comparative

39. Minutes of the Board of Directors of the Milwaukee Electric Railway and Light Company, 76, 82, 86, hereinafter cited as TMER&L Directors, Minutes. Executive and Financial Committee of the Milwaukee Electric Railway and Light Company, Minute Book, 15, hereinafter cited as TMER&L Minute Book. Wight, *Payne*, 60, 78. Gavett, "Labor Movement in Milwaukee," 180. *Milwaukee Sentinel*, May 14, 1896.

40. *Milwaukee Journal*, May 7, 1896. Wight, *Payne*, 62. McDonald, "Street Cars, Part I," 170, 206–7. W. D. Mahon to Gov. William Upham, telegram, n.d., "Strikes and Riots," Box 1, Wisconsin State Archival Series 1/1/8–9. *Arbitration Report, 1895 and 1896*, 16, 19, 23.

emptiness of these few, and the crowded streets at times when the cars have heretofore been *packed*. White ribbon, "I'll walk; will you?" "To Ride Gives Me a Payne" cards are worn by hundreds. Silk hats on delivery wagons, elegant dresses in 'busses, and the laborious efforts of the fat man as he loyally refuses to patronize the monopoly, and tests for the first time his "pedestrianistical" powers are among the many unusual street scenes just now, and all speak loudly for the strikers.

This general hostility toward the company astonished the New York directors. "We were surprised at the extent of the popular support and sympathy for the strikers," reported two directors after visiting Milwaukee. "No doubt it is the result of the prolonged agitation of the questions of taxation and a reduction of fares." Milwaukeeans were indeed angry. Grocers, butchers, and tobacconists refused to sell to the scabs; 127 businessmen petitioned the Common Council to annul TMER&L's franchises. Many stockholders urged Payne to compromise, but he refused and the boycott continued.[41]

The boycott might have lasted indefinitely—and it did continue with lessening support for several months—had the dispute not taken two new turns. First, radical political speakers incited mobs to violence. Following a rally on May 25, the audience cut wires, overturned cars, stabbed and beat several policemen—most of whom had been friendly to the strikers—and attacked scabs with bricks and clubs; workers fired at passengers in TMER&L's cars. It looked as though the revolution was erupting on the streets of Milwaukee. Such company foes as Butler and Rauschenberger urged a quick end to the whole dispute in order to preserve civil order. As a result, the battle shifted in a second direction, from the boycotted cars to the Common Council's chambers.[42]

The city administration elected in April had a decidedly progressive cast. When Rauschenberger became mayor, his brother-in-law Henry Baumgaertner, long-time enemy of

41. Aunt B. to Ada James, May 7, 1896, Box 3, Ada James Papers, Manuscripts Division, State Historical Society of Wisconsin. Wight, *Payne*, 60–62. McDonald, "Street Cars, Part I," 206–8. Butler, "Street Railway Problem," 213. TMER&L Directors, Minutes, 93, 105. TMER&L Minute Book, 26. *Appleton Weekly Post*, May 21, 1896. *Milwaukee Catholic Citizen*, May 30, 1896. *Our Church Life*, 2 (June 1896), 127.
42. *Milwaukee Sentinel*, May 24, 25, June 6, 1896. McDonald, "Street Cars, Part I," 208–10. *Arbitration Report, 1896*, 12. TMER&L Directors, Minutes, 92.

private utilities, was elected president of the Common Council. Baumgaertner appointed to chair the crucial railroad committee the city's most rabid enemy of TMER&L, George Thuering.[43] Payne enraged local officials when he refused to arbitrate with a board created by the Common Council or with the State Board.[44] In response to the strike and boycott, the city administration tried every means that had yet been proposed to assert popular control over the company. Mayor Rauschenberger's old proposal for a municipal lighting plant was defeated again for want of funds.[45]

With the attempts to arbitrate the differences stymied by Payne and the efforts to take the utilities under city management stopped by lack of money, city officials next confronted the most serious proposal to be offered. By the time they resolved it Milwaukee's Republicans would have created a self-conscious progressive movement. The idea of forcing TMER&L to lower its fares had been present since 1894. Reform-minded Republican aldermen like Thuering, Baumgaertner, and Rauschenberger had introduced fare-reduction ordinances several times over the past year,[46] but Republican aldermen had listened to Payne and had repeatedly killed them. Realizing that rate regulation was now a strong possibility, Payne had urged the directors to reissue commutation tickets, but the directors told him that the company could not afford them.[47] Payne then turned to attempts to silence the mounting demands in the Common Council for lower fares.

At this point Mayor Rauschenberger and Eugene S. Elliott, Republican city convention chairman, called a meeting of twelve prominent GOP leaders to map Republican strategy in the fight against TMER&L. It was the first time in several years that Republicans had decided party policy without considering Payne's wishes. With only Horace Rublee dissenting, they issued a "peremptory order" on Payne and TMER&L: Either settle the strike and rehire the old workers, or forfeit any economic, political, or moral hold on Milwaukee Republicans. Serving as the meeting's spokesman, Elliott blasted TMER&L:

43. *Milwaukee Sentinel,* April 29, 1896.
44. *Arbitration Report, 1896,* 11–12. McDonald, "Street Cars, Part I," 206–7.
45. *Milwaukee Sentinel,* April 22, 1896. McDonald, "Street Cars, Part I," 208.
46. For example, see *Milwaukee Sentinel,* February 17, 1895.
47. TMER&L Directors, Minutes, 72.

"It controlled the legislature and made a tool of the common council until the people are roused in righteous indignation." Milwaukee Republicans, he announced, would take the people's side.[48] When Payne rejected the peremptory order, Republican aldermen had to choose between two factions. The differences went deeper than the customary quarrels between "outs" and "ins," for, in fact, most city officials and party leaders opposed TMER&L's operation. The fight was over the principles of regulation and taxation of quasi-public corporations. The decision—ideological, not factional—was between the new mass politics and the old machine politics.

Most Republican aldermen sided with the progressives. William Cromwell, TMER&L president, called an emergency meeting of the directors at his Wall Street office on the evening of June 5 to report that "a hearing was no longer allowed to our representatives before [Common Council] committees, and that the introduction of any ordinance adverse to the Company's interest was tantamount to its passage." Payne, it was obvious, no longer dominated Republican aldermen. On June 9, 1896, by a 39 to 3 vote, the council passed an ordinance requiring TMER&L to return to its pre-1894 rates. Steered to passage by Mayor Rauschenberger, this ordinance represented the first fruits of the Municipal League-progressive Republican alliance. It was a declaration of independence from Payne by Milwaukee Republicans,[49] but the rejoicing was short-lived. TMER&L promptly enjoined the city from enforcing the ordinance and appealed the council's action. For the next two years the so-called four-cent ordinance remained in litigation.[50]

The defeat of the ordinance further enraged reformers and city officials and drove the Municipal League to support demands for a competitor. There was, as the *Sentinel* observed, no longer any difference between the programs of the Municipal League and those of the radical Populists and Federated Trades Council. When progressive city officials supported the project, the Common Council voted 30 to 11 to enfranchise the Milwaukee and Waukesha Electric Railway Company on July 21, reserving the right of the city to purchase its properties at a future

48. *Milwaukee Journal,* May 18, 1896.
49. *Milwaukee Sentinel,* May 26, June 6, 9, 1896. Butler, "Street Railway Problem," 213. "The Milwaukee Street Railway Decision," *Outlook,* 59 (June 18, 1898), 412. TMER&L Directors, Minutes, 105.
50. *Milwaukee Sentinel,* June 12, July 23, 1896, December 18, 1897, June 1, 1898.

date. Although TMER&L eventually prevented its erstwhile competitor from ever laying tracks by seizing control of all the viaducts leading to the city, the enfranchisement expressed Milwaukee's desperation with TMER&L in the summer of 1896. The company had driven all reform groups together,[51] and had been responsible for the city's enacting every anti-TMER&L proposal of the past two years.

IV

Perhaps the most significant outgrowth of the 1896 strike was the polarization of city and state Republicans. The May 18 meeting at which city Republican leaders defied Payne, marked the beginning of open warfare that swept across the state during the summer. The emerging reform Republican alliance operated on two levels. Milwaukee Republicans learned from the Municipal League that they could best curtail TMER&L's power by reform on the state level. Their concerns were both anti-TMER&L and ideological. At the same time there was a group of "out" politicians that had been feuding with Payne for six years over political matters. Its concerns were essentially factional, and its major interests were election to state office and control of patronage.

The first scene for the emerging coalition was the Republican National Convention at Saint Louis, where Payne was seeking re-election to a fifth four-year term as Wisconsin's national committeeman. Although Mark Hanna implored the delegation to return Payne, most of the state's Republican editors, reflecting the new mass politics, followed the *Sentinel*'s lead and opposed Hanna and his support of Payne. Complaining that recent events in Milwaukee had indicated that "his political influence becomes an ally of his personal private business and interests," they agreed with the *Appleton Post* that "his usefulness as a political leader is ended." The anger with Payne's corporate lobbying fitted perfectly into the ambitions of the "out" politicians, represented at Saint Louis by former Governor William D. Hoard and Robert M. La Follette. These politicians joined

51. The Common Councils of Milwaukee and Waukesha subsequently revoked the franchises because the competitor never built anything. Milwaukeeans were more desperate, waiting until November, 1897, long after Waukesha had surrendered, to kill the project. *Ibid.*, June 6, July 21, 29, 1896, November 9, 1897. TMER&L Minute Book, 33. McDonald, "Street Cars, Part I," 210.

Milwaukee Republicans in voting against Payne, but Payne still controlled enough of the delegation to win re-election. An important alliance was being forged. The La Follette faction had discovered a popular issue from the Milwaukeeans and the state press, an issue it could use in its battles for state offices.[52]

The alliance solidified after the delegates returned from Saint Louis. Republican wheel horse Eugene Elliott announced that the GOP had reached a crossroads: "I believe that the political methods that were so openly used during the last legislature, and which resulted in the passage of bills enacted in the interests of corporations to the detriment of the people, are pernicious to the welfare of our state, and must in the end be destructful to the Republican party." Elliott and prominent Republican and Milwaukee Leaguer Edward P. Bacon sought out the state's most active anticorporation Republican, Assemblyman Albert R. Hall, and pledged to join his campaigns for such programs for political democracy as a campaign for abolition of free passes. Republican progressives now realized that they would have to capture control of the state government. By the summer of 1896 progressive Republicans from Milwaukee and the rural western part of the state, now a self-conscious, ideological, anticorporation group, had formed a common bond to resist Payne's corporate lobbying. At the same time, the La Follette organization, which saw Payne only as the main enemy of its leader's political ambitions, reinforced its ties with the ideological progressives. The first triumph of this new alliance occurred when the Municipal League, Milwaukee progressives, radicals like Albert Hall, and leaders of the "out" faction like Hoard and La Follette persuaded William McKinley to reject Mark Hanna's pleas that he appoint Payne postmaster general.[53]

V

The 1897 legislative fights revealed the contradictory purposes of the political alliance that had formed the previous summer. When the La Follette faction did nothing to help the

52. *Milwaukee Sentinel,* June 10, 13, 16, 20, 1896. Wight, *Payne,* 88. *Appleton Weekly Post,* June 25, July 30, 1896.
53. *Milwaukee Sentinel,* July 4, November 19, 1896. Eugene Elliott to Albert R. Hall, July 20, 1896, Edward P. Bacon to Hall, August 7, 1896, Hall Papers, Manuscripts Division, State Historical Society of Wisconsin. Wight *Payne,* 90–91, 179. Lahman, "La Follette," 373–74. Butler, "The

ideological reformers, angry progressive city officials and the Municipal League managed the fights against TMER&L and the corporations. They worked closely with such progressive legislators as Milwaukee's Julius Roehr, who had signed the May, 1896, attack on Payne, and Albert Hall. The anticorporation bloc also included Charles W. Davis, William A. Jones, Herman C. Whipperman, Charles H. Baxter, James J. McGillivray, and other legislators whose communities had experienced similar problems in dealing with quasi-public corporations. The leading objective was to repeal the 1895 tax exemption act. Reminding Republican legislators that the Milwaukee 1896 platform promised repeal, the Milwaukee Common Council and city officials from Superior and Portage urged action at Madison. John A. Butler and Milwaukee's Tax Commissioner Thomas H. Brown were the chief lobbyists, with Hall and Roehr managing the floor fights. The result was a compromise that retained the license fee but raised TMER&L's taxes from $20,000 to $60,000. It was an extremely bitter fight. Butler recalled later that proponents had encountered "the greatest difficulty" in their attempts to treble the company's taxes, and Payne had telegraphed the syndicate's directors that he had barely prevented the reformers from repealing the 1895 act.[54] While the repeal fight cemented the bonds between members of the Municipal League and progressive officials, its main political significance was in uniting the antiutility forces in Milwaukee with those in other parts of the state.

The reformers had learned a crucial lesson in the repeal fight. The success of mass, ideological politics in winning structural changes desired by the reformers depended on the corporations' committing some tangible, arrogant act that could arouse public indignation. Without such an event, city officials and the Mu-

---

Place of the Council and of the Mayor in the Organization of Municipal Government," *Good City Conference,* Indianapolis, 173. William D. Hoard to H. P. Myrick, December 30, 1896, Hoard Letter Books, 52:128–29, Hoard Papers, Manuscripts Division, State Historical Society of Wisconsin. La Follette, *Autobiography,* 127–31.

54. *Milwaukee Sentinel,* January 16, March 3, 6, 10, 21, April 9, 1897. *Milwaukee Daily News,* March 10, 1897. Wisconsin, *Laws* (1897), chap. 223. Wisconsin, Legislative Petitions 1210A and 760S, 1897 Legislature, Box 59, Wisconsin State Archival Series 2/3/1/5–7. *Superior Evening Telegram,* March 23, 1897. Butler, "A General View," 93. TMER&L Directors, Minutes, 145. TMER&L Minute Book, 89, 92. Cf. McDonald, "Street Cars, Part I," 211, which distorts Payne's lobbying by its ignorance of the 1895 law.

nicipal League had little hope of winning popular support. As the memory of the 1896 events receded, voters would settle for an increase in TMER&L's taxes and would not demand repeal of the exemption act.[55] Because TMER&L had been circumspect in the months following the boycott, the repeal fight lacked the broad support that the four-cent ordinance and competing franchise had won. Clearly, reformers could effectively apply the progressive concept of "the public interest" only after obvious displays of corporate arrogance.

This fact was driven home to reformers in the municipal garbage crusade of 1897-1898, which shaped reformers' attitudes toward the trolley and light monopoly as well. Although the Municipal League, city officials, and Populists had promoted the municipal plant for several months, it took the bribery of an alderman to channel the public dissatisfaction. The garbage fight was important for several reasons. It was the first time all classes had united behind municipal ownership. Populists no longer challenged the motives of the Municipal League, and the league forgot its concern with low taxes when it sponsored a project that would cost the city $80,000. Leaders of the fight also developed the technique of the mass indignation meeting to apply the pressures of the new politics on politicians. Ethnic and class differences became irrelevant in the ideological politics. Wealthy bankers, union men, and *Turnverein* members spoke from the same platforms as Republican officials, Populists, and Municipal Leaguers. The audience at a mass meeting in Shooting Park ignored ethnic differences and urged speakers to "use any old language they were a mind to." Above all, it showed all reform-minded Milwaukeeans that they could win their goals and unite all classes—as consumers—when the companies committed some arrogant act.[56]

VI

While reformers were concentrating on the garbage fight, Payne and TMER&L were trying to repair the tainted image they had acquired in 1896. During 1897 Payne planted sympa-

55. *Milwaukee Sentinel,* March 21, April 9, 1897.
56. *Ibid.,* February 21, 25, March 31, April 10, June 3, July 31, August 6, 10, 12, 14, 15, 17, 18, 21, 27, September 8, 1897, January 17, March 1, 12, 1898. *League Bulletin,* 1 (February 19, 1898), and 2 (March 19, 1898). *Milwaukee Daily News,* March 29, 31, 1897, February 1, 15, March 12, 1898. *Milwaukee Catholic Citizen,* August 21, 1897, February 19, 1898. "Resolu-

thetic stories in Milwaukee newspapers and hinted to politicians that the company might soon reinstitute the four-cent commutation tickets. By December of 1897 the company's directors found a clearly favorable "change in public sentiment in Milwaukee towards this corporation."[57]

The municipal elections of 1898 reversed the direction of the company's public relations efforts and set the pattern of relations between TMER&L and the city for the rest of the decade. In preparation for the elections, the Municipal League urged voters to select only those men who promised "strict supervision" of the utilities, and it was delighted that most caucuses rejected aldermen who had opposed the municipal garbage plant. The league promoted the mayoral candidacy of radical Henry Baumgaertner; the Populists also nominated Baumgaertner, and it seemed certain that the Republicans, too, would nominate the front-running Baumgaertner when their platform promised municipal ownership.[58] But Henry Payne, haunted by the prospect of the city's oldest enemy of private utilities in the mayor's chair, called in all his debts and united his friends behind William Geuder, a mildly progressive sheet-metal manufacturer who would not, he hoped, appear too much a company tool, since he had voted against Payne in Saint Louis in 1896. By a 181 to 116 vote the Republican convention nominated Geuder. Fighting mad, Baumgaertner's friends roundly denounced Payne.[59]

With progressive Republicans sulking, Democrats nominated David S. Rose, a finished orator, on a municipal-ownership platform. Eager to punish the Republicans for rejecting Baumgaertner, the Populists also nominated Rose. While Geuder devoted his campaign to attacking Rose, Rose ran against TMER&L and Payne, telling voters that Geuder's election would "be equivalent to the election of the officers of the street railway company

tion of the People's Party to the Common Council, September 7, 1897," William L. Pieplow Papers, Milwaukee County Historical Society.

57. TMER&L Directors, Minutes, 201, 208. TMER&L Minute Book, 113–14, 122–23, 127, 133, 147–48.

58. *Superior Evening Telegram*, March 14, 1898. *League Bulletin*, 1 (February 19, 1898), and 2 (March 19, 1898). *Milwaukee Sentinel*, February 4, 8, 1898. Theodore Zillmer to Robert M. La Follette, February 12, 1898, La Follette Papers, Manuscripts Division, State Historical Society of Wisconsin.

59. *Milwaukee Sentinel*, March 8, 1898. Lahman, "La Follette," 423–24. Albert O. Barton, *La Follette's Winning of Wisconsin, 1894–1904* (Des Moines: Homestead Co., 1922), 116–32.

to the office of mayor." The campaign illustrated how the issue of popular control over utilities eclipsed all earlier differences. The *Catholic Citizen* told its readers that religious and ethnic issues were irrelevant and that the Catholic voter should elect enemies of utilities. It singled out "our venerable Methodist brother, Deacon Hyde," who had years earlier flirted with the nativist American Protective Association, as the kind of alderman who should be elected because he had steadfastly opposed TMER&L and the garbage company in more recent years. The paper attacked Democratic aldermen who were more indebted to the utilities than many Republicans. In what became a popular referendum on the utilities, Milwaukeeans gave Rose a landslide victory and awarded the Republicans only thirteen of the Common Council's forty-two seats.[60]

Rose won by carrying the antiutility vote. His election, observed the German Republican *Herold,* revealed "the same spirit of angry resentment which prompted the population of the city to walk rather than to patronize an excallant [*sic*] car system." Mayor Rauschenberger termed the election a protest against "the influence of lobbyists and dictators for the benefit of private enterprise against that of the public good." For Milwaukee voters it was reassertion of popular sovereignty. "The Republican party," Baumgaertner declared, "has been under a trolley car."[61]

Progressive Republicans decided they could no longer depend on traditional politics to defeat Payne, so they began after the election to prepare for future elections. They formed the Republican Club of Milwaukee County and elected banker C. F. P. Pullen as president. Club leaders like Rauschenberger, Fiebrantz, and Elliott argued that the 1898 election proved their warning of May 18, 1896, that voters would reject Republicans who were too closely allied to Payne and TMER&L. Cassius M. Paine, Municipal Leaguer and local chamber of commerce president, joined the old progressive Republicans. The question still remained: how to defeat Payne. Gradually, as the August, 1898, state Republican convention approached, they concluded that the best way to reassert popular control over corporations

60. Butler, "Street Railway Problem," 214. *Milwaukee Sentinel,* April 6, 1898. *Milwaukee Catholic Citizen,* February 19, March 12, 19, 26, April 9, 1898. McDonald, "Street Cars, Part I," 211–12.

61. McDonald, "Street Cars, Part I," 212. *Milwaukee Sentinel,* April 6, 1898. *League Bulletin,* 4 (April 16, 1898). *The Madison State,* April 8, 1898.

was to support La Follette's campaign for the governorship. The aroused Milwaukee voters had proved that Republicans would continue to lose elections until they demonstrated their independence from corporations. The Republican state platform of 1898 reflected the club's work by including three of four planks proposed by the club. Although La Follette was defeated in his gubernatorial ambitions at the convention, these progressive Republicans vowed to continue the fight against Payne and TMER&L for ignoring the majority of Republican voters in 1898.[62]

While Baumgaertner's progressive allies were forming their organization, Federal Judge William H. Seaman reopened the four-cent fare question and, at the end of May, threw out the 1896 four-cent fare ordinance. Apparently accepting the right of the city to regulate TMER&L, Seaman cast aside the ordinance on the narrow grounds that the company simply could not afford to charge only four cents a ride. As a result, most of the reaction centered around the question of whether TMER&L was prosperous enough in 1898 to afford what it could not afford in 1896. Noting that Detroit's street railway earned three times greater profits than TMER&L claimed by charging only 3.4 cents a ride, *Outlook* strongly hinted that Payne had lied in the statistics he presented to the court. If the company was so poor, why had Payne offered commuter tickets to prevent the aldermen from enfranchising a competitor in March of 1898? Seeking votes and believing that the company could now afford it, the Democratic city officials repassed the four-cent ordinance only a few days after Judge Seaman's decision. Once again TMER&L appealed; the fare question entered lengthy litigation a second time; and Milwaukeeans of all social backgrounds were again disappointed in their quest for lower fares. The New York directors again wondered why Milwaukee was so hostile to their company, and the *Sentinel* fired back an answer that the Municipal League endorsed: "The public is eager to secure legislation unfavorable to the company because the company has secured legislation unfavorable to the public." The company's "business has become an issue in politics" because the company's

---

62. Lahman, "La Follette," 423–24. Barton, *La Follette's Winning of Wisconsin*, 116–32. *Milwaukee Sentinel*, July 17, 28, August 1, 11, 1898. *Blue Book, 1899*, 711–12. Charles F. P. Pullen to James O. Davidson, December 15, 1898, Davidson Papers, Manuscripts Division, State Historical Society of Wisconsin. William D. Hoard to Cassius M. Paine, Hoard Letter Books, 52: 974.

"management has made politics an important part of its business."[63] The city's attitude toward the company was a simple cause-and-effect reaction.

Payne and TMER&L, correctly sensing that they were losing control of city and state politics, decided to wage an all-out fight for political immunity. To achieve "future harmonious relations and a cessation of hostilities," the company began to negotiate with the Democratic city council over the price of TMER&L's immunity. City officials saw in these negotiations a chance to pose as saviors of the city from the hated monopoly. On November 17, 1898, Mayor Rose triumphantly laid the results before the Common Council. In exchange for annual payments to the city treasury that would increase over five years from $50,000 to $100,000, the company was to be guaranteed an exclusive twenty-five-year franchise, a minimum five-cent fare, and an end to litigation for the four-cent ordinance. These terms were to be cemented by a binding contract. Democrats believed that the Rose-Payne compromise showed, in the words of the *Journal*, that "Mayor Rose has made a bargain for the city."[64]

Everyone else disagreed. Some hinted that TMER&L had bribed Rose, for why else would he have bargained away the city's right to regulate or buy the company for twenty-five years? In attacking the compromise, reform groups cooperated more closely than they ever had in the past. Rose's allies in the 1898 campaign, the Populists and Socialists, promptly withdrew their support of the mayor. At the other economic extreme the Merchants and Manufacturers Association unanimously rejected the proposition. Most important of all was the reaction of the Municipal League, which completely abandoned its old concern with lower taxes—offered by the compromise in the form of

63. Butler, "Street Railway Problem," 213–15. *League Bulletin*, 6 (June 4, 1898), and 8 (July 30, 1898). *Milwaukee Sentinel*, January 24, March 12, June 12, 1898, April 7, September 9, 1899. *Superior Evening Telegram*, March 26, 1897. "The Milwaukee Street Railway Decision," *Outlook*, 59 (June 18, 1898), 412. McDonald, "Street Cars, Part II," *Wisconsin Magazine*, 39 (Summer 1956), 253. There was probably some truth to the reformers' charges, for the directors' Executive and Financial Committee (p. 77) decided in February, 1897, not to provide detailed statistics of TMER&L's operations for *Poor's Manual and Commercial and Financial Chronicle*.

64. TMER&L Directors, Minutes, 187, 220–21, 223–29, 237–38, 242. Butler, "Street Railway Problem," 214. *Milwaukee Sentinel*, November 18, 1898. Quoted in McDonald, "Street Cars, Part II," 254–55.

annual payments to the city—in favor of lower fares, the traditional concern of workers. Declaring the proposal primarily an affront to "the working people and poorer classes," the league charged that it proved anew that TMER&L was the most serious threat to honest government in the city. The Populist *Daily News* praised the league's "very strong stand" and declared that John A. Butler's denunciation "should be read by every citizen of Milwaukee." Drawing on their successful experience in the garbage controversy of the previous summer, the reformers called mass protest meetings to compel the aldermen to reject the compromise. "We will not barter away our control over the street railway company for any price," cried Butler at one meeting. "Stand up for Milwaukee," screamed the Populists. The largest meeting was at the West Side Turner Hall, where 2,000 citizens saw on the platform the wedding of the Populists to the old Municipal League-progressive Republican alliance. For the first time in years, Populist Robert Schilling wholeheartedly agreed with the league in a major controversy. Astonished by these protests, Rose and Payne hastily disengaged themselves from the issue. So quickly did TMER&L withdraw the offer that the whole matter was dead by the end of December.[65]

The near-compromise was not forgotten, however, and its defeat cemented the partnership between Populists and labor unions with the Municipal League and progressive Republicans. The man who acted as a major bond was Henry Smith, former Labor party congressman, respected Populist leader, and the city's most progressive alderman in 1898. Smith delighted older Municipal Leaguers with his vigilance against municipal extravagance. In return, Municipal Leaguers like Cassius M. Paine warmly supported the radical Smith's campaign for appointment to the Board of Public Works in the spring of 1899. With closer league-Populist ties came closer ties between the league and labor unions. In mid-March Charles A. Harmel, secretary of the Milwaukee Feeders, Helpers, and Job Pressmen's Union, recognized these ties and thanked Butler for "the efforts of the league for the advancement of good municipal government."[66]

65. *Milwaukee Sentinel,* November 24, 26, 27, December 2, 6, 8, 1897. *Milwaukee Daily News,* November 26, 28, December 1, 1898. Butler, "Street Railway Probelm," 214. Butler, "Place of the Council and of the Mayor," 167–73. McDonald, "Street Cars, Part II," 256.

66. *Milwaukee Sentinel,* February 18, 1897, March 20, 29, April 2, 1899. Frederick I. Olson, "Henry Smith, Nestor of the Common Council," *His-*

The allies were preparing for the 1899 legislative battle. The anti-TMER&L lobby at Madison included the Municipal League and its infant, the League of Wisconsin Municipalities. Indistinguishable from them were progressive Republicans Baumgaertner and Theodore Zillmer, who had been selected at a December mass meeting to lobby at Madison. They, in turn, began to work more closely with progressive Republican legislators from other cities. The primary focus of the alliance was upon a bill requiring street railways and electric companies to file public statements of their financial situations. Payne fought passage hard because he recognized that Judge Seaman's decision made the bill the first step toward rate regulation, tax increases, and possibly municipal ownership, but he could no longer resist the mass pressures of the Milwaukee League, the Wisconsin League, progressive Republicans, the Populists, some Democratic aldermen, and a number of mayors—all of whom invoked the memory of TMER&L's recent effort to purchase political immunity. An amended bill passed;[67] the political power of TMER&L had galvanized the reform alliance. Spurred on by the Populists, progressive Republicans, and the Municipal League, the state's progressive Sen. Julius E. Roehr, an outspoken TMER&L opponent, secured a law that required all lobbyists to register and to file expense statements.[68] In the area of taxation, which had initially converted the Municipal League to the progressive camp, reformers once again raised the amount of taxes to be paid by street railways and electric companies and secured permanent status for the State Tax Commission, which a year earlier had blasted tax dodging by quasi-public corporations.[69] The lobby was less successful in its efforts for home rule, which, as the 1898 garbage and street railway protests showed,

torical Messenger, Milwaukee County Historical Society, 14 (March 1958), 2-6.

67. Milwaukee Sentinel, December 25, 1898, January 6, 12, 17, March 16, 20, 22, April 4, 7, 1899. Woodruff, "A Year's Advance," Good City Conference, Columbus, 1899, 176. Woodruff, "A Year's Municipal Development," Good City Conference, Milwaukee, 1900, 71. Milwaukee Social Economics Club, Minute Book, 102, Milwaukee County Historical Society. Wisconsin, Laws (1899), chap. 329. State Journal, January 6, 1899.

68. State Journal, February 17, 1899. Milwaukee Sentinel, April 28, 1899.

69. Milwaukee Sentinel, February 12, March 12, April 21, 1899. Wisconsin, Laws (1899), chaps. 206 and 354. Tax Report, 1898, 66–67, 122–23, 183. Emanuel L. Philipp and Edgar T. Wheelock, Political Reform in Wisconsin: An Historical Review of the Subjects of Primary Election, Taxation, and Railway Regulation (Milwaukee: privately published, 1910), 115–29.

offered reformers the best hope for regulating utilities. The companies were most vulnerable at the local level. The closest the reformers came was passage of a weak law that forced certain franchises to be submitted to popular referenda.[70]

Payne's lobbying was only one way TMER&L drove voters outside Milwaukee toward the city's reform coalition. As it recovered from the depression, the company extended its services to all of southeastern Wisconsin. It seemed to have learned nothing from its political problems in Milwaukee, and it used the same techniques in the new areas—with the same results. The Waukesha Common Council ordered TMER&L to lay only a single track on the city's main street because two tracks would interefere with farmers who hitched their wagons in front of merchants' stores. TMER&L promptly enjoined the city from enforcing its order and, in the predawn hours of July 1, 1899, began to lay a second track. Someone rang the fire bell, and the alarm brought the fire department and a mob, which played fire hoses on the workers. Seeing friends in the mob, the workers began to tear up the track. TMER&L's foreman stopped them, but the same scene was re-enacted a few hours later when TMER&L returned with new workers. The Common Council ordered the city's huge steam roller moved into the path of the proposed illegal track. Despite these efforts by the city and its citizens, TMER&L, through force and court orders, laid a 1,300-foot second track down Broadway. Merchants and editors felt the mobs had been justified, and the company's single-mindedness had infuriated all classes in Waukesha.[71]

Shortly after moving into Racine, TMER&L alienated that city's influential citizens also. The company ordered that all passengers drop their fares into a box, and to enforce the order it imported three carloads of Negroes and Italians as "spotters." The mere presence of the spotters angered passengers, but the city exploded in October when a spotter attacked a respected citizen, Louis Wishman, and threw him off the car. Mayor Michael Higgins, Jr., called the attack "an outrage and disgrace to Racine. . . ." "I feel," he exclaimed, "that to have negroes, Italians and hobos come here and placed on street cars, to assault taxpayers who never refused to pay fares, [is] a stain

70. McShane, "Milwaukee Street Railways," 123–24.
71. *Milwaukee Sentinel,* July 2, 4, 9, 14, 1899.

upon our fair name."[72] TMER&L's insistence on installing a double track and employing spotters drove influential citizens into the reform alliance. They now understood the arrogance that Milwaukeeans had been attacking for years, and they knew which side to take in the final and most spectacular act, which was about to be played in Milwaukee.

VII

As events seemed to close in and the political atmosphere became increasingly charged with demands to restrict TMER&L's activities, Payne made a last, desperate effort to buy immunity through compromise. This compromise, arrived at openly after discussions with the Common Council, provided that the company would grant a four-cent fare during rush hours (and a five-cent fare at all other times) until 1905 in exchange for immunity until 1934 and a grant of twelve new franchises covering sixteen miles of streets. That the compromise was to be cemented by a "contract" meant, in John Butler's words, that the "introduction of public ownership has been delayed for thirty-five years, the present company is established in its monopoly during that period, and the public right to regulate fares has been surrendered."[73]

While the proposition took shape in council committees, reformers bitterly denounced it. The Municipal League called even a permanent four-cent fare an "absurdly inadequate" concession for immunity. Populist Alderman Henry Smith warned: "We have against us the shrewdest men in the country. . . . Henry Payne is the shrewdest man in the state of Wisconsin today. . . . I tell you we are but pigmies [sic] in their hands." Suddenly, on November 7, 1899, TMER&L's directors approved the compromise and it became a proposed ordinance for passage by the aldermen.[74]

The resultant popular protest was unequalled anywhere in Wisconsin during the 1890s. Asking, "Who is representing the city or the public in these alleged negotiations?" the Sentinel charged that TMER&L had proved its "control of the city ad-

72. Ibid., October 3, 1899. Appleton Weekly Post, October 12, 1899.
73. Butler, "Street Railway Problem," 214–15. McDonald, "Street Cars, Part II," 256–57.
74. Milwaukee Sentinel, August 15, 16, September 9, October 18, 19, November 7, 1899.

ministration and a majority of the aldermen through manipulation of local politics." TMER&L and Payne had patently violated the limits of selfishness and arrogance and sabotaged "the public interest." The head of every German *Turnverein* in the city blasted the measure, and Congregational minister Judson Titsworth condemned the company's selfishness. The Municipal League sponsored several large protest meetings.[75]

When Butler announced that the league did not have enough money to "compete with an organization which represents millions," a new group, the Committee of Ways and Means, arose to lead the fight. Headed by two Municipal Leaguers and former Milwaukee chamber presidents, Edward Bacon and Cassius Paine, this group was based in the chamber, which donated the use of its rooms to the cause. The *Sentinel* donated a daily, front-page box. "Is a high handed assault upon the rights of the public to be allowed to triumph?" demanded Paine in his first column. "When public servants fail in their duty, good citizenship should rise in its might." Good citizenship took the form of mass meetings, sometimes five or six a night, sponsored by the Ways and Means Committee and the Municipal League, with the most popular speaker at the rallies being Henry Baumgaertner. Each word in the proposed ordinance, he declared, was worth a million dollars to the company. In one ward after another these meetings demanded that aldermen heed the voice of the people and kill the ordinance. The protestors converted even the city's leading Democratic organization, the Jefferson Club, which charged that the ordinance betrayed the party's 1898 municipal ownership plank. The Democratic *Journal*, which alone among the city's papers supported the ordinance, was forced to admit that a very large number of Milwaukeeans opposed it.[76]

Despite its obvious popularity, this protest movement was strangely ineffectual. One or two mass meetings had been enough to kill the garbage contract in 1897 and TMER&L's first proposition in 1898, but this time only one alderman, Democrat W. H. Graebner, converted to the reformers. On December 19 the Common Council passed the ordinance to a

75. *Ibid.*, November 7, 9, 15, December 2, 4, 1899. Butler, "Street Railway Problem," 214–15.

76. *Milwaukee Sentinel*, November 14, December 5, 8, 10, 13, 17, 1899. *Milwaukee Daily News*, December 8, 11, 14–16, 1899. Woodruff, "A Year's Municipal Development," 83–84. Butler, "Street Railway Problem," 214–16. McDonald, "Street Cars, Part II," 257, 271. Cf. Wight, *Payne*, 69–70.

third reading by a 25 to 17 vote, with the ordinance to become binding at the next meeting.[77]

The Common Council's vote split the Democratic coalition that had run the city since 1898. Following the actions of the Jefferson Club, which departed before the vote, the Populists declared in a fiery manifesto that they would never again cooperate with Democrats. The next day the Federated Trades Council, speaking for organized labor, bitterly condemned the ordinance. To these groups it appeared that Rose and the Democratic aldermen had sold out the city to TMER&L and Payne.[78] The issue transcended party lines, as it had for progressive Republicans in 1896.

With their new support, the reformers struck back at the aldermen. Charging the aldermen and TMER&L with conspiracy to defraud the people of Milwaukee by giving away valuable rights without sufficient compensation, they secured an injunction on December 21 that restrained city officials and the company from taking further action for twenty days. When TMER&L got an injunction forbidding enforcement of the reformers' order, the Ways and Means Committee secured two more injunctions to prohibit action on the ordinance and enforcement if it should pass. The trial judge upheld the reformers and restrained both the city and TMER&L from acting on the ordinances. This war of injunctions escalated until soon there were eleven relating to the issue.[79]

Reformers believed they had won a period of grace when the trial court ruled in their favor, but TMER&L was not intimidated. "To hell with the injunctions," roared General Manager John I. Beggs. In a crude effort to muzzle reformers and distract attention from the central issue in the last days before the final vote, Payne and Charles Pfister sued the *Milwaukee Sentinel* on December 29 for $100,000 damages, charging that the paper had libeled them and the company. In a succinct statement of the new civic consciousness, the *Sentinel* replied that it was the victim of "probably the most formidable and influential com-

77. *Milwaukee Sentinel*, December 17, 19, 1899. *Milwaukee Daily News*, December 19, 1899. McDonald, "Street Cars, Part II," 271.

78. *Milwaukee Daily News*, December 11, 1899. *Milwaukee Sentinel*, December 19, 1899. McDonald, "Street Cars, Part II," 271–72.

79. *Milwaukee Sentinel*, December 19, 21, 22, 31, 1899, January 2, 5, 9, 25, 1900. Butler, "Street Railway Problem," 215. McDonald, "Street Cars, Part II," 271–72.

bination of selfish interests ever found in the city of Milwaukee."[80]

On January 2, 1900, the Common Council defied the outspoken wishes of the *Turnvereine,* the Municipal League, the Populists, the Jefferson Club, the Federated Trades Council, the chamber of commerce-oriented Ways and Means Committee, all but one of the city's newspapers, a number of clergymen, and a trial court's injunction. It passed the ordinance, Mayor Rose quickly signed it, and TMER&L's directors approved it. The reformers were stunned; they had doubted that city officials would risk arrest by defying the injunction, and now they tried to punish them. When Superior Court Judge John C. Ludwig found the mayor, city clerk, and twenty-four aldermen in contempt of court, a Madison editor remarked that "Milwaukee may yet revel in the novelty of being run by a council behind bars." The state supreme court overturned Ludwig's ruling, however, and upheld the ordinance.[81] The streetcar issue was now removed from city politics for thirty-five years.

Their last hopes dashed by the court, reformers tried to analyze the entire proceedings. Why had the mass meetings and the public protests failed? Was the ordinance popular with particular groups in the city? What had influenced the aldermen's votes? First, the social composition of an alderman's ward evidently had little influence on his vote. Each ward had two aldermen, and the delegations from ten of the city's twenty-one wards had cast opposing votes. Both aldermen from four wards had opposed the ordinance, and both aldermen from seven wards had favored it. The two aldermen from the city's poorest ward, the fourteenth, which contained the highest proportions of Poles and unskilled workers and which usually turned out heavy Democratic majorities, divided on the issue. The same thing happened in the heavily native-born, middle-class sixteenth and the German, working-class twentieth. The seven wards whose two aldermen supported the ordinance ranked from 2

80. *Milwaukee Sentinel,* December 29, 30, 1899. Butler, "Street Railway Problem," 215. McDonald, "Street Cars, Part II," 273. *Appleton Weekly Post,* February 1, 1900. The suit was not settled until 1901 when Pfister bought the *Sentinel* to block the reformers' legislative program. Robert S. Maxwell, *La Follette and the Rise of the Progressives in Wisconsin* (Madison: State Historical Society of Wisconsin, 1956) , 32.

81. *Milwaukee Sentinel,* January 3, 5, 18, 20, February 28, 1900. TMER&L Directors, Minutes, 273–75. *State Journal,* January 18, February 27, 1900.

to 20 in concentration of native-born, from 1 to 21 in concentration of Germans, from 3 to 20 in proportion of professionals, from 2 to 20 in proprietors, from 2 to 21 in unskilled workers, from 2 to 21 in skilled workers, and from 2 to 19 in Democratic vote in 1900. The four wards whose aldermen opposed the ordinance were equally varied. The issue had, then, clearly transcended the old divisions between class, ethnic, and partisan backgrounds.[82]

The clash was essentially a confrontation between the old city politics of machines and the new, issue-oriented politics of ideological reformers. The reformers had lighted fires in every ward, class, ethnic group, and party. Milwaukeeans regarded the ordinance as the climax of six years of struggle against corporate ruthlessness and political domination. The popularity of the reformers' cause was demonstrated in the municipal elections four months later when voters re-elected fifteen of the seventeen aldermen who had opposed the ordinance and only seven of the twenty-five who had voted for it. The stakes were very high for Payne and TMER&L, who knew that defeat of the ordinance might well mean subsequent annihilation of the company. The company used every technique of the old politics —city contracts, political organization, and money—to sway the aldermen, and the reformers used every technique of mass politics—mass meetings, newspaper publicity, interviews, and petitions.

Each alderman faced a tremendous conflict. It was too much for Alderman George Hill of the first ward, who committed suicide on December 28 rather than suffer further attacks from his friends and constituents by casting a second, promised vote for the ordinance.[83] Mayor Rose and TMER&L won the vote of another alderman by awarding his company a city contract, even though his bid was $300 higher than a competitor's.[84] The use of bribery on this ordinance is unquestionable; its extent remains uncertain. A grand jury subsequently indicted one alderman for soliciting a $10,000 bribe for his vote on the

82. *Milwaukee Daily News*, December 19, 1899, January 3, 1900. *Milwaukee Sentinel*, January 3, 1900. Roger Simon graciously provided me with his indexes of demographic disproportion for the city's wards.
83. *Milwaukee Daily News*, December 28, 1899. Charles K. Lush, *The Autocrats: A Novel* (New York: Doubleday, Page, 1901), 310–12, 335.
84. *Milwaukee Daily News*, December 16, 1899.

ordinance.[85] A newsman who wrote a novel about the ordinance suggested that ten aldermen had been purchased outright and that others had pledged their votes in exchange for business and political favors.[86] The Democratic machine promised organizational support for aldermen who stood by the mayor, and Aldermen Cornelius Corcoran, from the traditional center of the machine—the downtown third ward—was Mayor Rose's leading lieutenant in seeking votes. In the end, the old politics of political organizations, city contracts, and money prevailed over the new politics of aroused consumers. The stakes had been so high for TMER&L that it could not afford to reject any traditional technique that might lead an alderman to ignore his constituents' outspoken demands.

If TMER&L got its ordinance, it lost public support throughout the state. Most Wisconsinites, who had been following the dramatic battle since November, sided with the reformers. Nearly every Wisconsin editor, familiar with similar events in his community, attacked TMER&L for its effort to win immunity from the mounting demands to regulate, tax, and possibly own the utility. They took their lead from the *Sentinel's* angriest editorial of fourteen years:

> The man whose gorge does not rise at such contemptuous indifference to the order of a court is a pretty feeble-spirited creature. Persons of this kidney are not numerous in Milwaukee. The Street Railway company has not only aggravated the indignation of men who were already disgusted at its tactics—a thing that anybody would have declared to be impossible. It has roused men who had been mere spectators. It has converted them into angry opponents. To a cynical defiance of public opinion they have now added an equally cynical defiance of the courts. We say this of them, rather than of [city officials] who are so subservient to their wishes, because there is no sane adult in Milwaukee who supposes that the mayor or the majority of the council would have disobeyed the injunction if Messers. Payne, Pfister, Beggs and Bigelow had asked them to show the courts a little respect.[87]

Excepting only a handful of rabidly Democratic newspapers

85. Duane Mowry, "The Reign of Graft in Milwaukee," *Arena,* 34 (December 1905), 592.

86. Lush, *The Autocrats,* especially 83–84, 102–3, 189, 278–79, 335.

87. *Milwaukee Sentinel,* January 4, 1900. Lush, *The Autocrats,* suggests that Payne desperately tried to purchase the *Sentinel* to prevent just such editorials.

like the *Milwaukee Journal,* the state's editors echoed the *Sentinel.* It was, declared the Republican *Vernon County Censor,* a simple "case of the 'people be d——d.' " To the *Appleton Post* "a more high-handed business has certainly never been attempted in this state by citizens who profess not to belong to the criminal classes." The passage of the ordinance climaxed the cumulative frustration Wisconsinites experienced as they concluded that the political arrogance of quasi-public corporations was the greatest menace to honest and popular government. The editors who denounced Payne, TMER&L, and the aldermen represented the entire political spectrum. Democratic papers like the *Marinette Argus, Kenosha Gazette, Oshkosh Times,* and *Kewaunee Enterprise* thundered opposition. Independents like the *Lancaster Teller* and *Reedsburg Times* blasted the ordinance. The chorus of protest from Republican editors ranged from the progressive *Milwaukee Sentinel, Durand Entering Wedge, Vernon County Censor, Jefferson County Union,* Madison *State,* and *Appleton Post* through the moderate *Eau Claire Telegram, Kenosha Daily News, Waukesha Press, Waupun Leader, Wausau Record, Racine Journal,* and *Marinette North Star,* to the conservative *Oshkosh Northwestern* and Madison *Wisconsin State Journal.*[88] The Milwaukee street railway ordinance of 1900 intensified Wisconsinites' determination to cast off the domination of the utilities. The political process had to be made responsive to citizens' needs.

Reformers now tried to channel infuriated public opinion toward the destruction of TMER&L and Payne's political influence. The Federated Trades Council and Populists worked closely with the merchant- and manufacturer-oriented Ways and Means Committee in what a Marinette editor termed "one of the most desperate fights in the history of Milwaukee civil government." Led by Populist Alderman Henry Smith, they demanded that the city construct a municipal lighting plant. "Public ownership kills the lobby and its demoralizing tendencies," roared Smith. "By the very conditions of their existence such corporations must have ignorance or villainy or both in the city government, and the worse it is, the more money they make." As the various reform groups rallied to support Smith's proposal, Republican and Democratic leaders inserted a munici-

88. These papers are all quoted in *Milwaukee Sentinel,* December 22, 24, 1899, January 6, 9, 10, 20, 1900. *Appleton Weekly Post,* January 11, 1900. *The State,* January 5, 1900.

pal lighting plank in their 1900 platforms. On March 26 the Common Council, trying to regain public favor a week before the election, submitted the project to the voters on the spring ballot.[89]

The reformers were more interested in stripping Payne of his political influence than in supporting the lighting plant. Once it was clear that the ordinance would pass, the Ways and Means Committee had formed the nonpartisan Citizens movement. For mayor the reformers wanted Henry Baumgaertner, the city's oldest enemy of the utilities and the man Payne had beaten in 1898. Municipal Leaguers like Butler and Bacon joined the Populists in sponsoring the Citizens movement. Progressive Republicans also supported the Citizens drive. The adoption of the term *Citizens* by Populists, progressive Republicans, and the Municipal League—a term that a few years earlier had been confined to retrenchment and blue law enforcement—and their joining to oppose both regular parties, illustrated just how far TMER&L had pushed them in five years.[90]

While the reformers were booming Baumgaertner, the Democrats met. "Mayor Rose," wrote Butler, "was the inevitable candidate of the 'Payne-Pfister Democracy.' " Reformers might denounce Rose for surrendering the city's right to regulation, but he could reply that the courts had sustained him and that "something had been done" to result in a four-cent fare. He was a credible person to stand justifiably on a municipal ownership platform because he had already secured the municipal garbage plant.[91]

Believing that Rose's renomination proved that TMER&L dominated the Democrats, the progressives fought even harder for Baumgaertner. They used the techniques of mass publicity in an unprecedented way by distributing 65,000 Baumgaertner circulars and announcing in advance which delegates to the Republican city convention would vote for their man. When they elected 140 of the city's 171 Republican delegates, Payne's candidate hastily withdrew and Baumgaertner was nominated by acclamation. The Citizens, Populists, and Municipal League

89. *Municipality*, 1 (June 1900), 41. Henry Smith, "Municipal Lighting for Milwaukee," *ibid.*, 1 (August 1900), 25–31.

90. *Milwaukee Sentinel*, January 7, February 2, 17, March 4, 7, 10, 1900. Butler, "Street Railway Problem," 216–17.

91. Butler, "Street Railway Problem," 216. McDonald, "Street Cars, Part II," 273.

rushed to his support; the reform coalition had reunited behind a progressive Republican.[92]

The campaign was extremely bitter. Payne's lieutenants and TMER&L's funds went to the Democrats, while Baumgaertner campaigned with slender resources. Rose, a flamboyant orator, projected a more impressive image than Baumgaertner, but Baumgaertner received considerable support from outside Milwaukee. The election was, to the *Appleton Post*, "a great fight for the public as against exclusive corporate interests," and a Beloit editor proclaimed that "Beloit . . . needs more Baumgaertners." Conversely, Baumgaertner angered those Republicans who believed that he was "merely the advance agent of La Follette" supporters in the party. Indeed, men like Elliott, Paine, and Baumgaertner himself had long since turned toward La Follette as the best way to destroy the influence of Payne and TMER&L over state government. The campaign, then, was a number of concurrent fights between Republicans and Democrats, Rose and Baumgaertner, reformers and TMER&L, and La Follette and Payne.[93]

Rose won the election, polling 23,542 votes compared to Baumgaertner's 21,695 and the Social Democratic candidate's 2,369. But his victory was no endorsement of the ordinance. Voters turned out eighteen of the twenty-five aldermen who had supported it and only two of the seventeen who had opposed it. Furthermore, the municipal lighting referendum passed by an 11 to 1 margin. Rose's percentage of the major party vote declined in fifteen wards from his 1898 showing and rose in only five.

Baumgaertner's defeat did not end the fight, although Rose and the Democrats went on to dominate Milwaukee politics for a decade. Protected by its new franchise, TMER&L continued its expansion program until it blanketed southeastern Wisconsin. The progressive Republicans, who had broken Payne's hold over their party when they nominated Baumgaertner, gathered enough influence to dominate state politics for fifteen years, during which time they enacted many programs that had derived from the Milwaukee wars. Henry Payne became postmaster general in Theodore Roosevelt's Administration at a

92. *Milwaukee Sentinel,* March 10, 14, 17, 20, 26, 1900.
93. Butler, "Street Railway Problem," 216–17. *Milwaukee Sentinel,* February 28, March 23, 24, 25, April 4, 1900. *Appleton Weekly Post,* March 29, 1900.

time when Wisconsin Republicans would not have elected him ward committeeman. Finally, the long fight proved to the private utilities that reformers were most to be feared at the local level, and they sought immunity from them there by establishing state-wide utility regulation, a campaign that would succeed in 1907.[94]

VIII

Milwaukee's six-year fight against its trolley and light monopoly was primarily a product of the depression. The depression forced TMER&L to adopt unpopular economies and city officials to seek additional tax sources. The first crusaders against TMER&L were, as a result, the city officials who were crushed between these conflicting pressures for economy.

The fight played a crucial part in defining the issues of Wisconsin progressivism. In this era before home rule, the issues that developed in Milwaukee became state issues. By converting the Municipal League in 1895, TMER&L produced an anti-corporation thrust in the only state-wide reform movement. Hostility toward utilities among state-wide reformers was accelerated by events in Milwaukee and by the creation of the League of Wisconsin Municipalities, with its frustrated local officials. First, reformers maintained, quasi-public corporations should be compelled to pay taxes on the same basis as other property owners. Second, reformers had lost their earlier enthusiasm for property rights and private services and their skepticism toward politics and government. If reformers recognized that their worst enemies were politicians like Payne, they knew their best friends were politicians like Brown and Baumgaertner. As a result of these identifications, they demanded that government begin to regulate prerogatives that had traditionally belonged to capitalists.

The most important contribution of the Milwaukee fight to Wisconsin progressivism was the new, insurgent mood of the reformers. TMER&L and its political allies in Milwaukee and Madison formed an imposing establishment. Even when the reform coalition included city officials, its members were es-

94. McDonald, "Street Cars, Part II." 273. McDonald, *Let There Be Light: The Electric Utility Industry in Wisconsin, 1881–1955* (Madison: American History Research Center, 1957), 114–25. Maxwell, *La Follette and the Rise of the Progressives*, 96–97. John R. Commons, "The Wisconsin Public Utility Laws," *Review of Reviews*, 36 (August 1907), 221–24.

sentially insurgents trying to make the political process responsive to the majority of voters. Voters were furious; they could not translate into policy their desire to restore service, fares, or taxes to prepanic levels if TMER&L opposed them. To counter the parliamentary skills, political organization, and money the establishment commanded, they developed the techniques of mass politics. They learned that their instruments of exposure, mass meetings, petitions, and publicity could defeat the establishment only if voters could directly express their wishes by such changes in political institutions as home rule, secret nominations, antilobby laws, and an end to free passes. They were trying to change the traditions and operations of city politics as much as anything else and in the process created a mass, issue-oriented politics whose perpetuation depended on reforms to democratize the political process.

The distinguishing social feature of the new mass, progressive politics was its unification of men from all classes as consumers, taxpayers, and citizens. By 1898, if not 1896, the progressive coalition combined workers and businessmen, foreign-born and native-born, Populists and Republicans, drinkers and abstainers, Catholics and Protestants. The separate class and ethnic bases that had underlain Milwaukee politics since the Civil War fused under the unifying pressures of corporate offenses—higher fares for streetcar riders, higher taxes for taxpayers, air pollution from the company's power station, and the company's defiant attitude toward the city's requests for even minor concessions.

More cautious politicians picked up the issues and mood generated by the Milwaukee progressives. In their declaration of independence from Payne in May, 1896, progressive Republicans had demanded equitable taxation and regulation of quasi-public corporations and measures to limit their political power. Their villain was not U.S. Sen. Philetus Sawyer, but Henry Payne, whose lobbying blocked popular government in Milwaukee and Wisconsin. More than a year later, when Robert M. La Follette was casting about for popular issues on which to base his gubernatorial ambitions and campaign for control of the Republican party, he adopted precisely the issues that the Milwaukee Progressives—Baumgaertner, Rauschenberger, Elliott, Paine, Brown, Roehr, and others—had long championed.

By converting municipal reformers and their state-wide organizations from mugwumpery to progressivism, by identifying the issues and personalities in the battle for state-wide political dominance, by forging a coalition of reformers dedicated to one goal, by generating the insurgent spirit among voters and giving thrust and tone to the movement, the Milwaukee street railway fight became the most important factor in the origins of Wisconsin progressivism.

Wisconsin progressivism derived its vitality from the political radicalism of city dwellers, whose lives were intimately touched by the utility corporations' evasion of taxes, political domination of local governments, and contempt for the common good. There was, at the local level, no possibility of compromise with unsafe water supplies, unprotected railroad crossings, and streetcars that killed and maimed passengers and school children, or tax dodgers whose nonpayments meant the closing of schools and curtailment of other public services. It was clear that popular and honest government would be possible only after voters terminated the power of quasi-public corporations. The political situation in cities like Milwaukee was potentially revolutionary as citizens demanded urgent relief from these ills but were denied it by governments that were in bondage to the corporations.

In this era before home rule the cities, powerless to fight the corporations and tax dodgers on their own ground, had to seek relief at the state level. In the distance that separated the local grievance from the state-wide solution can be seen the dilution of the originally radical thrust to progressivism. Reformers in the cities developed the new, ideological politics of mass publicity and pressure that fit the local conditions of aroused consumers and taxpayers, continuous city council meetings, less partisan elections, and newspaper influence. But political conditions at the state level were uniquely suited to the old politics of ethnically rooted partisanship and of corporate influence in their remoteness from localized problems, the partisan structure of the legislature and its brief meetings, and a greater receptivity to politically recognizable state-wide blocs of ethnic and producer groups.

The reformers' state-wide battles were thus conflicts between the new consumer-oriented, insurgent politics of the local level and the old ethnic- and producer-centered, partisan politics of the state level. If the new politics sometimes collapsed into futile demonstrations of mass pressure, the old politics sometimes collapsed into nonideological factional battles for the spoils. Nowhere were the tensions between the old and new politics more evident than in the emergence of Robert M. La

Follette as the political leader who merged the reformers' demands with traditional political methods. A consummate old-style politician, La Follette became ever more a new-style politician as he increasingly heeded local progressives in order to advance his career.

I

To his contemporaries Senator La Follette seemed the prototypical progressive of the new politics, the perfect reformer. His autobiography, published in 1911, confirmed the impression projected by his courage, determined countenance, and impassioned rhetoric. When contemporary writers and later scholars sought the origins of Wisconsin progressivism, they naturally came to focus on this remarkable man. Lincoln Steffens told it all in a title: "Wisconsin: A State Where the People Have Restored Representative Government—the Story of Governor La Follette."[1] Future historians were to add to his colors as a crusader the hues of a politician, but they would essentially vindicate Steffens' point that La Follette was a boss who dictated democracy. They would never question La Follette's own account of how he became a progressive. Popular legend explained that when Sen. Philetus Sawyer in 1891 offered what La Follette thought was a bribe, it confirmed to him the corruption of a political system he had observed in Congress and offended his sense of integrity. "Out of this awful ordeal came understanding," he wrote in his *Autobiography,* "and out of understanding came resolution. I determined that the power of this corrupt influence, which was undermining and destroying every semblance of representative government in Wisconsin, should be broken." Scholars would add that La Follette promoted the direct primary to further his political ambitions. From this point of view, then, Wisconsin progressivism began in 1900 when Robert M. La Follette had finally persuaded the state's voters of the justice of his reform proposals by energetic speaking campaigns and the growing power of his political organization. His major problem was to convince voters of the need for reform.[2]

1. *McClure's,* 23 (October 1904), 563–79.
2. Lincoln Steffens, *The Autobiography of Lincoln Steffens* (New York: Harcourt, Brace, 1931), 454–63. Robert M. La Follette, *La Follette's Autobiography: A Personal Narrative of Political Experiences* (Madison: Robert M. La Follette Co., 1913), 164. John Dos Passos, *The 42nd Parallel*

This interpretation of the rise of La Follette inverts the actual order of events and by so doing distorts the significance of both La Follette and state-wide reform in the origins of Wisconsin progressivism. Instead of converting the state's voters into progressives by his shimmering rhetoric and superb machine, La Follette was himself converted by the voters from the leader of an "out" faction into a progressive. While La Follette's decision to espouse the issues and style of the new politics was fairly natural and easy, he would offend many of the old-style politicians who comprised his "out" faction and expected different results from politics than did the reformers.

La Follette's early success as a politician derived from his natural sociability and zealous oratory. Nearly everyone who met him along his road to power was impressed by his personal warmth. His college classmates remembered him as "the chairman of the undergraduate greeters," and his main interest in college had been in his social life. In 1890, after three terms as a congressman, he was, said a reporter, "popular at home, popular with his colleagues, and popular in the house. . . . He is so good a fellow that even his enemies like him." Ten years

(New York: Harper and Bros., 1930), 377. Nils P. Haugen, *Pioneer and Political Reminiscences* (Madison: State Historical Society of Wisconsin, ca. 1930), 138, 151. Robert S. Maxwell, *La Follette and the Rise of the Progressives in Wisconsin* (Madison: State Historical Society of Wisconsin, 1956), 10–26, 56–73. Robert C. Twombly, "The Reformer as Politician: Robert M. La Follette in the Election of 1900" (M.A. thesis, University of Wisconsin, 1964), 13, 23–169. Stuart Dean Brandes, "Nils P. Haugen and the Wisconsin Progressive Movement" (M.S. thesis, University of Wisconsin, 1965), 52–109. Howard L. Smith, "The New Primary Law in Wisconsin," *Publications of the Michigan Political Science Association,* 6 (March 1905), 73. Ernst Christopher Meyer, *Nominating Systems: Direct Primaries versus Conventions in the United States* (Madison: privately published, 1902), 244. Carroll Pollock Lahman, "Robert Marion La Follette as Public Speaker and Political Leader, 1855–1905" (Ph.D. diss., University of Wisconsin, 1939), 396–494. Albert O. Barton, *La Follette's Winning of Wisconsin, 1894–1904* (Des Moines: Homestead Co., 1922), 69–164. Eugene A. Manning, "Old Bob La Follette: Champion of the People" (Ph.D. diss., University of Wisconsin, 1966), 34–53. Allen F. Lovejoy, *La Follette and the Establishment of the Direct Primary in Wisconsin* (New Haven: Yale University Press, 1941), 34–54. Kenneth C. Acrea, Jr., "Wisconsin Progressivism: Legislative Response to Social Change, 1891 to 1909" (Ph.D. diss., University of Wisconsin, 1968), 221–95, 350–52, 354–55, 359–60. Herbert F. Margulies, *The Decline of the Progressive Movement in Wisconsin, 1890–1920* (Madison: State Historical Society of Wisconsin, 1968), 3–50. Roger E. Wyman, "Voting Behavior in the Progressive Era: Wisconsin as a Case Study" (Ph.D. diss., University of Wisconsin, 1970), 236ff.

later friends and enemies alike commented on his "fascinating personality and manners which makes 'Bob' seem a synonym of friendship and good fellowship to all whom he exerts himself to please."[3]

With this sensitivity to the nuances in the personalities of his associates came a sympathy with their views and attitudes. In the two most famous early cases of what he would later describe as a lifelong battle against special privileges—his fight against the dominance of college fraternities and his opposition to Madison's postmaster, Elisha W. Keyes—La Follette waited until events and other men had defined and attacked the enemy before he enlisted in the battle.[4] As congressman from 1885 to 1891 La Follette was "the steadfast friend of every interest in his district," and he waged many battles to protect his district's dairy and tobacco farmers from competition by oleomargarine and foreign tobacco producers.[5] On questions of the tariff, currency, and Negro rights, La Follette was, like his district, a northern Republican partisan who represented his constituents' views.[6]

He followed public opinion on two questions that would subsequently be identified with progressivism. When the state's merchants, farm groups, and temperance advocates demanded

3. Albert O. Barton interview with James A. Peterson, February 8, 1893, Barton Papers, Manuscripts Division, State Historical Society of Wisconsin. Walter Davenport, "Fighting Blood," *Collier's*, 89 (April 23, 1932), 10–11, 46–48. *Milwaukee Sentinel*, March 30, 1890, July 10, 1897, August 5, 1900. Haugen, *Pioneer and Political Reminiscences*, 151.

4. David P. Thelen, *The Early Life of Robert M. La Follette, 1855–1884* (Chicago: Loyola University Press, 1966), 35–36, 63–72, 88–100.

5. Quotation is from *Milwaukee Sunday Telegraph*, quoted in *State Journal*, October 13, 1890. For information on dairy farmers, see, for example, *State Journal*, May 31, June 15, 1886. For tobacco growers, see *U.S. Congressional Record*, 49th Cong., 2d sess., 1886–1887, 269–70. *State Journal*, September 13, October 15, 1884, January 4, 7, February 17, October 29, December 20, 1886, January 11, February 15, July 19, August 10, 1888. *Milwaukee Sentinel*, June 8, 1890. *Stoughton Courier*, September 19, 1884.

6. *State Journal*, September 10, October 2, 24, 1884, February 10, October 20, 1886, February 2, March 15, June 14, July 16, 18, November 7, 1888, February 14, March 8, 1889, July 3, October 4, 13, 31, November 1, 4, 1890. *U.S. Congressional Record*, 49th Cong., 2d sess., 1886–1887, 269–70, 1300, 1883, 1921, 2700; 51st Cong., 1st sess., 1889–1890, 4473–82, Appendix, 467–69. *Eau Claire Daily Free Press*, April 10, 1886. *North American Review*, 146 (March 1888), 249–50. U.S. House of Representatives, *Revision of the Tariff: Hearings Before the Committee on Ways and Means*, 51st Cong., 1st sess., 1889–1890, House Misc. Doc. 176, 62, 173, 438, 443, 449, 596–97, 601–7, 1177, 1375.

thorough railroad regulation, his statement that the "prosperity of this country and of the railways are interdependent" sounded almost conciliatory, but he supported creation of the Interstate Commerce Commission.[7] The popular response to the rapid growth of trusts in the 1880s remained with him for the rest of his life. The result of investigations of national trusts in sugar, cattle, and oil and such local monopolies as the Milwaukee coal pool, the Appleton flour pool, railroad pools, and the express trust that steeply raised its prices to Wisconsin merchants, was a state antitrust bill and the national Sherman Act. Swept along by the mounting outcry against trusts, La Follette proclaimed the Sherman Antitrust Act "one of the most important acts ever conceived."[8] La Follette's views and votes on railroad regulations and trusts coincided with those of national and state Republican leaders, but he allowed his sensitivity to majority desires to lead him wherever it would—even to opposing his party's leaders. This occurred when he balked at such pork-barrel legislation as rivers and harbors appropriations. While every other Wisconsin congressman was seeking his piece of pork, La Follette was winning bipartisan applause from local and national editors for his championship of fiscal economy. This independence from other congressmen led the *Darlington Democrat* to note that "if you can't have a democrat from your district, you could fare much worse than to have 'Bob' La Follette." His stand against pork-barrel measures proved to his district's leading Republican paper that "he has in him the material for making a statesman."[9]

By the time La Follette was defeated in the Democratic landslide of 1890, he had shown that he instinctively followed popular opinion and that he would exalt that opinion over the

7. U.S. *Congressional Record*, 49th Cong., 2d sess., 1886–1887, Appendix, 185. *State Journal*, January 22, 1887. Milwaukee Chamber of Commerce, *30th Annual Report of the Trade and Commerce of Milwaukee*, 1888, 27. Gabriel Kolko, *Railroads and Regulation, 1877–1916* (Princeton: Princeton University Press, 1965), 32. *Presbyterian Minutes*, 1884, 7.

8. *Milwaukee Sentinel*, July 23, August 23, September 4, October 23, November 27, 1887, January 26, February 2, May 9, September 3, 13, 25, November 15, 1888, January 31, February 6, 1889, July 4, October 6, 1890. *State Journal*, October 5, 1890. Belle Case La Follette and Fola La Follette, *Robert M. La Follette*, 2 vols. (New York: Macmillan Co., 1953), 1:80.

9. U.S. *Congressional Record*, 49th Cong., 2d sess., 1886–1887, 250–51, 967–68, 1056–61, 2438. *State Journal*, April 23, 24, May 20, August 2, October 27, 1886, January 27, February 5, 1887, May 11, 1888. Lahman, "La Follette," 221.

wishes of party leaders. He was already a popular politician who had proven his receptivity to issues with demonstrated mass appeal, and it was possible to assume that he would continue to search out such issues in the future. Indeed, when he first championed the direct primary and railroad taxation in 1897, the *Milwaukee Sentinel* shrewdly classified him with "the party leaders who try to find out what the popular current is, what the people want. . . . They may give effect to forces already at work and they may profit, too, by their recognition and understanding of these forces."[10]

There was more to La Follette's personality than a respect for public opinion. Since childhood he had shown a tendency to see public affairs as polarized between Good and Evil, Right and Wrong. As a college student he had been influenced by John Bascom, who gave depth to his emerging judgmental streak. As Dane County district attorney between 1881 and 1884 he had developed his moralistic sense into the belief that the courtroom was an arena in which Truth battled Falsehood. His ruthless prosecution of drunks and vagrants made him "a standing terror among the criminal classes of Dane County."[11]

La Follette's extraordinary flair for oratory provided the vehicle for this moralistic zeal. A good part of the talent that had made him the champion collegiate orator of six states and was to impress auditors until his death was a flair for drama. "Although he did not speak so in ordinary conversation," recalled a college friend, "the minute he got on the platform he became the actor." The editor of a Madison newspaper described La Follette's style during a 1900 murder trial:

> All of the dramatic art of La Follette, now shaking an index finger at a witness, now half sitting upon the reports' table, now with a pointer in hand by the map on the wall—La Follette, ever restless, ever eager—always in deadliest earnest, had set his stage scenery. The calcium lights were ready. The curtain boy had been given the last word. . . . Now his face was calm—now a thunder cloud—now full of sorrow. Here his voice arose almost to a shriek—there it sank to a whisper. Yet he was not acting. It was the artist in the orator, painting the colors on the words as they sprang from his soul.[12]

10. *Milwaukee Sentinel*, August 3, 1898.
11. Thelen, *Early Life of La Follette*, 23–24, 46–49, 73–87.
12. *Ibid.*, 31–32, 33, 42–45, 104. *State Journal*, February 1, 3, 1900.

It was on the platform that La Follette fused his dramatic oratorical talents with his growing judgmental tendencies. He gave his Gilded Age audiences the grandiose and self-righteous oratory he knew they liked. It was his primary political asset at first, and local Republican leaders chose him for the district attorneyship because of his oratorical skills. He never disappointed them; although Democrats mocked his oratory at first ("He talked for all the world like a strolling play actor.") , they soon felt the sting of his moralistic words. By 1884 the Madison Democratic editor reserved for La Follette alone the epithet *demagogue*. It was a label that would follow him for the rest of his life; it was accurate to the extent that it described a politician who was extremely effective in persuading audiences that his (and their) cause was just and that the opposition was composed of fools and knaves.[13]

Established as a zealous foe of Democrats, drunkards, and vagrants, La Follette used his moralistic oratory to further causes in Congress that were popular among his constituency. Because of Wisconsin's dairy interests, the hated oleomargarine became a "monstrous product of greed and hypocrisy," and he sponsored in the national legislature measures to limit its production. His slashing partisan attack on House Speaker John Carlisle in the summer of 1888 impressed even the cynical Thomas B. Reed, who subsequently appointed La Follette to the Ways and Means Committee as a reward.[14] So zealous was La Follette in prosecuting any cause he espoused that the 1888 election, in which he was re-elected, was largely fought over the issue of whether he was a demagogue.[15]

After his defeat in the Democratic landslide of 1890, La Follette became the state's leading Republican orator. Even when his political ambitions clashed with those of his party's leaders, the leaders still begged him to speak for the party. His sworn journalistic enemy, the *Wisconsin State Journal,* conceded that he was a "rattling campaigner," and party leaders ignored his various attacks in the campaign of 1896 to ask him to give twenty-five speeches in support of the ticket.[16]

13. Thelen, *Early Life of La Follette,* 104–6.
14. *State Journal,* June 15, 1886, July 16, 18, 19, 1888. *Milwaukee Sentinel,* July 21, 1888, December 13, 1889. La Follette, *Autobiography,* 99–102.
15. *State Journal,* September 16, October 21, 1886, October 25, November 2, 4, 1890. *Milwaukee Sentinel,* May 21, July 3, 1890.
16. *State Journal,* July 30, 1896. *Milwaukee Sentinel,* November 3, 1896.

During the 1890s he used his oratorical talents to build a profitable law practice, and his reputation as a brilliant pleader before juries attracted a number of clients. A *Chicago Times-Herald* reporter called him "foremost among the jury lawyers of the state." When La Follette won damages for a client whose hand had been lost in an industrial accident, the defeated corporation lawyer angrily recalled that "he could not have made humanity's case any more desperate if it had been the hand of Providence that was lost."[17] His most publicized case was his assistance to Milwaukee County's district attorney Leopold Hammel in that city's prosecution of the embezzler of the South Side Bank in 1893–1894. The defense lawyer spent five minutes warning the jurors against La Follette's oratory; La Follette was in good form:

> So the money of the merchant and the laboring men pour into the coffers of the bank; but suppose some morning that community wakes up and finds that for 25 years it has been deceived, that this man has all that time been living a lie? Now that trust is destroyed; men distrust each other; they look with suspicion on each other; their business and social relations in a measure are destroyed, simply on account of this man. . . . [The accused's] love of [his family] had been forgotten in the years of crime in which he was steeped.

By pinning all the social unrest of the depression on a single banker who, according to La Follette, was so wicked that criminal desires outweighed love of his family, La Follette won the case and earned a fee of $1,627.[18] Even in the courtroom he tied his oratory to popular attitudes.

While at first glance there might seem to be a contradiction between the pleasant La Follette who adapted to men and majorities on the one hand and the moralistic orator on the other, there was no real dichotomy in his life. When he stepped down from the platform after delivering a fiery speech he resumed his genial demeanor, and his associates—whether friends or foes—discovered anew that the passionate orator was also a "royal good fellow" and a confirmed compromiser. In a speech at Oshkosh in the summer of 1897 he thoroughly roasted the machine's leader Philetus Sawyer for provoking interruptions

Lahman, "La Follette," 329–34, 389–93.
17. Lahman, "La Follette," 302–3.
18. *Milwaukee Sentinel,* January 23–25, 1894. Lahman, "La Follette," 291–92.

of his speech, but after the speech he sought out Sawyer, chatted warmly with him for several minutes, and took upon himself the blame for the misunderstanding.[19] In a rare cynical moment he explained his detachment from his oratory to a cousin by saying that he gave speeches mainly "to stir the animals up."[20]

From this interplay between the sociable politician and the zealous orator came La Follette's major strengths as a popular factional leader in the years before 1900. By contrast with such machine leaders as Sawyer and Payne, who hesitated to meet people and avoided crowds, La Follette loved crowds. "I am an old picnicer [sic]," he told local politicians.[21] The speeches he gave at the political picnics persuaded audiences that he was the best person to implement long-popular causes. "You get nearer the people every time you publicly assail their enemies and betrayers," observed a friend.[22] His warm personality and demagogic oratory rewarded him with broad mass appeal.

La Follette's personality fitted him to become a leader of the new, popular, issue politics. While he espoused no especially progressive ideas before 1897, he had shown that he would espouse ideas whose popularity others had established. Furthermore, his reliance on direct contacts with voters through oratory made him receptive to the mass appeals of the new politics.

But La Follette knew that oratory was not the main road to political success. Coming from a family that had long prized political office, he also knew the traditional ingredients for victory.[23] He was equally comfortable with the old methods of courting local politicians who fancied themselves community leaders, of making his supporters anticipate a patronage plum for their efforts, of reconciling feuds, and, above all, of luring those men and groups who felt snubbed by the dominant faction.[24] His personality was a great asset in these activities. "One

19. *Milwaukee Sentinel,* September 30, October 2, 1897. La Follette, *Autobiography,* 206–7.

20. Robert M. La Follette to Charles La Follette, January 6, 1900, La Follette Papers, Manuscripts Division, State Historical Society of Wisconsin.

21. Robert M. La Follette to D. C. Hayes, August 24, 1897, *ibid.*

22. A. C. Wallin to Robert M. La Follette, August 30, 1897, *ibid.*

23. John H. La Follette, *History of the La Follette Family in America* (Ottumwa, Iowa: Charles F. Lang, 1898), 4, 8, 9, 14, 16, 23. La Follette and La Follette, *Robert M. La Follette,* 1: 8. *State Journal,* September 4, 1886, August 9, 1888. *Stevens Point Daily Journal,* August 4, 1900. Samuel A. Harper to Harvey La Follette, December 20, 1896, La Follette Papers. Thelen, *Early Life of La Follette,* 7–11, 16–17.

24. For his uses of such techniques, see Margulies, *Decline of Progressive*

can't shake hands with the man without a quiet feeling that he can get on the payroll any time he pleases," commented a Superior editor.[25] His direct and flattering appeals ("It would please me greatly to have you come to the state convention.") attracted local politicians. He spent three days at the Milwaukee Summer Carnival in 1898 in a continuous reception at the Plankinton House for politicians who might support his gubernatorial ambitions at the state convention a month later.[26]

He began to construct a faction out of disgruntled groups. From 1891, when he first denounced Sawyer publicly, until 1897, when he embraced progressive issues, the faction was essentially an old-style collection of outs trying to get in; its major goal was to win control of the party—and its patronage—from the dominant machine. Sour charges of bossism certainly did not presage a reform administration; they were simply the traditional rhetoric of out factions.

La Follette had little trouble in locating disgruntled groups. One man who burned with hatred of the machine and became a key leader of the out faction in the mid-nineties was former Governor Hoard. A prominent spokesman for the state's rapidly growing numbers of dairy farmers, Hoard felt that the machine, and particularly Payne, had betrayed dairymen by its subservience to the oleomargarine interests and had betrayed Hoard personally by not enthusiastically backing his re-election campaign in 1890. So completely did Hoard and the dairymen color the intentions of the La Follette faction that as late as 1896 one reform-minded editor complained that "Hoard and his man for governor, Mr. La Follette" should learn that "there are more momentous issues involved in the present campaign than the dairy cow."[27] La Follette also attracted large numbers of young men, particularly University of Wisconsin alumni, who saw little and slow opportunity for advancement in the machine and

Movement, 22–23, 34–35, 41. Maxwell, *La Follette and the Rise of the Progressives,* 15–26. Twombly, "Reformer as Politician," as a case study.

25. *Superior Evening Telegram,* July 31, 1900, in Lahman, "La Follette," 475.

26. Robert M. La Follette To David Taylor, June 19, 1900, La Follette to M. J. O'Dwyer, June 18, 1900, La Follette to Samuel H. Jones, June 18, 1900, La Follette Papers. *Milwaukee Sentinel,* June 30, 1898. *The Madison State,* May 25, 1900. *Wausau Daily Record,* July 28, 1898.

27. William D. Hoard to H. P. Myrick, December 30, 1896, Hoard Letter Books, 52: 128–29. Hoard to E. J. Hooper, February 26, 1897, 52: 344; Hoard to Hollon Richardson, February 26, 1897, 52: 346–47; Hoard to A. L. Fontaine, February 26, 1897, 52: 381–82; Hoard to G. E. Bryant,

admired the popular alumnus.[28] Large numbers of individual politicians felt snubbed by the old guard and brought their followers to the out faction. The most important of these was millionaire lumberman Isaac Stephenson, who began to bankroll the faction in 1899 after the machine killed his hopes to become United States Senator.[29]

The voting base of the La Follette faction came from the Scandinavians. Although they had consistently supported the Republican party since the 1850s, they were by the end of the century coming to feel, and justifiably, that the machine took their loyalty too much for granted and denied them overdue political recognition. Sawyer, Payne, Spooner, and the machine leaders obviously believed that the German Protestants were the pivotal voters in Wisconsin and geared issues and patronage in the 1880s toward winning the German Lutherans. This growing discontent among Scandinavians surfaced in the 1890 election when the machine seemed willing to sacrifice even the party in its subservience to German Protestants. That year machine leaders only reluctantly supported Hoard's re-election campaign because the governor had alienated German Lutheran voters (as well as others) by binding the party to an 1889 law that the Germans believed would destroy their most important cultural institution—the parochial school. Not vitally interested in the 1889 law, the Scandinavians interpreted the machine's inaction in 1890 as proof that it was indifferent to them.[30] While they continued to vote Republican in general elections, they flocked to the out faction to assert their political

April 25, 1897, 52: 501, Hoard Papers, Manuscripts Division, State Historical Society of Wisconsin. *Appleton Weekly Post*, July 30, 1896. *Madison Old Dane*, December 3, 1897. *Milwaukee Sentinel*, August 6, 1896. Maxwell, *La Follette and Progressives*, 62. D. C. Whitney to Robert M. La Follette, May 28, 1900, La Follette Papers.

28. La Follette, *Autobiography*, 207–8. Margulies, *Decline of Progressive Movement*, 19–22.

29. For examples, see *Milwaukee Sentinel*, August 1, 1896. *Ashland Daily News*, June 22, 1900. La Follette, *Autobiography*, 226–28. Margulies, *Decline of Progressive Movement*, 45. Maxwell, *La Follette and Progressives*, 15, 24, 60–62.

30. For information on the machine's interest in German Protestants, see *Milwaukee Catholic Citizen*, March 8, June 14, November 8, 1890. Roger E. Wyman, "Wisconsin Ethnic Groups and the Election of 1890," *Wisconsin Magazine of History*, 51 (Summer 1968), 272, 275. Wyman, "Voting Behavior," 59, 82, 534. Dorothy Ganfield Fowler, *John Coit Spooner: Defender of Presidents* (New York: University Publishers, 1961), 146–50. Richard N. Current, *Pine Logs and Politics: A Life of Philetus Sawyer* (Madison: State Historical Society of Wisconsin, 1950), 254.

maturity. La Follette candidly explained why he had promoted Norwegian-born Nils P. Haugen as the faction's first gubernatorial candidate in 1894: "I knew [the Scandinavians] felt a certain national pride in Congressman Haugen's prominence and success, and I counted on their giving him very strong support." From 1894, when they were simply backing an out politician, until at least 1910, when that politician was a significant progressive, the Scandinavians provided many of the votes for the La Follette faction. On his part, La Follette rewarded their desire for political recognition.[31]

By 1895 La Follette was clearly the leader of this informal coalition of assorted out groups and politicians. His natural charm, organizational skill, oratorical ability, and driving ambition to become governor made him the natural leader. It was probably also true, as a Democratic editor claimed, that La Follette was the only possible leader because the diverse types of people in the faction were "a large number of chiefs, each about as unavailable as the other and all jealous of their fellows."[32] La Follette's election became the sole aim of the faction because it was the only goal that could reward all the groups.

By 1897 it was also clear that La Follette was adept enough as an old-style politician to win the governorship at some future point. In 1896 his faction had been sufficiently skillful in the timing and packing of caucuses and in the art of winning convention delegates to win the lead on the first nominating ballot. Time, too, was on La Follette's side, for age and political blunders were taking their toll among the machine leaders. Sawyer was eighty years old, and after 1896 Payne faced continuing open revolt from the majority of Republicans in his home base of Milwaukee.

No one at this point comprehended the central tension in the out faction between its leader's personality and the objectives of its constituents. La Follette would almost inevitably sponsor

31. La Follette, *Autobiography,* 176–78. Most of the following accounts explain Scandinavian support for La Follette's faction as a reflection of that nationality's inherent progressivism: Margulies, *Decline of Progressive Movement,* 26–28. Jörgen Weibull, "The Wisconsin Progressives, 1900–1914," *Mid-America,* 47 (July 1965), 191–221. Maxwell, *La Follette and Progressives,* 59–61. Wyman, "Ethnic Groups," 275. Wyman, "Voting Behavior," 332–33, finds patronage a major reason for Scandinavian support, which is elsewhere (Wyman, pp. 494, 503–4, 592–671, 935) explained as their progressivism. See also Robert M. La Follette to Mrs. N. Haugen, February 5, 1898, La Follette Papers.

32. *Milwaukee Journal,* July 22, 1898, in Lahman, "La Follette," 423.

popular issues and practice the new politics, while his followers maintained their interest in the rewards of the old politics. La Follette, it seemed, could not or would not simply perfect his organization.

II

The year 1897 marked the turning point in the development of Wisconsin progressivism, for it was then that La Follette began to promote on a state-wide basis the issues that local progressives had identified. La Follette had watched the vocal and well-organized reformers show, during the 1897 legislature, how reform issues could reveal Payne, his enemy within the party, as a popular villain. He had seen the spokesmen of mass politics—reform groups and editors—attack politicians who blocked popular campaigns against corporate arrogance and tax dodging, so he took up these popular issues in the summer of 1897. The eleven proposals he placed on the masthead of his newspaper were a catalog of early progressive proposals. He added his voice to the clamor for equitable taxation of quasi-public corporations in several speeches at county fairs. Corporate tax dodgers, he warned, undermined "the will of the people and threaten the very principles of Representative Government." He advocated repeal of the license fee tax on railroads, which taxpayers, city officials, and reformers had been denouncing for years. His second new program was institution of the direct primary—an attempt to break the control of quasi-public corporations over the political process. The direct primary would make nominations for office less dependent on the will of corporations, executed in secret, and more dependent on mass appeals by reformers and orators in public.[33]

Friends and enemies alike agreed that La Follette's new issues had been popular long before he espoused them. Conservatives charged that he was one of those politicians "who keep their ears to the ground and govern their actions by what they hear. These are the statesmen who ride upon the crest of the wave of public opinion." The *Oshkosh Northwestern* declared that La Follette's nomination demonstrated that "politicians are power-

33. La Follette, *Autobiography*, 185–86, 196–210. Pencil copy of speech by La Follette in July 1–15, 1897 Folder, La Follette Papers. *Milwaukee Sentinel*, September 6, 11, 25, 1897, July 17, 1898. *Ashland Daily Press*, April 12, 1899. Amos Parker Wilder, "Governor La Follette and What He Stands For," *Outlook*, 70 (March 8, 1902), 631–34.

ful only when they follow the wishes of the people."[34] Progressives were openly uneasy at his sudden conversion to their views. Why, they wondered, had he waited until after the 1897 legislature had adjourned to announce his program? The *Milwaukee Sentinel* complained that he had ignored reform issues during the legislative session "when it might have been possible to avoid or correct those manifest legislative errors."[35] Since the recent legislative session had raised taxes on quasi-public corporations and established secret primary elections in the cities, the progressive *Appleton Post* worried that La Follette's "new" issues were "not very new questions" and that "it is only recently that Mr. La Follette has become fully awakened to these dangers."[36]

Although the reformers were uneasy at La Follette's conversion, they had nowhere else to go. As events increasingly exposed Payne as the villain who blocked their campaigns for popular government, they flocked to La Follette. But they were the least comfortable group in his coalition. The classic tension between the ambitious politician and the dedicated reformer intervened and, not comprehending his natural sociability, they failed to see how he could denounce a man from the platform one day and make a deal with him the next. In 1896, at the very time Milwaukee progressives were roasting Payne and TMER&L for their arrogance and La Follette was publicly calling for Payne's resignation as national committeeman, La Follette was privately writing Payne, "I know of no sufficient reason why we should not have been friends."[37] Reformers were deeply unhappy when La Follette and his lieutenants held several conferences with Payne and railroad executives in 1900 to assure their opponents that La Follette was not as radical as he sounded on the platform.[38] The issue-oriented reformers could not be happy with politicians' deals nor could they accept his pragmatism.

34. Emanuel L. Philipp and Edgar T. Wheelock, *Political Reform in Wisconsin: A Historical Review of the Subjects of Primary Election, Taxation, and Railway Regulation* (Milwaukee: privately published, 1910), 240. *Oshkosh Northwestern*, quoted in *Milwaukee Sentinel*, July 26, 1900.
35. *Milwaukee Sentinel*, September 6, 1897.
36. *Appleton Weekly Post*, October 7, 1897. See also May 25, 1899.
37. Robert M. La Follette to Henry C. Payne, June 10, 1896, La Follette Papers.
38. Maxwell, *La Follette and Progressives*, 15–17, 36, 46. Lahman, "La Follette," 454, 469–70. Margulies, *Decline of Progressive Movement*, 47–48.

The alliance posed even deeper problems for the reformers, problems that were associated with who was to shape the reform movement. Once converted, La Follette followed many of the reformers in developing a special progressive concept of political leadership that transcended the role of the factional leader. He came to believe that his election to the governorship was a necessary first step for progressive reform. The unchallenged factional leader now insisted that he was also the reform leader. In a political situation in which ordinary men were warped or broken by the utilities to defeat the popular will it made good sense to develop the myth of a superman who could succeed where others had failed. The reform leader had to be a political Moses. Believing that his election alone could express "the will of the people" and bring reform, La Follette became a filter for all reform issues. His original reason for pursuing only two issues was that "we had found it important to keep the field of discussion narrowed to the subjects which could be treated adequately in a single address."[39] This oratorical technique of the new politics thus served to limit the program of the reform leader whose primary goal was election to the governorship.

The progressives had different goals in their state-wide reform movement. The reformers, less interested in who was governor than in passing laws to curb the corporations, end their tax evasions, and free their cities from the grasp of quasi-public corporations, were less than enthusiastic about defining the progressive program around only two issues. During the 1897 and 1899 legislative sessions, when the progressives were fighting for such broad programs as corrupt practices acts, abolition of the license fee tax, home rule, financial statements by utilities, abolition of railway passes and other forms of bribery, La Follette ignored their causes and worked only for the direct primary, which would improve his chances for nomination.[40] His own paper, *Old Dane,* virtually ignored the legislative reformers and used its columns to promote the election of La Follette's law partner to the county bench.[41] La Follette's new paper, *The State,* similarly interpreted Benjamin

39. La Follette, *Autobiography,* 238–39.
40. *State Journal,* March 30, 1897. *Superior Leader,* March 27, 1897. *Milwaukee Sentinel,* December 6, 1896, September 6, 1897, July 28, 1900. Philipp and Wheelock, *Political Reform,* 20, 21. Meyer, *Nominating Systems,* 244–47. Smith, "The New Primary Law in Wisconsin," 73.
41. For example, see *Old Dane,* April 9, 1897.

Harrison's 1898 demand for an inheritance tax as an endorsement of La Follette for governor.[42] His reaction to the 1899–1900 drive by Payne and TMER&L for political immunity in Milwaukee also illustrated the tension between La Follette and the progressives. Instead of emphasizing Payne's defiance of public opinion or the need for taxation and regulation, as the progressives did, La Follette said that the ordinance proved the necessity of electing him governor.[43] The goals of the progressives and the goals of La Follette were different enough to cause serious tension in the relationship.

At the same time that La Follette picked up the progressives' issues, he continued to practice the old politics as he built his faction. This fact helps to explain why he could hold his followers of disparate persuasions for his brand of politics and definition of the issues. His faction was basically indifferent to ideological issues; his old supporters were more interested in political recognition than reform, and they were willing to let their leader use any issues he wanted. By distributing patronage and other forms of recognition to eager Scandinavians, La Follette gave political rewards to a major group denied acceptance by the old machine.[44] By building his machine in the politically immature rural areas, La Follette brought the excitement and satisfactions of politics to neglected voters while he escaped the savage wars between machines and issue-oriented reformers in the cities. Less involved in issues, rural voters preferred to follow community leaders. La Follette already knew the accuracy of the *Wausau Record*'s 1902 definition of a farmer as "one who does not know that there is a fight on between the stalwarts and the half breeds."[45] His followers wanted different things from politics than legislative programs, and they let him shape the program.

The La Follette faction was an unstable merger between the old politics and the new. La Follette himself took some issues from the progressives and increasingly used their styles of mass pressure—newspaper publicity, direct contacts with the mass of voters, denunciations of the alliances between corporations and politicians that subverted popular government, and, in general, appeals to public opinion on consumer and taxpayer issues. He

42. *The State,* June 24, 1898.
43. *Ibid.,* January 5, 1900.
44. See note 31.
45. Quoted in Wyman, "Voting Behavior," 807.

305

also continued to practice the old, ethnic- and producer-based politics by rewarding Scandinavians with patronage and ultimately the Milwaukee Chamber of Commerce with railroad regulation.[46] In the years between 1897 and 1900 the constituents of both the old and new politics could unite behind La Follette to defeat the Payne machine. Old-style politicians received such patronage as the faction could muster from friendly state and national officials, and the reformers were free to define whatever issues they wanted in the legislature because the conservative governor, Edward Scofield, was indifferent, if not hostile, toward all their goals. Both groups could look forward to that day in 1900 when La Follette's election would weaken the machine that defied both reformers and recognition-hungry politicians.

"Success, for a new movement," as La Follette declared, "often presents quite as serious problems as defeat." With his increasingly messianic conception of political leadership—a natural result of his 1900 victory, the strength of the opposition, his moralistic streak, and the new mass politics—he would insist on becoming the legislative leader of Wisconsin progressivism. Now the function of his program became, in his words, to "hold back and keep together the enthusiasts in our ranks."[47] The early progressives had championed state reforms to restore power in order to solve their local problems in their communities with the techniques they best understood, but the new governor wanted state reforms to strengthen the power of the state government and his organization. As a result, Wisconsin lagged far behind other "progressive" states in giving power to its cities, and home rule would not come until 1924. The state that the National Municipal League had expected to pioneer in establishing the means for popular city government was, in fact, to trail her sisters badly.

If La Follette's conversion in 1897 made the flower that bloomed significantly different than might have been predicted from its roots, the fact remains that a flower did bloom. La Follette's own genius was in accomplishing something of a political revolution by blending the old ethnic politics with the new issue politics. His greatness came from the fact that he was

46. Stanley P. Caine, "Railroad Regulation in Wisconsin, 1903–1910: An Assessment of a Progressive Reform" (Ph.D. diss., University of Wisconsin, 1967), 19–22, 24–26, 34, 43–46, 111, 117.
47. La Follette, *Autobiography*, 237.

responsive enough to public opinion to incorporate the programs of the early progressives.

III

While this account may explain La Follette's enthusiasm for certain progressive programs, it does not explain why those programs had become too popular for La Follette to ignore them. The answer to the question lies in responses to the depression of 1893–1897. The depression struck Wisconsin with special ferocity because it forced the state's residents to recognize, for the first time, the social and political results of the sudden urbanization and industrialization of the previous decade. The results were hurried, pragmatic efforts to adjust institutions to rapid demographic and economic changes and the collapse of social barriers that had previously separated Wisconsinites. The new progressive coalitions gained power because they united diverse groups with disparate backgrounds. Because the corporations' ignoring of the cities' needs and their evasion of taxes presented both new and urgent problems during the depression, opposition to them lent force and direction to the political coalitions. The railroads' tax dodging and their control of politicians had become such burning issues among so many different groups that the state's politicians would inevitably have been driven to confront them even if La Follette had never come to the fore.

In addition to providing progressive issues for La Follette, early reformers had achieved significant victories on their own. The war against the corporations had produced municipal ownership of various utilities, rate regulation on the local level, consumer-owned utilities, prohibitions on free passes for aldermen and legislators, requirements for financial statements by utilities, registration of corporate lobbyists, and enforcement of health and safety requirements. The taxation crusade had forced some wealthy individuals and companies to pay their delinquent taxes, created ad valorem taxation of sleeping-car and express companies, raised taxes significantly on the remaining quasi-public corporations and insurance companies, established a state tax commission, and passed a state inheritance tax. The state's political climate was profoundly influenced by civil service laws, regulation of party nominations, attempted prohibitions on corporate activities, referenda on some utility questions, and, above all, the increasingly competent, conscientious, and responsive local officials who campaigned against corporate privilege and tax exemptions.

The greatest achievement of the early Progressives was not their ability to exploit the new civic consciousness and the multiplying abuses that accompanied the depression. Their major accomplishment was the creation of a yardstick—"the public interest"—that provided the thrust to Wisconsin progressivism as it united diverse groups against selfish and special interests in their communities. It pointed out for subsequent reformers and politicians a new way for evaluating the behavior of individuals and corporations, a way that bridged the social chasms of occupation, partisanship, nativity, religion, age, and sex. The significant point about the concept of the public interest was that it created a new mass politics that united men as consumers and taxpayers in opposition to the old politics that was based on ethnic and producer identities.

Wisconsin had several features that distinguished it, in degree at least, from other states and helped to shape its peculiar form of progressivism. First, social barriers could be more easily crossed during the late nineties because Wisconsin's citizens had been relatively less divided in the years before the panic. For this reason, groups like the American Protective Association made fewer inroads into Wisconsin than into neighboring Michigan and Minnesota. Second, Wisconsin had only one large city, sparing her rivalries like those between Cleveland and Cincinnati and between Kansas City and Saint Louis, that retarded reform in other midwestern states. Third, the social unrest of the depression was probably deeper in Wisconsin because the state's urbanization and industrialization had been concentrated in the twenty years since the last depression. Fourth, Wisconsin developed more institutional directions for the depression's developing civic consciousness because of a proud and pioneering heritage of adult education. The popular farmers' institutes of the 1880s provided a useful model for the new social scientists. Richard T. Ely's ambition and enthusiasm guaranteed that the state would have enough progressive social scientists to meet the demand after 1893. Fifth, the remarkable personality and organizational genius of Robert M. La Follette aided early progressives after 1897. Sixth, few municipal reform groups in the country matched the Milwaukee Municipal League and its brilliant leader John Butler in ability to focus local issues on the state level. Finally, the corporations' disregard of civic responsibilities and the domination of private utilities over state politics became more burning issues in Wisconsin because few state-wide political bosses were either more powerful or more subservient to the utilities than Henry Payne.

But these features were, after all, only differences of degree. Without the depression of 1893–1897 there would have been no Wisconsin progressivism. The depression experience created programs for tax reform, popular control over quasi-public corporations, and direct democracy, and the popularity of those programs confirmed La Follette as a progressive. The most important feature in the origins of Wisconsin progressivism was that the issues of corporate irresponsibility and tax evasion transcended the social barriers that had divided individuals and groups before the depression. The progressive issues were rooted not in social backgrounds—the ethnic, occupational, partisan, class, and religious affiliations that had motivated political behavior before 1893—but in local problems that threatened everyone. Because the trauma of the depression was local and immediate—the closing of local factories, loss of jobs by friends and neighbors, strikes at nearby plants, death-dealing impure water, increased streetcar fares, higher local taxes, criminal local bankers, fatal accidents at unguarded railway crossings, and declining income for everyone—the reaction was also local and immediate. Instead of looking toward national ethnic, professional, or partisan organizations, which were not oriented toward such crises, Wisconsinites worked with their fellow townspeople of all backgrounds to alleviate suffering among their unfortunate neighbors and to control arrogant local individuals and corporations. Most Wisconsin groups were menaced by the new and manifest challenges of tax evasion and corporate insolence and by the political power of the offenders. Political progressivism enlisted workers and bosses, merchants and bankers, Protestants, Catholics, and Jews, immigrants and native-born, young men and old, farmers and city-dwellers, and both friends and enemies of the saloon.

The local and immediate nature of the social and political crises that accompanied the depression created new forms of political action that were to challenge the classic assumption that men develop political programs and rhetoric on the basis of their identification with a class or status group. None of the indexes of social origins—occupation, nativity, age, education, ethnic background, or size of home town—predicted which of 360 Republican legislators between 1897 and 1903 would become progressives and which would become conservatives.[1] The crises were so immediate that progressive rhetoric and programs were derived from the common features of men—as consumers of water, riders of streetcars, payers of taxes, as "citizens," in that favorite progressive word, and in the common emotions of anger and fear.

As a result, early progressives began with the assumption that the depression's social unrest had already aroused Wisconsinites, and that their task was to focus that unrest and bridge the new-

1. David P. Thelen, "Social Tensions and the Origins of Progressivism," *Journal of American History*, 56 (September 1969) , 330–33.

found social chasms by uniting men and women in an assault on common enemies and common problems. They assumed that their communities were potentially united against unjust and unsafe social tensions from within and against the ruthlessness of selfish interests. More firmly than earlier reformers, the early progressives relied on the civic consciousness created by the depression to sustain confidence in their abilities to reach men as angry, fearful consumers. Without the new civic consciousness their moralistic and patriotic campaigns never would have overcome the natural thrust of industrialization toward organization along class and professional lines.

Sensing that their movements depended on a crisis psychology, early Wisconsin progressives realized that their campaigns were vulnerable precisely because they were rooted in the spirit of the aroused consumer and not in the natural divisions of industrial society. They realized that their mechanism for change ran counter to the natural identifications that accompanied the spread of cities and factories. Because they could not appeal to natural economic divisions or interest groups, they had to build a new mass politics that reached all citizens across the traditional political barriers of ethnic and interest groups. Their target, the consumer, could become either so aroused that he would overthrow powerful political machines or so apathetic that the early progressives would be alone in their efforts. Their eventual success depended on their abilities to exploit acts of arrogance to arouse Wisconsinites as consumers and taxpayers and to strike while they were still incensed. The early progressives taught this lesson well to the popular muckraking journalists of the next decade; the muckrakers learned to base their articles on the hard, local, immediate facts of corporate and political disregard of the common interest instead of on class appeals. Where most reformers in the depression of the 1930s would assume that the power for change resided in interest groups, the early progressives and muckrakers were such firm believers in and products of this classless civic consciousness that they could sustain their faith in the consumer's power and in the strength of common emotions of anger and fear to bring change. There was a vital, potent public interest that united men and that needed to be upheld. The techniques of their mass politics—exposure, publicity, petitions, oratory, mass meetings—could work so long as the threats and solutions were local and immediate. When the desire for final solutions to these problems led them to the state and national level, they would discover—too late—that mass politics was relatively less effective in political arenas where ethnic tensions, partisanship, and new producer and professional groups were firmly entrenched. Men cared less deeply about and could compromise over railway rates; there was no compromise on the issue of death-bearing water.

Early Wisconsin progressives were conservatives and radicals at the same time. They were conservative in that their desperate campaigns to reunite the social order and to emphasize common threats sometimes barred them from helping the neediest victims of the factories and cities to organize and gain power on their own initiative. But they also made important contributions to the radical tradition: the more tightly quasi-public corporations fastened their holds on the political process in order to block the early progressives' demands for such minor changes as lower electric rates or lower taxes, the angrier reformers and citizens became. Out of that anger came radical economic programs like municipal ownership and income taxes and radical political programs like the direct primary, the initiative, and home rule. The angrier the Progressives became, the more clearly they viewed the enemy as an establishment of corporations and politicians that deliberately thwarted the will of the people and refused to respond to change. Unlike a subsequent depression generation, when the political system appeared responsive to the people's needs, this depression generation had itself to place heavy emphasis on political reform and direct democracy, on restoring power to the people because government was unresponsive. Before they could inaugurate economic reforms, the early progressives had to break the political power of this establishment. Journalists of the next decade would describe their mood as the "insurgent" spirit. This insurgency against political establishments was the progressive's contribution to the radical tradition.

ESSAY ON THE SOURCES

PRIMARY SOURCES

NEWSPAPERS

This book leans heavily on newspapers. Often reformers themselves, Wisconsin editors liked to publish the reformers' communications and describe the movement. The following selection of newspapers represents an attempt to balance geographic and partisan differences to get a cross section of editorial and popular opinion. An intensive study of a few cities and their newspapers in this case has revealed better the pressures for and against reform than would a cursory examination of dozens of cities and their newspapers.

The *Milwaukee Sentinel* (1886–1900) was the most important single newspaper for my research. Not only did it have the largest circulation of any paper and serve the state's metropolis, but the daily editorials of Horace Rublee (1886–1896) and H. P. Myrick (1896–1900) also reflected the popular conversion from social Darwinism and mugwumpery to more progressive attitudes. While less partisan than many newspapers, the *Sentinel* serves as a good source because it provided Republican legislators with their basic political intelligence for the entire state. By reporting events from other cities and reprinting opinions from other editors, the *Sentinel* was Wisconsin's closest approximation to a state-wide newspaper.

Two other Milwaukee newspapers with circulation in other parts of the state complemented the *Sentinel*'s coverage. While the *Milwaukee Catholic Citizen* (1887–1900) addressed itself to the minority of Catholics who spoke English, its social gospeler editor, Humphrey Desmond, covered the activities of German Catholics as well as the political developments in the city and state. The *Citizen* reflected the depression's influence in thawing ethnic and religious barriers. For the thoughts and activities of workers and Populists, this book leans on the *Milwaukee Daily News* (1893–1900). The conversion of the *Daily News* from bitter criticism of the Milwaukee Municipal League into ardent support reflected the desperate events at Milwaukee and the growing consensus to advocate progressivism.

Four other newspapers offered unique features. The *Superior Sunday Forum* (1895–1898), while not of the same journalistic caliber as many other papers, was consistently the most radical. In 1895–1896 its editor was a Populist; in 1897–1898 its editor was the state's best spokesman for the progressive municipal reformers. Although more conservative than most newspapers, the *Madison, Wisconsin State Journal* (1880–1890, 1895, 1897, 1899–1900) had three unique features: the best coverage of the state legislature; editorials

313

that often reflected the views of Amos P. Wilder, a prominent national mugwump and reform lecturer; and the most complete, if hostile, reporting of Robert M. La Follette's activities. La Follette's own newspapers, the *Madison Old Dane* (1897–1898) and *The State* (1898–1900), presented the views of his organization on various events.

Some of the other Wisconsin newspapers were noteworthy for their sprightly styles, good features, or complete reporting. These included the *Appleton Post* (1892–1900), the *Ashland Daily News* (1890–1891, 1895–1896, 1899–1900), the *Grand Rapids Wood County Reporter* (1893–1897), the *La Crosse Chronicle* (1895), the *Madison Democrat* (1880–1884, 1895), the *Menomonie Dunn County News* (1890–1891), the *Milwaukee Journal* (1895–1896), the *Sun Prairie Countryman* (1880–1884), the *Superior Evening Telegram* (1893, 1895–1898), the *Superior Leader* (1893, 1895–1898), and the *Wausau Daily Record* (1898–1900). Of relatively lesser quality were the *Ashland Daily Press* (1898–1900), the *Ashland Weekly Press* (1895), the *Eau Claire Daily Free Press* (1896), the *Sheboygan Herald* (1893–1894), the *Stanley Republican* (1900), and the *Stevens Point Daily Journal* (1896, 1898, 1900).

Some newspapers were used almost exclusively to provide information about La Follette's collegiate and early political careers: *Black Earth Advertiser* (1884), *Boscobel Dial* (1884), *Dodgeville Chronicle* (1884), *Dodgeville Star* (1884), *Lancaster Grant County Herald* (1884), *Madison Third District Republican* (1884), *Madison University Press* (1875–1880), *Monroe Sun* (1884), *Mount Horeb Blue Mounds Weekly News* (1884), and the *Stoughton Courier* (1880–1884).

SPEECHES, ARTICLES, AND PAMPHLETS

Because the leading reformers emphasized in this book left no manuscript collections and rarely held official posts, they are most easily approached through their articles and speeches. Publicists by temperament, they exploited every opportunity to express their views.

A few articles reveal the basic strands of mugwumpery. For a Milwaukee Municipal Leaguer's statement of the evils of partisan politics, see F. C. Winkler, "Municipal Government of Milwaukee," *Proceedings of the Second National Conference for Good City Government, 1894* (Philadelphia: National Municipal League, 1895), 119–24. Amos Parker Wilder, "The Citizen and Law and Order Movement," *Lend a Hand,* 14 (June, 1894), 437–41, presents a vice crusader's view. N. S. Gilson, "Municipal Debts, Expenditures and Taxation," *Municipality,* 1 (June, 1900), 1–14, is useful for study of the economic bases of mugwumpery and progressivism. Charles R. Beach, "What Can the Government Legitimately Do for the Farmer?" *Wisconsin Farmers' Institutes, A Handbook of Agriculture*, bull. no. 5 (1891), 77–82, is a good agrarian, self-help, mugwump statement. J. A. Monger's remarks in *Proceedings of the Second National Conference for Good City Government, 1894*, 12–14, reflect the moral and economic elements of mugwumpery. *Municipal Reform Movements in the United States*, William H. Tolman, ed. (New York: Fleming H. Revell, 1895), includes the constitutions and descriptions of early activities of mugwump organizations at Beloit and Milwaukee.

President John A. Butler of the Milwaukee Municipal League was the state's most important municipal reformer. His conversion from mugwumpery to progressivism, reflected in his annual speeches, parallels the development of municipal reform throughout the state during the 1890s. Butler's speeches include his remarks in the *Proceedings of the First Annual Meeting of the National Municipal League* (Philadelphia: National Municipal League, 1895), 194–98; "A Single or Double Council?" *Proceedings of the Second Annual Meeting of the National Municipal League*, 252–62; "The Place of the Council and of the Mayor in the Organization of Municipal Government," in *Proceedings of the Indianapolis Conference for Good City Government* (Philadelphia: National Municipal League, 1898), 167–73; "A General View of the New Municipal Program," in *Proceedings of the Columbus Conference for Good City Government* (Philadelphia: National Municipal League, 1899), 87–95; and "Some Essential Features of the New Municipal Program," *Proceedings of the Milwaukee Conference for Good City Government* (Philadelphia: National Municipal League, 1900), 94–105.

Two speeches discussed important facets of political progressivism. Charles Noble Gregory's *Corrupt Use of Money in Politics and Laws for Its Prevention* (Madison: Historical and Political Science Association of the University of Wisconsin, 1893) was presented countless times between 1893 and 1897 in support of a corrupt practices act. Amos Parker Wilder's "Primary Election Laws," *Proceedings of the Milwaukee Conference for Good City Government*, 212–25, partially explains how the direct primary had become inevitable in Wisconsin by 1900.

The dominant strand of political progressivism was still the crusade against quasi-public corporations. Reformers publicly cried for help in their battles against corporate arrogance. The two best general articles on this problem are one by Charles E. Monroe, angry secretary of the Milwaukee Municipal League, "The Time to Deal with Corporations Asking Public Franchises," *Municipality,*

1 (August, 1900), 5–14, and Richard T. Ely, "Natural Monopolies and Local Taxation," *Lend a Hand,* 4 (March, 1889), 178–92, an early statement of the problem. Other problems in city-utility relations are discussed by John F. Burke, "The Improper Influence on Legislation by Public Service Companies," *Proceedings of the Milwaukee Conference for Good City Government,* 157–63, and by Richard T. Ely, "Natural Monopolies and the Workingman," *North American Review,* 158 (March, 1894), 294–303.

Articles on particular fights best reveal the reformers' desperation with quasi-public corporations. The generalizations of Monroe and Burke derived from the Milwaukee league's crusades against the street railway, lighting, and garbage monopolies of that city. The best account of the Milwaukee street railway fight is John A. Butler's "Street Railway Problem in Milwaukee," *Municipal Affairs,* 4 (March, 1900), 212–18. The company's viewpoint is represented by "The Milwaukee 4-Cent Fare Decision," *Street Railway Journal,* 16 (November 10, 1900), 1122–25, and "The Electric Railway System of Milwaukee and Eastern Wisconsin," *ibid.,* 15 (June, 1899), 339–52. The Milwaukee fight is placed in the perspective of city-utility relations in other cities by "The Milwaukee Street Railway Decision," *Outlook,* 59 (June 18, 1898), 412. Duane Mowry's "The Reign of Graft in Milwaukee," *Arena,* 34 (December, 1905), 589–93, describes the "old politics" of Milwaukee aldermen. A very useful if somewhat unreliable behind-the-scenes look at the Milwaukee fight is afforded in a novel by a Chicago newspaperman, Charles K. Lush's *The Autocrats: A Novel* (New York: Doubleday, Page, 1901). Populist Alderman Henry Smith pleads for "Municipal Lighting in Milwaukee," in *Municipality,* 1 (August, 1900), 25–31. Background material for Ashland's three-year fight with its water company appears in "The Ashland Water Pollution Case," *Engineering Record,* 39 (December 24, 1898), 67–68.

By the late 1890s cities had begun to generate alternatives to private utility monopolies. Three articles describe obstacles in the path toward municipal ownership. Gustav Meissner, "Electric Lighting Plant of the City of Oconomowoc," *Municipality,* 1 (October, 1900), 15–18, and W. C. Leitsch, "Municipal Electric Lighting at Columbus," *ibid.,* 1 (April, 1900), 32–36, describe cities that created municipal utilities without ever having experienced private ones. A. D. Davis, "The Removal of Mayor Mansfield," *Municipality,* 1 (December, 1900), 30–31, appraises South Milwaukee's campaign against a mayor who refused to heed popular pressures for a municipal plant. The consumer-owned cooperative company was a second alternative to private monopolies. The cooperative utility movement is discussed in Albert H. Sanford, "A Co-operative Telephone System," *Municipality,* 1 (October, 1900), John Gaynor,

"The Local Telephone Service," *ibid.*, 1 (February, 1901), 14–16, and Gaynor, "Wisconsin Valley Plan," *Municipal Monopolies,* Edward W. Bemis, ed. (New York: Thomas Y. Crowell, 1899), 358–61.

There also were problems with city-operated utilities. Two case studies are "Water Rates in Milwaukee," *Engineering Record,* 38 (July 30, 1898), 177–78, and "The New Water Rates in Milwaukee," *ibid.,* 39 (December 31, 1898), 90.

The League of Wisconsin Municipalities, primarily representing city officials who were groping with the problems of taxation and corporate arrogance, directed much of the state-wide progressive campaign at the end of the decade. The league is described by Joshua Stark in "The New Municipal Program and Wisconsin Cities," *Proceedings of the Milwaukee Conference for Good City Government,* 106–18; by John A. Butler in "The Model City Charter and Its Relation to Wisconsin Cities," *Proceedings of the Convention Held at Fond du Lac, June 26–27, 1899,* bull. no. 3 (Madison: League of Wisconsin Municipalities, 1899), 10–24; and by early leader Ford H. MacGregor, *The League of Wisconsin Municipalities: Its History, Activities, and Accomplishments* (Madison: privately published, 1925). The Butler and MacGregor items are available only at the league's Madison office.

The league's president A. S. Douglas declared "The Need of Legislation for Wisconsin Cities," in *Municipality,* 1 (October, 1900), 8–14. The league's secretary Samuel E. Sparling wrote several descriptions of the organization: "League of Wisconsin Municipalities," *Annals of the American Academy of Political and Social Science,* 14 (September, 1899), 116–17; "The Importance of Uniformity for Purposes of Comparison," *Proceedings of the Columbus Conference for Good City Government,* 136–47; "Uniform Accounting for Wisconsin Cities," *Proceedings of the Convention Held at Fond du Lac,* 41–46; and "The Small City and the Municipal Program," *Proceedings of the Milwaukee Conference for Good City Government,* 127–35.

The social effects of the depression received less comment. The best appraisals of unemployment, which place Wisconsin in a national context, are Carlos C. Closson, Jr., "The Unemployed in American Cities," *Quarterly Journal of Economics,* 7 (January, 1894), 168–217, 257–60, and 8 (July, 1894), 453–77, and 499–502, and Albert Shaw, "Relief of the Unemployed in American Cities," *Review of Reviews,* 9 (1894), 29–37, 179–91. Aspects of the depression's social unrest and civic consciousness can be traced in Richard T. Ely, "Schools and Churches in their Relation to Charities and Correction," *Charities Review,* 4 (December, 1894), 57–64, and Edward D. Jones, "Methods of Teaching Charities and Correction at the University of Wisconsin," *ibid.,* 5 (April, 1896), 289–

93. The syllabi of University of Wisconsin extension courses were also useful: Richard T. Ely, *Socialism,* bull. no. 4 (1892) ; William A. Scott, *Economic Problems of the Present Day,* bull. no. 1 (1892) and 26 (1894) ; B. H. Meyer, *An Introduction to Economic Problems,* bull. no. 31 (1895) ; and Amos P. Wilder, *The Government of Cities,* bull. no. 41 (1895). Annabell Cook Whitcomb's *Report of the Boys' Busy Life Club: Story of the Boys' Club and the Boy Problem* (Milwaukee: privately published, 1899), reveals the impact of the depression on a voluntary charity and the pressures that led Milwaukee to pioneer in the juvenile court movement.

PROCEEDINGS, DIRECTORIES, BULLETINS, AND PERIODICALS

Many of the articles described above appeared in the periodicals and reports used by reformers to disseminate ideas and share experiences. The *Proceedings* of the National Municipal League, *Publications of the Association of Collegiate Alumnae,* and *Charities Review* helped to place Wisconsin reformers in a national context. Frank Parson's exhaustive compendium of progressive programs, *The City for the People* (Philadelphia: C. F. Taylor, 1901 ed.) also provided important national perspective.

All that remain of the dozens of bulletins and circulars published by the Milwaukee Municipal League are *The Municipal League Bulletin,* Nos. 1–2, 4–12 (1898–1899), which are housed in the Reference Collections of the Milwaukee Public Library. The League of Wisconsin Municipalities left only a slightly better record: of the league's four conventions held during the 1890s, only the *Proceedings of the Convention Held at Fond du Lac, June 26–27, 1899* remains and is located at the league's Madison office. Beginning in 1900 the league published *Municipality,* a bimonthly magazine whose files exist at the State Historical Society of Wisconsin Library at Madison.

The state's interest groups revealed their attitudes toward reform in their proceedings and magazines. While the Congregationalist magazine *Our Church Life* (1895–1900) reflects the shift from mugwumpery to progressivism, the proceedings of most state-wide religious organizations reveal the continuing popularity of mugwumpery among clergymen: *Minutes of the [Presbyterian] Synod of Wisconsin* (1884–1897) ; *Minutes of the Wisconsin Annual Conference of the Methodist Episcopal Church* (1891–1896) ; *Minutes of the Annual Meetings of the Congregational Convention of Wisconsin* (1890–1896) ; *Minutes of the Wisconsin Baptist Anniversaries* (1889–1895) ; *Proceedings of the Wisconsin Baptist Anniversaries* (1896–1900).

While the women's clubs left a much fainter trace than the clergy-men, the *Minutes of the Annual Meetings of the Woman's Christian Temperance Union of Wisconsin* (1882–1887), the descriptions of local clubs in Jane C. Croly's *History of the Woman's Club Movement in America* (New York: H. G. Allen, 1898), and the *Directory of the Founders of the Wisconsin State Federation of Women's Clubs, January 1897,* are useful.

The development of Wisconsin's most powerful local association of businessmen was followed through the Milwaukee Chamber of Commerce, *Annual Reports of the Trade and Commerce of Milwaukee* (1888–1900). All that remains from the Wisconsin Federation of Labor is the *Official Wisconsin State Federation of Labor Directory* for 1896–1897 and for 1899–1900. Farmer opinion was approached through the *Proceedings of the Annual Sessions of the Wisconsin State Grange Patrons of Husbandry* (1881–1900) and the *Wisconsin Farmers' Institutes; A Handbook of Agriculture* (1891–1900).

Two useful sources for identifying Wisconsin charities are the American Association of Societies for Organizing Charity, *Directory of Charity Organization Societies. . . .* (New York, 1917) and John Palmer Gavitt, *Bibliography of College, Social, and University Settlements* (Cambridge, 1896).

The following city directories list the occupations of residents and frequently the officers of social and religious clubs: *Ashland City Directory* (1895, 1897), *La Crosse City Directory* (1895), *Wright's Directory of Milwaukee* (1888–1900), *Madison, Wisconsin, City Directory* (1894–1895), and *City of Superior Directory* (1891–1892 through 1899).

MANUSCRIPTS

Manuscript collections are of relatively little use as sources for this study. While the major Wisconsin depositories have collected the papers of politicians, they have ignored early reformers. There are no manuscript collections for any officers of the Milwaukee Municipal League, early progressive city officials from any city, or any other reformers. Neither the State Historical Society at Madison nor the league's Madison office has any papers from the League of Wisconsin Municipalities. Unless otherwise indicated, the collections mentioned hereinafter are housed at the State Historical Society.

The manuscript collections on political reform are generally disappointing. The Charles Noble Gregory Papers (1882–1903) consist entirely of personal and family affairs, and there are only a few useful items on Milwaukee's labor politicians in the thin collections of Robert Schilling (1852–1922), and William L. Pieplow (1896–1900), the latter at the Milwaukee County Historical Society. The Papers of the Milwaukee Chamber of Commerce (1893–1900), at the Milwaukee County Historical Society, emphasize the businessmen's fight for railroad regulation, not their campaigns against the local street railway. The papers of two mugwumps, William F. Allen and Henry A. Miner, are of little use, and the Henry Demarest Lloyd Papers from Illinois (1894, 1899) have surprisingly little correspondence with neighboring Wisconsin.

While the collections of the state's politicians are frequently more substantial, they are considerably more useful for information on state-wide political organization than for reform. The major exception is the collection of Albert R. Hall (1863–1909), which, while small in volume, contains correspondence from reformers. The voluminous Robert M. La Follette Papers (1880–1900) are remarkable primarily for the absence of any concern with reform; they are mainly political. The collections of James O. Davidson (1885–1900), Henry Cullen Adams (1870–1902), and Nils P. Haugen (1895) primarily comprise correspondence with other politicians. Although William D. Hoard's Papers (1897–1899) include correspondence outside the world of politics, they contain relatively few letters from reformers. Some collections were useful for facts about La Follette's early collegiate and political careers: Charles R. Van Hise (1875–1881), Willet S. Main (1879–1884), Elisha W. Keyes (1880–1884), Lucius Fairchild (1884), William Freeman Vilas (1880–1884), and Burr Jones (1882–1884).

Perhaps the most revealing and informative collections on political progressivism are those housed at the Wisconsin Electric Power Company in Milwaukee. These collections include the Minutes of Meetings of the Committee on Operations of The Milwaukee Street Railway Company, 1895–1899, the Minutes of the Board of Directors of the Milwaukee Electric Railway and Light Company, 1896–1900, and the Minute Book of the Executive and Financial Committee of the Milwaukee Electric Railway and Light Company, 1896–1900. While these sources rarely included communications between the directors and the Milwaukee managers, they often revealed the thinking, as well as the decisions, of the company's owners and managers.

A number of manuscript collections reveal the character of civic consciousness in the depression. While the voluminous Richard T. Ely Papers (1892–1900) are primarily composed of correspondence with national religious, journalistic, educational, and business colleagues, they contain considerable correspondence with Wisconsinites. Few of the depression's discussion clubs left records, but the Club (1877–1900), and the Madison 6 O'Clock Club (1899–1900), at the Milwaukee County Historical Society, the Madison Literary Club (1877–1900), and the Madison 6 O'Clock Club (1899–1900), at the State Historical Society, composed mainly of meeting programs, do remain and are of use. The Michael V. O'Shea Papers (1892–1901) are too thin to reveal much.

There are two excellent, if small, collections for study of progressivism. The Ada James Papers (1885–1900), which include the minutes of the Wisconsin Woman Suffrage Association, contain correspondence from most of the state's outstanding suffragettes. The Lizzie Black Kander Papers (1875–1901) reflect the thinking of a leader in Milwaukee's Jewish charities, the main promoter of The Settlement house in that city. The Minute Books of the Milwaukee Woman's Industrial Exchange (1888–1900), at the Milwaukee County Historical Society, emphasize business and employee problems. Of no benefit were the Papers of the Wisconsin State Federation of Woman's Clubs (1899–1900).

The State Historical Society made a major effort to collect the records of labor organizations. Among those collections the Minute Books of the Superior Trades and Labor Assembly (1892–1896), the Racine Typographical Union, Local 324 (1894–1904), and the Madison Typographical Union, Local 313 (1892–1894) were more revealing than the Papers of the American Federation of Musicians, Kenosha Local 59 (1897–1900), the International Alliance of Theatrical Stage Employees, Milwaukee Local 18 (1894–1901), and the Brotherhood of Railroad Trainmen, Chippewa Falls Local 410 (1897–1900).

While the State Historical Society also houses the papers of a number of religious organizations, those collections reveal more information on mugwumpery than on progressivism. The broadening of the vice crusades during the depression can be traced in the Papers of the Wisconsin State Federation of Reforms and the Wisconsin Federation of Churches and Christian Workers (1898–1901). The Eugene G. Updike Papers (1890) reveal how temperance sentiments drove ministers to desert the Methodist church. The Minutes of the Fond du Lac Ministers' Association (1884–1900), in Box 7 of the John N. Davidson Papers, show the planning that went behind the organization of the vice crusades. Business affairs dominate the Minutes of the Milwaukee District Congregational Convention Councils (1885–1901), the Madison District Convention of Congregational Churches and Ministers (1890–1900), and the Milwaukee Hanover Street Congregational Church (1889–1900), but they do contain the programs of ministers' meetings.

GOVERNMENT DOCUMENTS

Several government documents are invaluable reference sources. Because the commission itself was the product of a long campaign by both mugwumps and progressives and because its proposals were adopted by the progressives, the *Reports of the Wisconsin State Tax Commission* (1898, 1900) are essential for data on the taxation crusade. Statistics on local budgets and taxes can be found in the *Biennial Reports of the Secretary of State* (1890–1900) and the *Third Biennial Report of the State Board of Control* (1896). The *Biennial Reports of the Railroad Commissioner* (1886–1900) contain valuable information on railroad taxes and labor legislation, while the *Biennial Reports of the Bureau of Labor Statistics,* later called the Bureau of Labor, Census, and Industrial Statistics (1883–1900), contain perceptive observations and many interviews with workers. Testimony on strikes is reproduced in the *Biennial Report of the State Board of Arbitration and Conciliation* (1896). The State Superintendent of Public Instruction wrote his own comments on education in the *Biennial Reports of the State Superintendent of the State of Wisconsin* (1891–1892 through 1899–1900), and he included the reports of county school superintendents. The *Reports of the President of the University of Wisconsin* (1895–1900) provide added comment on university extension.

For legislative history, the *Senate* and *General Assembly Journals of the Wisconsin Legislature* (1895–1903) are important for both the history of bills and the roll call votes; the bills themselves are bound as *Legislative Bills* (1895–1899), while those that passed are the *Laws of Wisconsin* (1874–1899). Biographical information on legislators and party platforms is included in several volumes of *The Blue Book of the State of Wisconsin* (Milwaukee: Northwestern Litho Co., 1895–1903).

A few local documents are also of some value. A discussion of the ordinance relating to fights with utilities is included in *Charter and Ordinances of the City of Superior* (1896, 1908). *The Annual Report of the Police Department of the City of Milwaukee* (1893) contains numerous useful statistics. The depression's social progressivism, as well as arguments for manual training, parent-teacher cooperation, and flexible groupings, are revealed in Richard B. Dudgeon's *Annual Reports of the Public Schools of the City of Madison, Wisconsin* (1891–1892 through 1905–1906).

La Follette's congressional career can be traced through the *Congressional Record* (49th through 51st Congresses), and the *Revision of the Tariff: Hearings Before The Committee on Ways and Means,* 51st Cong., 1st sess., House of Representatives Misc. Doc. 1796 (1890), which is also a good account of his role in the McKinley Tariff.

ESSAY ON THE SOURCES

UNPUBLISHED ARCHIVAL SOURCES

One of the most valuable approaches to new civic consciousness is through the J. H. Raymond Files of General Correspondence, 1895–1897, in the collections of the University of Wisconsin Extension Division, University of Wisconsin Archival Series 18/1/1–4, housed in the Memorial Library. The Petitions to the Legislature, State of Wisconsin Archival Series 2/3/1/5–7 (1895–1899), do not include all the petitions received. The folders in Investigation of Charges, Surveys, Relief, Disasters, and Social Unrest, State of Wisconsin Archival Series 1/1/8–1, contain helpful reports on the use of state troops in labor disturbances and the conditions in state charitable institutions.

Several other collections in the State Archives are valuable for data on La Follette's early life. The condition of the family's farm is revealed in Dane County Tax Rolls (Series 013/2/2) and Dane County Probate Files (013/10/6). His official activities as district attorney can be found in Dane County Municipal Court Case Records (013/11/6), Dane County District Attorney's Indictment Book (013/9/5–1), and the Dane County Circuit Court Case Records (013/9/6). Two useful sources for La Follette's collegiate extramural activities are in the University of Wisconsin Archives, Minutes of the Athenaean Literary Society, and Bills of Exercise of the Athenaean Society.

AUTOBIOGRAPHIES AND REMINISCENCES

Robert M. La Follette, *La Follette's Autobiography: A Personal Narrative of Political Experiences* (Madison: Robert M. La Follette Co., 1913) is one of the most sprightly and pugnacious of the progressive reminiscences. Written to further La Follette's presidential ambitions, the book grossly distorts his thinking and behavior at the time events actually occurred.

Pioneer and Political Reminiscences (Madison: State Historical Society, ca. 1930), by Nils P. Haugen, one of La Follette's most important lieutenants in the 1890s, is a useful corrective to La Follette's *Autobiography*. More disillusioned and bitter toward La Follette than Haugen's account is Rasmus B. Anderson's *Life Story of Rasmus B. Anderson* (Madison: privately published, 1915). John Strange, an Oshkosh lumberman and former La Follette ally, wrote his "Autobiography" (Microfilm Collections, Manuscripts Division, State Historical Society) from the same viewpoint as did Anderson and Haugen.

Other valuable reminiscences include John Bascom, *Things Learned by Living* (New York: G. P. Putnam's Sons, 1913), Richard T. Ely, *Ground Under Our Feet* (New York: Macmillan Co., 1938),

Lucy Thompson, "To Robert M. La Follette, My Friend," *La Follette's Magazine* (September, 1926), and Sidney Dean Townley, *Diary of a Student of the University of Wisconsin, 1886 to 1892* (Stanford, Calif.: privately published, 1939).

SECONDARY SOURCES

Wisconsin's history has been studied in depth. A valuable survey of theses and dissertations is Robert C. Nesbit and William Fletcher Thompson, *A Guide to Theses on Wisconsin Subjects* (Madison: State Historical Society of Wisconsin and University of Wisconsin Extension Division, 1964), whose major omissions are rectified in *A Supplement to A Guide to Theses on Wisconsin Subjects* (1966). The following list of books, theses, and articles, a few of which are not technically "secondary," includes only those that deal primarily with Wisconsin. Works on other states or national events are cited in the footnotes.

Abell, Aaron I., *American Catholicism and Social Action: A Search for Social Justice, 1865–1950* (Garden City, 1960).

Acrea, Kenneth C., Jr., "Wisconsin Progressivism: Legislative Response to Social Change, 1891 to 1909" (Ph.D. diss., University of Wisconsin, 1968).

Altmeyer, A. J., *The Industrial Commission of Wisconsin* (Madison: University of Wisconsin Studies in the Social Sciences and History, No. 17, 1932).

Andersen, Theodore A., *A Century of Banking in Wisconsin* (Madison: State Historical Society of Wisconsin, 1954).

Anderson, William J., "The Tax Problem in Wisconsin," *Outlook,* 70 (January 11, 1902), 128–30.

Baird, Russell Norman, "Robert M. La Follette and the Press, 1880–1905" (M.A. thesis, University of Wisconsin, 1947).

Barton, Albert O., *La Follette's Winning of Wisconsin, 1894–1904* (Des Moines: Homestead Co., 1922).

Berthrong, Donald J., "Social Legislation in Wisconsin, 1836–1900" (Ph.D. diss., University of Wisconsin, 1951).

Birr, Kendall, "Social Ideas of Superior Business Men, 1880–1898" (M.S. thesis, University of Wisconsin, 1948).

Boyer, William W., Jr., "Church-State Relations in Wisconsin" (Ph.D. diss., University of Wisconsin, 1953).

Brandes, Stuart Dean, "Nils P. Haugen and the Wisconsin Progressive Movement" (M.S. thesis, University of Wisconsin, 1965).

Bremer, Gail D., "The Wisconsin Idea and the Public Health Movement, 1890–1915" (M.S. thesis, University of Wisconsin, 1963).

Brethouwer, Melvin W., "Safety Legislation in Wisconsin: Legislative Enactments on Safety in Factories and Detailed History of the General Orders on Sanitation and the Industrial Lighting Code" (M.A. thesis, University of Wisconsin, 1928).

Brownsword, Joann Judd, "Good Templars in Wisconsin, 1854–1880" (M.A. thesis, University of Wisconsin, 1960).

Burton, William L., "The First Wisconsin Railroad Commission: Reform or Political Expediency?" (M.S. thesis, University of Wisconsin, 1952).

Caine, Stanley P., "Railroad Regulation in Wisconsin, 1903–1910: An Assessment of a Progressive Reform" (Ph.D. diss., University of Wisconsin, 1967).

Campbell, Ballard, "The Good Roads Movement in Wisconsin, 1890–1911," *Wisconsin Magazine of History*, 49 (Summer, 1966), 273–92.

Clough, Gates, *Superior: An Outline of History* (Superior: Evening Telegram Co., 1954).

Commons, John R., "Claims of the Candidates: Robert M. La Follette," *North American Review*, 187 (May, 1908), 672–77.

———, "The Wisconsin Public Utility Law," *Review of Reviews,* 36 (August, 1907), 221–24.

Cosmas, Graham A., "The Democracy in Search of Issues: The Wisconsin Reform Party," *Wisconsin Magazine of History*, 46 (Winter, 1962–1963), 93–108.

Crafer, Thomas W. B., "The Administration of Public Poor Relief in Wisconsin" (M.A. thesis, University of Wisconsin, 1907).

Current, Richard Nelson, *Pine Logs and Politics: A Life of Philetus Sawyer* (Madison: State Historical Society of Wisconsin, 1950).

Curti, Merle and Vernon Carstensen, *The University of Wisconsin: A History*, 2 vols. (Madison: University of Wisconsin Press, 1949).

Davenport, Walter, "Fighting Blood," *Collier's,* 89 (April 23, 1932), 10–11, 46–48.

Davidson, Raymond C., "The History and Development of State Administered Probation and Parole in Wisconsin" (M.S. thesis, University of Wisconsin, 1950).

Derby, William Edward, "A History of the Port of Milwaukee, 1835–1910" (Ph.D. diss., University of Wisconsin, 1963).

Deutsch, Herman J., "The Ground Swell of 1873," *Wisconsin Magazine of History*, 15 (March, 1932), 282–96.

———, "The Liberal Republican Movement," *Wisconsin Magazine of History*, 15 (December, 1931), 168–81.

———, "Railroad Politics," *Wisconsin Magazine of History*, 15 (June, 1932), 391–411.

Doland, Robert T., "Enactment of the Potter Law," *Wisconsin Magazine of History,* 33 (September, 1949), 45–54.

Donoghue, James R., *How Wisconsin Voted, 1848–1954* (Madison: Bureau of Government, University of Wisconsin Extension Division, 1956).

Dorau, Herbert B., "The Rise and Decline of Municipal Ownership in the Electric Light and Power Industry of Wisconsin," *Journal of Land and Public Utility Economics,* 3 (May, 1927), 173–82.

Earnest, Robert C., *History of Savings and Loan Associations in Wisconsin* (Milwaukee: Wisconsin Savings and Loan League, 1956).

Elliott, Frank N., "The Causes and the Growth of Railroad Regulation in Wisconsin, 1848–1876" (Ph.D. diss., University of Wisconsin, 1956).

Flynn, Eleanor J., "The Development of Wisconsin's Administration of Charities and Correction and Present Trends in the United States" (M.Ph. thesis, University of Wisconsin, 1926).

Fowler, Dorothy Ganfield, *John Coit Spooner: Defender of Presidents* (New York: University Publishers, 1961).

———, "The Influence of Wisconsin on Federal Politics, 1880–1907," *Wisconsin Magazine of History,* 16 (September, 1932), 3–25.

Fries, Robert F., *Empire in Pine: The Story of Lumbering in Wisconsin, 1830–1900* (Madison: State Historical Society of Wisconsin, 1951).

Gavett, Thomas W., "The Development of the Labor Movement in Milwaukee" (Ph.D. diss., University of Wisconsin, 1957).

Glover, Wilbur H., *Farm and College: The College of Agriculture of the University of Wisconsin, A History* (Madison: University of Wisconsin Press, 1952).

Glyer, George A., "A Report of the Conditions of the Rural Schools of Douglas County, Wisconsin" (M.A. thesis, University of Wisconsin, 1915).

Goes, Edmund, "Milwaukee, the German City of America," *The Chautauquan,* 27 (September, 1898), 659–61.

Gregory, John G., *History of Milwaukee, Wisconsin* (Chicago: S. J. Clarke Publishing Co., 1931).

———, *Southwestern Wisconsin: A History of Old Crawford County,* 4 vols. (Chicago: S. J. Clarke Publishing Co., 1932).

Hantke, Richard Watson, "The Life of Elisha Williams Keyes" (Ph.D. diss., University of Wisconsin, 1942).

Harvey, Alfred S., "The Background of the Progressive Movement in Wisconsin" (M.Ph. thesis, University of Wisconsin, 1933).

Helgeson, Arlan C., "The Promotion of Agricultural Settlement in Northern Wisconsin, 1880–1925" (Ph.D. diss., University of Wisconsin, 1952).

———, "The Wisconsin Treasury Cases," *Wisconsin Magazine of History*, 35 (Winter, 1951), 129–36.

Herrmann, William H., "The Rise of the Public Normal School in Wisconsin" (Ph.D. diss., University of Wisconsin, 1953).

Hesseltine, William B., "Robert Marion La Follette and the Principles of Americanism," *Wisconsin Magazine of History*, 31 (March, 1948), 261–67.

Howard, Leora M., "Changes in Home Life in Milwaukee from 1865 to 1900" (M.A. thesis, University of Wisconsin, 1923).

Howe, Frederick C., *Wisconsin: An Experiment in Democracy* (New York: Charles Scribner's Sons, 1912).

Hunt, Robert S., *Law and Locomotives: The Impact of the Railroad on Wisconsin Law in the Nineteenth Century* (Madison: State Historical Society of Wisconsin, 1958).

Hurst, James Willard, *Law and Economic Growth: The Legal History of the Lumber Industry in Wisconsin* (Cambridge: Harvard University Press, 1964).

Jackson, Penrose B., "The Development of Public Health Administration in Wisconsin" (M.A. thesis, University of Wisconsin, 1950).

Johnson, William Robert, "Municipal Reform in Milwaukee, 1900–1912" (B.A. thesis, University of Wisconsin, 1965).

Kaiser, Norman J., "A History of the German Theater of Milwaukee from 1850 to 1890" (M.S. thesis, University of Wisconsin, 1954).

Keith, George M., "An Historical View of the Taxation of Telephone Utilities in Wisconsin" (M.A. thesis, University of Wisconsin, 1931).

Kellogg, Louise Phelps, "The Bennett Law in Wisconsin," *Wisconsin Magazine of History*, 2 (September, 1918), 3–25.

Keppel, Ann M. and James I. Clark, "James H. Stout and the Menomonie Schools," *Wisconsin Magazine of History*, 42 (Spring, 1959), 200–210.

Kern, Alexander C., "Farms, Loans and Farm Mortgage Foreclosures in Dane County, 1867–1875" (M.A. thesis, University of Wisconsin, 1933).

Knapp, Hugh H., "The Social Gospel in Wisconsin, 1890–1912" (M.A. thesis, University of Wisconsin, 1968).

Korman, Adolf Gerd, "A Social History of Industrial Growth and Immigrants: A Study with Particular Reference to Milwaukee, 1880–1920" (Ph.D. diss., University of Wisconsin, 1959).

Krueger, Leonard Bayliss, *History of Commercial Banking in Wisconsin* (Madison: University of Wisconsin Press, 1933).

La Follette, Belle Case and Fola La Follette, *Robert M. La Follette,* 2 vols. (New York: Macmillan Co., 1953).

La Follette, John H., *History of the La Follette Family in America* (Ottumwa, Iowa: Charles F. Lang, 1898).

Lahman, Carroll Pollock, "Robert Marion La Follette as Public Speaker and Political Leader, 1855–1905" (Ph.D. diss., University of Wisconsin, 1939).

Lampard, Eric E., *The Rise of the Dairy Industry in Wisconsin: A Study in Agricultural Change, 1820–1920* (Madison: State Historical Society of Wisconsin, 1963).

Larson, Laurence M., *A Financial and Administrative History of Milwaukee* (Madison: University of Wisconsin Bull. No. 242, 1908).

Lovejoy, Allen F., *La Follette and the Establishment of the Direct Primary in Wisconsin* (New Haven: Yale University Press, 1941).

Lutz, Harley Leist, *The State Tax Commission: A Study of the Development and Results of State Control over the Assessment of Property for Taxation* (Cambridge: Harvard University Press, 1918).

Magnuson, Toni, "Private Charity and Public Welfare Services in Cleveland, Ohio, and Milwaukee, Wisconsin, 1880–1905" (B.A. thesis, University of Wisconsin, 1964).

Main, Jackson T., "History of the Conservation of Wild Life in Wisconsin" (M.A. thesis, University of Wisconsin, 1940).

Manning, Eugene A., "Old Bob La Follette: Champion of the People" (Ph.D. diss., University of Wisconsin, 1966).

Margulies, Herbert F., *The Decline of the Progressive Movement in Wisconsin, 1890–1920* (Madison: State Historical Society of Wisconsin, 1968).

Marsden, K. Gerald, "Patriotic Societies and American Labor: The American Protective Association in Wisconsin," *Wisconsin Magazine of History,* 41 (Summer, 1958), 287–94.

Maxwell, Robert S., *La Follette and the Rise of the Progressives in Wisconsin* (Madison: State Historical Society of Wisconsin, 1956).

McDonald, Forrest, *Let There Be Light: The Electric Utility Industry in Wisconsin, 1881–1955* (Madison: American History Research Center, 1957).

———, "Street Cars and Politics in Milwaukee, 1896–1901," *Wisconsin Magazine of History,* 39 (Spring, 1956), 166–70, 206–12, and (Summer, 1956), 253–57, 271–73.

McNamara, Sallee, "The Record Re-examined: The Stalwarts, the Progressives, Education and Public Welfare in Wisconsin" (M.A. thesis, University of Wisconsin, 1965).

McShane, Clay, "The Growth of Electric Street Railways: Milwaukee, A Case Study, 1887–1900" (M.A. thesis, University of Wisconsin, 1970).

Merk, Frederick, *Economic History of Wisconsin During the Civil War Decade* (Madison: State Historical Society of Wisconsin, 1916).

Merrill, Horace Samuel, *William Freeman Vilas: Doctrinaire Democrat* (Madison: State Historical Society of Wisconsin, 1954).

Meyer, Ernst Christopher, *Nominating Systems: Direct Primaries versus Conventions in the United States* (Madison: privately published, 1902).

Miller, John Lester, "A History of the Telephone Industry as a Regulated Business in Wisconsin" (Ph.D. diss., University of Wisconsin, 1940).

Nelson, E. Clifford and Eugene L. Fevold, *The Lutheran Church Among Norwegian–Americans: A History of the Evangelical Lutheran Church,* 2 vols. (Minneapolis: Augsburg Publishing House, 1960).

Olson, Frederick I., "Henry Smith, Nestor of the Common Council," *Historical Messenger of the Milwaukee County Historical Society,* 14 (March, 1958), 2–6.

———, "The Socialist Party and the Union in Milwaukee, 1900–1912," *Wisconsin Magazine of History,* 44 (Winter, 1960–1961), 110–16.

Orsi, Richard Jean, "Humphrey Joseph Desmond: A Case Study in American Catholic Liberalism" (M.S. thesis, University of Wisconsin, 1965).

Otterson, Joseph O., "History and Civil Government in the Public Schools of Illinois, Indiana, Michigan, Ohio, and Wisconsin, 1860–1890" (M.A. thesis, University of Wisconsin, 1931).

Pen and Sunlight Sketches of Duluth, Superior, and Ashland (Chicago: Phoenix Press, 1892).

Philipp, Emanuel L. and Edgar T. Wheelock, *Political Reform in Wisconsin: A Historical Review of the Subjects of Primary Election, Taxation, and Railway Regulation* (Milwaukee: privately published, 1910).

Pike, Frederic A., *A Student at Wisconsin Fifty Years Ago* (Madison: privately published, 1935).

Pitz, Herbert G., "Governmental Policies toward the Blind: State and National" (M.Ph. thesis, University of Wisconsin, 1938).

Purcell, Mary J., "Self Government in Colleges and Universities and the History of the Women's Self Government Association at the University of Wisconsin" (M.A. thesis, University of Wisconsin, 1947).

Pyre, J. F. A., *Wisconsin* (New York: Oxford University Press, 1920).

329

Rader, Benjamin G., *The Academic Mind and Reform: The Influence of Richard T. Ely in American Life* (Lexington: University of Kentucky Press, 1966).

Raney, William F., "The Building of Wisconsin Railroads," *Wisconsin Magazine of History,* 19 (June, 1936), 387–403.

———, *Wisconsin: A Story of Progress* (New York: Prentice-Hall, 1940).

Roe, Gilbert E., "Senator La Follette and Representative Government," *Independent,* 44 (April 2, 1908), 717–25.

Rosentreter, Frederick M., *The Boundaries of the Campus: A History of the University of Wisconsin Extension Division, 1885–1945* (Madison: University of Wisconsin Press, 1957).

Russell, Ralph, "The Grange in Wisconsin" (M.S. thesis, University of Wisconsin, 1929).

Saucerman, Kathryn, "A Study of the Wisconsin Library Movement, 1850–1900" (M.A. thesis, University of Wisconsin, 1944).

Sayre, Wallace S., "Robert M. La Follette: A Study in Political Methods" (Ph.D. diss., New York University, 1930).

Schlabach, Theron F., "An Aristocrat on Trial: The Case of Richard T. Ely," *Wisconsin Magazine of History,* 47 (Winter, 1963–1964), 146–59.

Schumacker, Waldo, "The Direct Primary in Wisconsin" (Ph.D. diss., University of Wisconsin, 1923).

Secher, Herbert P., "The Law and Practice of Municipal Home Rule in Wisconsin Under the Constitutional Amendment of 1924" (M.A. thesis, University of Wisconsin, 1949).

Small, Milton M., "Biography of Robert Schilling" (M.A. thesis, University of Wisconsin, 1953).

Smith, Howard L., "The New Primary Law in Wisconsin," *Publications of the Michigan Political Science Association,* 6 (March, 1905) 73–92.

Snider, Guy E., "History of the Taxation of Railway Corporations in Wisconsin" (B.Lett. thesis, University of Wisconsin, 1901).

Spahr, Walter E., "The Wisconsin Primary Election Law" (M.A. thesis, University of Wisconsin, 1917).

Steffens, J. Lincoln, "Wisconsin: A State Where the People Have Restored Representative Government—the Story of Governor La Follette," *McClure's,* 23 (October, 1904), 563–79.

Still, Bayrd, *Milwaukee: The History of a City* (Madison: State Historical Society of Wisconsin, 1948).

"Tattler" (pen name), "Robert M. La Follette," *Nation,* 101 (October 21, 1915), 493–94.

Thelen, David P., *The Early Life of Robert M. La Follette, 1855–1884* (Chicago: Loyola University Press, 1966).

————, "Social Tensions and the Origins of Progressivism," *Journal of American History*, 56 (September, 1969) , 323–41.

Twombly, Robert C., "The Reformer as Politician: Robert M. La Follette in the Election of 1900" (M.A. thesis, University of Wisconsin, 1964) .

Ulrich, Robert J., "The Bennett Law of 1889: Education and Politics in Wisconsin" (Ph.D. diss., University of Wisconsin, 1965) .

Updegrove, William Walter, "Bibles and Brickbats: Religious Conflict in Wisconsin's Public School System During the Nineteenth Century" (M.A. thesis, University of Wisconsin, 1969) .

Usher, Ellis Baker, *Wisconsin: Its Story and Biography, 1848–1913,* 8 vols. (Chicago: G. W. Lewis Publishing Co., 1914) .

Waligorski, Ann Shirley, "Social Action and Women: The Experience of Lizzie Black Kander" (M.A. thesis, University of Wisconsin, 1969) .

"Washington Journalist" (pen name) , "Insurgents We are Watching," *Independent,* 67 (March 31, 1910) , 693–94.

Weibull, Jörgen, "The Wisconsin Progressives, 1900–1914," *Mid-America,* 47 (July, 1965) , 191–221.

Whyte, William F., "The Bennett Law Campaign in Wisconsin," *Wisconsin Magazine of History,* 10 (June, 1927) , 363–90.

————, "The Watertown Railway Bond Fight," *Proceedings of the State Historical Society of Wisconsin,* 64 (1917) , 268–307.

Wight, William W., *Henry Clay Payne: A Life* (Milwaukee: privately published, 1907) .

Wilder, Amos Parker, "Governor La Follette and What He Stands For," *Outlook,* 70 (March 8, 1902) , 631–34.

Wolner, Helen M., "The History of Superior, Wisconsin to 1900" (M.A. thesis, University of Wisconsin, 1939) .

Wyman, Roger E., "Voting Behavior in the Progressive Era: Wisconsin as a Case Study" (Ph.D. diss., University of Wisconsin, 1970) .

————, "Wisconsin Ethnic Groups and the Election of 1890," *Wisconsin Magazine of History,* 51 (Summer, 1968) .

Youmans, Theodora W., "How Wisconsin Women Won the Ballot," *Wisconsin Magazine of History,* 5 (September, 1921) , 3–32.